Berlin Mitte
Downtown Berlin

DIPL.-ING. R. WILKENS
Brunnenstraße 24
10119 Berlin ☎ 238 64 70

Annegret Burg

Berlin Mitte
Die Entstehung einer urbanen Architektur
Downtown Berlin
Building the Metropolitan Mix

herausgegeben von   edited by   Hans Stimmann

Bauwelt
Berlin

Birkhäuser Verlag
Berlin Basel Boston

Wir danken den folgenden
Unternehmen, die diese Publikation
finanziell unterstützt haben.
We thank the following companies
who kindly sponsored this publication.

Unternehmensgruppe Roland Ernst
sowie and
Berliner Kraft- und Licht (Bewag)-
Aktiengesellschaft
debis Immobilienmanagement
Anno August Jagdfeld
Tishman Speyer Properties
Victoria Versicherungen

Redaktionelle Mitarbeit
Editorial Assistance
Dorothea Balzer
Rosemarie Frank
Carola Ode

Redaktionsschluß: August 1994
Main contributions
and data submitted prior
to August 1994

Übersetzungen ins Englische
Translations into English
Ingrid Taylor
Christian Caryl
Robin Benson

Der Übersichtsplan auf S. 22/23 wurde
freundlicherweise von der
Senatsverwaltung
für Bau- und Wohnungswesen zur
Verfügung gestellt.
The Senate Construction and Housing
Department kindly provided the map
on p. 22/23.

Entwurf und Gestaltung
Design
Nicolaus Ott + Bernard Stein

Gesamtherstellung
Production
Reiter-Druck

Der Vertrieb über den Buchhandel
erfolgt ausschließlich über den
Birkhäuser Verlag.
World Distribution by Birkhäuser
Publishers, excluding orders from
Bauwelt and other journals' subscribers
and readers.

A CIP catalogue record for this book is
available from the Library of Congress,
Washington, D.C., U.S.A.

Deutsche Bibliothek Cataloging-in-Publication Data

Burg, Annegret:
Berlin Mitte - die Entstehung einer urbanen Architektur = Downtown Berlin
- building the metropolitan mix / Annegret Burg. Hrsg. von
Hans Stimmann. - Berlin ; Basel ; Boston : Birkhäuser, 1995
    ISBN 3-7643-5063-6 (Basel ...)   brosch.
    ISBN 0-8176-5063-6 (Boston) brosch.
    ISBN 3-7643-5062-8 (Basel ...) Gb.
    ISBN 0-8176-5062-8 (Boston) Gb.

This work is subject to copyright. All
rights are reserved, whether the whole
or part of the material is concerned,
specifically the rights of translation,
reprinting, re-use of illustrations,
recitation, broadcasting, reproduction
on microfilms or in other ways, and
storage in data banks. For any kind of
use permission of the copyright owner
must be obtained.

©1995 Bertelsmann Fachzeitschriften
GmbH, Gütersloh, Berlin und
Birkhäuser Verlag, Berlin, Basel, Boston
Printed on acid-free paper produced of
chlorine-free pulp
Printed in Germany
ISBN 3-7643-5062-8 (hard cover)
ISBN 0-8176-5062-8 (hard cover)
ISBN 3-7643-5063-6 (soft cover)
ISBN 0-8176-5063-6 (soft cover)

9 8 7 6 5 4 3 2 1

Inhalt
Contents

6   Hans Stimmann
    Neue Berliner Büro- und Geschäftshäuser
    New Berlin Office and Commercial Buildings

24 Annegret Burg
    Das Geschäftshaus als Baustein der Stadt
    The Commercial Building: An Urban Component

30 I Der kombinierte Entwurf: Prinzip Baukasten –
    Prinzip Collage
    I The Combined Design:
    »Set of Blocks« – »Collage«

38 Hofgarten am Gendarmenmarkt
    Josef Paul Kleihues, Berlin
40 Hofgarten am Gendarmenmarkt
    Jürgen Sawade, Berlin
42 Hofgarten am Gendarmenmarkt
    Müller Reimann Scholz Architekten, Berlin
44 Hofgarten am Gendarmenmarkt · Hans Kollhoff, Berlin
48 Hofgarten am Gendarmenmarkt
    Max Dudler, Berlin–Frankfurt am Main–Zürich
52 Quartier Schützenstrasse · Aldo Rossi, Milano
60 Gendarmenmarkt (BEWAG)
    Max Dudler, Berlin–Frankfurt am Main–Zürich
64 Gendarmenmarkt · Josef Paul Kleihues, Berlin
66 Gendarmenmarkt
    Hilmer & Sattler Architekten, München
68 Triangel · Josef Paul Kleihues, Berlin

70 II Blockergänzung
    II Block Completion

76 Haus Pietzsch · Jürgen Sawade, Berlin
78 Haus Dussmann · Miroslav Volf, Saarbrücken
80 Deutsches Bibliotheksinstitut
    German Library Institute
    Modersohn und Freiesleben, Berlin
82 Geschäftshäuser Friedrichstadt
    Josef Paul Kleihues, Berlin
84 Deutscher Industrie- und Handelstag
    Association German Chambers of Industry
    and Commerce
    Architekten Schweger + Partner, Hamburg
88 Unter den Linden · Klaus Theo Brenner, Berlin
90 Glinkastrasse · Jürgen Sawade, Berlin
92 Bürohaus Deutscher Bundestag
    Brands Kolbe Wernik Architekten, Berlin
96 Rosmarin Karree · Böge + Lindner, Hamburg
    Kahlfeldt Architekten, Berlin

100 III Großblock
    III The Large Block Form

106 Friedrichstadt Passagen · AJN Jean Nouvel, Paris
112 Friedrichstadt Passagen
    Pei Cobb Freed & Partners, New York
118 Friedrichstadt Passagen · O. M. Ungers & Partner, Berlin
124 VICTORIA · Thomas van den Valentyn, Köln
130 Centre Paris-Berlin · Claude Vasconi, Paris
134 Ludwig Erhard Haus · Grimshaw & Partners, London
138 Lindencorso · Christoph Mäckler, Berlin–Frankfurt am Main

142 IV Turm und Hochhaus: Fixpunkte im Stadtbild
    IV Tower and Tower Block:
    Fixed Points in the Urban Scene

148 Frankfurter Allee · HPP, Berlin SOM, Chicago
152 Zoofenster · Richard Rogers Partnership, London
156 Treptower Park (Allianz) · Gerhard Spangenberg, Berlin
160 Treptower Park · Georg Kieferle & Partner,
    Stuttgart-Berlin
164 Kynaststrasse · Klaus Theo Brenner, Berlin

166 V Potsdamer Platz: Die neue Mitte?
    V Potsdamer Platz: The New Centre?

174 Daimler-Benz/debis
    Renzo Piano Building Workshop, Paris–Genova
180 Daimler-Benz/debis · Hans Kollhoff, Berlin
184 Daimler-Benz/debis · Richard Rogers Partnership, London
188 Daimler-Benz/debis · Arata Isozaki & Associates, Tokyo
194 A+T · Giorgio Grassi, Milano
200 A+T · Architekten Schweger + Partner, Berlin
204 A+T · Jürgen Sawade, Berlin
206 A+T · Diener & Diener Architekten, Basel

208 Schluß: Vom Bauboom zum Bautyp
    Conclusion: From Building Boom to Building Type

214 43 weitere Projekte
    43 Other Projects

223 Bildnachweis
    Acknowledgements

Hans Stimmann
Neue Berliner Büro- und Geschäftshäuser

Der Neubau einer Stadtmitte

Wer im Herbst 1994, fünf Jahre nach Öffnung der Berliner Mauer und vier Jahre nach der tatsächlichen Wiedervereinigung, Berlin vom Frankfurter Tor im Osten bis zur Messe am westlichen Rand des Stadtrings durchfuhr, konnte nicht daran vorbei: Aus der Stadt der kaum übersehbaren Pläne, Konzepte und Projekte ist Mitte der neunziger Jahre eine Stadt der Kräne, Baufahrzeuge und Baustellen geworden.

Der Fall der Mauer hat einen milliardenschweren Bauinvestitionsboom ausgelöst, in dem sich der fundamentale Strukturwandel Berlins zur hauptstädtischen Dienstleistungsmetropole ausdrückt. Die politische Entscheidung des deutschen Parlaments vom 20. Juni 1991 sowie die gesetzlichen Festlegungen vom März 1994, mit denen der Umzug von Parlament und Regierung eingeleitet wurde, hat diesem Strukturwandel eine solide Grundlage verschafft.

Sieht man einmal vom Wohnungsbau ab, so konzentriert sich das komplexe Baugeschehen auf die Citybereiche in den Stadtbezirken Mitte, Tiergarten und Charlottenburg. Den Schwerpunkt in Berlins Mitte bildet die schnurgerade Friedrichstraße: Über 800.000 m² Bruttogeschoßfläche mit einem Investitionsvolumen von ca. 6 Mrd. DM werden hier von 1995 an fertiggestellt. Das zweite Zentrum der innerstädtischen Modernisierung entsteht seit Sommer 1994 am Potsdamer Platz. Er bildet den Mittelpunkt einer ca. 50 ha großen Stadtbrache, die noch immer etwas vom ambivalenten Charme des früheren Grenzortes vermittelt. Die stadtstrukturelle Reichweite des neuen Quartiers ist wegen der konzeptionell und technisch damit verbundenen unterirdischen Verkehrsbauwerke für Fernbahn, S-, U-, Straßenbahn und Straße sowie wegen der zentralen Lage zwischen City West und City Ost ungleich größer als in der Friedrichstraße. In den Jahren, da sich der Zustand dieser faszinierenden innerstädtischen Peripherie täglich verändert, spiegelt sie besser als jeder andere Ort den gründerzeitlichen Gegenwartszustand dieser Stadt wider.

Dabei geht es in Berlin nicht wie bei La Défense (Paris), Canary Wharf (London) oder in Lille um die Errichtung einer zweiten City neben den traditionellen Innenstädten. Vielmehr wird hier am Ende des 20. Jahrhunderts noch einmal die Frage nach Struktur und Gestalt des Zentrums einer europäischen Hauptstadt und Dienstleistungsmetropole gestellt. Berlin ist der Ort, wo aus den praktischen Erfahrungen mit den städtebaulichen und architektonischen Konzepten von Frühmoderne, Moderne, Nachkriegsmoderne und Postmoderne theoretische und entwurfliche Konsequenzen gezogen werden können. Berlin ist aber auch der Ort, an dem sowohl im kapitalistischen Westen als auch im sozialistischen Osten die Stadtkonzepte der Nachkriegsjahrzehnte mit ihrer radikalen Entmischung der Funktionen, der Ignoranz gegenüber den parzellären Eigentumsverhältnissen und der autoorientierten Verkehrsplanung erprobt wurden und gescheitert sind. Berlin war die Stadt mit dem nur aufgrund seiner jüngeren politischen Geschichte als Hauptstadt im NS-Deutschland nachvollziehbaren Willen zur konsequenten Auslöschung des historischen Stadtgrundrisses im Zentrum. Die Architekten- und Politikergenerationen der Nachkriegszeit lebten »aus Vergangenheitshaß und Fortschrittsglauben. Mit der Hinterlassenschaft des Dritten Reiches sollten auch die städtebaulichen Restbestände der bürgerlichen Welt abgeräumt werden«[1]. Aber Berlin war in den achtziger Jahren – insbesondere durch die Internationale Bauausstellung (IBA) – auch der Ort intensiver Wiederentdeckung des Stadtgrundrisses und der architektonischen Qualität des 19. und frühen 20. Jahrhunderts.[2]

An diese Erfahrungen der vergangenen Jahrzehnte anknüpfend sind die rahmensetzenden Bedingungen für die Bauprojekte der neunziger Jahre
- das stadtplanerische City-Konzept,
- das städtebauliche Konzept der »Kritischen Rekonstruktion«,
- das Leitbild der »europäischen Stadt«,
- die Wiedereinführung privaten Grundbesitzes im Ostteil der Stadt sowie
- der Hauptstadtbeschluß und die damit gewonnene Klarheit über die wirtschaftlichen Perspektiven.

Büroflächen: Bestand und Bedarf

In Berlin befanden sich 1994 etwa 1,6 Mio. m² Büroflächen im Bau bzw. in umfassender Modernisierung. Bis Mitte 1995 sollten davon ca. 600.000 m² fertiggestellt

Hans Stimmann
New Berlin Office and Commercial Buildings

The Rebuilding of a City Centre
A visitor to Berlin in the fall of 1994 – five years after the opening of the Berlin Wall and four years after reunification – who traveled through the city from Frankfurter Tor in the east to the fairgrounds on the western edge of the city ring, could not fail to note a fundamental development: in the middle of the 1990s the city known earlier for its bewildering array of plans, concepts and projects has become a city of cranes, building machinery and construction sites.

The fall of the Wall has triggered a construction investment boom worth billions of dollars, expressing the fundamental structural transformation of Berlin into the national capital and a centre of service industry. The political decision of the German parliament on June 20, 1991 and the follow-up legislation of March 1994, which initiated the move of parliament and government, have provided this structural transformation with a solid basis.

With the exception of housing construction, the complex building activities are concentrated in inner-city areas in the boroughs of Mitte, Tiergarten and Charlottenburg. The focal point in Berlin's central district of Mitte is the straight line of Friedrichstrasse: more than 800,000 square metres of gross area with an investment volume of ca. 6 thousand million DM will be completed here from 1995 on. The second centre of inner-city modernisation has been under construction since the summer of 1994 at Potsdamer Platz. It comprises the centrepiece of a fallow urban area approximately 50 hectares in size which still conveys something of the ambivalent charm of the once-divided city. The effects of this new quarter on the urban structure of the city are significantly more far-reaching than in the case of Friedrichstrasse due to the conceptually and technically connected below-ground transport projects for long-distance railroads, urban mass transit and streets as well as because of the site's central position between the eastern and western city centres. In these years, while the condition of this fascinating inner-city periphery is changing daily, it reflects the present incipient state of this city better than any other site.

Unlike La Défense in Paris, Canary Wharf in London or the urban expansion in Lille, Berlin does not confront us with the construction of a second downtown area adjacent to a traditional inner city. The question being posed here is instead, at the end of the 20th century, once again that of the structure and form of the centre of a European capital and service metropolis. Berlin is the place where theoretical and design consequences can be drawn from the practical experience of the urban planning and architectural ideas of early modernism, modernism, postwar modernism and postmodernism. Yet Berlin is also the place where the urban planning strategies of the postwar decades, with their radical separation of functions, their ignorance toward the ownership conditions of individual lots and their automobile-oriented traffic planning were tested and failed – in the capitalist west as well as in the socialist east. Berlin was the city whose recent political history as the capital of Nazi Germany imbued it with the understandable desire for consistent destruction of the historical urban plan in the centre. The architects and politicians of the postwar era lived »from hatred of the past and belief in progress. The urban remnants of the bourgeois world were to be wiped out along with the legacy of the Third Reich.«[1] But Berlin in the 1980s was also – particularly due to the International Building Exhibition (IBA) – the site of intensive re-discovery of the urban ground plan and the architectural quality of the 19th and early 20th centuries.[2]

Based on this experience of past decades, the fundamental parameters for the building projects of the 1990s are as follows:
- The urban planning concept for the inner city;
- The urban planning concept of »Critical Reconstruction«;
- The guiding image of the »European city«;
- The re-introduction of private real-property ownership in the eastern part of the city; and
- The German parliamentary resolution to make Berlin the capital and the corresponding clarity of economic prospects for the city.

werden. Diese Menge entspricht bis zum Jahre 2010 dem geschätzten mittleren Jahresbedarf an neu zu errichtenden Büroflächen. Daraus ergibt sich rein rechnerisch – also nicht differenziert nach Lage, Projektgröße, Miethöhe usw. – ein Wachstumspotential von ca. 10 Mio. m² Bruttogeschoßfläche. Ausreichend Potential also, um nötigenfalls aus den städtebaulichen, architektonischen und wirtschaftlichen Defiziten der Mitte der neunziger Jahre realisierten Projekte Konsequenzen zu ziehen.

Struktur und Quantität des Bedarfs ergeben sich aus
– dem Nachhol-, Erweiterungs- und Ersatzbedarf,
– dem wirtschaftlichen Strukturwandel sowie
– dem Bedeutungszuwachs Berlins als deutscher Hauptstadt.

Die real in Berlin vorhandenen Büroflächen machen den im Vergleich zu anderen Städten großen Nachholbedarf und die Notwendigkeit des wirtschaftlichen Strukturwandels deutlich.[3]

Stadt	Büroflächenbestand/BGF Mio. m²	Ende 1993 m²/EW
Berlin	12,4	3,6
Frankfurt	8,4	12,7
München	10,5	8,3
Hamburg	11,0	6,5
Düsseldorf	4,5	7,8
Stuttgart	4,8	8,0
Leipzig	1,3	2,6

Zu diesem strukturellen Nachholbedarf kommen besonders in Ost-Berlin gravierende Defizite im Ausstattungsstandard des Bestandes. Dies geht in der Regel einher mit einem sehr niedrigen Raumangebot pro Büroarbeitsplatz. Es beträgt in Ost-Berlin derzeit ca. 15 m², in West-Berlin 21 m² und im westdeutschen Mittel ca. 25 m² Bruttogeschoßfläche pro Beschäftigten. Das geringe Raumangebot ist vor allem eine Folge der relativen Überalterung des Bestandes, von dem etwa die Hälfte älter als 70 Jahre ist.

Aufgaben, Vorgaben und Ziele der Stadtplanung

Die Entscheidungsträger in Politik und Verwaltung der Jahre 1989/90 sahen sich vor außergewöhnliche Probleme gestellt. Große Teile des bis zum Ende des Zweiten Weltkrieges dicht bebauten und hochkomplexen Zentrums befanden sich im Zustand der Verwahrlosung, bildeten eine innere Peripherie. Hinzu kamen mehrere hundert Hektar Brachflächen sowie nach dem Ende des DDR-Staates leerstehende Regierungsgebäude in einer Größenordnung, die die sofortige Unterbringung einer kompletten Regierung eines mittelgroßen europäischen Staates ermöglicht hätte. Auf diese fragmentarisierten Areale richteten sich die Wünsche und Begehrlichkeiten der Investoren aus der alten Bundesrepublik, aber auch aus den USA, England, Frankreich, Schweden, Japan u.a. Den Auftakt für einen wahren Projektrausch bildete das noch im Juli 1990 vom West-Berliner Bürgermeister Walter Momper eingeleitete Grundstücksgeschäft mit der Daimler-Benz-Tochter debis über 67.000 m² Stadt am Potsdamer Platz.

Als Pendant fand in Ost-Berlin das erste und zugleich größte Investorenauswahlverfahren über 18.500 m² statt für drei schon zu DDR-Zeiten als zusammenhängender Komplex geplante Blöcke in der Friedrichstadt, die sogenannten Friedrichstadt-Passagen (Quartiere 205, 206, 207). Die städtebaulichen Rahmenbedingungen für dieses Projekt wurden im November 1990, also noch unter dem ersten und letzten frei gewählten Magistrat von Ost-Berlin, festgelegt. Die wenigen Regeln (Einhaltung der Baufluchtlinien, Höhenbegrenzung auf 22 m Trauf- bzw. 30 m Firsthöhe sowie ein nicht quantifizierter Wohnanteil) waren die Grundlagen[4] für einen internationalen, kombinierten Investoren- und Architektenwettbewerb unter zunächst 22 und dann in der zweiten Stufe fünf Bewerbern mit jeweils drei unterschiedlichen Architektengruppen. Dem französischen Unternehmen Galeries Lafayette wurde zugestanden, einen nur auf das »Quartier 207« bezogenen Entwurf einzureichen. Auslober war hier zum ersten Mal die seit Juni 1990 über die Grundstücke verfügende Treuhandanstalt in Absprache mit der Senatsverwaltung für Bau- und Wohnungswesen. Von einer Jury wurden unter der Leitung von Josef Paul Kleihues drei Investoren mit jeweils einem Architekten ausgewählt[5]: Galeries Lafayette mit Jean Nouvel, Paris; Bouygues Immobilier mit Pei Cobb Freed & Partners, New York; und Tishman Speyer Properties mit Oswald Mathias Ungers, Köln. Die einzige deutsche Gruppe (DGI Deutsche Grundbesitzinvestmentgesellschaft) konnte mit der internationalen Konkurrenz nicht mithalten.

Diese Großprojekte aus der Periode zwischen dem Fall der Mauer und der Bildung des ersten gemeinsamen Berliner Senats im Jahre 1991 sprengten nicht nur die Dimensionen der historischen Parzellen, sondern – mit der Idee einer parallel zur Friedrichstraße angeordneten oberirdischen Passage – auch den Maßstab der friedrichstädtischen Blöcke. Sie bildeten den Auftakt und leider

Office Space: Availability and Demand

In Berlin in 1994 roughly 1.6 million square metres of office space are under construction or undergoing comprehensive modernisation. Of these, approximately 600,000 square metres are scheduled for completion by the middle of 1995. This amount corresponds to the estimated average annual demand for newly built office space until the year 2010. In purely arithmetic terms – that is, without differentiation by site, project size, rent levels, etc. – this means a growth potential of approximately 10 million square metres of gross floor area – adequate potential, therefore, for drawing lessons from the urban planning, architectural and economic deficiencies of the projects implemented in the mid-90s.

The structure and quality of demand derives from:
- The need for supplementation, expansion and replacement;
- The transformation of economic structure; and
- The growing significance of Berlin as the German capital.

The office space actually available in Berlin clearly demonstrates the extent to which it still lags behind other cities and the need for transformation of economic structure.[3]

City	Existing office buildings /gross floor area end of 1993	
	Mil. m²	m² per capita
Berlin	12,4	3,6
Frankfurt	8,4	12,7
Munich	10,5	8,3
Hamburg	11,0	6,5
Düsseldorf	4,5	7,8
Stuttgart	4,8	8,0
Leipzig	1,3	2,6

Much of this structural demand derives from the substandard quality of existing buildings in East Berlin. This generally goes along with very low amounts of available space per office workplace. In East Berlin at present this amount is approximately 15 square metres, compared with 21 square metres in West Berlin and the average West German figure of approximately 25 square metres of gross floor area per employee. The low amount of available space is above all a result of the relative aging of the existing buildings, of which roughly half are older than seventy years.

Tasks, Requirements and Aims of Urban Planning

The decision-makers in politics and administration of the years 1989/90 faced exceptional problems. Large parts of the extremely complex city centre, densely developed until the end of the Second World War, were in a state of neglect, forming an »inner periphery«. The problems were increased by several hundred hectares of fallow land as well as the empty buildings of the GDR, which would have immediately provided enough space for the entire government of a mid-sized European country. This fragmented area is the focus of interest for investors from the old West Germany, but also from the U.S.A., England, France, Sweden, Japan and so on. The starting point for a frenzy of projects came in July 1990 with the real-estate deal concluded by the West Berlin mayor, Walter Momper, with the Daimler-Benz subsidiary debis for 67,000 square metres at Potsdamer Platz.

The East Berlin counterpart to this project got underway with the first and largest investors selection procedure for over 18,500 square metres for the three blocks – planned as a coherent complex already during the GDR period – in the Friedrichstadt area, the so-called Friedrichstadt Passagen (blocks 205, 206, 207). The urban planning parameters for this project were set in November 1990 under the first and last freely elected city government of East Berlin. The few rules (maintenance of frontage lines, height restrictions of 22 metres to eaves, 30 metres to ridge, and an unspecified percentage of housing) served as the bases[4] of an international competition combining investors and architects with at first twenty-two applicants (by the second stage reduced to five, each with three different groups of architects). The French company Galeries Lafayette was allowed to submit a plan based on Block 207 only. For the first time, the competition organiser here was the Treuhand (the agency for privatisation of former state-owned property from the GDR), which had control of the property since June 1990, in consultation with the Senate Construction and Housing Department. A jury under the direction of Josef Paul Kleihues selected three investors, each with one architect[5]: Galeries Lafayette with Jean Nouvel, Paris; Bouygues Immobilier with Pei Cobb Freed & Partners, New York; and Tishman Speyer Properties with Oswald Mathias Ungers, Cologne. The sole German group (DGI, Deutsche Grundbesitzinvestmentgesellschaft) proved unable to keep up with the international competition.

auch den Maßstab für eine ganze Reihe weiterer Projektideen privater Investoren für den Bereich des historischen Zentrums zwischen Alexanderplatz und Potsdamer Platz. Für diese stadt- und wirtschaftspolitisch gewollten, städtebaulich aber höchst problematischen Projekte mußten aus dem Stand heraus Regeln für die Bereitstellung der Grundstücke, aber auch stadtplanerische und städtebauliche Vorgaben definiert werden.

Die Entwicklung stadtplanerischer Vorgaben war in der Kürze der zur Verfügung stehenden Zeit nicht in den geordneten und gestuften Kategorien der bundesdeutschen Bauleitplanung (Flächennutzungsplan für das gesamte Stadtgebiet und daraus abgeleitete Bebauungspläne für Teilgebiete) möglich. Der erste Gesamtberliner Flächennutzungsplan wurde erst im Sommer 1994 verabschiedet. Der Ost-Berliner Generalbebauungsplan wurde nicht als Flächennutzungsplan für die 11 Ost-Berliner Bezirke übergeleitet, da seine auf eine sozialistische Gesellschaft orientierten Inhalte überholt waren. Andere Planungen, die als Bebauungsplan hätten bestätigt werden können, gab es nicht.

Eine wichtige Rolle spielte die Entwicklung der Eigentumsverhältnisse. Trotz der weitestgehenden Verfügungsberechtigung über die ehemals volkseigenen Grundstücke durch die Treuhandanstalt, die Oberfinanzdirektion oder den Senat erwies sich die Reprivatisierung und damit die Aufteilung der vordem großflächig arrondierten Grundstücke als das zentrale Hemmnis vieler Projektträume. Andererseits bestand mit dem »Gesetz über besondere Investitionen im Gebiet der ehemaligen DDR« und dem »Gesetz zur Regelung offener Vermögensfragen« mit dem Einigungsvertrag die Möglichkeit, zur »Sicherung oder Schaffung von Arbeitsplätzen, insbesondere durch Errichtung einer gewerblichen Betriebsstätte oder eines Dienstleistungsunternehmens« und zur »Deckung eines erheblichen Wohnbedarfs der Bevölkerung« »volkseigene« Grundstücke trotz der vermögensrechtlichen Ansprüche der Alteigentümer zu veräußern. Diese wirtschaftlich begründeten Möglichkeiten zur Beschleunigung des arbeitsplatzschaffenden investiven Baugeschehens bildeten die Grundlage für die vielfach großen, parzellenübergreifenden Hauseinheiten relativ homogener Nutzung.

Obwohl eine rechtskräftige Bauleitplanung fehlte, bestand rechtlich gesehen eine Entscheidungsgrundlage für jede konkrete Bauabsicht: Auch in Ost-Berlin galten mit dem Einigungsvertrag die Vorschriften des bundesdeutschen Baugesetzbuches und damit dessen §34 als genehmigungsrechtliche Grundlage. Seine Anwendung entscheidet sich danach, ob ein beabsichtigtes Vorhaben in einem »im Zusammenhang bebauten Ortsteil« im sogenannten Innenbereich liegt und sich in die Eigenart der näheren Umgebung einfügt. Um Kriterien für diese »Einfügung« von Neubauten in der Dorotheen- und Friedrichstadt zu erhalten, waren zunächst zwei grundsätzliche Fragen zu beantworten:

1. Sollte es sich bei dem Gebiet der historischen Friedrichstadt auch in Zukunft um ein Citygebiet handeln?
2. Sollten als Maßstab für die Einfügung der Neubauten die Fragmente der historischen Stadt im Grund- und Aufriß oder aber die Hochhausbebauungen an der Leipziger Straße und am Bahnhof Friedrichstraße gelten?

Über die zukünftige Art der Nutzung gab es zu keinem Zeitpunkt Zweifel: Dorotheen- und Friedrichstadt sollten wieder Zentrum der Metropole Berlin werden. Planungsrechtlich bedeutete dies eine Ausweisung als »Kerngebiet«, wie sie im Flächennutzungsplan von 1994 entsprechend vorgenommen wurde: Zulässig sind Geschäfts-, Büro- und Verwaltungsgebäude, Einzelhandelsbetriebe, Hotels usw.; als Ausnahme werden auch Wohnungen zugelassen.

Die zweite Frage war ebenso schnell wie unumstritten im Sinne einer Kritischen Rekonstruktion des Stadtgrundrisses beantwortet. Nach den gescheiterten Experimenten mit den neuen Stadtideen war nicht die Sehnsucht nach einer abermals neuen Stadt das vorherrschende Gefühl. Vielmehr dominierte in Ost und West gleichmaßen der Wunsch nach Wiederaufnahme der städtebaulichen Tradition, nach dem Zusammenwachsen im Mauerstreifen und nach einer gemeinsamen Zukunft in einem neue Identität stiftenden Zentrum. Gegenstand dieser Sehnsucht waren insbesondere historische Orte wie der Pariser Platz, der Potsdamer Platz, der Checkpoint Charlie und der Spittelmarkt.

Natürlich gab und gibt es gerade in Berlin unter Architekten auch eine andere Tradition, nämlich die offener Stadtkonzepte. Diese Position artikulierte sich nach dem Fall der Mauer in zwei Veröffentlichungen: 17 international renommierte Architekten entwarfen für die Frankfurter Allgemeine Zeitung in Kooperation mit dem Deutschen Architekturmuseum »Das Berlin von morgen« und hier insbesondere das »Herz einer großen Stadt«[6]; etwas später zog die Zeitschrift GEO mit 8 weiteren Entwürfen nach.[7] Das wirklich Neue an diesen Projekten war weniger die städtebauliche Radikalität im Zugriff auf die historische Mitte, sondern vielmehr die Tatsache, daß die Pläne von Medien bestellt und vertrieben wurden, aufge-

These large-scale projects from the period between the fall of the Wall and the formation of the first joint Berlin Senate in 1991 not only vastly exceeded the dimensions of the historical lots but also – with the idea of an above-ground passage running parallel to Friedrichstrasse – the scale of the blocks of the historical Friedrichstadt district. They set the stage, and unfortunately also the scale, for an entire series of project ideas from private investors for the area of the historical centre between Alexanderplatz and Potsdamer Platz. These projects, promoted for reasons of city and economic politics, but highly problematic in their effects on urban design, meant that rules for making property available, as well as urban planning and urban-design specifications, had to be defined spontaneously.

It proved impossible in the short time available to develop urban planning specifications according to the established procedures and categories of federal physical development laws (land use plan for the entire urban area and development plans for sub-areas derived from it). The first overall Berlin land use plan was passed in the summer of 1994. The East Berlin general development plan was not used as a basis for the land use plan for the eleven boroughs of East Berlin because its contents, oriented to a socialist society, had become outmoded. There were no other plans that could have been confirmed as development plans.

The development of ownership conditions played an important role. Despite the wide-ranging authority of disposition over the formerly state-owned properties granted to the Treuhand, to the city finance authorities, or to the Senate, reprivatisation and the associated dividing up of formerly large-scale properties proved the primary barrier to many project dreams. On the other hand, the Law on Special Investments in the Area of the Former GDR and the Law for the Regulation of Open Property Questions in connection with the Unification Treaty allowed the sale of the former state-owned properties, despite the claims of former owners, for »the purpose of creating or guaranteeing jobs, especially through the creation of commercial production facilities or of a service company« and for »meeting a significant demand for housing among the population.« These economically motivated possibilities for speeding up investment in building activities leading to job creation served as the basis for the many large, multi-lot buildings with relatively homogeneous uses.

Despite the lack of a legislatively approved physical development plan, the legal situation nonetheless offered an adequate basis for every concrete construction project: the Unification Treaty brought the rules of the federal German Construction Law into force in East Berlin as well, with Article 34 as the basis for approval. This article is applied according to whether an intended project lies in a »coherently developed city district« in the so-called inner zone and lends itself to integration into the specific conditions of the nearby area. In order to establish criteria for this »integration« of new buildings in the Dorotheenstadt and Friedrichstadt districts, two fundamental questions first had to be answered:

1. Should the area of the historical Friedrichstadt continue to be an inner-city area in the future?

2. Which scale should serve as the basis for integration of the new buildings: the fragments of the historical city in the elevation and plan or the high-rise buildings on Leipziger Strasse and Friedrichstrasse Station?

At no time was there any doubt about the future type of use: Dorotheenstadt and Friedrichstadt were to become once again the centre of the Berlin metropolis. For planning law this implied definition of a »core area« of the type ultimately provided by the land use plan of 1994: admissible are commercial, office and administrative buildings, shops, hotels, etc. Housing is also allowed as an exception.

The second question was answered equally quickly and uncontroversially: in favour of a strategy of »Critical Reconstruction« oriented to the historical city plan. Following the failure of experiments with new ideas of the city, there was little desire for yet another new city. Instead, both east and west displayed a desire for resumption of the urban planning tradition, for urban regeneration along the course of the former Wall and for a joint future in a centre that would provide a new identity. This yearning focused particularly on historical sites such as Pariser Platz, Potsdamer Platz, Checkpoint Charlie and Spittelmarkt.

Naturally there was and is precisely in Berlin also another tradition among architects, namely that of open concepts of the city. This position was articulated after the fall of the Wall in two publications: 17 internationally known architects, commissioned by the Frankfurter Allgemeine Zeitung newspaper in cooperation with the German Architecture Museum, designed »The Berlin of Tomorrow«, and in particular the »Heart of a Great City«[6]; somewhat later GEO magazine joined

macht wie ein »Versandhauskatalog in Sachen Architektur für Politiker und Investoren, der ihnen Lust zum Bauen machen soll« (Bruno Flierl).[8] Daß dieser Appell durchaus ernstgenommen wurde, belegen die kurz darauf von Developern vorgestellten und inzwischen schon wieder vergessenen hypertrophen Bauprojekte für viele exponierte Stellen in der Mitte Berlins[9].

Die Kritische Rekonstruktion

Die städtebauliche Methode der Kritischen Rekonstruktion hatte sich in der Zeit der IBA als Grundlage für die Neubebauung in der Südlichen Friedrichstadt durchgesetzt und war auch unter Ost-Berliner Architekten als Leitbild anerkannt. Die Konkretisierung und Weiterentwicklung dieser Methode erfolgte nach der Wende parallel zur Grundstücksrückgabe, parallel aber auch zu gutachterlich erstellten Planungsvorgaben für einzelne Bereiche (Pariser Platz, Spittelmarkt, Bahnhof Friedrichstraße, Mehringplatz) und schließlich für die gesamte Dorotheen- und Friedrichstadt im Auftrag der Senatsbauverwaltung[10]. Dabei ging es nicht um eine mechanische Übertragung der zu Mauerzeiten in der Südlichen Friedrichstadt angewandten städtebaulichen Strategie. Ziel war vielmehr die Weiterentwicklung dieses theoretischen Prinzips in seiner Anwendung auf die stadtbaugeschichtlich, nutzungsstrukturell und eigentumsrechtlich andersartige Situation. Unter den veränderten Bedingungen der Einheit ist die Hauptnutzung in den betreffenden Gebieten nicht mehr wie zur Zeit der IBA der öffentlich geförderte Wohnungsbau, sondern es sind typische innerstädtische Nutzungen: Bürohäuser, Hotels, Warenhäuser, Ministerien, Universitätsbauten.

Bei der Kritischen Rekonstruktion ging und geht es weder um die Wiederherstellung historischer Zustände noch um ein nostalgisches Stadtbild, sondern um die Ausbildung einer differenzierten und zeitgenössischen Stadtstruktur. Das Zentrum Berlins soll in seinen historischen Schichten und Maßstäblichkeiten, seinen Abfolgen städtischer Räume und seiner differenzierten Nutzungsvielfalt, aber auch als Ort zeitgenössischer Architektur und wirtschaftlicher Verhältnisse wieder erfahrbar werden. Die geplante Nutzungsstruktur unterscheidet zwischen Geschäftsstadt, Regierungsbezirken, Universitätsviertel bzw. den zentralen kulturellen Einrichtungen, setzt aber auch auf die Mischung innerhalb der einzelnen Stadtquartiere und fordert grundsätzlich die Integration des innerstädtischen Wohnens. Dabei läßt sich die städtebauliche Methode der Kritischen Rekonstruktion auf wenige Regeln reduzieren:

- Das historische Straßennetz und im Zusammenhang damit die historischen Baufluchten der Straßen und Plätze sind zu respektieren bzw. zu rekonstruieren.
- Die maximal zugelassene Höhe der Bebauung beträgt bis zur Traufe 22 m und bis zum First 30 m.
- Als Voraussetzung für die Erlangung der Baugenehmigung wird der Nachweis eines Anteils von ca. 20 % der Bruttogeschoßfläche an Wohnnutzung gefordert.
- Die Bebauungsdichte (GFZ) wird nicht vorgeschrieben. Sie ergibt sich durch die oben genannten Rahmenbedingungen, die Art der Nutzung und die Festlegungen der Bauordnung und liegt in der Regel bei 5,0.
- Ziel der Neubebauung ist das städtische Haus auf einer Parzelle; die maximal zugelassene Parzellengröße ist der Block.

Die Rekonstruktion des historischen Stadtgrundrisses mit dem damit verbundenen Rückbau überbreiter Straßen (Leipziger Straße, Glinkastraße, Friedrichstraße etc.) enthält zugleich ein verkehrspolitisches Programm, weil der Rückbau von Straßen bei gleichzeitiger intensiver Geschäftsnutzung nur bei entsprechendem Ausbau des öffentlichen Personennahverkehrs (politisch angestrebt sind 20 % Individualverkehr / 80 % öffentlicher Verkehr) und radikaler Änderung der Stellplatzpolitik möglich war. An der Auseinandersetzung über die Stellplatzverordnung zeigten sich exemplarisch die unterschiedlichen Auffassungen vom Charakter der Stadt. Die große Mehrheit der neuen Bauherren/Investoren beharrte, in der Logik der Tradition offener Stadtkonzepte mit vielspurigen Straßen, auf dem Bau der zuvor bauordnungsrechtlich geforderten Stellplätze. In dem knappen Straßenraum der barocken Friedrichstadt hätte dies ein permanentes Verkehrschaos zur Konsequenz gehabt. Um den Widerspruch zwischen bauordnungsrechtlicher Forderung und verkehrspolitisch begründetem Verzicht aufzulösen, wurde 1994 die auf die Reichsgaragenordnung von 1939 zurückzuführende Berliner Stellplatzverordnung so novelliert, daß auf die staatliche Forderung nach Stellplätzen ganz verzichtet wurde. Nur Wohnungsbauten sind von dieser Regelung ausgenommen.

Leistungen und Grenzen der Kritischen Rekonstruktion

Die praktischen Ergebnisse im Umgang mit den zentralen Forderungen der Kritischen Rekonstruktion zeigen den relativen Erfolg, aber auch die Problematik und die Grenzen dieser städtebaulichen Methode.
Leichter gefordert als realisiert war die Rekonstruktion des historischen Stadtgrundrisses, weil seine Zerstörung

in with eight additional plans.[7] What was truly new about these projects was less the urban planning radicalism in their handling of the historical centre than the fact that they had been ordered and distributed by the media, presented like a »mail-order catalogue of architecture for investors and politicians designed to stimulate their appetite for building« (Bruno Flierl).[8] The extent to which this call was taken seriously can be seen in the hypertrophic construction projects presented by developers shortly after, and since forgotten, for many prestigious sites in the centre of Berlin.[9]

Critical Reconstruction

The urban planning method of Critical Reconstruction became established during the International Building Exhibition (IBA) in Berlin as a basis for redevelopment of Southern Friedrichstadt and as such also served as a source of orientation to East Berlin architects. This method was elaborated and continuously developed after the peaceful revolution in East Germany parallel to the restitution of property, but also parallel to the planning rules based on expertises for individual areas (Pariser Platz, Spittelmarkt, Bahnhof Friedrichstrasse, Mehringplatz) and finally for the entire Dorotheenstadt and Friedrichstadt as commissioned by the Senate Construction and Housing Department.[10] Here the aim was not a mechanical transfer of the urban planning strategy applied in Southern Friedrichstadt during the years of the Wall. Work now focused on the continued development of this theoretical principle in its application to the completely different historical, functional and legal situation. Under the changed conditions of unity, the main use in the affected areas is no longer subsidized housing construction, as it was at the time of the IBA, but rather typical inner-city uses: office buildings, hotels, department stores, ministries, university buildings.

Critical Reconstruction has never aimed either at the restoration of historical conditions or at a nostalgic urban plan, but rather at the formation of a differentiated and contemporary urban structure. The centre of Berlin should once again be made perceptible in its historical scales and layerings, its sequences of urban spaces and its differentiated variety of uses, but also as a site of contemporary architecture and of economic conditions. The planned structure of uses differentiates between commercial city, government areas, university quarter and central cultural facilities, but also promotes mixtures within the individual urban quarters and fundamentally supports the integration of inner-city housing. Here the urban planning method of Critical Reconstruction can be reduced to a few rules:

- The historic street network and the associated historic frontage lines of the streets and squares should be respected or restored.
- The maximum admissible height of development should be 22 metres to eaves and 30 metres to ridges.
- Certification of a share of approximately 20% of the gross floor area for housing use is required as the condition for approval.
- The density of development (floor space ratio) is not prescribed. It is yielded by the parameters named above, the type of use and the specifications of the building code. As a rule it is 5.0.
- The aim of new development is the urban house on one lot; the maximum admissible lot size is the block.

Reconstruction of the historical urban plan with the associated re-narrowing of excessively wide streets (Leipziger Strasse, Glinkastrasse, Friedrichstrasse etc.) also implies a traffic-policy programme, because the narrowing of streets with intensive commercial use has been possible only with corresponding expansion of the public mass-transit network (the policy targets are 20% individual transport vs. 80% public transport) and radical transformation of policy in respect to parking spaces. The conflict over parking-space regulations showed in exemplary fashion the differing conceptions of the city's character. The great majority of the new clients/investors followed the logic of the tradition of open city concepts with multi-lane streets by insisting on the construction of the parking places demanded by the former building codes. In the narrow streets of the baroque Friedrichstadt the result would have been permanent traffic chaos. In order to soften the contradiction between the demands of building codes and the changed aims of traffic policy, a 1994 reform of the Berlin parking regulations (based on the 1939 parking-place ordinance) did away completely with state requirements for the supply of parking spaces. Only residential buildings are exempted from this rule.

Achievements and Limits of Critical Reconstruction

The practical results achieved in the use of the central principles of Critical Reconstruction demonstrate the relative success but also the problems and limits of this urban planning method.

nicht kriegsbedingt, sondern der Logik der Stadt- und Verkehrsplaner zur Anpassung der Straßenbreiten an eine neue Verkehrsnachfrage entsprungen war. Am erfolgreichsten wurde diese Rekonstruktion am Pariser Platz durchgesetzt, dessen Neubebauung wegen seiner besonderen Bedeutung ausnahmsweise durch eine Gestaltungssatzung geregelt werden soll,[11] sowie im Kreuzungsbereich Friedrichstraße / Unter den Linden. Dort wurde, um das Raumgefühl der Dorotheenstadt zurückzugewinnen, der Rückbau auf eine Straßenbreite von 14 m zur Grundlage der privaten Bauprojekte gemacht; beide Projekte nördlich und südlich der Straße Unter den Linden verfügen über eine 5 m breite, zweigeschossige Fußgängerarkade. Schwierig gestaltete sich dagegen der Umgang mit dem so wichtigen Kreuzungsbereich Leipziger Straße / Friedrichstraße, der sich innerhalb des Berliner Koalitionssenates zum Gegenstand einer verkehrspolitischen Grundsatzauseinandersetzung entwickelte.

Relativ einfach ließ sich auf der Grundlage der Genehmigung nach §34 die Beschränkung der Bebauungshöhe durchsetzen. Die Bauordnung von 1897, auf deren Grundlage sich die Citybildung im historischen Zentrum vollzog, hatte bei 5 Geschossen eine max. Traufhöhe von 22 m festgelegt und forderte außerdem, daß an öffentlichen Straßen nur in der Baufluchtlinie oder parallel dazu gebaut werden durfte. Die jetzige Regelung von ebenfalls 22 m Traufhöhe, aber max. 30 m Firsthöhe, bei möglicher Rückstaffelung der Geschosse unter einem Winkel von 60°, orientiert sich aber an der Berliner Bauordnung von 1929, die erstmals Staffelgeschosse anstelle des traditionellen Daches erlaubt hatte. Auf dieser Grundlage waren z. B. die Aufstockung des Mossehauses von Mendelsohn, sein berühmtes Columbushaus am Potsdamer Platz oder Alfred Grenanders Bürogebäude in der Dircksenstraße entstanden. Die Bauordnung von 1929 hatte aber auch erstmalig das Wohnen ausdrücklich ausgeschlossen und damit die Umnutzung der ursprünglich als Wohnstadt geplanten Friedrich- und Dorotheenstadt in eine Geschäftsstadt besiegelt. Dieser Prozeß war durch den umfangreichen Bau von Sozialwohnungen sowohl in der Südlichen Friedrichstadt (ehemals West-Berlin) als auch in der Nördlichen Friedrichstadt (ehemals Ost-Berlin) umgekehrt worden. Aus der dichten City einer Metropole war eine Wohnstadt mit vorstädtischem Ambiente geworden. Mit dem Neubau von Geschäftshäusern mit einem mindestens 20prozentigen Wohnanteil wird nun ein neues Blatt in der Geschichte der historischen Innenstadt aufgeschlagen.

Von zentraler Bedeutung ist auch die Forderung nach dem Bau selbständiger Häuser auf eigenständigen Parzellen. Diese theoretisch kaum umstrittene Forderung bildet die Grundlage für die Weiterentwicklung der Innenstadt im Sinne eines europäischen Stadtsystems. In diesem System ist das städtische Grundstück das den städtebaulichen Kontext stiftende Bindeglied zwischen der Stadtanlage und dem privaten Haus. Wie man im Zentrum der großen europäischen Metropolen Paris, Mailand oder Wien sehen kann, hebt die Zusammenlegung von Parzellen dieses System der europäischen Stadt nicht automatisch auf, sondern dehnt es nur aus. Der Bruch dagegen erfolgte, als Konsequenz neuer städtebaulicher Leitbilder in Berlin (West) und Berlin (Ost), durch die gewaltsame Einführung entmischter Nutzungsstrukturen und kommunaler bzw. städtischer Eigentumsverhältnisse und nicht – wie oft behauptet – durch den der Marktwirtschaft innewohnenden Konzentrationsprozeß. Die Wiedereinführung kleinteiliger Eigentumsverhältnisse und damit das Anknüpfen an die besonders im Zentrum der Stadt unterbrochene Stadtentwicklung hätte eindeutige politische und rechtliche Vorgaben erfordert, die es wie beschrieben in dieser Form nicht gab. Schließt man die bloß oberflächliche Scheinvielfalt von Fassaden aus, bleibt nur die Möglichkeit, in Zusammenarbeit mit den neuen Bauherren eine nutzungsstrukturell begründete Vielfalt als Grundlage für den Entwurf selbständiger Häuser zu entwickeln. Dies wurde beim Hofgarten am Gendarmenmarkt, dem Kontorhaus Mitte, dem Gendarmenmarkt und dem Gebäude Schützenstraße / Markgrafenstraße umgesetzt. Jedes dieser Projekte ist als eigentumsrechtliche Einheit ein Ausdruck der realen Besitzverhältnisse und der ökonomisch-politischen Zwänge, obwohl jedes aus funktional und bauordnungsrechtlich selbständigen Häusern verschiedener Architekten besteht. Eine Variante dieses Prinzips bildet das Projekt Schützenstraße von Aldo Rossi, da hier von nur einem Architekten die Collage einer städtischen Struktur mit 20 individuellen Häusern entworfen wurde.

Leitbild europäische Stadt

Parallel zur Kritischen Rekonstruktion der Dorotheen- und Friedrichstadt stellte sich die Aufgabe der Neuinterpretation weitestgehend freigeräumter, nur noch mit Resten der historischen Substanz bebauter zusammenhängender Areale im Zentrum. Dabei ging es um so unterschiedliche Bereiche wie

Reconstruction of the historical ground plan of the city proved easier to demand than to implement. The reason: the destruction of the ground plan was not a result of the war, but arose from planners' efforts to adapt street widths to new traffic demand. This reconstruction proved most successful at Pariser Platz, whose redevelopment is regulated by a formal statute (an exception due to its special significance)[11], and also in the area of the junction of Friedrichstrasse and Unter den Linden. In order to restore the spatial sensation of the Dorotheenstadt, a reduction of the street to a width of 14 metres was made the basis of the private construction projects; both projects to the north and south of Unter den Linden have 5-metre-wide, 2-storey pedestrian arcades. The crucial intersection of Leipziger Strasse and Friedrichstrasse, on the other hand, proved much more difficult to resolve, and this issue became the subject of a battle over traffic policy within the coalition Senate governing Berlin.

In contrast, restricting the height of construction on the basis of approval according to Article 34 proved relatively simple. The building code of 1897, which had served as the basis for formation of the inner city within the historical urban centre, had specified a maximum eaves height of 22 metres with 5 storeys and additionally required that buildings could only be built on public streets in the line of development or parallel to it. The present rules, which likewise provide for eaves heights of 22 metres, but for maximum ridge heights of 30 metres, with possible set-backs of storeys under a 60° angle, is oriented to the Berlin Building Code of 1929, which for the first time allowed stepped-back storeys in place of the traditional roof. This was the basis, for example, of the additional floors on top of the Mossehaus of Mendelsohn, his famous Columbus House on Potsdamer Platz or Alfred Grenander's office building in Dircksenstrasse. The 1929 Building Code also expressly excluded housing for the first time, thus permanently confirming the functional transformation into a commercial district of Dorotheenstadt and Friedrichstadt, which were originally planned as residential areas. This process was reversed by the extensive construction of public housing both in Southern Friedrichstadt (formerly West Berlin) and Northern Friedrichstadt (formerly East Berlin). The dense inner city of a metropolis was transformed into a residential city with a suburban atmosphere. The new construction of commercial buildings with a minimum housing share of 20% now opens a new page in the history of the historical inner city.

Also of central significance is the requirement for the construction of independent buildings on individual lots. This condition, scarcely disputed in theory, forms the basis for further development of the inner city according to a European city system. In this system the urban lot is the source of urban context, the connecting element between the city as a whole and the individual private building. As one can see in the centres of the great European metropolises of Paris, Milan or Vienna, the fusion of lots does not automatically suspend this system of the European city, but merely extends it. The violation of this principle occurred as a consequence of new urban planning concepts in Berlin (West) and Berlin (East) and the violent introduction of the separation of structures and of government ownership – and not, as is often claimed, thanks to the process of concentration implicit to the market economy. The re-introduction of small-scale ownership conditions, and thus the return to the pattern of urban development formerly abandoned particularly in the city centre, would have required clear political and legal rules, which, as we have described here, were not provided in this form. If one excludes the purely superficial formal variety of façades, then the only possibility is that of developing diversity based on use structures, in cooperation with the new clients, leading to the design of independent buildings. This approach was used in the case of the Hofgarten on the Gendarmenmarkt, the Kontorhaus Mitte, the Gendarmenmarkt and the building at Schützenstrasse/Markgrafenstrasse. Each of these projects expresses, as a distinct ownership unit, the real ownership conditions and political-economic constraints, even though each consists of buildings by different architects that are independent both in their functions and in terms of the building code.

A variant of this principle is represented by Aldo Rossi's Schützenstrasse project, since here a single architect designed the collage of an urban structure with twenty individual buildings.

The European City as a Model
Parallel to the Critical Reconstruction of Dorotheenstadt and Friedrichstadt, planners confronted the task of reinterpreting areas in the centre which had been largely cleared of buildings and contained only a few

- den Potsdamer Platz im ehemaligen Grenzbereich zwischen West-Berlin und Ost-Berlin,
- den Alexanderplatz im Übergangsbereich zwischen der Mitte und den ehemaligen östlichen Vorstädten,
- den Spreeinselbereich im Zentrum der historischen Stadt mit dem Palast der Republik auf dem historischen Standort des Schlosses,
- den Spreebogen als neuem Zentrum für Parlament und Regierung und schließlich
- den Bereich des neuen Stadtquartiers am Lehrter Fernbahnhof.

Für all diese Bereiche wurden städtebauliche Wettbewerbe in engster Absprache mit den künftigen Nutzern bzw. Investoren ausgeschrieben. Generell wurde dabei das Leitbild der »europäischen Stadt« mit ihrer strikten Trennung der öffentlichen Straßen, Plätze und Parkanlagen von den privaten Flächen vorgegeben. Dem widerspricht der Wunsch vieler Investoren nach halböffentlichen »Shopping-malls«. Die Gefahr, daß dieser Typus zur Grundlage neuer Bebauungen hätte werden können, war besonders groß, weil das städtische Grundstück als kleinste operative Einheit des städtischen Hausbaus in den zur Neuordnung anstehenden Gebieten weitestgehend fehlte. Auf dem etwa 50 ha großen Wettbewerbsgebiet des Potsdamer Platzes bestand die Aufgabe darin, mit den relativ wenigen neuen Grundstückseigentümern (debis, Sony, Wertheim, ABB) eine Neuinterpretation des Typus der europäischen Stadt auf der Grundlage eines kerngebietstypischen Bauprogramms zu versuchen. In der Wettbewerbsauslobung wurde daher die Auseinandersetzung mit der Parzelle verlangt: »Der Topos der Parzelle bzw. der Parzellenstruktur könnte sich für die weiteren Überlegungen als Schlüsselbegriff erweisen, wenn er über seine ursprüngliche historische Überwindung hinaus als Chiffre für funktionale, strukturelle und gestalterische Maßstäblichkeit und Mischung verstanden wird.« Die Mischung sollte ausdrücklich nicht durch Integration in eine Großform, sondern wo immer denkbar in kleinteiliger parzellenbezogener Anordnung erzielt werden.[12] Die Sieger der ersten Stufe des städtebaulichen Wettbewerbs – die Münchener Architekten Hilmer & Sattler – formulierten dies in der Erläuterung zu ihrem Entwurf: »Nicht das weltweit verwendete amerikanische Stadtmodell der Hochhausakkumulation, sondern die Vorstellung von der kompakten, räumlich komplexen europäischen Stadt liegt dem Entwurf zugrunde.« Städtisches Leben sollte sich nicht im Inneren großstrukturierter Gebäudekomplexe, sondern auf Straßen und Plätzen, d.h. im Stadtraum entfalten. Auf der Basis dieser Stadtidee entwarfen Hilmer & Sattler einen neuen Blockraster in der Größenordnung von 50x50 m. Das Raumprofil der öffentlichen Straßen hatte bei einer Gebäudehöhe von 35 m und einer Straßenbreite von 17,50 m ein Verhältnis von 2:1. Damit wurde in diesem Entwurf nicht nur die Berliner Traufhöhe von 22 m auf 35 m angehoben, sondern auch die städtische Atmosphäre durch ein senkrechtes Straßenprofil entscheidend verändert. Auf der Grundlage dieses Projektes wurde in Berlin und am Beispiel Berlin eine sehr gründliche und international beachtete Diskussion über die Zukunft der europäischen Innenstadt geführt.

Berlinische Geschäftshausarchitektur

Architektur als soziale Kunst braucht Regeln als Ausdruck gesellschaftlicher Stadtvorstellungen. Dies gilt insbesondere für die architektonische Darstellung gesellschaftlich wichtiger Nutzungen wie Rathäuser, Museen, Kirchen, Bahnhöfe etc. Doch mit jeder Rahmensetzung beginnt erst die eigentliche Arbeit und Verantwortung der Architekten und ihrer Bauherren.

Am Beginn dieser Arbeit steht der Appell, die in den 30er Jahren unterbrochene Tradition des großstädtischen Berliner Büro-, Geschäfts- und Warenhauses aufzugreifen und fortzuschreiben. Für diese Berliner Tradition stehen Namen wie Peter Behrens, Wilhelm Cremer, Emil Fahrenkamp, Alfred Grenander, Ludwig Hoffmann, Paul Mebes, Alfred Messel, Erich Mendelsohn, Hermann Muthesius, Bruno Paul, Hans Poelzig, Otto Rudolf Salvisberg, Johann Emil Schaudt, Max Taut, Richard Wolffenstein und andere. Als Befürworter der Großstadt entwarfen sie – anders als Bruno Taut, Hans Scharoun oder Ludwig Hilberseimer mit ihren radikalen Alternativen – Geschäftshäuser für die bestehende Stadt, deren Modernität sie in zeitgemäßer Architektur zum Ausdruck bringen wollten.

Die Modernität der großmaßstäblichen Grund- und Aufrisse zeigte sich in der Anwendung modernster Stahl- bzw. Stahlbetonkonstruktionen, im Entwurf großzügiger, leicht lesbarer Erschließungssysteme und großflächiger, horizontal gegliederter Fassaden mit großformatigen Elementen. Der architektonische Ausdruck dieser reinen Büro- und Geschäftshäuser war regelmäßig der eines Hauses mit deutlich ablesbarem Eingang, mit seriellen Fensterformaten und für Berlin typischen Fassadenmaterialien wie gelblich-grauem Sandstein, Muschelkalk, Kalkstein, aber auch Travertin oder keramischer Verkleidung und, seltener, hartgebranntem Klinker.

remnants of the historical substance of coherent developments. This involved such different areas as:
- Potsdamer Platz in the former border area between West Berlin and East Berlin;
- Alexanderplatz in the transitional area between the centre and the former peripheral areas of the east;
- The Spreeinsel area in the centre of the historical city with the Palast der Republik on the historical site of the imperial palace;
- The Spreebogen as the new centre for parliament and government; and finally
- The area of the new urban quarter at Lehrter Bahnhof train station.

Urban planning competitions were conducted for all these areas in close consultation with future users or investors. In general the guiding principle of the »European city,« with its strict division between public streets, squares and parks on one hand and private lots on the other, was a central requirement. This is contradicted by the wish of many investors for semi-public shopping malls. The risk of this building type becoming the basis for new developments was especially great because the urban property, as the smallest operative unit of urban construction, was largely absent in the areas subject to re-organisation.

On the roughly 50-hectare competition site of Potsdamer Platz, the main task consisted of attempting a new interpretation of the type of the European city on the basis of a core-area construction programme along with the relatively small number of new property-owners (debis, Sony, Wertheim, ABB). The competition brief thus required an awareness of the original lot sizes: »The topos of the lot or lot structure could prove a key concept for further considerations if it is understood as a cipher for functional, structural and formal scales and mixtures rather than merely as an overcome historical value.« The mixture was to be achieved expressly not through integration into a large form, but rather, wherever conceivable, in a small-scale, lot-related arrangement.[12] The winners of the first stage of the urban planning competition – the Munich architects Hilmer & Sattler – formulated this in the explanation of their project: »The plan is based not on the American urban model of high-rise accumulation used around the world, but rather on the idea of the compact, spatially complex European city.« Urban life should not arise in the interior of large-structured building complexes, but on streets and squares, that is, in urban space. On the basis of this idea of the city Hilmer & Sattler designed a new block grid of 50x50 metres. The spatial profile of the public streets had a proportion of 2:1, with building heights of 35 metres and a street width of 17.5 metres. Thus this plan not only raised the Berlin eaves height from 22 metres to 35 metres, but also decisively changed the urban atmosphere with a vertical street profile. This project triggered a very thorough and internationally noted discussion about the future of the European inner city.

Berlin Commercial Architecture

Architecture as a social art needs rules as the expression of society's ideas of the city. This applies particularly to the architectural representation of socially important functions, such as town halls, museums, churches, train stations, etc. But establishing a set of criteria is only the beginning of the real work and responsibility of the architects and their clients.

At the beginning of this work stands the call to resume and continue the tradition of metropolitan Berlin commercial architecture that was interrupted in the 1930s. This Berlin tradition is represented by names such as Peter Behrens, Wilhelm Cremer, Emil Fahrenkamp, Alfred Grenander, Ludwig Hoffmann, Paul Mebes, Alfred Messel, Erich Mendelsohn, Hermann Muthesius, Bruno Paul, Hans Poelzig, Otto Rudolf Salvisberg, Johann Emil Schaudt, Max Taut, Richard Wolffenstein and others. As adherents of the big city, they – unlike Bruno Taut, Hans Scharoun, or Ludwig Hilberseimer with their radical alternatives – designed commercial architecture for the existing city, whose modernity they wanted to express in up-to-date architecture.

The modernity of the large-scale ground plans and elevations was manifested in the application of modern steel or reinforced steel constructions, in the design of roomy, easily readable access systems and spacious, horizontally organised façades with large-format elements. The architectural expression of these office and commercial buildings was, as a rule, that of a building with a clearly readable entrance, with serial window formats and façade materials typical of Berlin, such as yellow-gray sandstone, shell limestone and limestone, as well as travertine or ceramic facing, or, more rarely, fired clinker brick.

These office and commercial buildings, erected in the context of existing blocks, stand as examples of the current demand for a »stone« architecture.[13] This

Diese im Kontext bestehender Blöcke errichteten Büro- und Geschäftshäuser stehen beispielhaft für die aktuelle Forderung nach einer »steinernen« Architektur.[13] Dieser Forderung liegt die Überzeugung zugrunde, daß es eine betonte Materialität der Stadt gibt. Ausschließlich aus gläsernen oder die konstruktiven Elemente nachzeichnenden High-Tech-Gebäuden kann keine Stadt im traditionellen Sinne entstehen. Eine europäische Stadt braucht Wände und Öffnungen, die den Übergangsbereich zwischen Haus und Stadt markieren.

Der Appell[14] zur Entwicklung »steinerner Fassaden« bedeutet nicht die Forderung nach einer einschichtig aufgebauten Wand. Die tragenden Konstruktionen der berühmten Beispiele Berliner Geschäfts- und Warenhäuser waren immer verkleidet, innen wie außen. Wirklich neu am Thema Verkleidung ist die konstruktive und architektonische Verarbeitung der Wärmedämmung zwischen der Verkleidung und den tragenden Elementen. Es geht nicht um das »ob«, sondern darum, »wie« eine Verkleidung in handwerklich sauberer Art in eine dauerhafte Verbindung zur Konstruktion gebracht wird. Dies richtet sich auch gegen gestalterische Willkür, anonyme Glätte und dekorative Verkleidung durch extrem dünne und mit offenen Fugen vor die Wärmedämmung gehängte Natursteinmaterialien. All dies ist eine Herausforderung für die Architekten – und ihre Bauherren –; architektonische Qualität kann nicht von einer auch langfristigen wirtschaftlichen Bewertung der Bau- und Bewirtschaftungskosten getrennt werden.

Öffentliche Diskussion und Kritik

Der Planungs-, Projektierungs- und Realisierungsprozeß der Berliner Bauprojekte wurde von Beginn an von Kritik begleitet. Die politische Kritik reibt sich am Umfang, der schieren Größe, den Verkehrs- und Umweltbelastungen sowie den alltäglichen Begleitumständen riesiger Großbaustellen im Zentrum der Stadt. Die Fachkritik hingegen richtet sich gegen drei zentrale Aspekte des städtebaulichen und architektonischen Umsetzungsprozesses:
- das städtebauliche Konzept der Kritischen Rekonstruktion,
- das Insistieren auf Wiederaufnahme der europäischen Stadtbautradition,
- und die Forderung nach dem Anknüpfen an die Architekturtradition Berliner Büro- und Geschäftshäuser der Frühmoderne und Moderne.

Daran entzündete sich eine thematisch weitreichende und auch von einer breiten Öffentlichkeit verfolgte Debatte. Sie richtete sich auf das Verhältnis von Architektur, Städtebau und Politik, auf die Frage, welche Einflüsse die heute entstehende Großstadtarchitektur tatsächlich bestimmen oder aber bestimmen sollten, und insbesondere darauf, ob es möglich und sinnvoll ist, den typischen Charakter einer Stadt wie Berlin städtebaulich und architektonisch zu erfassen, zu bewahren und womöglich zu stärken.[15]

Die Kritik ist wegen der großen Zahl der Projekte und vor dem Hintergrund der überwiegend negativen Erfahrungen, die man in Berlin im Umgang mit weitreichenden Neugestaltungskonzepten aus der Kriegs- und Nachkriegszeit gemacht hat, verständlich und in konstruktiver Form willkommen. Mit den seit 1991 regelmäßig durchgeführten »Berliner Architekturgesprächen« bietet die Senatsbauverwaltung den Beteiligten und den Kritikern ausdrücklich Gelegenheit zur Auseinandersetzung. Jede Kritik wird jedoch maßstabslos, wenn sie die Produktionsbedingungen für Architekturprojekte außer acht läßt. Deshalb soll dieses Buch auch zur Versachlichung einer Architekturdebatte beitragen, in der ästhetische und politische Kategorien zuweilen leichtfertig vermischt oder gleichgesetzt werden.[16] Es vermittelt einen Eindruck von der enormen Anstrengung der beteiligten Architekten, Planer, Ingenieure, Verwaltungen und vor allem Bauherren und Investoren, die unter extremem Zeitdruck und schwierigsten Umständen Projekte baureif zu entwickeln hatten. Nicht zuletzt dokumentiert es das Ergebnis einer außergewöhnlich großen wirtschaftlichen Konkurrenz mittlerer und großer Architekturbüros, aber auch einer von der Senatsbauverwaltung ausdrücklich unterstützten, die regionalen und nationalen Grenzen sprengenden, offenen Architekturpolitik. Sie zeigt sich nicht zuletzt darin, daß z.B. 1994/95 allein im Zentrum ca. 150 Architekten aus 11 Ländern tätig waren.

Offenheit darf jedoch nicht verwechselt werden mit Beliebigkeit, Experiment nicht mit Zerstörung der städtebaulichen Struktur. Metropole wird nur diejenige Stadt, die sich als Ort ihrer Geschichte behauptet. Es ist deswegen nicht das Ziel, herausragende Architekturleistungen wie in einem Museum zu kollektionieren. Neue Architektur muß sich auf die Stadt, auf den historischen und städtebaulichen Kontext, auf die architektonische Tradition beziehen, um die Identität der Stadt zu stärken. Architektonischer Fortschritt entsteht nicht im Bruch, sondern in der Weiterentwicklung bewährter Traditionen, Typologien und Technologien.

demand is based on the conviction that an urban atmosphere derives from the emphasised materiality of the city. High-tech buildings consisting solely of glass or displaying all their structural elements cannot allow the creation of a city in the traditional sense. A European city needs walls and openings that mark the transition between building and city.

The call[14] for development of »stone façades« does not mean the demand for a single-layer wall. The load-bearing structures of the famous examples of Berlin commercial buildings and department stores were always clad, inside and out. One genuinely new aspect of cladding is the structural and architectural exploitation of thermal insulation between the facing and the supporting elements. At issue here is not »whether«, but rather »how« cladding can be brought into a durable connection with the structure in a cleanly crafted fashion. This is also directed against formal randomness, anonymous smoothness and decorative claddings by means of extremely thin natural-stone materials suspended with open joints in front of the insulating material. All this is a challenge for the architects as well as for their clients; architectural quality cannot be separated from a long-term economic assessment of construction and management costs.

Public Discussion and Criticism

The planning and implementation process of the Berlin building projects has been accompanied by criticism from the very beginning. The political criticism objects to the scope, the sheer enormity, the enormous traffic load, the ensuing pollution and other damage to the environment and the everyday side effects of gigantic construction sites in the centre of the city. The architectural criticism, on the other hand, is directed against three central aspects of the urban planning and architectural implementation process:

- The urban planning strategy of Critical Reconstruction;
- The insistence on resumption of the European tradition of urban development; and
- The demand for continuation of the architectural tradition of the Berlin office and commercial architecture of early modernism and modernism.

These objections triggered a broad debate that was also followed by a wide public audience. Discussion revolved around the relationship between architecture, urban development and politics, the question of which influences define or should define the architecture of the contemporary big city and in particular whether it is possible or reasonable to define, preserve and perhaps even strengthen the typical character of a city such as Berlin in terms of architecture and urban planning.[15]

When we consider both the large number of projects and the predominantly negative experience in Berlin with far-reaching urban redevelopment strategies during and after the war, these criticisms are understandable and, when made constructively, welcome. With the »Berlin Architecture Talks« conducted regularly since 1991, the Senate Construction and Housing Department has expressly offered participants and critics a chance to speak their minds. Any criticism becomes disproportionate, however, when it fails to account for the conditions to which architecture projects are subject. For the same reason this book should also contribute to objectify an architectural debate in which aesthetic and political categories are often casually mixed or conflated.[16] It conveys an impression of the immense efforts of the participating architects, planners, engineers, administrations and especially of the clients and investors, who had to bring projects right up to the point of construction under extreme time pressure and the most difficult conditions. Not least it documents the result of exceptionally strong competition among large and mid-sized architectural offices, as well as of an open architectural policy expressly supported by the Senate Construction and Housing Department and reaching far beyond national and regional limits. This is demonstrated not least by the fact that around 150 architects from 11 countries were active in the central area alone in 1994/95.

However, openness should not be confused with randomness, and experimentation should not become equivalent to destruction of the urban planning structure. The category of »metropolis« can be claimed only by that city which asserts itself as a site of history. For this reason it is not the aim to collect outstanding architectural achievements as if in a museum. New architecture must relate to the city, to the historical and urban planning context and to architectural tradition, in order to reinforce the identity of the city. Architectural progress evolves from the continued development, and not from the complete renunciation, of traditions, typologies and technologies.

Zu diesem Buch

Was mit dieser Dokumentation in Zeichnungen und Modellen vorliegt, ist eine architektur- und städtebautheoretische Zwischenbilanz großstädtischer Büro- und Geschäftshäuser – mit und ohne Wohnanteil –, die in der Zeit nach 1989 entworfen wurden. Die Veröffentlichung soll die vorgestellten Projekte während der Zeit ihrer Ausführung, Fertigstellung und Aufnahme in das Stadtbild und das städtische Leben begleiten. Sie erfolgt daher zu einem Zeitpunkt, zu dem noch kein einziger der gezeigten Bauten fertiggestellt ist. Dadurch bietet sich zugleich die Möglichkeit, die Entwürfe vor allem unter konzeptionellen und typologischen Aspekten zu betrachten, wie es in den einzelnen Kapiteln geschieht. So können diese unter vergleichbaren Bedingungen konzipierten Projekte im Quervergleich gelesen und bewertet werden.

Dies wird durch die Vereinheitlichung des Maßstabes von Ansichten, Grundrissen und Schnitten (in der Regel 1:750) erleichtert.

Die Auswahl der Projekte des Hauptteils erfolgte ausschließlich unter qualitativen Gesichtspunkten; die Projekte sollten zum Thema einen eigenständigen architektonischen oder typologischen Beitrag leisten und im Bau oder mindestens baureif sein, und es mußte möglich sein, in aller Regel den zur Ausführung bestimmten Planungsstand zu zeigen. Im Anhang werden 43 weitere nach 1989 geplante Büro- und Geschäftshäuser aufgeführt.

Die Gesamtheit der Beispiele ist nicht zuletzt ein Beleg dafür, daß es möglich ist, technologische Komplexität und architektonische Tradition in Einklang zu bringen. Tradition und Innovation sind kein Widerspruch.

---

1 Wolf Jobst Siedler, »Stadtgedanken«, München 1990, S. 27
2 Josef Paul Kleihues, »Südliche Friedrichstadt: Rudimente der Geschichte, Ort des Widerspruchs, Kritische Rekonstruktion«, in: »Internationale Bauausstellung Berlin 1984/87, Die Neubaugebiete, Dokumente, Projekte«, Stuttgart 1987, S. 11-28.
3 Siehe dazu: Aengevelt Research, »City Report, Region Berlin Nr. IV«, Berlin, Juli 1994.
4 Beschluß des Magistrats von Berlin vom 6. 11. 1990
5 Mitglieder der Jury waren Prof. Kleihues, Prof. Hollein (Wien), Prof. Kiessler (München), Prof. Marg (Hamburg), Prof. Sawade (Berlin), Hr. Ahlrichs (Treuhand), Hr. Haase (Bezirksbürgermeister), Hr. Klein (SenBauWohn), Hr. Dahlhaus (SenStadtUm).
6 Die von November 1990 an laufende Serie der FAZ wurde dokumentiert in AD »Berlin Tomorrow«, Vittorio Magnago Lampugnani (Hrsg.), London 1991.
7 »Kleine Buletten für das neue Berlin – 8 Architekten und Künstler entwerfen eine andere Stadt«, in: Geo-Spezial: »Metropole Berlin«, Hamburg 6.2.1991.
8 Bruno Flierl, »Hochhäuser für Berlin – wozu und wo?«, in: »Die Stadt als Gabentisch«, Leipzig 1992, S. 457.
9 Siehe dazu Bauwelt Nr. 39/18. Oktober 1991: »66 Bauwünsche für die Mitte Berlins«, S. 2098ff.
10 Durch Dieter Hoffmann-Axthelm und Bernhard Strecker. Senatsverwaltung für Bau- und Wohnungswesen, Berlin, Hans Stimmann (Hrsg.), »Städtebaulicher Strukturplan« (Heft 6 der Reihe »Städtebau und Architektur«, Berlin 1992)
11 Die Grundlage für die Satzung bildet ein Gutachten von Bruno Flierl und W. Rolfes (unveröffentlicht), Berlin 1993.
12 Ausschreibung Potsdamer und Leipziger Platz, internationaler engerer Wettbewerb, Berlin, Juli 1991.
13 Diese Forderung hat gerade in Berlin zu vielfältigen Mißverständnissen geführt, da sie die 1930 von Werner Hegemann am Hobrechtplan vorgetragene Kritik am »Steinernen Berlin« zu relativieren schien. Hegemanns umstrittene Kritik bezog sich jedoch nicht auf die Architektur von Bürohäusern, sondern auf die bauordnungsrechtlich mögliche Dichte der Wohnhäuser.
14 Es gibt in Berlin – mit der erwähnten Ausnahme »Pariser Platz« – keinerlei behördliche Gestaltungs- und Materialvorschriften.
15 Siehe dazu ARCH+, Nr. 122, Juni 1994: »Von Berlin nach Neuteutonia«, und »Neue Berlinische Architektur: Eine Debatte«, herausgegeben von Annegret Burg, Berlin Basel Boston 1994.
16 Siehe dazu exemplarisch ARCH+, a. a. O.

Die hier vorgetragenen Gedanken wurden in kürzerer Form an verschiedenen Stellen veröffentlicht. Für Anregungen danke ich U. Luther und den Mitarbeitern und Mitarbeiterinnen der Architekturwerkstatt B. Hoidn, M. Sauerzapfe, B. Kalthöner sowie D. Hoffmann-Axthelm, J. P. Kleihues und H. Kollhoff.

About This Book

The drawings and models shown in this documentation present a cross-section of architectural theory and urban planning applied to metropolitan office and commercial buildings – with and without housing – in the period after 1989. The publication is designed to accompany the presented projects during the period of their construction, completion and integration into the urban scenery and the life of the city. It therefore appears at a moment when not one of the buildings shown has been completed. At the same time this offers a chance to study the designs according to conceptual and typological aspects, as is done here in the individual chapters. Thus all the projects planned under comparable conditions can be read and assessed in cross-comparison. This is also facilitated by standardisation of the scale of elevations, floor plans and sections (usually 1:750).

The selection of the projects of the main section was made solely by qualitative criteria: the projects were required to make an independent architectural or typological contribution to the subject at hand, to be under construction or at least ready for construction and to show wherever possible the state of planning approved for implementation. 43 additional office and commercial buildings planned after 1989 are shown in the Appendix.

Taken together, these examples demonstrate that it is possible to bring technological complexity and architectural tradition into harmony: tradition and innovation are no opposites.

---

1 Wolf Jobst Siedler, »Stadtgedanken«, Munich 1990, p. 27.
2 Josef Paul Kleihues, »Südliche Friedrichstadt: Rudimente der Geschichte, Ort des Widerspruchs, Kritische Rekonstruktion«, in: »Internationale Bauausstellung Berlin 1984/87, Die Neubaugebiete, Dokumente, Projekte«, Stuttgart 1987, pp. 11-28.
3 See here: Aengevelt Research, »City Report, Region Berlin No. IV, « Berlin, July 1994.
4 Resolution of the Berlin Magistrate of November 6, 1990.
5 Members of the jury were Prof. Kleihues, Prof. Hollein (Vienna), Prof. Kiessler (Munich), Prof. Marg (Hamburg), Prof. Sawade (Berlin), Mr. Ahlrichs (Treuhand), Mr. Haase (district mayor), Mr. Klein (Senate Construction and Housing Department), Mr. Dahlhaus (Berlin Ministry for Urban Development and Environmental Protection).
6 The series in the Frankfurter Allgemeine, which began in November 1990, was documented in AD, »Berlin tomorrow«, Vittorio Magnago Lampugnani (ed.), London 1991.
7 »Kleine Buletten für das neue Berlin – 8 Architekten und Künstler entwerfen eine andere Stadt«, in: Geo-Spezial: »Metropole Berlin«, Hamburg, February 6, 1991.
8 Bruno Flierl, »Hochhäuser für Berlin – wozu und wo?«, in: »Die Stadt als Gabentisch«, Leipzig 1992, p. 457.
9 See Bauwelt No. 39 October 18, 1991: »66 Bauwünsche für die Mitte Berlins,« p. 2098ff.
10 By Dieter Hoffmann-Axthelm and Bernhard Strecker. Senate Construction and Housing Department, Berlin, Hans Stimmann (ed.), »Städtebaulicher Strukturplan«, (vol. 6 of the series »Städtebau und Architektur«, Berlin 1992).
11 The basis for the statute is an expertise by Bruno Flierl and W. Rolfes (unpublished), Berlin 1993.
12 Competition brief for Potsdamer Platz and Leipziger Platz, international restricted competition, Berlin, July 1991.
13 Precisely in Berlin this demand has led to many misunderstandings, seeming as it did to relativise Werner Hegemann's 1930 criticism of the »stone Berlin« represented by the Hobrecht Plan. Hegemann's controversial critique was not aimed at the architecture of office buildings, but at the possible density of residential buildings allowed by building codes.
14 Except for the example of Pariser Platz mentioned here, there are no government rules on design or material use in Berlin.
15 See here ARCH +, No. 122, June 1994: »Von Berlin nach Neuteutonia«, and »Neue Berlinische Architektur: Eine Debatte«, edited by Annegret Burg, Berlin Basel Boston 1994.
16 For a representative example, see ARCH+, loc cit.

The ideas presented here were published in shorter form in various places. My thanks for suggestions go to U. Luther; to B. Hoidn, M. Sauerzapfe, B. Kalthöner, all members of the Architecture Workshop; and to D. Hoffmann-Axthelm, J. P. Kleihues and H. Kollhoff.

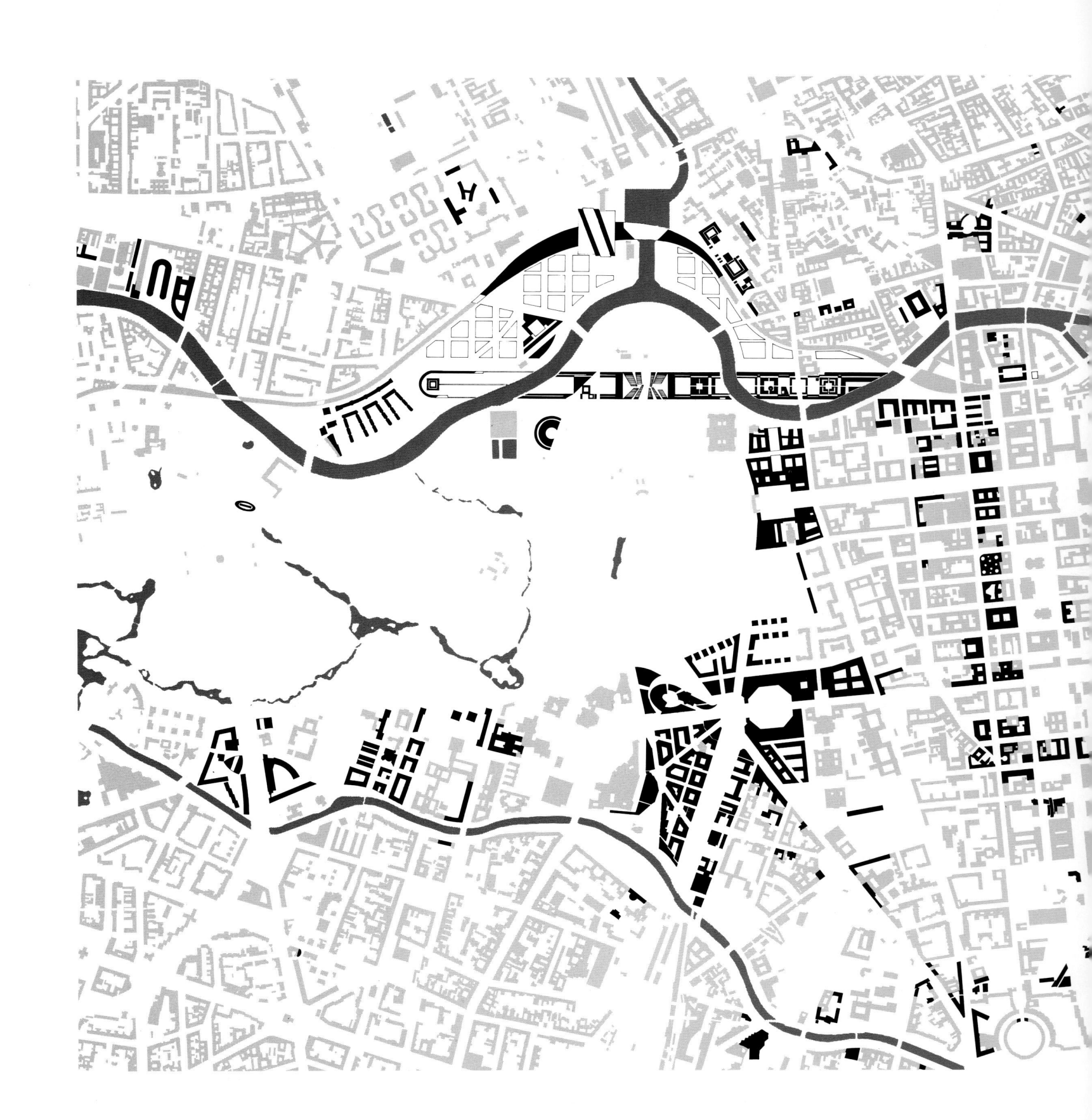

Projekte in der Stadtmitte, Stand 1994 (Architekturwerkstatt, Senatsverwaltung für Bau- und Wohnungswesen)
Projects in the city centre as of 1994 (Architecture Workshop, Senate Construction and Housing Department)

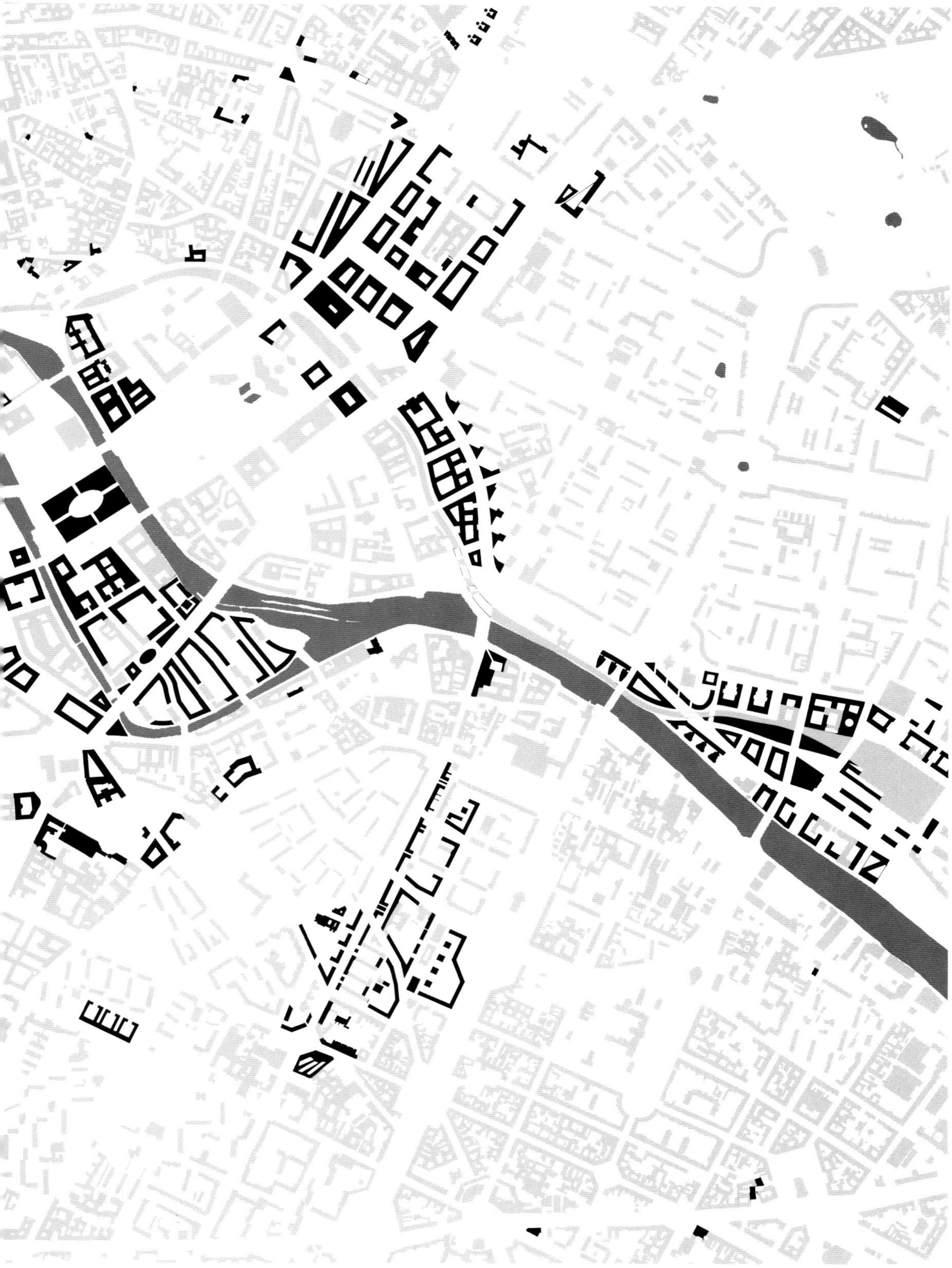

Das Geschäftshaus als Baustein der Stadt

Berlin verändert sein Gesicht. Dorotheen- und Friedrichstadt werden von Baukränen bevölkert, im Spreebogen entsteht ein neues Parlamentsviertel und zwischen Potsdamer Platz, Kemperplatz und Landwehrkanal ein ganzes Büro- und Geschäftsviertel in der Größenordnung eines Stadtzentrums. Auch die City West und wichtige Verkehrsverbindungen wie die Hauptradialen der Stadt oder der S-Bahnring erleben mit Planungen und Baustellen in nicht unerheblichem Umfang eine tiefgreifende Veränderung ihrer Physiognomie und Nutzungsstruktur.
Bedeutender architektonischer Baustein ist dabei das Büro- und Geschäftshaus, das vom einfachen Haus in der Baulücke über die vollständige Blocküberbauung bis zum Hochhaus oder Geschäftskomplex in allen denkbaren städtischen Dimensionen entsteht. Durch den hohen Anteil, den dieser Gebäudetyp insbesondere in den innerstädtischen Bereichen am Gesamtbauvolumen hat, trägt er die städtebaulichen und stadtstrukturellen Veränderungen wesentlich mit und zeigt in exemplarischer Weise den Zusammenhang zwischen einer neuen urbanen Architektur und einem im Werden befindlichen Stadtbild, das das Leben in der Metropole Berlin bis weit ins nächste Jahrtausend hinein bestimmen wird.
Das Büro- und Geschäftshaus hat in Berlin eine vergleichsweise junge Tradition. Während es in Handelsstädten wie Hamburg eine stetige Entwicklung vom Kaufmannshaus über das Kontorhaus bis zum modernen Bürogebäude gab, setzte der Bau von Geschäftshäusern in Berlin spät und abrupt ein, umfaßte dann aber rasch ein weites Spektrum unterschiedlicher Bautypen. Diese sprunghafte und stürmische Entwicklung stand in unmittelbarem Zusammenhang mit dem Ausbau zur Hauptstadt des Deutschen Kaiserreiches und zu einer der führenden europäischen Metropolen. Dabei kam dem Geschäftshaus von Anfang an besondere Bedeutung gerade in den innerstädtischen Bereichen zu.
Wie sehr sich das Bild der Stadt um die Jahrhundertwende mit der Einführung dieses neuen Gebäudetyps zu wandeln begann, wird deutlich, wenn man sich die damals entstandenen Häuser im Nebeneinander zu der vorangegangenen Bebauungsgeneration vergegenwärtigt. Die Bürofassaden folgten immer seltener den Gesetzmäßigkeiten der bürgerlichen Wohnhausfassade mit stehenden Fensterformaten und repräsentativem Fassadenschmuck. Statt dessen setzten sich horizontale Fenster oder Fensterbänder durch, die der auf strenger Addition standardisierter Büroräume aufgebauten Rasterstruktur des Gebäudetragwerks folgten.
Besonders tiefgreifend war – verstärkt auch durch die Umnutzung vorhandener Gebäude – der funktionale Umbau der Stadt auf dem Weg von der Wohnstadt zur Geschäftsstadt. Die Wohnstadt mit

The Commercial Building: An Urban Component

The face of Berlin is changing. Cranes cluster in Dorotheenstadt and Friedrichstadt, a new parliament quarter is being built on a bend of the river, the »Spreebogen«, and a whole new business district, as big as a town centre, is springing up between Potsdamer Platz, Kemperplatz and the Landwehr Canal. Also in the City West and along important communications links such as the main roads into the city and the S-Bahn urban railway ring, new projects bring about considerable changes in terms of appearance and structure of use.

A cornerstone in this new architectural development is the office and commercial building, which can be anything from a simple infill for a building gap to a complete new block development, or a high-rise or integrated business complex. The presence of a high percentage of this type of building in the inner city in particular, means that it has a considerable influence on the new face of Berlin; it is a good example of the relationship between a new urban architecture and an emerging cityscape which will determine life in the metropolis of Berlin until far into the next millenium.

The office and commercial building is a relatively new phenomenon in Berlin. While in commercial centres such as Hamburg there had been a continuous development from merchant's houses to early purpose-built offices for trading companies and then the modern office block, the spread of office buildings was a rather late and sudden development in Berlin, and one which quickly came to encompass a wide spectrum of different building types. This rapid, stormy development was in connection with the expansion of Berlin as the capital city of the German Empire and as a major European metropolis. Thus right from the beginning the office and commercial building took on particular significance in the inner city areas.

The extent to which this new type of building began to change the turn-of-the-century face of the city becomes clear when we compare the new structures with the development which had taken place during the previous century. Office façades were departing more and more from the vertical fenestration and ornate, prestigious style common in middle-class housing at the time. Instead horizontal windows or bands of fenestration started to appear, in line with the regular structural grids into which series of standardised office units were slotted.

A major functional change was taking place – a former residential city was becoming a centre of business, a trend aided by the conversion of many existing buildings for commercial use.

Läden und Cafés nur in den Erdgeschossen der Hauptstraßen oder Plätze entwickelte sich bis zur Jahrhundertwende zunächst zu einer durchmischten großstädtischen City mit noch immer einem erheblichen Anteil an Wohnungen und kleineren Läden, mit Theatern und Museen, mit Regierungsgebäuden und Botschaften, aber vor allem auch großstädtischen privatwirtschaftlichen Nutzungen wie Kaufhäusern und Einkaufspassagen, Bankgebäuden und Verlagshäusern sowie vermietbaren oder vom Bauherrn eigengenutzten Büro- und Geschäftshäusern. Diese Mischnutzung war eine der großen – heute wiedererkannten – Qualitäten der europäischen Stadt des späten 19. Jahrhunderts. Im städtebaulichen Wettbewerb »Groß-Berlin« 1910/11 dachte man aber bereits an die Entwicklung einer Geschäftsstadt im engeren Sinn. In den Jahren der Weimarer Republik wurde die damit verbundene Verdrängung der Wohnnutzung aus der City mit der neuen Berliner Bauordnung festgeschrieben. Die kürzeren Wege und die unmittelbare räumliche Nachbarschaft der Geschäftspartner waren vor unserem Zeitalter der Medienkommunikation ein nicht zu unterschätzender Wirtschaftsfaktor. Erst in der Nachkriegszeit hielt der Wohnungsneubau erneut Einzug in die Innenstadt, in erheblichem Umfang vor allem in die Friedrichstadt.

Seit der Wiedervereinigung ist das Geschäftshaus wieder wichtiger städtebaulicher Baustein. Straßenränder, Blockecken, Plätze, Sichtachsen und Höhendominanten werden im Zuge des Wiederaufbaus der City-Bereiche fast ausschließlich durch diesen Gebäudetyp nachgezeichnet oder neu definiert. Die historischen Stadtgrundrisse insbesondere der für die europäische Stadtbaugeschichte bedeutenden barocken Gründungen Dorotheen- und Friedrichstadt werden mit seiner Hilfe rekonstruiert.

Unabhängig von der Dimension des einzelnen Gebäudes ist der innere Funktionsaufbau der neuen Büro- und Geschäftshäuser meist ähnlich. In den unteren Geschossen befinden sich Läden, Gastronomie oder kulturelle Einrichtungen, in den Obergeschossen bis zur Traufe liegen die Büro- oder Verwaltungsetagen, und in den Attikageschossen oder in einem unabhängigen und eigenständigen Bauteil liegt der von der Senatsbauverwaltung zur Auflage gemachte 20prozentige Wohnanteil. Dabei sind die unteren und die oberen Geschosse sowohl gestalterisch als auch durch ihren engen Bezug zur Stadt, zur Straße und zur Dachlandschaft, von besonderem Interesse.

Die untere Zone ist in der Regel mehrgeschossig. Zusätzlich zum Erdgeschoß umfaßt sie – je nach Lagegunst und Größenordnung des Projektes – ein oder mehrere Obergeschosse und ein oder mehrere Untergeschosse, die im Gebäudeinneren durch Hallen, Säle oder Passagen räumlich miteinander verbunden sein können. Oberhalb der Trauflinie finden sich formale Übereinstimmungen in der Baukörperausbildung, die sich durch die Abstandsflächen ergeben. Ein, zwei oder drei Geschosse werden von der Fassade zurückgestaffelt und erhalten schmale vorgelagerte Terrassen oder

Up until the turn of the century the residential city with shops and cafés along the main streets and around the squares gradually took on a more mixed urban character, still with a considerable residential proportion and smaller shops, theatres, museums, government buildings and embassies, but above all also private businesses such as department stores, shopping arcades, banks and publishers, as well as rented or owner-occupied office and commercial space. This mix of use was one of the main, today newly recognised characteristics of the European city in the late nineteenth century. In the »Gross-Berlin« urban development competition in 1910/11 the trend was already towards the formation of a business city in the narrower sense. During the years of the Weimar Republic the displacement of residential districts to outside the inner city area, an inevitable consequence of the new thinking, was even laid down in Berlin's building regulations. Proximity to business partners was a considerable economic factor in the days before modern telecommunications. It was not until after the Second World War that apartments were again built in the inner city, most being concentrated in Friedrichstadt.

Since reunification the office and commercial building again occupies a central place in urban development. In the process of urban renewal, it is almost exclusively this type of building that we see lining streets, marking out city blocks and squares and defining lines of sight and height. This building type plays a major role in reinstating the former urban layout, particularly in the reconstruction of Dorotheenstadt and Friedrichstadt, districts founded in the Baroque period and representing a significant development in the history of European cities.

Regardless of the dimensions of the individual buildings, the internal arrangement of functions is generally the same in the new office and commercial buildings: the lower floors are taken up with shops, cafés and restaurants or cultural facilities, above which are general office and administrative areas up to the level of the eaves. The 20 % residential proportion required by the Berlin Senate Construction and Housing Department is incorporated either in the attic storeys or in an independent, separate section. Of particular interest here are the lower and upper storeys, both in terms of their design and their reference to the urban situation, to the street and to the roofscape.

The area encompassing shops, restaurants, cafés and cultural facilities can incorporate one or more upper storeys and one or more basement levels, all of which can be spatially linked with each other by means of halls and arcades. Above the level of the eaves there are distinct formal similarities in building design, resulting from the required spacings. One, two or three attic storeys rise up in steps back from the façade above the continuous eaves line, thus creating flat roofs, sometimes used as narrow terraces, in front of the attic levels. In a number of

Flachdachbereiche. Das Thema der Staffelgeschosse wird z.T. auch im Blockinneren des Gebäudekomplexes durchgespielt, um kleinen oder engen Höfen Weite zu verleihen.

Der Gebäudetyp mit zurückgesetzten Attikageschossen war in Berlin wie auch in anderen europäischen Städten bereits in den 20er Jahren vertreten. Er war durch die Bauordnung untermauert, aber darüber hinaus wurden die Staffelgeschosse bei einer Reihe von Projekten zum formgebenden Leitmotiv der Gebäudekonzeption. 1922 entwarfen die Brüder Luckhardt einen Baukörper am Bahnhof Friedrichstraße mit zurückgestaffelten Attikageschossen und horizontaler Betonung gestapelter Geschosse. Otto Kohtz hatte zwei Jahre zuvor ein den Spreebogen beherrschendes Reichshaus am Königsplatz ganz aus der Geometrie der Stufenpyramide entwickelt; bei seinem 1927/28 teilrealisierten Entwurf für das Scherl-Haus schuf er eine plastisch durchgeformte Baukörpergliederung, bei der die Staffelgeschosse mit Vor- und Rücksprüngen in der Fassade und mit dem vertikalen Akzent des Turmes verbunden sind. Bei dem 1930/31 errichteten Shell-Haus von Emil Fahrenkamp werden Staffelgeschosse, die subtil und elegant mit der Baukörperstaffelung der Fassade verschmelzen, noch eindeutiger zur Artikulation des Formwillens eingesetzt. Außerhalb Berlins ist eines der schönsten Beispiele das 1922–1924 errichtete Chilehaus von Fritz Höger in Hamburg, das bis heute nichts an seiner zeitlosen Modernität und an weltstädtischem Ausdruck und Maßstab verloren hat.

Dennoch waren Geschäftshäuser mit Staffelgeschossen im Berlin der 20er und 30er Jahre noch die Ausnahme. Während Dachräume der Berliner Gründerzeithäuser als Abstellböden dienten und Neubauten der Moderne mit ungenutzten Flachdächern endeten, gab es in Paris längst lichtdurchflutete Künstlerateliers über den Dächern der Stadt, in Rom Dachterrassen mit Pergolen und Altanen, und im Mailand der 20er und 30er Jahre entwickelten sich aus den Themen »Haus auf dem Haus« und »Gestapelte Villa« völlig neue Gebäudetypen, bei denen die Geschosse oberhalb der Trauflinie sich von der Geometrie des Baukörpers zu lösen begannen. Mit der Einführung des Aufzuges wurde die Beletage in die obersten Geschosse verlagert, wo sie – als luxuriöse Stadtwohnung oder Chefetage – von ihrer hellen Lage, von Dachgärten und von der Aussicht über die Stadt profitierte.

Besichtigte man einige der Büro- und Geschäftshäuser der Berliner Innenstadt im Rohbauzustand, so konnte man sich angesichts der einzigartigen Ausblicke über die historische Mitte hinweg auf die Dächer, Kuppeln und Türme fragen, warum diese Lagegunst bisher so wenig erkannt wurde und warum meist kleinen, wenig attraktiven und sehr teuren Wohnungen innerhalb des Geschäftshauses der Vorzug gegeben wird. Die Suche nach einer Nutzungsmischung innerhalb des Geschäftshauses, bei der jeder Bereich aus seinen besonderen Lagebedingungen entwickelt ist und in eine eigene Beziehung zur Stadt tritt, steht erst an ihrem Beginn.

projects this theme of stepped levels is further expanded within the building complex, as a means of giving width to small or narrow courtyards.

Inner city buildings with stepped attic storeys were already a recognised building type in Berlin and other European cities in the 1920s. It was supported by the building regulations, and the idea of upper storeys stepped back from the façade was even used as a design leitmotif in a whole range of projects. In 1922 the Luckhardt brothers proposed a building at Friedrichstrasse station with stepped attic storeys and a distinct horizontal layering. Two years previously, in a proposal for a high-rise Reichshaus dominating the Spreebogen at Königsplatz, Otto Kohtz's design was entirely influenced by the geometry of a terraced pyramid; in his 1927/28 design, partly realised, for the Scherl House, he created a sculptured, vertical, high-rise form which combined stepped levels with projecting and indented sections of the façade. In Emil Fahrenkamp's Shell House, erected in 1930/31, the height differences in the storeys blend elegantly and subtly with the articulation of the façade to express a particular form. Outside Berlin one of the most successful examples is Fritz Höger's Chile House, built in 1922-24 in Hamburg; to this day this building has lost none of its timeless modernity and cosmopolitan scale, nor its expressive quality.

And yet, office and commercial buildings with stepped storeys were still the exception rather than the rule in Berlin during the 1920s and 1930s. While in this city the attics of late 19th century houses were used just for storage, and the flat roofs of Modern buildings were largely unused, Paris had for many years enjoyed light-filled artists studios at rooftop level and in Rome roof terraces with pergolas and balconies were quite common. In Milan in the 1920s and 1930s completely new building types were being developed on the theme of a »house on top of a house« and »stacked villas«; here the geometry of the storeys above the eaves line was beginning to depart from that of the main levels below. As a result of the introduction of the lift the Bel Étage was transferred to the top of the building, where, either as exclusive town apartments or as the management floor, these rooms could enjoy the benefits of roof gardens and the view over the city.

When visiting the office and commercial buildings under construction in the inner city in Berlin, one is tempted to wonder why this favoured situation with unique views over the historic core of the city, its roofs, domes and towers, has been so little regarded, and why mostly small, not very attractive, yet expensive apartments within office blocks are being preferred. For the commercial building, the search for a mixture of uses in which each area is developed in accordance with its particular locational circumstances and able to set up its own relationship with the city, is only just beginning.

I
Der kombinierte Entwurf:
Prinzip Baukasten – Prinzip Collage

Bebauung auf historischer Parzellierung, Leipziger Straße/Ecke Mauerstraße, Foto 1909
Development on historic lot structure, corner of Leipziger Strasse and Mauerstrasse, 1909 photograph

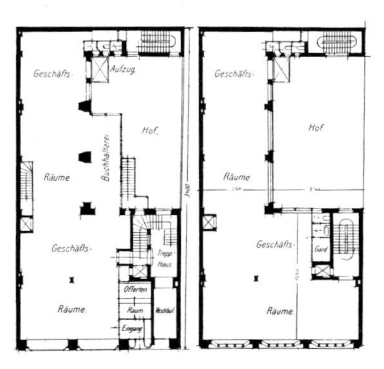

Felix Lindhorst, Geschäftshaus P. Lindhorst auf einer Blockrandparzelle, Oranienstraße 125, 1905/06, historische Aufnahme und Grundrisse
Felix Lindhorst, P. Lindhorst commercial building on a block edge site, Oranienstrasse 125, 1905/06, contemporary photograph and ground plans

Zu Beginn der nach der Wende einsetzenden Bautätigkeiten in der Friedrich- und Dorotheenstadt waren viele Blöcke durch brachliegende Flächen gekennzeichnet. Diese Brachen waren zum Teil eine Hinterlassenschaft des Sozialismus, wurden aber auch durch neue Abrisse erweitert. Abgerissen wurden nicht unter Denkmalschutz stehende Altbauten, schwer umnutzbare oder sanierbare Gebäude aus der Zeit der DDR und Rohbaukonstruktionen nicht fertiggestellter Plattenbauten. Dennoch waren die Blöcke zum Teil nicht komplett freigeräumt, sondern besaßen nach wie vor zumindest punktuell vorhandene Baukörper. Dadurch war die Planungssituation in der Regel komplexer als bei vollkommen freigeräumten Flächen oder bei Baulücken. Als Fragmente nicht nur der Stadt der Vergangenheit, sondern – durch ihren Erhalt – auch der Stadt der Zukunft, brachten die historischen Bauten Maßstab, Proportion und Nutzungsvielfalt der alten Parzellenstruktur mit in die Planung und das Erscheinungsbild des neuen Blockes ein. Die Besitzverhältnisse der angrenzenden Blockflächen hingegen hatten – begünstigt zunächst durch die Enteignungen des Sozialismus, dann durch die Konzentration des Immobilienkapitals – die kleinteilige historische Parzellenstruktur überwunden. Die Investoren tendierten bei der Bebauung zu wirtschaftlicheren zusammenhängenden Grundstücksflächen.

Um diese widersprüchlichen Realitäten auf ein und demselben Block in Einklang zu bringen, bedurfte es kombinatorisch angelegter Entwurfsstrategien. Es entstanden das »Prinzip des Baukastens« von Josef Paul Kleihues und die Strategie der »Collage« von Aldo Rossi, die bei drei Projekten in der Friedrichstadt Anwendung fanden: Block 109 (Kontorhaus Mitte) und Block 208 (Hofgarten) folgten nach dem Prinzip des Baukastens Gesamtentwürfen von Kleihues, das Quartier 275 (Quartier Schützenstraße) dem Prinzip der Collage nach dem Entwurf von Rossi.

Die Gemeinsamkeit beider Strategien liegt – bei deutlicher Verschiedenheit der Architekturen – in der Frakturierung des Blockes und der Realisierung einer Kombination von Einzelhäusern. Dadurch erfährt der Gebäudekomplex auf einem eigentumsrechtlich zusammengefaßten Blockgrundstück eine Elementierung, die auf praktikable Weise Grundlage für Vielfalt im architektonischen Ausdruck und im Spektrum der Nutzungen ist und eine relativ unproblematische Integration sowohl der Altbauten als auch eigenständiger und von der Erschließung der Bürogebäude getrennter Wohnhäuser ermöglicht.

Aldo Rossi bleibt bei diesem Experiment der historischen Parzellenstruktur und dem Charakter einzelner, in ihrem Ausdruck völlig

I
The Combined Design: »Set of Blocks« – »Collage«

At the beginning of building activity following the fall of the Berlin wall there were many areas of wasteland in the Friedrichstadt and Dorotheenstadt districts, where once complete blocks had stood. These empty spaces were partly a legacy from the socialist era but they were also further extended by demolition of existing structures. The types of buildings demolished during this period included older structures without listed building status, buildings constructed during the time of the GDR regime which were now difficult to convert or renovate, and unfinished slab buildings. However, some of the blocks were not completely cleared, but still retained one or two of the older buildings, dotted around the site. This fact, of course, made planning usually more complex than if the site had been completely free, or if it were simply a matter of filling in a largely intact block structure. These remaining older structures – fragments from the city's past, but also, through their preservation, part of the city's future – introduced an element of scale, proportion and diversity from the older block structure into the planning and appearance of the new block. However, as a result of the expropriation of land and property under the GDR regime and the concentration of real estate capital, the ownership situation of these sites no longer corresponded to the original, more fragmented lot structure. In planning new development the investors preferred to work with larger scale, single, and thus more economic units.

To reconcile these conflicting realities in one and the same block, a combined design strategy was required. Two different strategies can be distinguished: the »set of blocks« strategy used by Josef Paul Kleihues and the »collage« strategy of Aldo Rossi; these approaches were used for three projects in Friedrichstadt: Block 109 (Kontorhaus office building) and Block 208 (Hofgarten office building on Gendarmenmarkt), the overall design of these two following Kleihues' »set of blocks«, and Block 275 (on Schützenstrasse) which take Rossi's collage principle.

Although the architectures involved are considerably different, both strategies share a certain fragmentation of the block and a combining of individual buildings. This division of the building complex into separate units, on what is basically one whole site in single ownership, forms the basis for a variety of architectural expression and a wide spectrum of uses. Furthermore it enables a relatively easy integration of both the existing buildings and the new apartment blocks whose circulation system is typically separate from that of the office space.

Robert Leibnitz, Geschäftshaus Moritz Mädler, Eckparzelle Leipziger Straße 29 / Friedrichstraße 58, 1908/09, historische Aufnahme und Grundrisse
Robert Leibnitz, Moritz Mädler commercial building, corner lot Leipziger Strasse 29 / Friedrichstrasse 58, 1908/09, contemporary photograph and ground plans

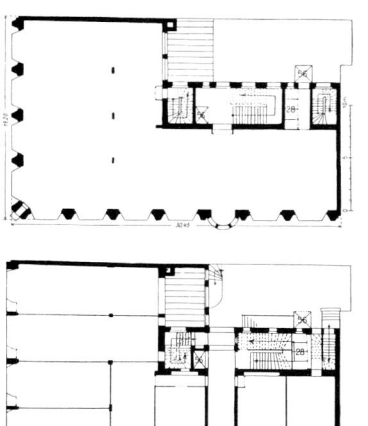

Josef Paul Kleihues, Kontorhaus Mitte, schematische Darstellung des Prinzips Baukasten
Josef Paul Kleihues, Kontorhaus Mitte building, sketch showing »set of blocks« principle

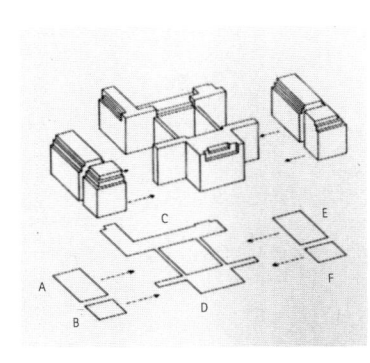

Haus Building A, C, D Josef Paul Kleihues

Haus Building B Klaus Theo Brenner
Haus Building F Walther Stepp

Haus Building E Vittorio Magnago Lampugnani/ Marlene Dörrie

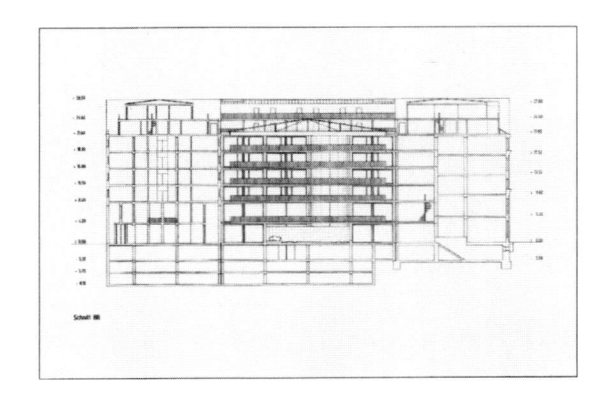

Josef Paul Kleihues, Kontorhaus Mitte, Gebäudeschnitt, Wettbewerbsplanung 1991
Josef Paul Kleihues, Kontorhaus Mitte building, section, competition planning 1991

Klaus Theo Brenner, Kontorhaus Mitte, Haus B, perspektivische Ansicht Friedrichstraße/ Ecke Kronenstraße
Klaus Theo Brenner, Kontorhaus Mitte building, Block B, perspective elevation of the corner of Friedrichstrasse and Kronenstrasse

individueller Häuser sehr eng verpflichtet. Obwohl die Eigentumsverhältnisse mit einem alleinigen Bauherren für das gesamte Quartier Schützenstraße nicht mehr denen der historischen Stadt entsprechen, collagiert er ein Stadtbild, das auf verblüffend freie und unbefangene Art eine Reinterpretation der gestalterischen Vielfalt des Stadtbildes der Gründerzeit ist und die Themen »Berliner Block« und »Berliner Innenhof« verfolgt. Der Ausdruck von Lebendigkeit und Vielfalt wird durch einen spielerischen und malerischen Umgang mit den Themen, mit Formen, Farben und Materialien erzielt. Die vom Grundriß vermittelte Geschlossenheit der Blockrandbebauung wird im Aufbau frakturiert: Sprünge in der Trauflinie, der Wechsel von Sattel-, Walm- und Flachdächern, gestaffelten Attikageschossen und Türmen betont auch in der volumetrischen Gestalt die Eigenständigkeit des einzelnen Hauses. Die integrative Kraft dieses Prinzips hat schon in der Vergangenheit gewirkt, als Gebäude unterschiedlicher Epochen, unterschiedlicher Handschrift und unterschiedlicher Bauhöhe durch die normativen Bedingungen der Parzelle und des Blockes zusammengehalten wurden. Es greift auch im Quartier an der Schützenstraße. Hier stehen, integriert in die Neubauplanung, zwei jener alten Gebäude von – wie Aldo Rossi schreibt – »vermutlich nicht sehr großem historisch-künstlerischem Wert«, die jedoch bezeichnend waren für jenen Ausdruck, den »die Stadt vor dem Krieg aufwies und den wir den Geschichtsbüchern entnehmen können.«[1] Häuser dieser Art, von denen in Berlin mitunter nur noch die unteren Geschosse oder die bloßen Fassaden stehen und die häufig keinen Auflagen seitens der Denkmalpflege unterliegen, sind nach Rossis Überzeugung »zu restaurieren, um jenen Zusammenhang mit der Vergangenheit wiederzufinden, der nicht nur mit den großen Denkmälern restauriert werden kann.«[2] Damit nimmt der Mailänder Rossi eine restriktivere Haltung im Umgang mit historischen Bauten ein als die meisten seiner Berliner Kollegen.

Die architektonische Vielfalt im Quartier an der Schützenstraße wird allein durch den Wunsch des Architekten und des Bauherrn nach dieser Vielfalt hervorgebracht. An anderen Stellen der Stadt – wie bei der dem Deutschen Dom gegenüberliegenden Blockrandbebauung an der Markgrafenstraße – ergibt sie sich noch, wie in der Vergangenheit, durch das Vorhandensein von drei selbständigen Parzellen mit jeweils eigenem Bauherrn und Architekten.

Um eine ähnliche Vielfalt der Architektur und des Stadtbildes auch im Theoriegerüst des Prinzips Baukasten zu verankern, beteiligte Kleihues bei zwei in der Gesamtkonzeption von ihm selbst entworfenen Blöcken in der Friedrichstadt andere geistesverwandte Architekten am »Spiel mit dem Baukasten«: beim Kontorhaus Mitte Klaus Theo Brenner, Walther Stepp und Vittorio Magnago Lampugnani & Marlene Dörrie, bei den Neubauten zum Hofgarten Hans Kollhoff, Jürgen Sawade und Max Dudler; für den

In this experiment Aldo Rossi adheres closely to the historic fragmented lot structure and the typical features of individual buildings with very distinct identities. Although the present ownership structure of the Schützenstrasse block, i.e. one owner, is no longer the same as in earlier days, the new pattern still manages to present a collage-like urban image. This makes for an astonishingly free and uninhibited reinterpretation of the city's appearance during the days of industrial expansion at the end of the last century; the imagery takes up Berlin's traditional architectural theme of »block« and »inner courtyard«. Liveliness and variety are expressed through a playful, artistic treatment of the themes, of forms, colours and materials. The impression of solidity and unity given by the ground plan for the block is gradually fractured at the higher levels: variations in the eaves height, the change from shed roof to hipped and flat roofs, the stepped attic storeys and towers all emphasise the individual design of the building volume.

The integrative power of this principle was also effective in the past when buildings from different epochs, with different styles and different heights were held together through the standardising influences resulting from a particular site or block situation. This holds true also in the Schützenstrasse block. Here, integrated in the new plan are two such older buildings, which, in the words of Aldo Rossi, »are presumably of little historical and artistic value«, yet which nevertheless are characteristic for the »face of the town after the war, a face we can read about in history books.«[1] This type of building, of which in Berlin sometimes only the lower storeys or the façades are still intact, and which have had no special preservation order, are, in the opinion of Rossi, »to be restored, in order to rediscover the link with the past, a past which cannot be retrieved only through the preservation of large monuments.«[2] With this approach the Milan architect takes a more restrictive stance in dealing with historic building substance than the majority of his Berlin colleagues.

The architectural variety in the block on Schützenstrasse was the result of the common wish of both the architect and the client. In other parts of the city, as for example at the Markgrafenstrasse block opposite the Deutscher Dom, this result has arisen as a consequence of the existence of three independent lots, each with a different architect and client.

In order to achieve the same diversity of architecture and cityscape within the theoretical framework of the set of blocks principle, Kleihues brought in like-minded architects in two of the Friedrichstadt blocks for which he had produced the overall design: these architects are Klaus Theo Brenner, Walther Stepp and Vittorio Magnago Lampugnani & Marlene Dörrie for the Kontorhaus, Hans Kollhoff, Jürgen Sawade and Max Dudler for

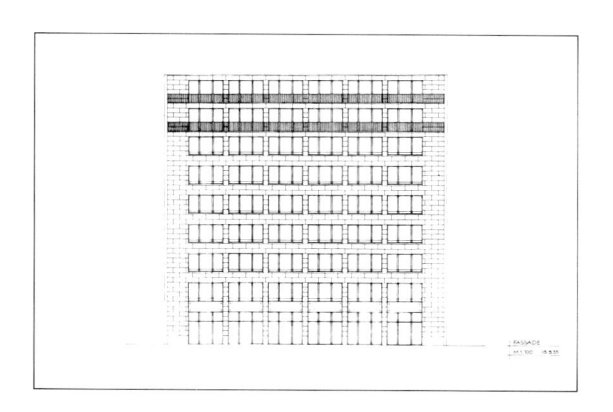

Vittorio Magnago Lampugnani/ Marlene Dörrie, Kontorhaus Mitte, Haus E, Ansicht Mohrenstraße
Vittorio Magnago Lampugnani/ Marlene Dörrie, Kontorhaus Mitte building, Block E, Mohrenstrasse elevation

Walther Stepp, Kontorhaus Mitte, Haus F, perspektivische Ansicht Friedrichstraße/ Ecke Mohrenstraße
Walther Stepp, Kontorhaus Mitte building, Block F, perspective elevation of the corner of Friedrichstrasse and Mohrenstrasse

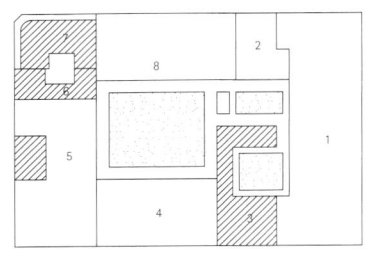

Josef Paul Kleihues, Hofgarten am Gendarmenmarkt, Lageplankonzept.

Josef Paul Kleihues, Hofgarten on Gendarmenmarkt, site plan concept.

Gebäude 1, 2
Building 1, 2
Josef Paul Kleihues
Altbau Existing buildings 6, 7
Gebäude 8
Building 8
und
Max Dudler
Gebäude 4
Building 4
Jürgen Sawade
Gebäude 5
Building 5
Hans Kollhoff

Josef Paul Kleihues, Hofgarten, perspektivische Ansicht des Hotelgebäudes, Französische Straße / Ecke Charlottenstraße

Josef Paul Kleihues, Hofgarten, perspective elevation of the hotel, corner of Französische Strasse and Charlottenstrasse

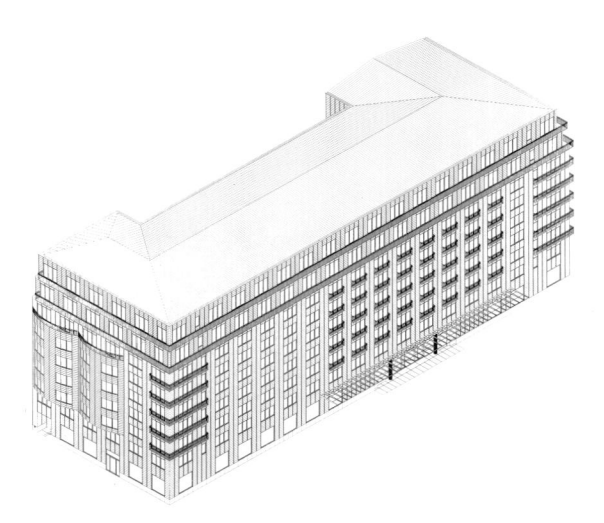

Hans Kollhoff, Hofgarten, perspektivische Ansicht der Häuser an der Friedrichstraße

Hans Kollhoff, Hofgarten, perspective elevation of the buildings on Friedrichstrasse

Umbau des Hauses Borchardt kamen die Architekten Müller Reimann Scholz hinzu. Wie jedes Spiel der Regeln bedarf, so verfügt das »Spiel mit dem Baukasten« über die Konvention eines klaren funktionalen und formalen Regelwerks, das die Kombination der individuellen Gebäudeeinheiten zu einem Ganzen möglich macht.

Bei beiden Baukasten-Projekten gruppieren sich die Häuser der einzelnen Architekten zusammen mit den Altbauten um zentrale Höfe von sehr unterschiedlicher Nutzung und Gestalt. Beim Kontorhaus Mitte wird der quadratische Hof zu einer auf Höhe der Trauflinie glasüberdachten Halle – einem »Wintergarten« –, der als zentraler Erschließungsraum dient, aber auch zum Verweilen und Flanieren einlädt. Beim Projekt Hofgarten definieren die Einzelhäuser hingegen einen rechteckigen grünen Gartenhof. Um diesen Gartenhof möglichst großzügig und zusammenhängend gestalten und gärtnerisch anlegen zu können, hatte Kleihues in einem ersten Entwurfskonzept den Abriß von Hinterhaus und Seitenflügel des 1900 erbauten Weinhauses Borchardt vorgeschlagen, sich mit diesem Konzept aber nicht gegenüber den Entscheidungen der Denkmalpflege durchsetzen können. Auch der komplette Abriß des – mit Ausnahme der Fassade und der ersten Raumschicht – maroden Altbaus an der Friedrichstraße war in einer der anfänglichen Konzeptvarianten angedacht worden. Grundsätzlich – so Kleihues – setzt Kritische Rekonstruktion »keineswegs voraus, daß alles erhalten wird, nur weil es noch existiert, sondern verlangt nach Entscheidung im Einzelfall«.[3]

Beim Kontorhaus Mitte wurden wichtige Baukastenelemente von Kleihues selbst entworfen: die Halle als Gebäudekern einschließlich ihrer Zugänge und der angrenzenden, durch die Randbebauung »gesteckten« Erschließungselemente, das mittlere Haus an der Friedrichstraße mit dem Haupteingang zum Kontorhaus und das Torhaus an der Kronenstraße mit dem Zugang zu der blockdurchquerenden Privatstraße. Beim Hofgarten hingegen gibt es kein solches architektonisches Gerüst, dem weitere Häuser angekoppelt oder eingesteckt werden, sondern ein additiveres Nebeneinander der Einzelhäuser. Darin ähneln sie der Parzellierung der Blockränder des Quartiers Schützenstraße, unterliegen aber strengeren Konventionen: ähnlichen Dachformen mit Staffelgeschossen, gemeinsamer Trauflinie und Gebäudehöhe, einem klassischen, horizontal betonten Fassadenaufbau in Sockelzone mit Läden, horizontal betonter Hauptzone und 2-geschossiger Attika. Dennoch wirkt die Fassade an der Friedrichstraße durch die unterschiedlich hohen Altbauten ähnlich bewegt wie Rossis in der Höhe springende Neubauten.

Trotz der für den Hofgarten vereinbarten Konventionen sind alle Häuser in Nutzung und Architektur – trotz der Geistesverwandtschaft der Architekten – nuanciert unterschiedlich und individuell. Jürgen Sawade entwarf ein in Fassade und Grundriß strenges, einfaches Haus mit zentraler kreuzförmiger Erschließung im Erd-

the new buildings on Hofgarten, with the addition of Müller Reimann Scholz Architects for the conversion of the Borchardt building. Every game has rules, and the set of blocks principle also follows certain clear, functional and formal conventions, which make it possible to combine individual building units into one whole.

In both »set of blocks« projects the buildings of the individual architects, together with the existing buildings, are grouped around central courtyards with very different uses and design. In the Kontorhaus project the square courtyard becomes a glass-roof covered hall rising to eaves height; like a kind of winter garden, it acts both as a communications axis for all parts of the building, and as a place to rest a while and relax. In the Hofgarten project, on the other hand, the individual buildings are arranged around a square, open garden courtyard. With the aim of creating as extensive and continuous a garden courtyard as possible Kleihues' first design concept had proposed demolishing the back building and wing of the turn-of-the-century Borchardt building, but he had been unable to carry this proposal through in the face of opposition from the Historic Buildings Commission who decided that these sections should be preserved. One of Kleihues' early design variants had even included the complete demolition of the rather ailing Friedrichstrasse building, with the exception of the façade and the first layer of rooms. In Kleihues' view, critical reconstruction »in no way demands that everything should be preserved, simply because it exists, but it requires decisions to be taken from case to case.«[3]

In the Kontorhaus important sections were designed by Kleihues himself: the hall forming the core of the building, including access to it and the neighbouring communications axes »piercing« the edge of the block, the central building on Friedrichstrasse with the main entrance to the office building and the gatehouse on Kronenstrasse with the entrance to the private road crossing the block. In the Hofgarten there is no such architectural framework to which the buildings are attached or with which they intersect, but it is instead an additive arrangement of individual buildings. In this it resembles the lot structure of the Schützenstrasse perimeter block, but is subject to stricter conventions: similar roof forms with stepped storeys, shared eaves heights and building heights, a classic, horizontal façade construction at base level with shops, strongly horizontal main zone and 2-floor attic level. Yet the varying heights of the existing buildings lend the Friedrichstrasse façade an impression of movement in the same way as the differentiated heights on Rossi's new buildings.

Despite the agreed conventions for the Hofgarten the character and use of the buildings are all slightly different and highly

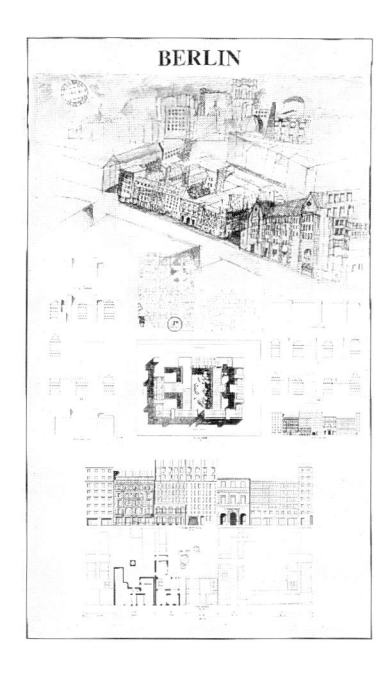

Aldo Rossi, Quartier Schützenstraße, Wettbewerbsentwurf zum Block 275
Aldo Rossi, Schützenstrasse block, competition design for Block 275

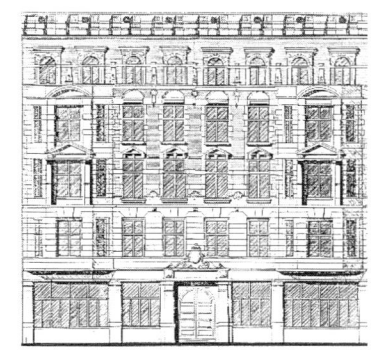

Aldo Rossi, Quartier Schützenstraße, Ansicht des rekonstruierten Gebäudes B an der Schützenstraße
Aldo Rossi, Schützenstrasse block, elevation of the reconstructed Block B on Schützenstrasse

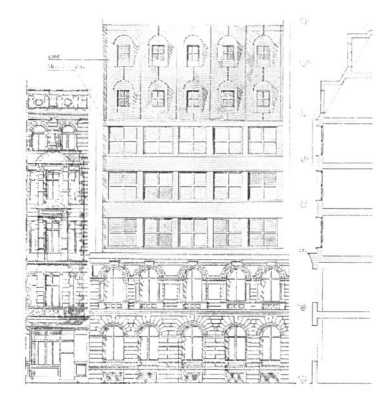

Aldo Rossi, Quartier Schützenstraße, Ansicht des restaurierten und aufgestockten Gebäudes C an der Schützenstraße
Aldo Rossi, Schützenstrasse block, elevation of restored and heightened Block C on Schützenstrasse

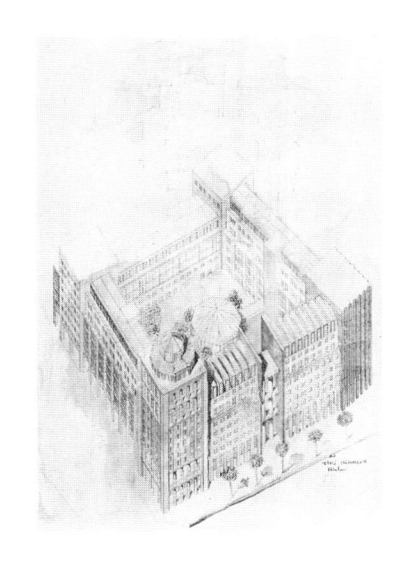

Aldo Rossi, Geschäftshäuser Landsberger Allee, Skizze
Aldo Rossi, commercial buildings on Landsberger Allee, sketch

geschoß und – oberhalb der Ladennutzung – reinen dreibündigen Büroetagen. Die Rückstaffelung der Attikageschosse wird mit 60 Zentimeter tiefen Sprüngen fast nur angedeutet. Das Rechteckraster der kargen Fassade folgt streng der Gebäudestruktur. Dies gilt ähnlich für die Fassade von Max Dudler, der jedoch einen Teil seines Hauses turmartig über die Trauflinie zieht, um die Garageneinfahrt zu betonen und zwischen den unterschiedlichen Gebäudehöhen der Nachbarhäuser zu vermitteln. Das Haus ist oberhalb der Läden ein reines Wohnhaus mit großzügigen, meist zweigeschossigen Stadtwohnungen, die ein Spektrum unterschiedlicher Grundrißtypen – im wesentlichen für Maisonette-Wohnungen – umfassen. Durch die Anordnung von innenliegenden Erschließungs- und Nebennutzflächen ergibt sich ein freier Bezug der Grundrisse zur Fassade; damit wird dasselbe strukturell bedingte Rechteckraster des Bürohauses von Sawade auch für das Wohnhaus möglich und erlaubt eine vollflächige Verglasung der Wohnräume sowohl zur Straße als auch zur Gartenfassade mit ihren Südbalkonen.

Kleihues entwarf für die Behrenstraße ein schmales Atelierhaus mit einer filigranen Glasfassade, die hinter eine schmale Reling zurücktritt. Die Rundung der Reling taucht als Thema in der angrenzenden Hotelfassade als Erker auf. Der Hotelbau wirkt massiv, introvertiert und steinern. Dadurch bildet die Glasfassade einen spannungsreichen Kontrast, wie ähnlich bei der ganz verglasten Südwestfassade des ansonsten steinernen Triangel. Die Hotelfassade besteht aus vorgefertigten, geschuppt angeordneten Natursteinpaneelen, die die Oberfläche des Hauses strukturieren.

Auch Kollhoff widmet der tektonischen Gliederung und Strukturierung der steinernen Gebäudeoberfläche besondere Aufmerksamkeit; auch hier werden die Platten der Steinverkleidung nicht stumpf gestoßen, sondern überlappend verlegt. Das Gebäude entstand für eine nicht einfache Situation: Nachdem die Entscheidung für den Erhalt der Fassade und der ersten Raumschicht des Altbaus Friedrichstraße 79a gefällt war, mußte er mit dem Neubau verschmolzen werden. Wie ein eigenes Baukastenelement ist der historische Baukörper in eine nischenartige Aussparung des Neubaus eingesteckt. Die drei so entstehenden Fassadenabschnitte ein und desselben Gebäudes stehen formal im Dialog miteinander. Der eingeschobene Altbau scheint den Rhythmus der ebenfalls vertikalen Fensterformate der nördlich benachbarten Neubaufassade zusammenzuschieben, um Platz zu finden. Damit trägt Kollhoff eine subtile ironisierende Note in seinen Entwurf. »Die Gebäude« – so Hans Kollhoff – »wollen im besten Sinne konventionell sein: zusammen mit ihresgleichen eine Straße, eine Stadt bilden. Sie werden erst auf den zweiten Blick die Aufmerksamkeit an sich ziehen.«[4]

1 Aldo Rossi, Erläuterungen zum Quartier Schützenstraße.
2 ebd.
3 Josef Paul Kleihues, »Auf dem Weg zur Metropole Berlin«, im »Tagesspiegel« vom 27. September 1992 (Sonntagsbeilage »Weltspiegel«).
4 Hans Kollhoff, Erläuterungen zum Projekt Hofgarten.

individual, for all the architects' spiritual affinity. Jürgen Sawade designed a building with simple, clear lines in both façade and ground plan, a central, cross-shaped communications axis in the ground floor, and, above the shops, offices arranged in threes around the stair wells. The attic storeys recede from the façade plane in almost nominal 60-cm steps. The rectangular grid of the sparse façade rigidly traces the building frame. This is also true of the façade by Max Dudler who develops part of the building into a tower-like section projecting above the eaves height; this has the effect of giving added emphasis to the garage entrance and acting as an integrating link between the different heights of the neighbouring buildings. Above the shops the building contains only apartments, mostly large city maisonettes with a wide variety of different ground plans. The arrangement of interior communications areas and ancillary spaces in the ground plans results in a very free relationship to the façade; this allows the same structurally determined rectangular grid used in Sawade's office building to be used for the apartment block. It also permits fully glazed façades in the living areas, both facing the street and also on the side with the south-facing balconies overlooking the courtyard.

For Behrenstrasse Kleihues designed a narrow studio house with a filigree glass façade protected by a narrow railing. The curve of the railing is also a theme in the neighbouring hotel façade, where it is developed more into a bay. The hotel seems monolithic, introverted and stone-like, an effect heightened by the contrast with the glass façade. A similar contrast is achieved with the fully glazed southwest façade of the »Triangle« building, a structure which otherwise presents a »stone-like« image. The hotel façade consists of prefabricated natural stone panels arranged in »scales« which structure its surface.

Kollhoff, too, pays particular attention to the tectonic division and structuring of the stone building surface; here, too, the stone cladding panels are not butted together, but overlap. The building was designed for a rather difficult situation: after the decision had been taken to retain the façade and first layer of rooms of the old building at Friedrichstrasse 79a, it then had to be integrated with the new building. Like a separate, individual building unit the historic building structure is inserted into a niche-like opening in the new building. The resulting three different façade sections of one and the same building enter into a formal dialogue with each other. The older section, sandwiched between the newer ones, seems to squeeze together the vertical fenestration of the building on its north side, in order to make room for itself. This lends rather an ironic touch to the design. »The buildings«, says Hans Kollhoff, »seek to be conventional in the best sense, they want to form part of a street together, part of the urban scene. They will only attract attention, if one looks a little more closely.«[4]

Ansicht der historischen Bebauung an der Markgrafenstraße vis-à-vis dem Deutschen Dom mit dem ersten öffentlichen Kraftwerk Deutschlands, Foto um 1885

Elevation of the original development on Markgrafenstrasse opposite the Deutscher Dom, with the first public power station in Germany, photograph ca. 1885

1 Aldo Rossi, Explanatory notes Block Schützenstrasse.
2 ebd.
3 Josef Paul Kleihues, »Auf dem Weg zur Metropole Berlin«, in »Tagesspiegel«, September 27, 1992 (Sunday supplement »Weltspiegel«).
4 Hans Kollhoff, Explanatory notes Hofgarten project.

| Büro- und Geschäftshaus 1 Office Building 1 | Hofgarten am Gendarmenmarkt | Josef Paul Kleihues Berlin mit with James Akin (Projektleitung project manager) Dirk Blomeyer Juan Beldarrain | Landschaftsarchitektur Landscape architecture Josef Paul Kleihues Berlin (Entwurf design) Clemens-Guido Szamaztolski + Partner Berlin (Ausführungszeichnungen Construction drawings) |

Bauherr:
Hofgarten Real Estate B.V.
Amsterdam

Projektentwicklung:
HINES
Grundstücksentwicklung GmbH
Berlin

Planungstermine:
Entwurfsplanung seit 1992
Baubeginn 1993
Voraussichtlicher Bezug 1995

Nutzung:
2 Läden mit
75 m² Nutzfläche
16 Büros mit
134 m² Nutzfläche

Geschosse (IX):
EG Läden
1.-8. OG Büros

Untergeschosse Gesamtprojekt (V):
fünfgeschossiger Keller
(18.026 m²)
1. UG Technik, Lieferung
2.-5. UG Tiefgarage
(380 Pkw-Stellplätze)

Grundstücksgröße
(Gesamtprojekt):
ca. 8.400 m²

Überbaute Fläche:
ca. 326 m²

Bruttogeschoßfläche:
2.765 m²

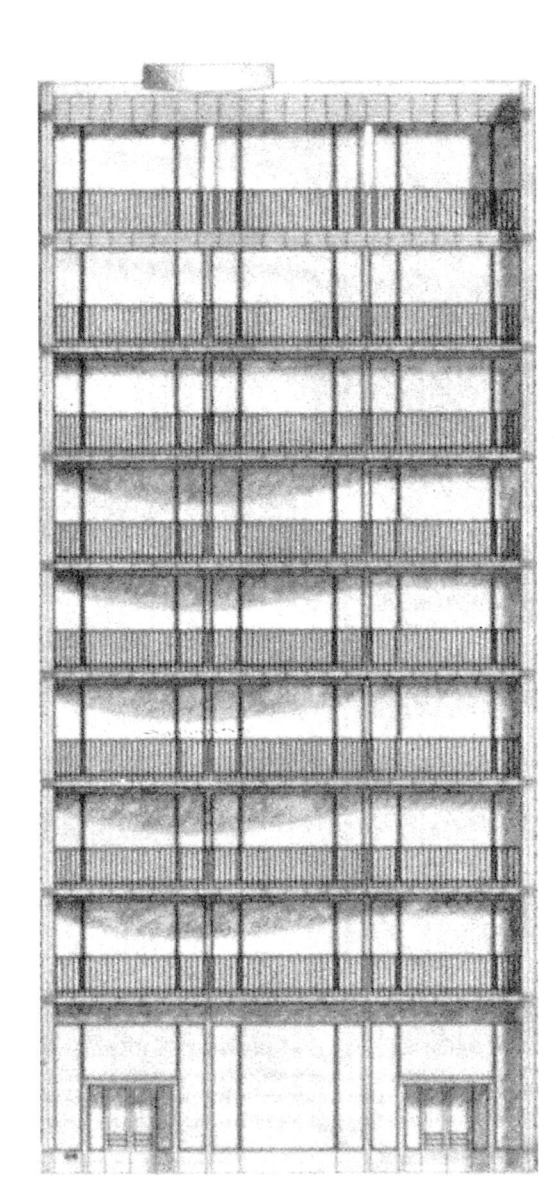

Ansicht Behrenstraße
von Norden
North elevation
Behrenstrasse

1:200

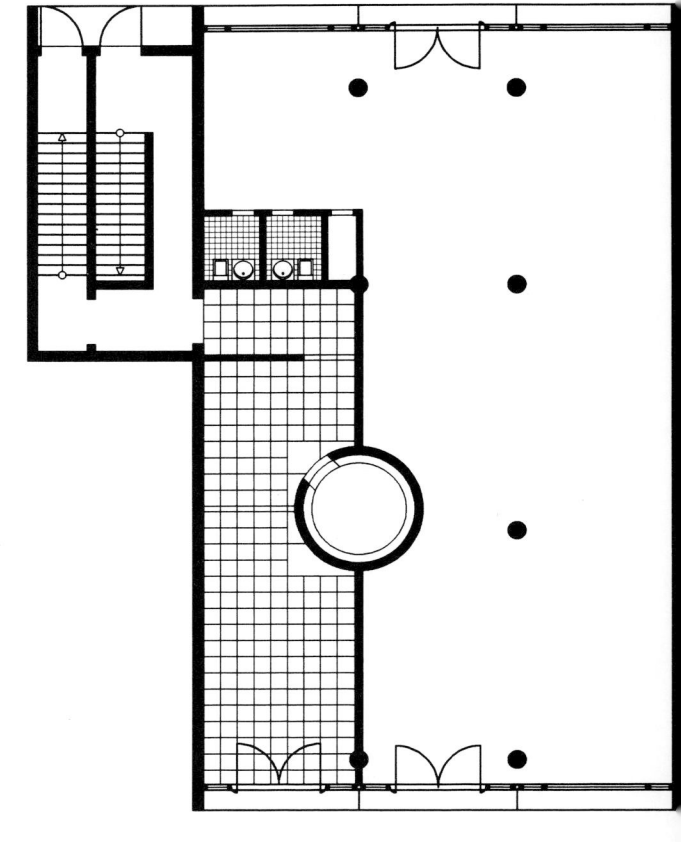

Grundriß Erdgeschoß
mit Ladennutzung
Ground floor plan
retail

1:200

Das Haus fügt sich auf einer schmalen Parzelle in die Blockrandbebauung der Behrenstraße und übernimmt Traufhöhe und Gebäudetiefe der Nachbarbebauung. Geschoßhohe Verglasungen sorgen für lichtdurchflutete Büroräume und für eine im wesentlichen durch das Tragwerk strukturierte Fassade, die Transparenz und architektonische Eigenständigkeit vermittelt.

Projektadresse:
Location:
Behrenstrasse 26
in
10117 Berlin–Mitte

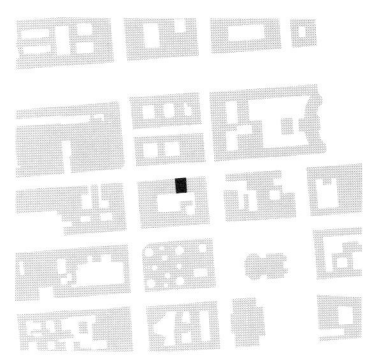

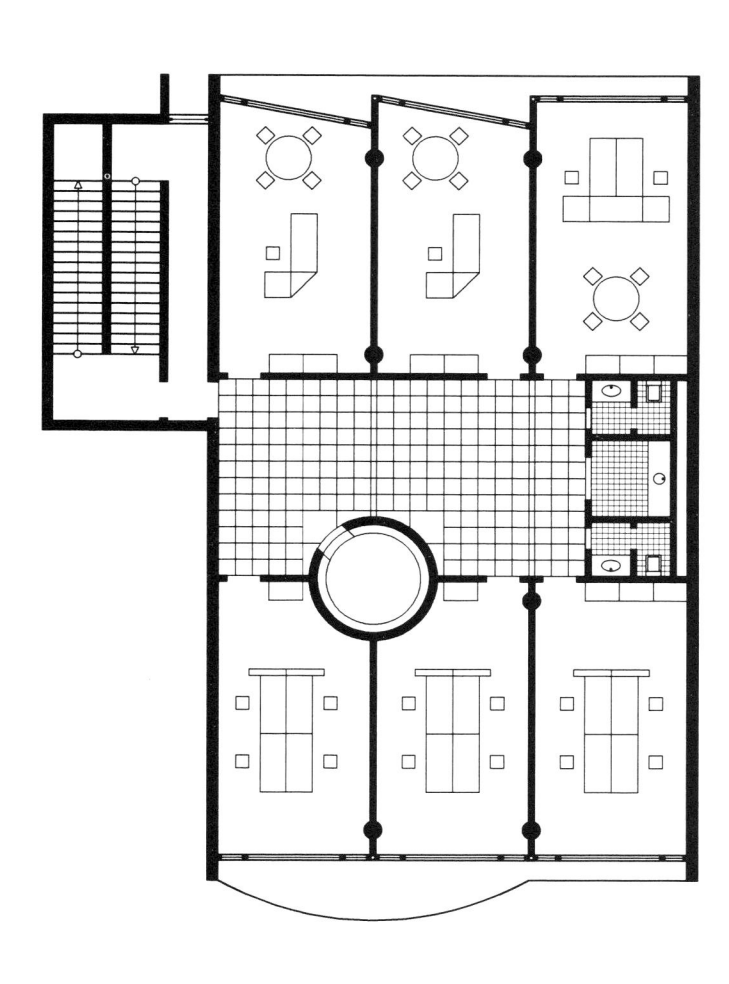

**Grundriß 1. Obergeschoß
mit Büronutzung**
1st floor plan offices

1:200

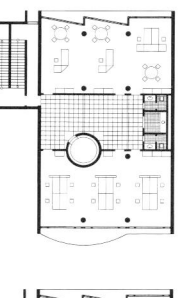

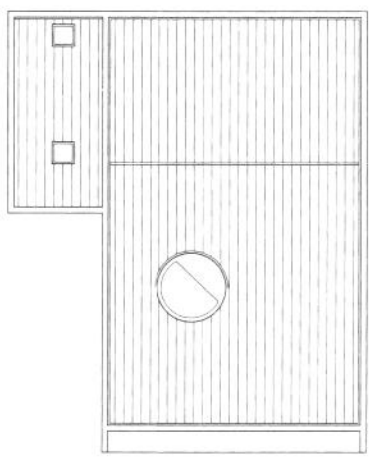

**Grundriß 2. Obergeschoß
mit Büronutzung**
2nd floor plan offices

**Grundriß 8. Obergeschoß
mit Büronutzung**
8th floor plan offices

Dachaufsicht
Top view of roof

1:750

Client:
Hofgarten Real Estate B.V.
Amsterdam

Project Development:
HINES
Grundstücksentwicklung GmbH
Berlin

Project Stages:
Design development from 1992
Start of construction 1993
Expected completion 1995

Building Use:
2 shops
à 75 m² useable area
16 offices
à 134 m² useable area

Upper Floors (IX):
Ground floor shops
1st-8th floor offices

Basement Floors
(Whole project) (V):
Five-floor basement (18026 m²)
1st basement with building
services and delivery zone
2nd-5th basement car park
levels with spaces for 380 cars

Site Area (Whole project):
ca. 8400 m²

Built Area:
ca. 326 m²

Gross Floor Area:
2765 m²

The building is slotted into a narrow site as part of a block edge development on Behrenstrasse. Taking its eaves height and building depth from the immediate surroundings, the new building has floor-to-ceiling glazing to admit maximum light into the office interiors. The façade, structured largely by the building's support frame, thus achieves transparence and a distinct architectural expression.

Büro- und
Geschäftshaus 4
Office Building 4

Hofgarten am Gendarmenmarkt

Jürgen Sawade
Berlin

Mitarbeit staff
Joachim Kleine Allekotte
(Projektleitung project manager)

Bauherr:
Hofgarten Real Estate B.V.
Amsterdam

Projektentwicklung:
HINES
Grundstücksentwicklung GmbH
Berlin

Planungstermine:
Entwurfsplanung seit 1992
Baubeginn 1993
Voraussichtlicher Bezug 1996

Nutzung:
2 Läden mit
insgesamt 408 m²
Büros (variable Größe) mit
insgesamt 4.473 m²

Geschosse (VIII):
EG Läden
1.-7. OG Büros

Untergeschosse (II):
1. UG Technik
2. UG Tiefgarage
mit Privatparkplätzen
(Planung Büro Kleihues)

Grundstücksgröße
(Gesamtprojekt):
ca. 8.400 m²

Überbaute Fläche:
789,60 m²

Bruttogeschoßfläche:
6.183 m²

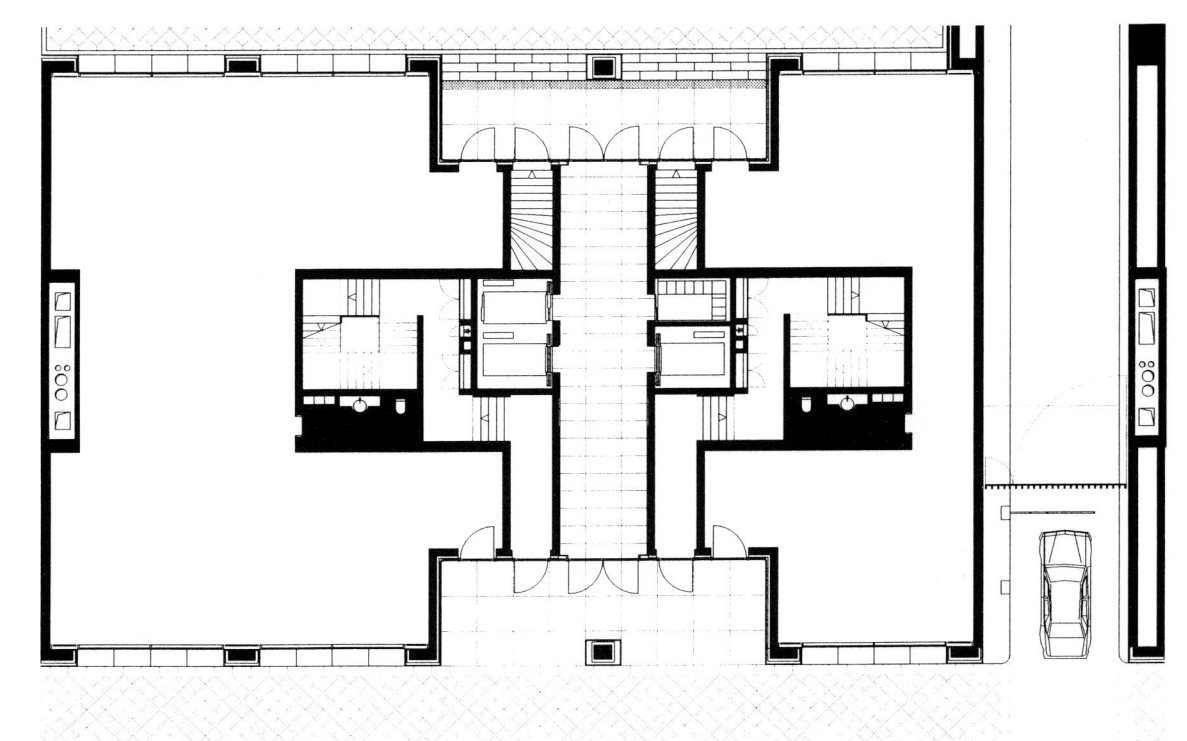

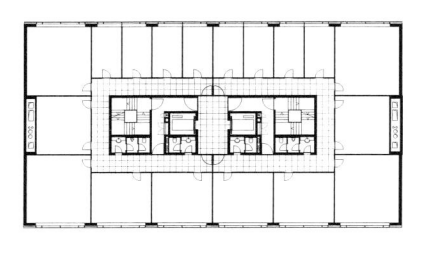

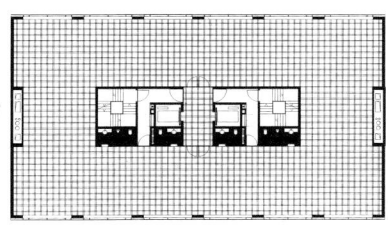

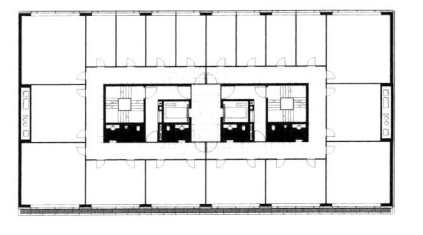

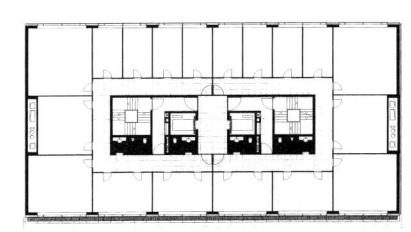

Das mit grau-weißem unpoliertem Granit verkleidete Haus orientiert sich bis zum 5. Obergeschoß an der Trauflinie der Anschlußbauten. 6. und 7. Obergeschoß sind als Staffelgeschosse mit 60 cm tiefen Rücksprüngen konzipiert. Oberhalb der beiden Läden im Erdgeschoß ist reine Büronutzung vorgesehen.

Grundriß Erdgeschoß
mit Ladennutzung
Ground floor plan retail

1:200

Grundriß Normalgeschoß
(2.-5. Obergeschoß)
mit Büronutzung
Typical floor plan
(2nd to 5th floors) offices

Grundriß 2.-5. Obergeschoß
Bandraster
Plan of 2nd to 5th floors
Grid plan

1:750

Grundriß 6. Obergeschoß
(Staffelgeschoß)
mit Büronutzung
6th floor plan offices

Grundriß 7. Obergeschoß
(Staffelgeschoß)
mit Büronutzung
7th floor plan
offices

1:750

Projektadresse:
Location:
**Französische Strasse 48
in
10117 Berlin-Mitte**

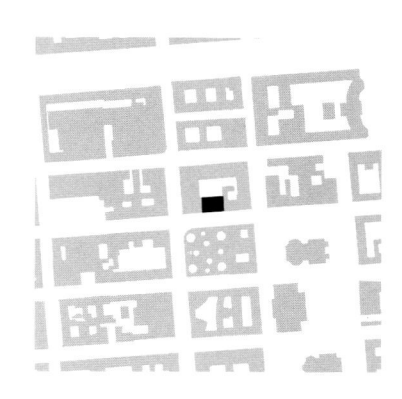

Client:
Hofgarten Real Estate B.V.
Amsterdam

Project Development:
HINES
Grundstücksentwicklung GmbH
Berlin

Project Stages:
Design development from 1992
Start of construction 1993
Expected completion 1996

Building Use:
2 shops totalling
408 m^2
Offices (various sizes) totalling
4473 m^2

Upper Floors (VIII):
Ground floor shops
1st-7th floor offices

Basement Floors (II):
1st basement services
2nd basement car park with
private car parking spaces
(Planning Büro Kleihues)

Site Area (Whole project):
ca. 8400 m^2

Built Area:
789.60 m^2

Gross Floor Area:
6183 m^2

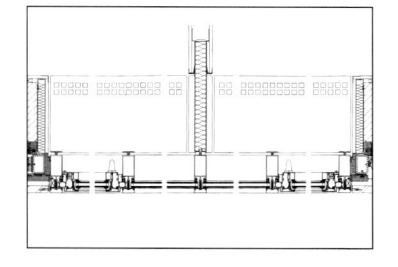

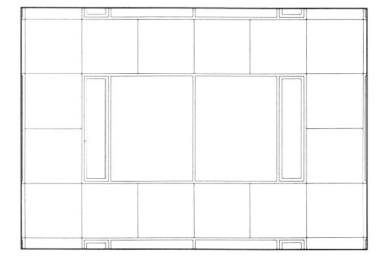

**Perspektive des Gebäudes
an der Französischen Straße
von Süden**
Perspective drawing of the building
on Französische Strasse
from the south

**Fensterdetails
(Schnitt und Ansicht)**
Window details
(section and elevation)

Clad with grey and white unpolished granite this building reaches the same eaves height as the surrounding buildings at 5th floor level, but above that, the 6th and 7th storeys are each set back 60 cm from the façade plane. Apart from the two shops at ground floor the building is intended for office use.

Büro- und
Geschäftshaus
Borchardt
Office Building
Borchardt

Hofgarten am Gendarmenmarkt

Müller Reimann Scholz
Architekten
Berlin
Thomas Müller
Ivan Reimann
Andreas Scholz

Mitarbeit staff
Antje Petersen
Victoria Larson

Bauherr:
Hofgarten Real Estate B.V.
Amsterdam

Projektentwicklung:
HINES
Grundstücksentwicklung GmbH
Berlin

Planungstermine:
Entwurfsplanung seit 1993
Baubeginn 1994
Voraussichtlicher Bezug 1995

Nutzung:
1 Restaurant mit
375 m²
8 Büroeinheiten
(4 à 274 m², 3 à 83 m²,
1 à 213 m²)

Geschosse (VI):
EG Restaurant Borchardt
1.-4. OG Büros
5. OG Technik, Abstellräume

Untergeschoß (I):
Restauranträume
Technik

Grundstücksgröße:
712,52 m²

Überbaute Fläche:
545,22 m²

Bruttogeschoßfläche:
4.060,47 m²

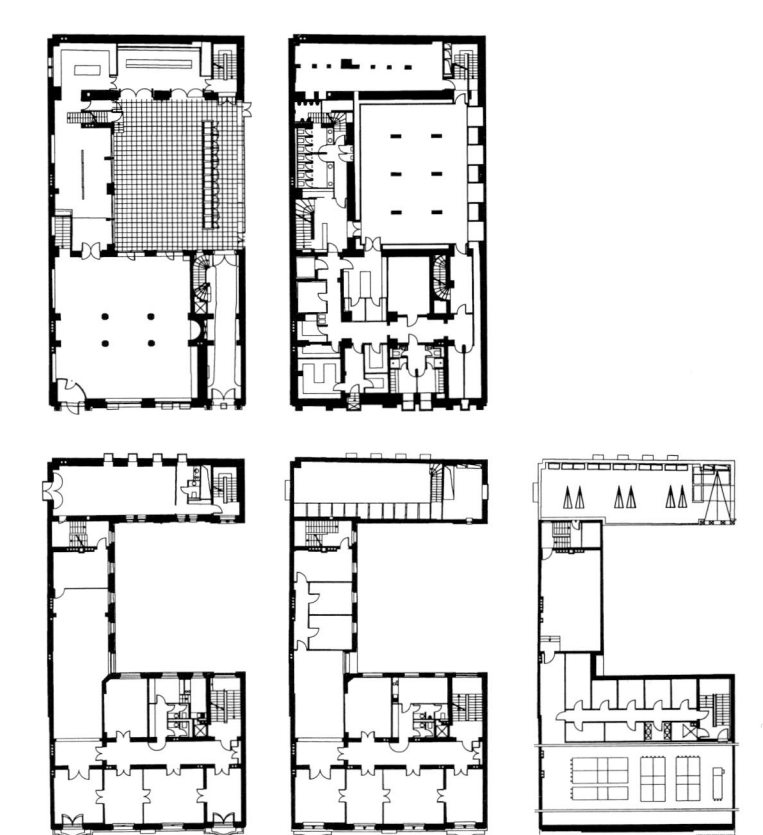

oben above
**Grundrisse Erdgeschoß
und Untergeschoß
mit Restaurant Borchardt**
Plans of ground floor
and basement
with Restaurant Borchardt

**Grundrisse 1. und 4. Obergeschoß
mit Büronutzung**
Plans of 1st and 4th floors
offices
**Grundriß Dachgeschoß
mit Wohnnutzung**
Plan of attic floor
apartments

1:750

Umbau und Modernisierung des 1900 errichteten Wohn- und Geschäftshauses der Weinhandlung F. W. Borchardt. Die im Originalzustand erhaltenen Fassaden und Innenräume, insbesondere Treppenhäuser und Durchfahrt werden restauriert. Nord- und Westfassade des Quergebäudes werden architektonisch neu geordnet. Das Restaurant Borchardt im Erdgeschoß erhält einen weiteren Gastraum im Untergeschoß.

Projektadresse:
Location:
Französische Strasse 47
in
10117 Berlin-Mitte

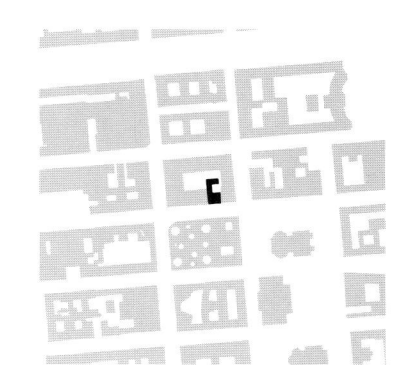

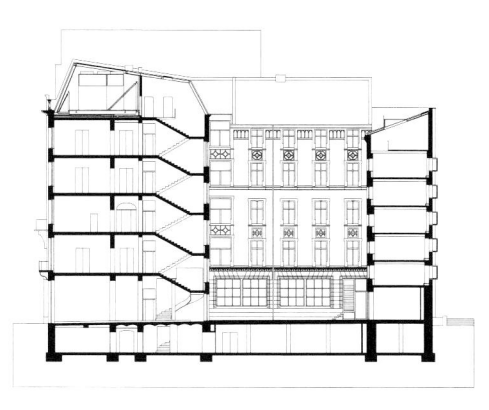

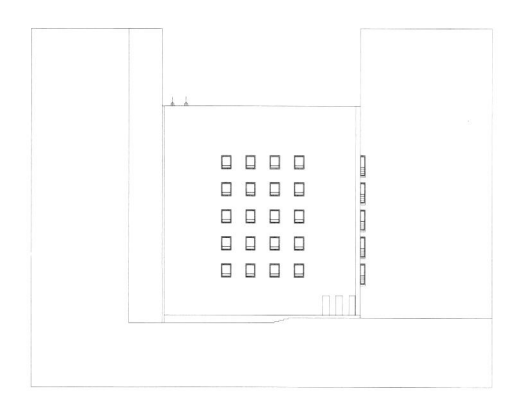

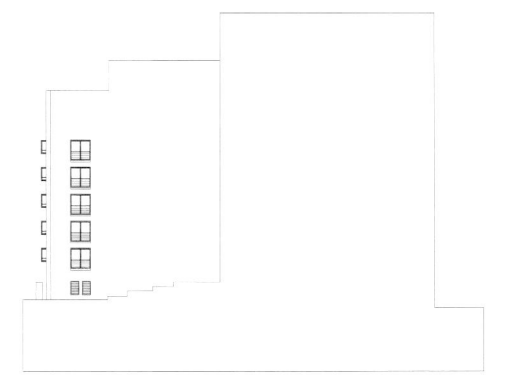

Client:
Hofgarten Real Estate B.V.
Amsterdam

Project Development:
HINES
Grundstücksentwicklung GmbH
Berlin

Project Stages:
Design development from 1993
Start of construction 1994
Expected completion 1995

Building Use:
1 restaurant of
375 m²
8 office units
(4 à 274 m², 3 à 83 m², 1 à 213 m²)

Upper Floors (VI):
Ground floor restaurant Borchardt
1st-4th floor offices
5th floor services, storerooms

Basement Floor (I):
Restaurant use
Services

Site Area:
712.52 m²

Built Area:
545.22 m²

Gross Floor Area:
4060.47 m²

Ansicht Französische Straße von Süden
South elevation
Französische Strasse

Hofansicht des Querflügels von Norden
Courtyard, north elevation of transverse wing

1:750

Hofansicht des Seitenflügels von Osten mit Schnitt durch Haupt- und Quergebäude
Courtyard, east elevation of wing with section through main and transverse buildings

Hofansicht des Seiten- und Querflügels von Westen mit Schnitt durch das Nachbargebäude an der Französischen Straße
Courtyard, west elevation of side and transverse wings with section through neighbouring building on Französische Strasse

1:750

Conversion and modernisation of the office and residential building of the vintners F. W. Borchardt, built in 1900. The original façade sections and interiors, in particular the staircase and the access passage through to the inner courtyard will be renovated. The north and west façades of the lateral building are architecturally restructured. The Borchardt restaurant on the ground floor is extended by an extra room in the basement.

Büro- und
Geschäftshaus 5
Office Building 5

Hofgarten am Gendarmenmarkt

Hans Kollhoff
Berlin
mit with
Michael Vöchting

Bauherr:
Hofgarten Real Estate B.V.
Amsterdam

Projektentwicklung:
HINES
Grundstücksentwicklung GmbH
Berlin

Planungstermine:
Entwurfsplanung seit 1992
Baubeginn 1994
Voraussichtlicher Bezug 1996

Nutzung:
Läden mit
920 m² Hauptnutzfläche
Büros mit
ca. 8.653 m²
Bruttogeschoßfläche

Geschosse (VIII):
EG Läden
1.-7. OG Büros

Untergeschoß (I):
1. UG Technik, Lager
(ca. 1.354 m²
Bruttogeschoßfläche)
(Planung Büro Kleihues)

Grundstücksgröße
(Gesamtprojekt):
ca. 8.400 m²

Überbaute Fläche:
ca. 1.353 m²

Bruttogeschoßfläche:
ca. 10.200 m²

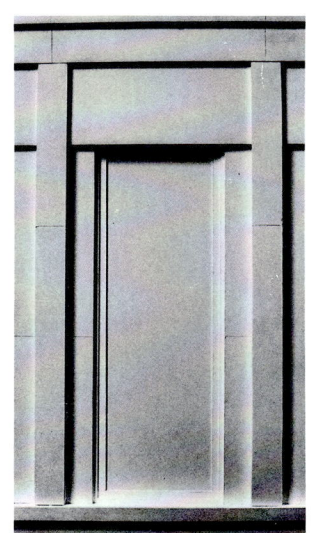

**Modell:
Ansicht Friedrichstraße
von Westen**
Model:
West elevation
Friedrichstrasse

Fassadenmodell Ausschnitt
Detail of façade model

Projektadresse:
Location:
Friedrichstrasse 79-80
in
10117 Berlin-Mitte

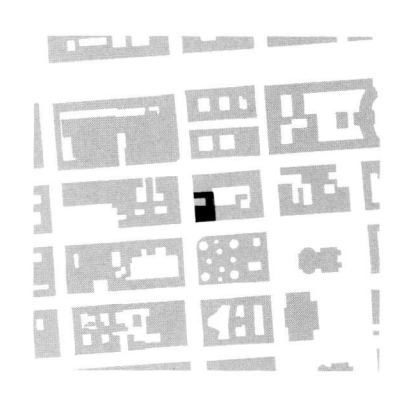

Client:
Hofgarten Real Estate B.V.
Amsterdam

Project Development:
HINES
Grundstücksentwicklung GmbH
Berlin

Project Stages:
Design development from 1992
Start of construction 1994
Expected completion 1996

Building Use:
Shops with
920 m² main floor space
Offices totalling
ca. 8653 m² gross floor area

Upper Floors (VIII):
Ground floor shops
1st-7th floor offices

Basement Floor (I):
1st basement
(ca. 1354 m² gross floor area)
with services, storage space
(Planning Büro Kleihues)

Site Area (Whole Project):
ca. 8400 m²

Built Area:
ca. 1353 m²

Gross Floor Area:
ca. 10200 m²

**Perspektive des Gebäudes
an der Kreuzung Friedrichstraße /
Französische Straße**
Perspective drawing of the corner of
Friedrichstrasse and Französische
Strasse

**Ansicht Friedrichstraße
von Westen**
West elevation
Friedrichstrasse

1:750

Büro- und Geschäftshaus 5
Office Building 5

Hofgarten am Gendarmenmarkt

Die Hauptfassade und die erste straßenseitige Zimmerflucht des Altbaus werden in die Gebäudekonzeption integriert; für die hofwärtige Altbausubstanz war aufgrund des maroden Zustandes der Abriß notwendig. Das Gebäude wird vom Straßenraum aus als Abfolge eines breiten Eckhauses, eines Altbaus und einer schmalen Baulückenschließung wahrgenommen; zum Hof besitzen die drei Bauteile eine gemeinsame neue Fassade. Das Eckhaus und die Lückenbebauung werden separat erschlossen; sie funktionieren als getrennte Hauseinheiten, zeigen aber deutlich ihre konzeptionelle Zusammengehörigkeit.
Oberhalb der Trauflinie sind die Attikageschosse in einem Winkel von 60° zurückgestaffelt.
Die mit graugrünem geflammtem Granit verkleideten Fassaden werden mit einer flachen Reliefstruktur tektonisch gegliedert. Erdgeschoß und 1. Obergeschoß sind monolithisch ausgebildet und wirken als Sockelzone der Fassade. Darauf bauen sich die Wandscheiben, Lisenen und Gesimse der weiteren Obergeschosse auf.

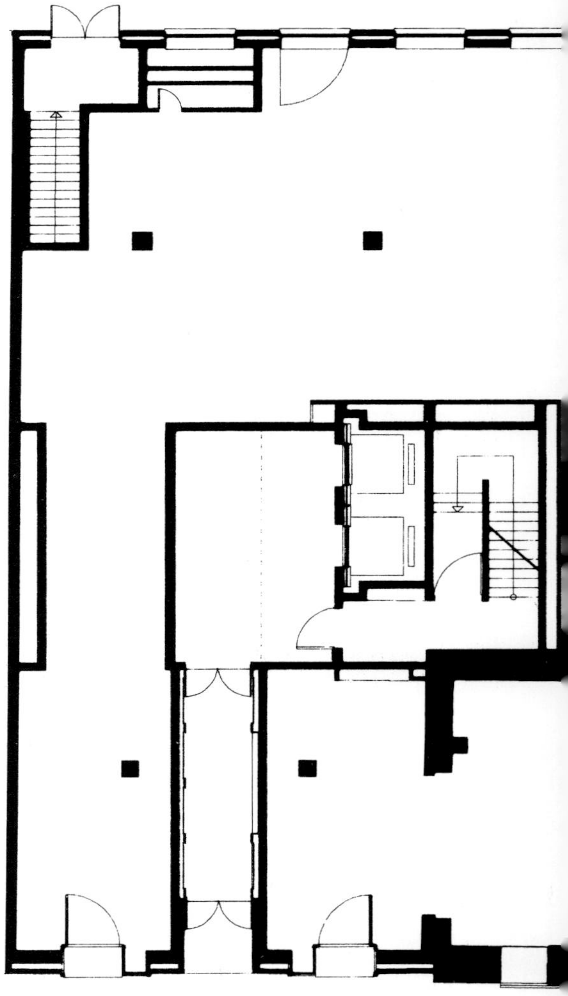

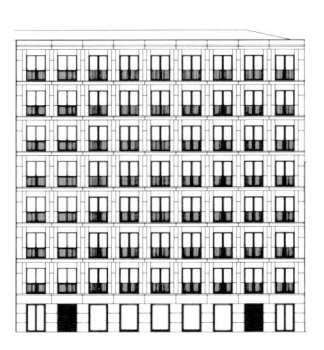

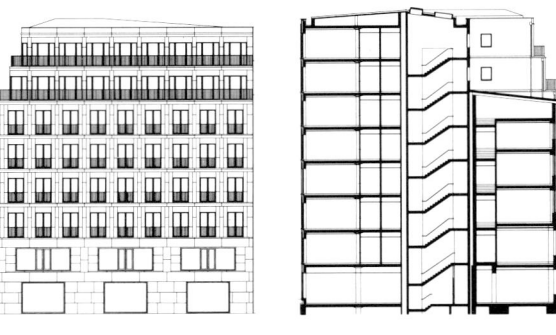

Hofansicht von Osten
East elevation courtyard

Ansicht Französische Straße von Süden
South elevation
Französische Strasse

Gebäudequerschnitt
Cross section of building

1:750

Grundriß Erdgeschoß mit Ladennutzung
Ground floor plan retail

1:200

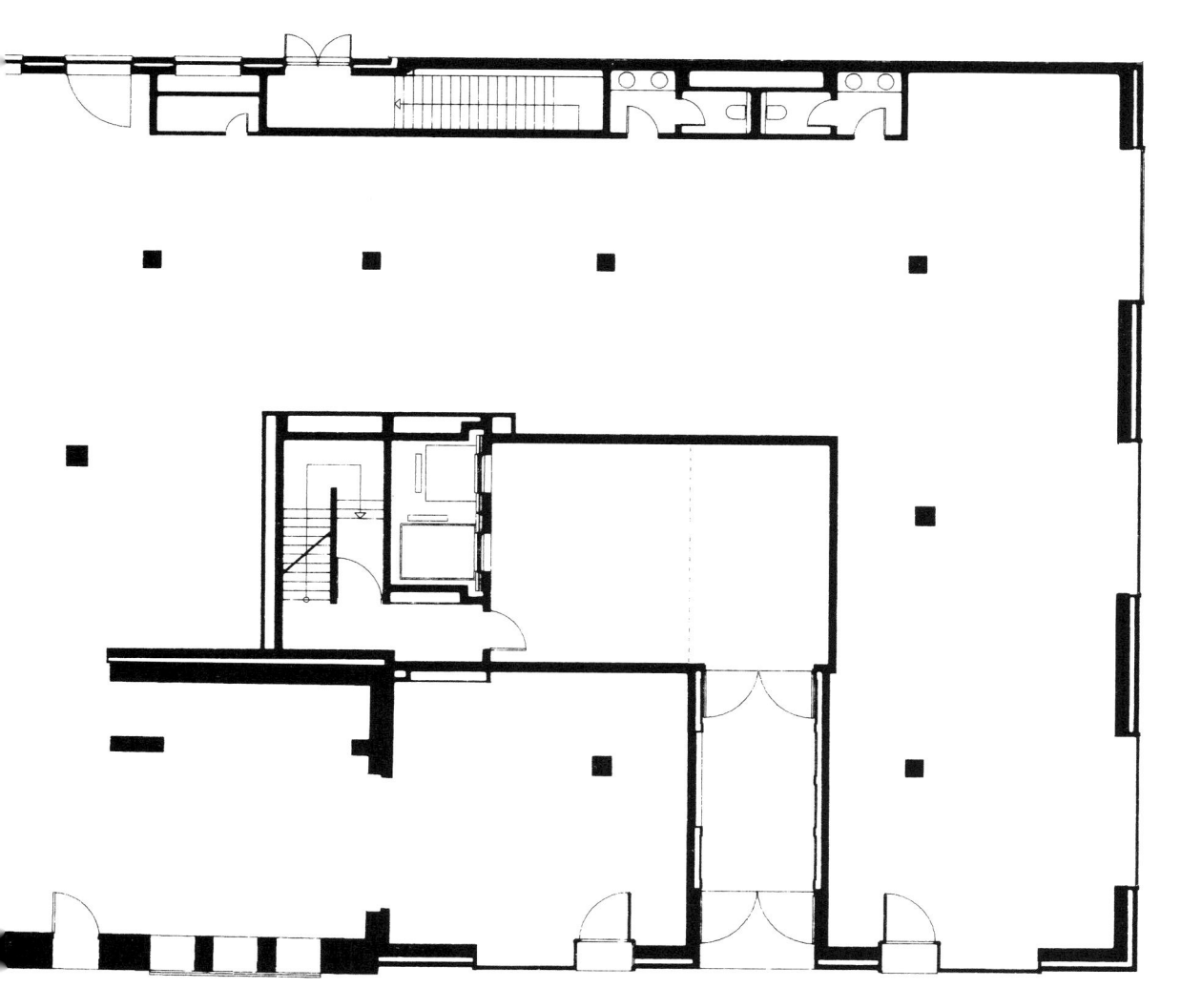

The main façade and the first street-side line of rooms of the existing building were taken up in the design of the building; however, the poor condition of the courtyard side of the existing building made it necessary to demolish it. On the street side the new building forms part of a row of buildings including a wide corner block, an older building and a narrow building closing up a gap; towards the courtyard the three buildings share a new façade. The corner block and the tall, narrow building function as separate entities, with separate access, yet are clearly based on the same overall design principles.

Above the eaves height the attic storeys recede at an angle of 60° from the main façade plane.

The grey-green, flamed granite-clad façades are structured by means of an irregular raised surface relief. The ground floor and first floor have a monolithic appearance and form a kind of plinth zone on the façade. On this base sit the outer walls with the lisenes and the cornices of the other floors.

Grundriß 1. Obergeschoß mit Büronutzung
1st floor plan offices

Grundriß Normalgeschoß (2.–5. Obergeschoß) mit Büronutzung
Typical floor plan (2nd to 5th floors) offices

Grundriß 7. Obergeschoß mit Büronutzung
7th floor plan offices

1:750

Wohn- und Geschäftshaus 8
Apartment and Office Building 8

Hofgarten am Gendarmenmarkt

Max Dudler
Berlin
mit with
Brigitta Weise

Mitarbeit staff
Maria Araujo
Andrea Deckert
Klaus Frey
Achim Grube
Philip Peterson
Nicola Romerio
Moritz Schneider
Michael Schultz
Heike Simon
Corado Signorotti
Jaques Vink
Antje Voigt

Bauherr:
Hofgarten Real Estate B.V.
Amsterdam

Projektentwicklung:
HINES
Grundstücksentwicklung GmbH
Berlin

Planungstermine:
Entwurfsplanung seit 1992
Baubeginn 1993
Voraussichtlicher Bezug 1996

Nutzung:
Läden mit
472 m² Verkaufsfläche
46 Wohnungen mit
45–210 m²

Geschosse (IX):
EG Läden
1.–8. OG Wohnungen

Untergeschosse (V):
1. UG Technik
2.–5. UG Tiefgarage
(Planung Büro Kleihues)

Grundstücksgröße
(Gesamtprojekt):
ca. 8.400 m²

Überbaute Fläche:
ca. 976 m²

Bruttogeschoßfläche:
ca. 8.500 m²

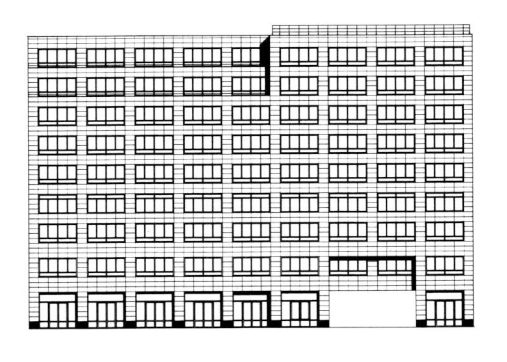

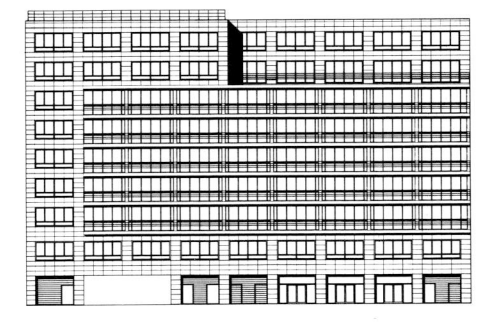

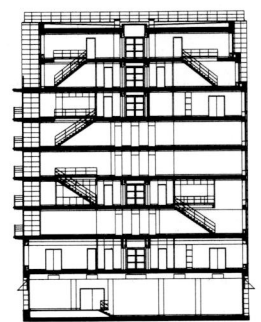

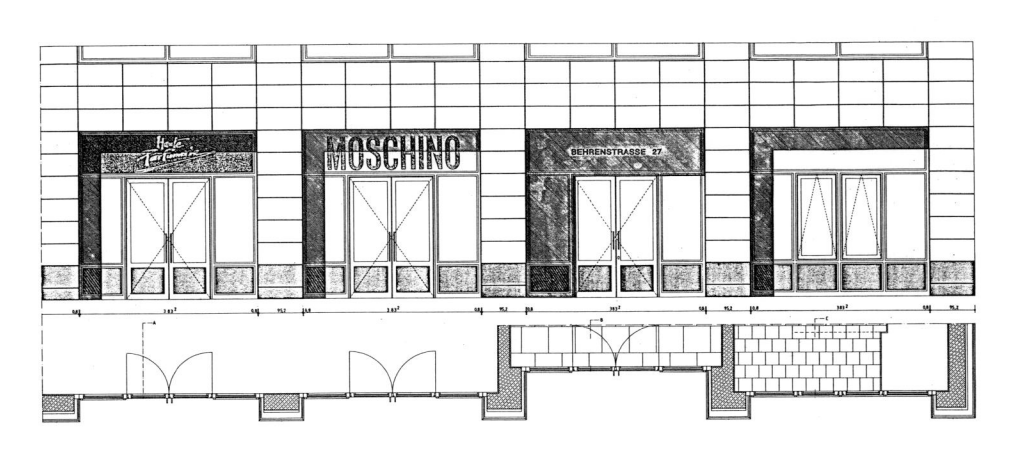

Fassadenausschnitt
und horizontaler
Fassadenschnitt
Façade detail
and horizontal
façade section

oben above
Ansicht Behrenstraße von Norden
North elevation Behrenstrasse

Hofansicht von Süden
South elevation courtyard

Gebäudequerschnitt im Bereich
interner Wohnungserschließungen
Cross section of building through
internal circulation areas of
apartments

1:750

Projektadresse:
Location:
**Behrenstrasse 27
in
10117 Berlin-Mitte**

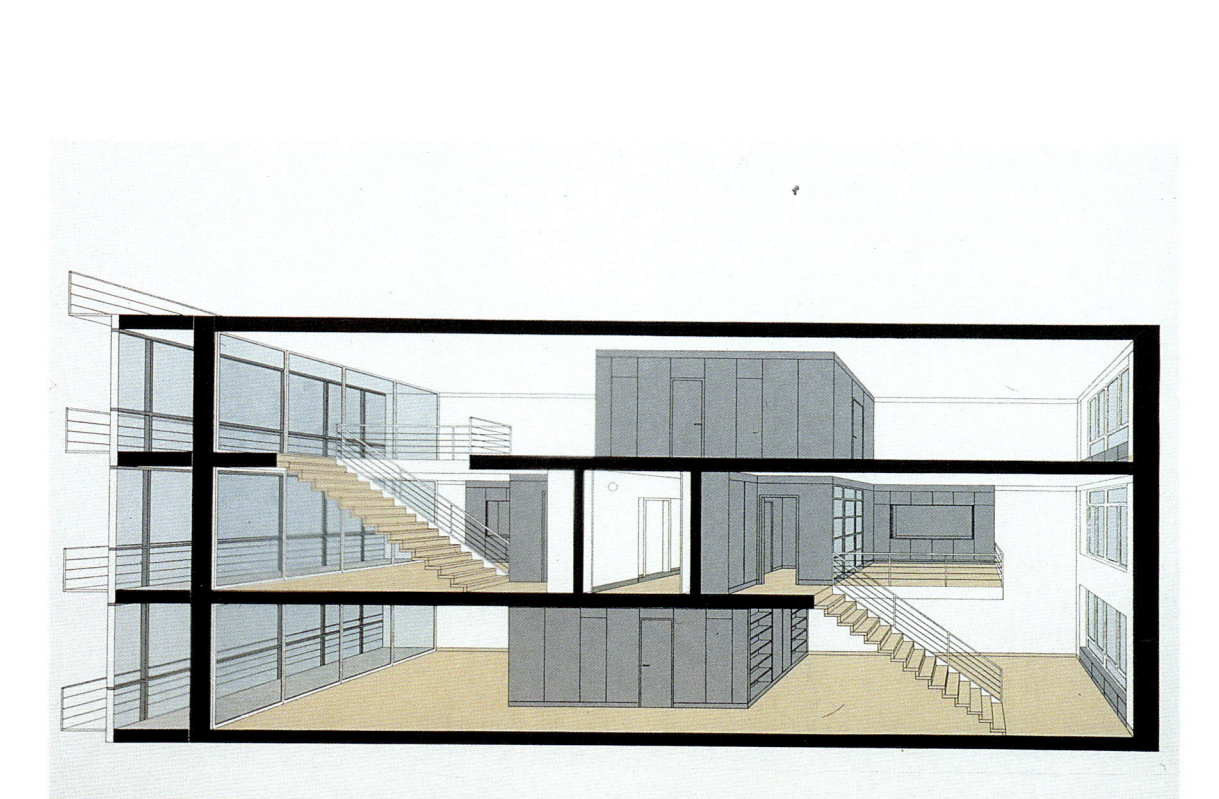

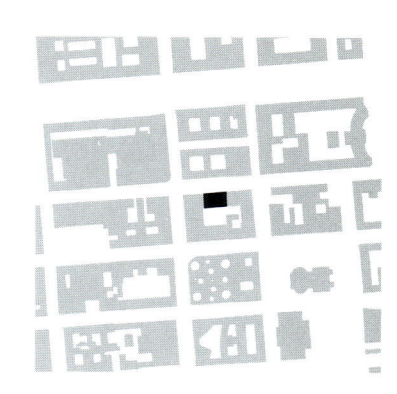

Client:
Hofgarten Real Estate B.V.
Amsterdam

Project Development:
HINES
Grundstücksentwicklung GmbH
Berlin

Project Stages:
Design development from 1992
Start of construction 1993
Expected completion 1996

Building Use:
Shops with a total sales area of 472 m^2
46 apartments
à 45-210 m^2

Upper Floors (IX):
Ground floor shops
1st-8th floor apartments

Basement Floors (V):
1st basement services
2nd-5th basement car park
(Planning Büro Kleihues)

Site Area (Whole project):
ca. 8400 m^2

Built Area:
ca. 976 m^2

Gross Floor Area:
ca. 8500 m^2

Schnittperspektive:
zwei Maisonette-Wohnungen
mit zentralem Erschließungsflur
Perspective section:
two maisonette apartments
with central corridor

Wohn- und Geschäftshaus 8
Apartment and Office Building 8

Hofgarten am Gendarmenmarkt

Oberhalb der Ladenzone im Erdgeschoß erfüllt Haus 8 als reines Wohngebäude die Forderung nach 20prozentigem Wohnanteil innerhalb des Bauvorhabens Hofgarten. Es verfügt über anspruchsvolle Stadtwohnungen mit unterschiedlicher Größe und Grundrißtypologie. Neben den »Durchsteck-Maisonetten« mit Nord-Süd-Ausrichtung in den mittleren Obergeschossen gibt es einseitig orientierte Etagenwohnungen im 1. Obergeschoß und, zur Hofseite, im 6. Obergeschoß sowie klassische Maisonette-Wohnungen mit ebenfalls einseitiger Orientierung zum Hof in den beiden obersten Staffelgeschossen.

Zu beiden Seiten wird die jeweilige Traufhöhe der Nachbargebäude übernommen und gemeinsam mit den beiden darüber angeordneten Attikageschossen bis an einen turmartigen Baukörper in der Gebäudemitte geführt, der zwischen den unterschiedlichen Gebäudehöhen vermittelt.

Das Gebäude ist als »Steinhaus« mit Lochfassade konzipiert: Es besitzt eine Natursteinfassade mit stark zurückgesetzten Stahl-Sprossenfenstern.

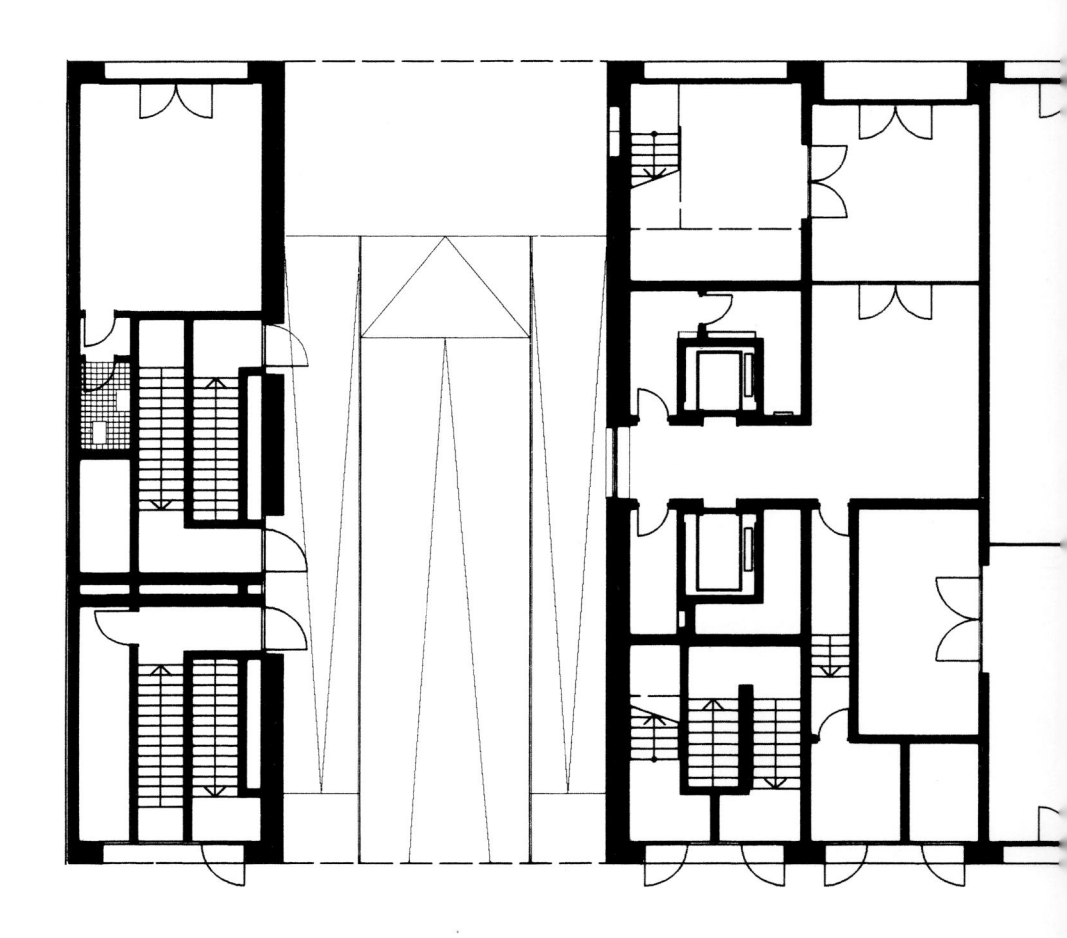

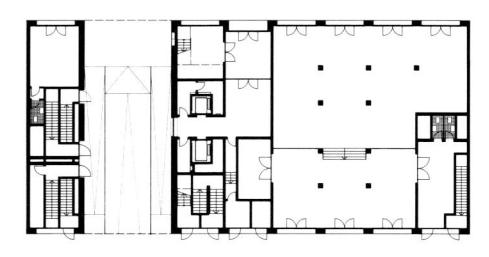

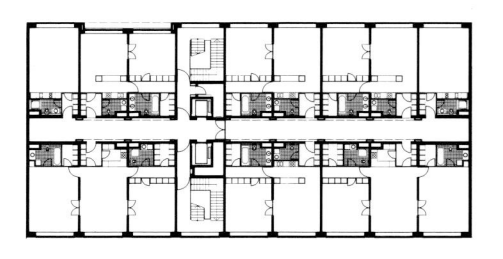

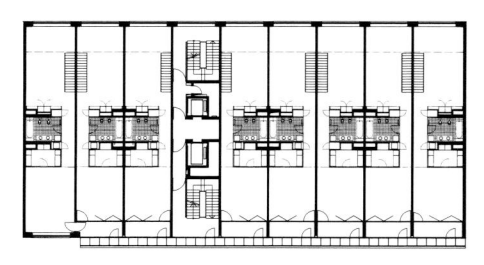

Grundriß Erdgeschoß mit Ladennutzung und Tiefgaragenzufahrt
Ground floor plan
retail
and entrance
to underground
car park

1:200
1:750

Grundrisse 1. und 2. Obergeschoß mit Wohnnutzung
Plans of 1st and 2nd floors
apartments

1:750

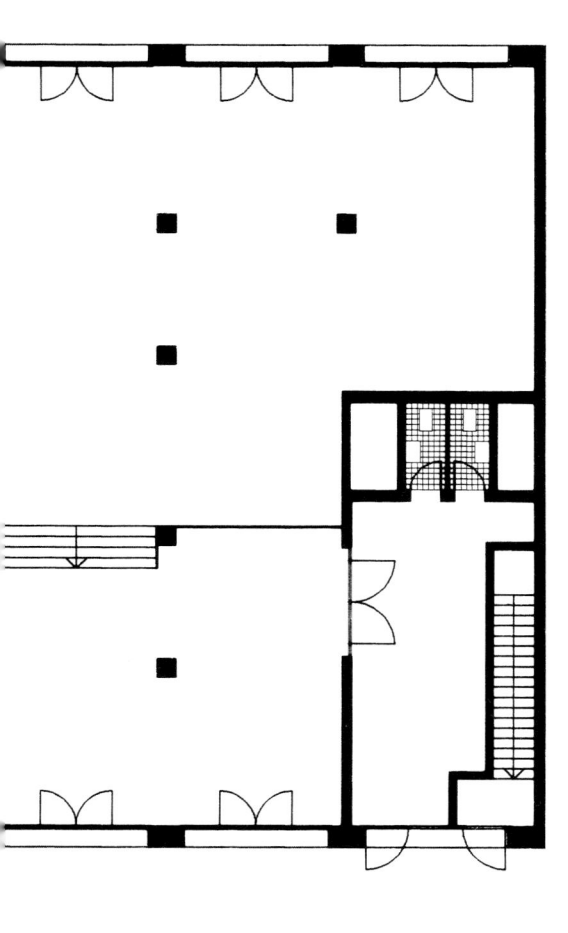

Above the ground floor shops this block is apartments, thus meeting the requirement for 20% residential use in the Hofgarten building project. The apartments are intended for the upper end of the market. They have varying sizes and ground plans. In the middle storeys there are maisonette apartments piercing the building from north to south, on the 1st storey and facing the courtyard on the 6th storey are single-level apartments, and on the top two levels are standard maisonette apartments overlooking the courtyard.

On both sides the eaves height of the neighbouring buildings is adopted for the new block, with the top two attic storeys forming in the centre of the building a tower-like structure which links the differing building heights.

The building is conceived as a »stone house« with a punctuated façade; clad with natural stone it has patent glazed windows inset in the façades.

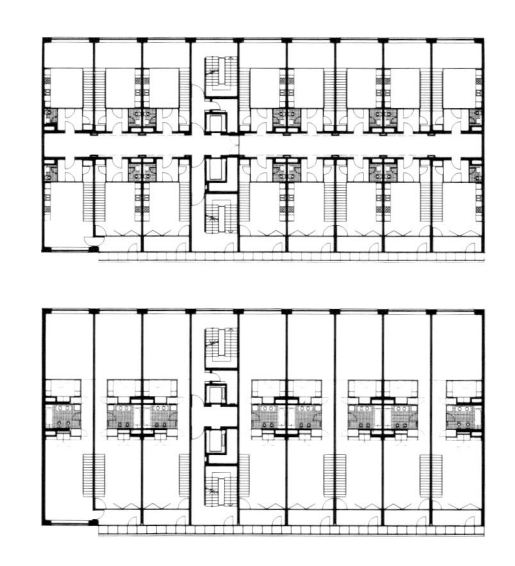

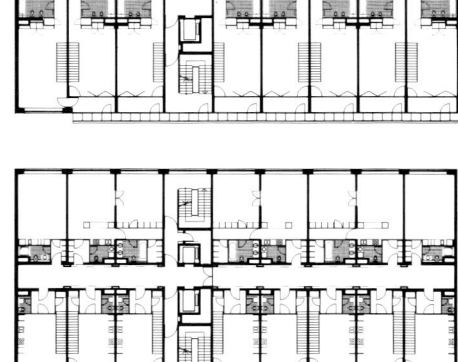

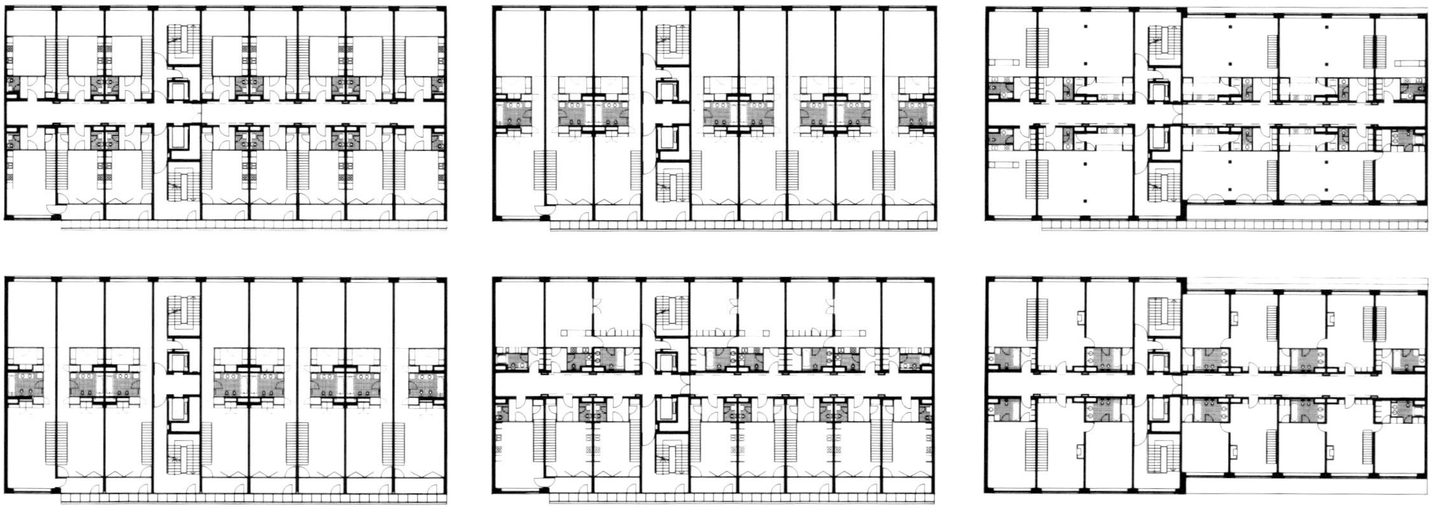

Grundrisse 3.–8. Obergeschoß mit Wohnnutzung
Plans of 3rd to 8th floors apartments

1:750

Büro-, Wohn- und Geschäftshäuser Office and Apartment Buildings	Quartier Schützenstrasse	Aldo Rossi Milano mit with Architektenbüro Bellmann + Böhm Berlin	Projekt Haus 12 Project house no. 12 Luca Meda, Milano Projekt Haus 10 Project house no. 10 Bellmann + Böhm, Berlin

Bauherr:
Dr. Peter und Isolde Kottmair GbR
Berlin

Planungstermine:
Entwurfsplanung seit 1992
Baubeginn Ende 1994
Voraussichtlicher Bezug
Anfang 1996

Nutzung:
Ladenfläche mit
ca. 5.110 m^2
Bürofläche mit
ca. 23.538 m^2
Wohnfläche mit
ca. 5.945 m^2

Geschosse:
Haus 1,5,6,7,9,10,11,12
(VI+II):
EG Läden
1.-6. OG und DG Büros
Haus 2 »Palazzo« (III+I):
EG – 2. OG gewerbliche
Sondernutzung
DG Büros
Haus 3 (VII+II)
EG Läden
1.-6. OG und DG Wohnungen
Haus 4 (V):
EG Läden
1.-4. OG Büros
Haus 8 (VII+II)
EG Büros
1.-6. OG und DG Wohnungen

Untergeschosse (IV):
1. UG (Souterrain) Läden
2. UG Technikzentrale
3.-4. UG Tiefgarage

Grundstücksgröße:
8.468 m^2

Überbaute Fläche:
6.765 m^2

Bruttogeschoßfläche:
ca. 43.000 m^2
(ohne Basement)

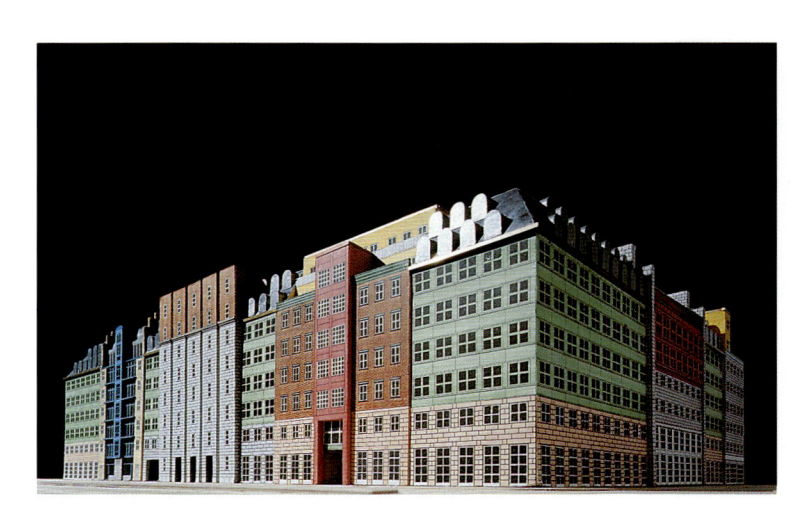

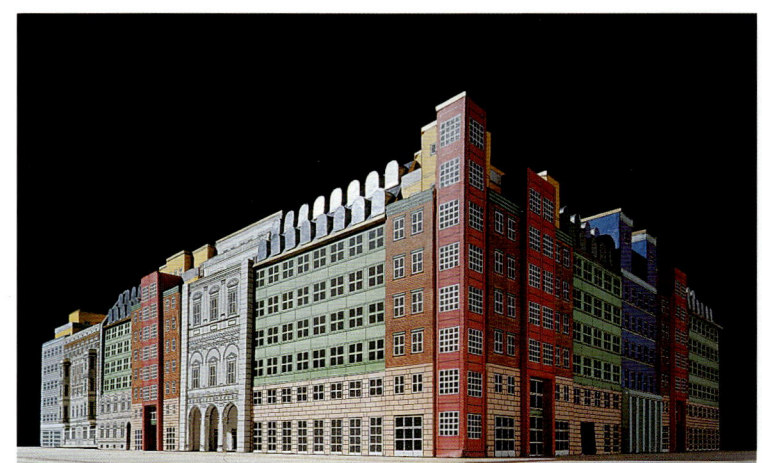

Entwurfsskizze Charlottenstraße
1993
Design sketch
Charlottenstrasse
1993

Entwurfsskizze Aldo Rossi
1993
Aldo Rossi design sketch
1993

oben above
Blick von Südosten
Zimmerstraße / Ecke Markgrafenstraße
Modellfoto 1992
View from the southeast of the corner
of Zimmerstrasse and Markgrafenstrasse
Model photo 1992

Blick von Nordwesten
Schützenstraße / Ecke Charlottenstraße
Modellfoto 1992
View from the northwest of the corner
of Schützenstrasse and Charlottenstrasse
Model photo 1992

Mitarbeit staff
Studio Aldo Rossi
Massimo Scheurer (Assistent assistant)
Marc Kocher (Assistent assistant)
Mauro Broglia
Sergio Gianoli
Elisabetta Pincherle

Projektadresse:
Location:
**Schützenstrasse/
Markgrafenstrasse/
Zimmerstrasse/
Charlottenstrasse
in
10117 Berlin-Mitte**

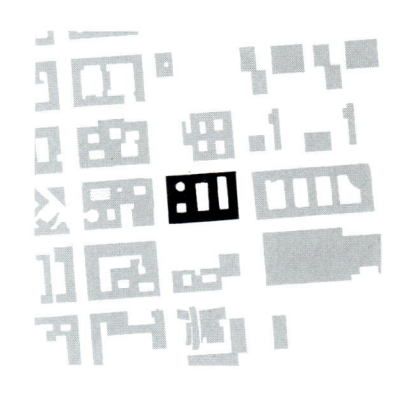

Client:
Dr. Peter und Isolde Kottmair GbR
Berlin

Project Stages:
Design development from 1992
Start of construction end 1994
Expected completion early 1996

Building Use:
Lettable retail space
ca. 5110 m^2
Lettable office space
ca. 23538 m^2
Lettable residential space
ca. 5945 m^2
Basement ca. 3152 m^2

Upper Floors:

Blocks 1,5,6,7,9,10,11,12 (VI+II):
Ground floor shops
1st-6th floor and top floor offices

Block 2 »Palazzo« (III+I):
Ground floor – 2nd floor
special commercial use
Top floor offices

Block 3 (VII+II):
Ground floor shops
1st-6th floor and top floor
apartments

Block 4 (V):
Ground floor shops
1st-4th floor offices

Block 8 (VII+II):
Ground floor offices
1st-6th floor and top floor
apartments

Basement Floors (IV):
1st basement shops
2nd basement services centre
3rd and 4th basement car park

Site Area:
8468 m^2

Built Area:
6765 m^2

Gross Floor Area:
ca. 43000 m^2
(excluding basement)

**Blick auf das Gesamtmodell von Osten
Fassaden Markgrafenstraße im
Vordergrund
Modellfoto 1992**
View of model of whole project
seen from the east
Façade Markgrafenstrasse in the
foreground
Model photo 1992

Büro-, Wohn- und
Geschäftshäuser
Office and
Apartment Buildings

Quartier Schützenstrasse

Das Projekt nimmt einen großen rechteckigen Berliner Block ein. Der Blockrand wird durch eine Randbebauung mit Berliner Traufhöhe und zwei Dach- bzw. Mansardgeschossen vollständig geschlossen. Dahinter ordnen Gebäudeflügel das Blockinnere und fassen vier große Höfe, die in der Tradition der Berliner Innenhöfe verstanden werden.

Die beiden einzigen historischen Gebäude des Blockes an der Schützenstraße – Haus 11/12 und das nur 2-geschossig erhaltete Haus Nr. 10 – integrieren sich nach ihrer Restaurierung in die neue Bebauung.

Das Projekt folgt dem Prinzip der architektonischen Collage und greift die frühere Parzellenstruktur des Blockes auf. Es beabsichtigt keine geschlossene Inszenierung der historischen Stadt, sondern sucht vielmehr eine lebendige Vielfalt von Typologien, um den unterschiedlichen Nutzungen – Büros, Geschäfte, Kunstgalerien, Wohnungen – gerecht zu werden. Der als Auflage geforderte 20prozentige Wohnanteil ist in einzelnen, eigens als Wohnhäuser konzipierten Gebäuden untergebracht.

oben above
Ansicht Zimmerstraße von Süden
South elevation
Zimmerstrasse

Ansicht Schützenstraße von Norden
North elevation
Schützenstrasse

1:750

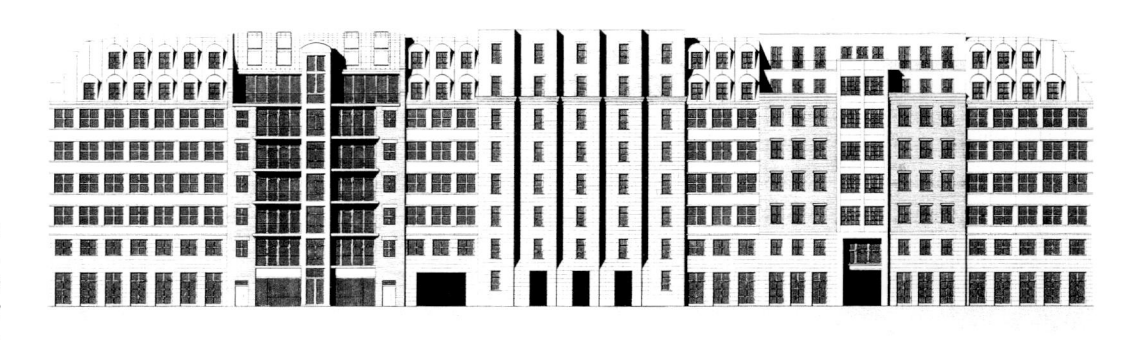

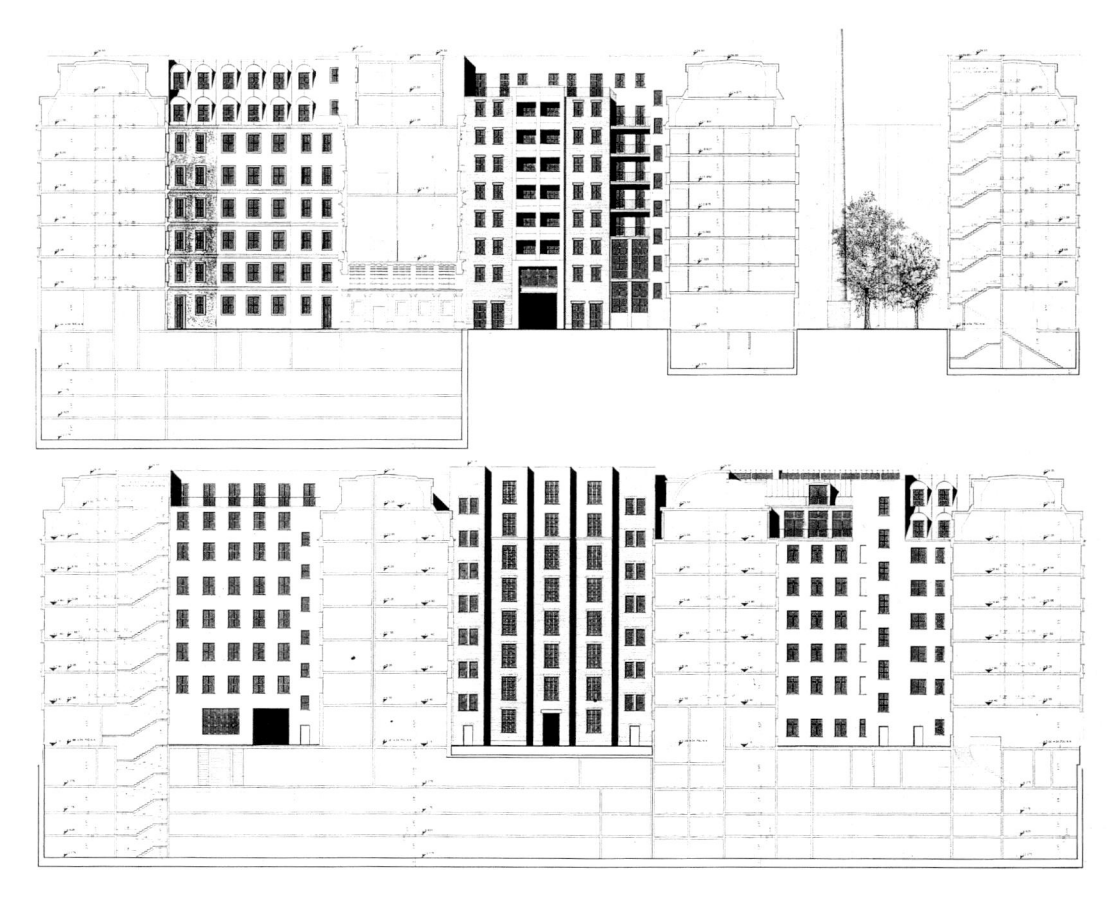

Längsschnitt durch den Block mit Hofansichten der Gebäude an der Schützenstraße von Süden
Longitudinal section through the block with courtyard elevations of the buildings seen from the south

1:750

Längsschnitt durch den Block mit Hofansichten der Gebäude an der Zimmerstraße von Norden
Longitudinal section through the block with courtyard elevations of the buildings on Zimmerstrasse seen from the north

1:750

**Ansicht Markgrafenstraße
von Osten**
East elevation
Markgrafenstrasse

**Ansicht Charlottenstraße
von Westen**
West elevation
Charlottenstrasse

1:750

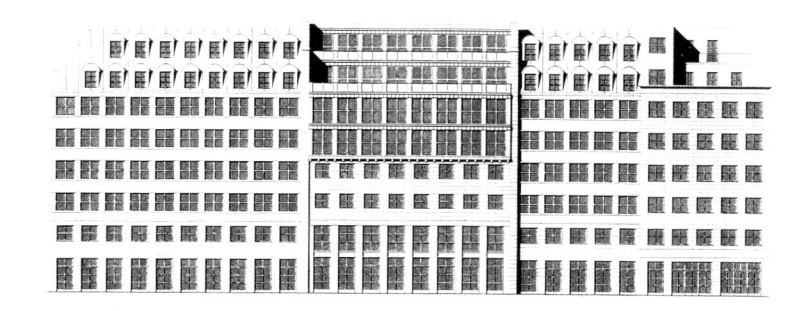

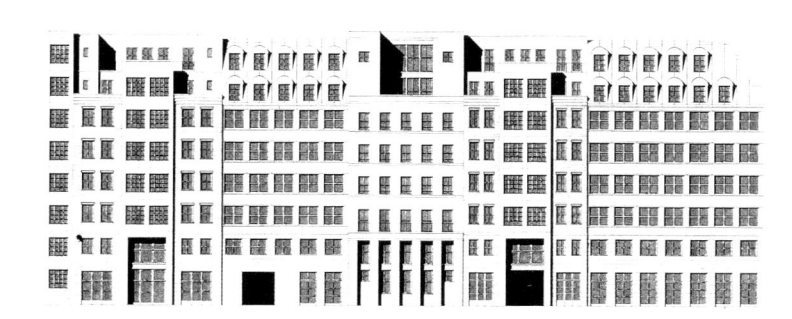

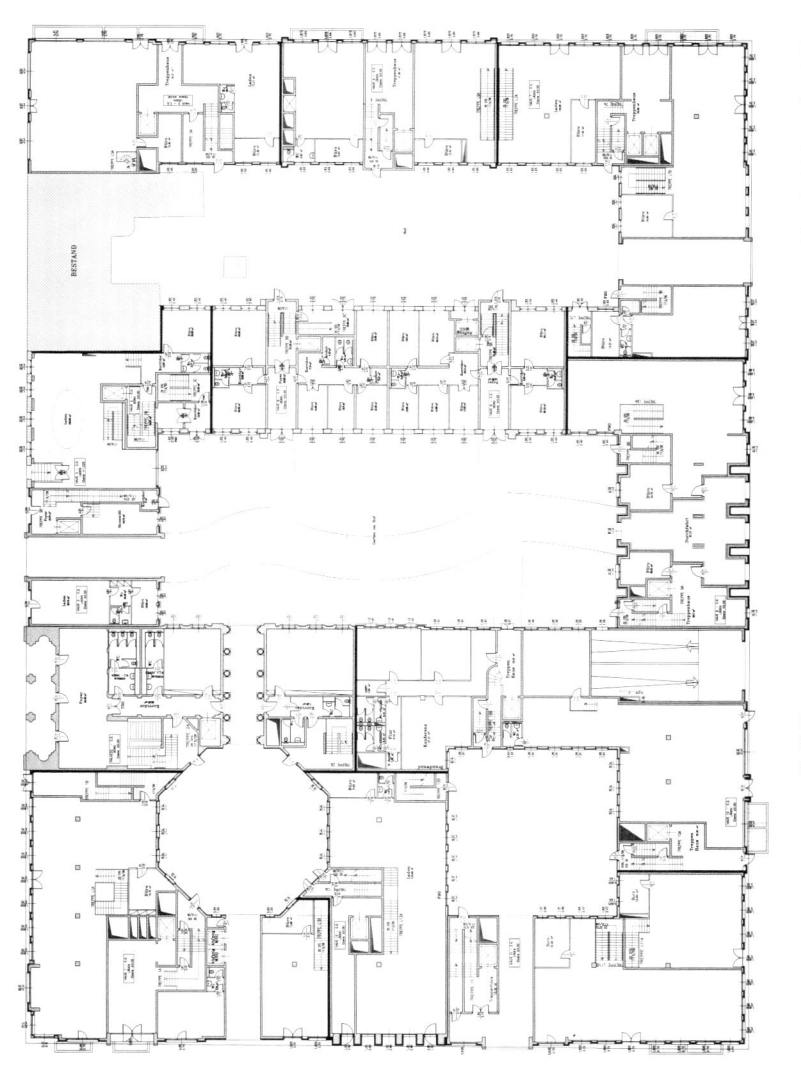

The site for the project occupies a large rectangular city block. Buildings completing the perimeter of the block have the traditional Berlin eaves height and two roof or mansard storeys. Inside this rim the courtyard area is divided into four by wings projecting into the centre, thus forming inner courtyards in keeping with the local architectural tradition. The only two older buildings to be preserved in the block are on Schützenstrasse, no. 11/12 and a 2-storey building at no. 10. After renovation these are to be integrated into the new development.

The project follows the principle of architectural collage and takes up the theme of the earlier lot structure of the block. It is not intended as a mere reenactment of the historic town, but rather seeks a lively variety of building types and different uses – offices, shops, art galleries and apartments. The requisite 20% proportion for residential use is found in separate apartment blocks specially designed for this purpose.

Grundriß Erdgeschoß der Gesamtanlage
Ground floor plan of the whole complex

1:750

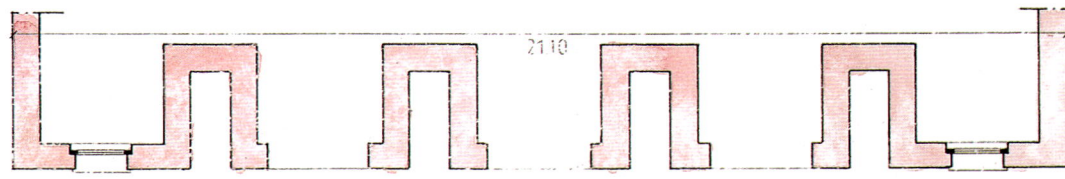

Büro-, Wohn- und Geschäftshäuser
Office and Apartment Buildings

Quartier Schützenstrasse

Fassadenstudien Gebäude P
Façade studies Building P

**Hofansicht
von Norden**
Courtyard elevation
seen from the north

**Ansicht Zimmerstraße
von Süden
mit Fassadenschnitt**
South elevation
Zimmerstrasse
with façade section

Fassadenstudien Gebäude G
Façade studies Building G

**Ansicht Charlottenstraße
von Westen**
West elevation
Charlottenstrasse

**Ansicht Schützenstraße
von Norden**
North elevation
Schützenstrasse

Büro-, Wohn- und Geschäftshäuser
Office and Apartment Buildings

Quartier Schützenstrasse

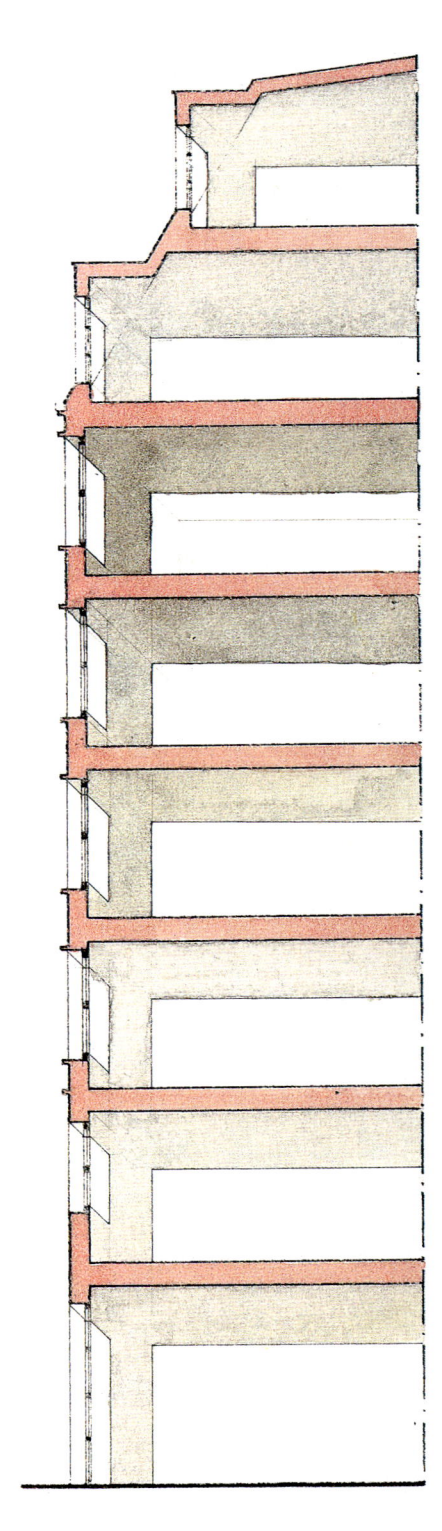

Fassadenstudien
Gebäude F, H, M, O, Q, S und U
Façade studies
Buildings F, H, M, O, Q, S and U

Ansicht und Schnitt
Elevation and section

Fassadenstudien Gebäude T
Façade studies Building T

**Ansicht Markgrafenstraße
von Osten und Schnitt**
East elevation
Markgrafenstrasse
and section

BEWAG-Geschäftssitz
Büro-, Wohn- und
Geschäftshaus   Gendarmenmarkt
Office and Apartment
Building of BEWAG

Max Dudler
Berlin – Frankfurt a. M. – Zürich

Mitarbeit staff
Hans-Achim Grube
Paul Holt-Seeland
Phil Peterson
Manfred Kunz

Bauherr:
Berliner Kraft- und Licht
(Bewag)-AG Berlin

Planungstermine:
Gutachten 1993
Entwurfsplanung seit 1993
Baubeginn Mitte 1994
Voraussichtlicher Bezug
Ende 1995

Nutzung:
5 Läden mit
750 m²
5 Bürogeschosse mit
jeweils 838 m²
(insgesamt 4.190 m²)
11 Wohnungen mit
insgesamt 1.060 m²

Geschosse (VIII):
EG Läden
1.-5. OG Büros
6.+7. OG Wohnungen

Untergeschosse (II):
1. UG Tiefgarage, Technik
2. UG Tiefgarage

Grundstücksgröße:
1.466 m²

Überbaute Fläche:
1.146 m²

Bruttogeschoßfläche:
9.980 m²

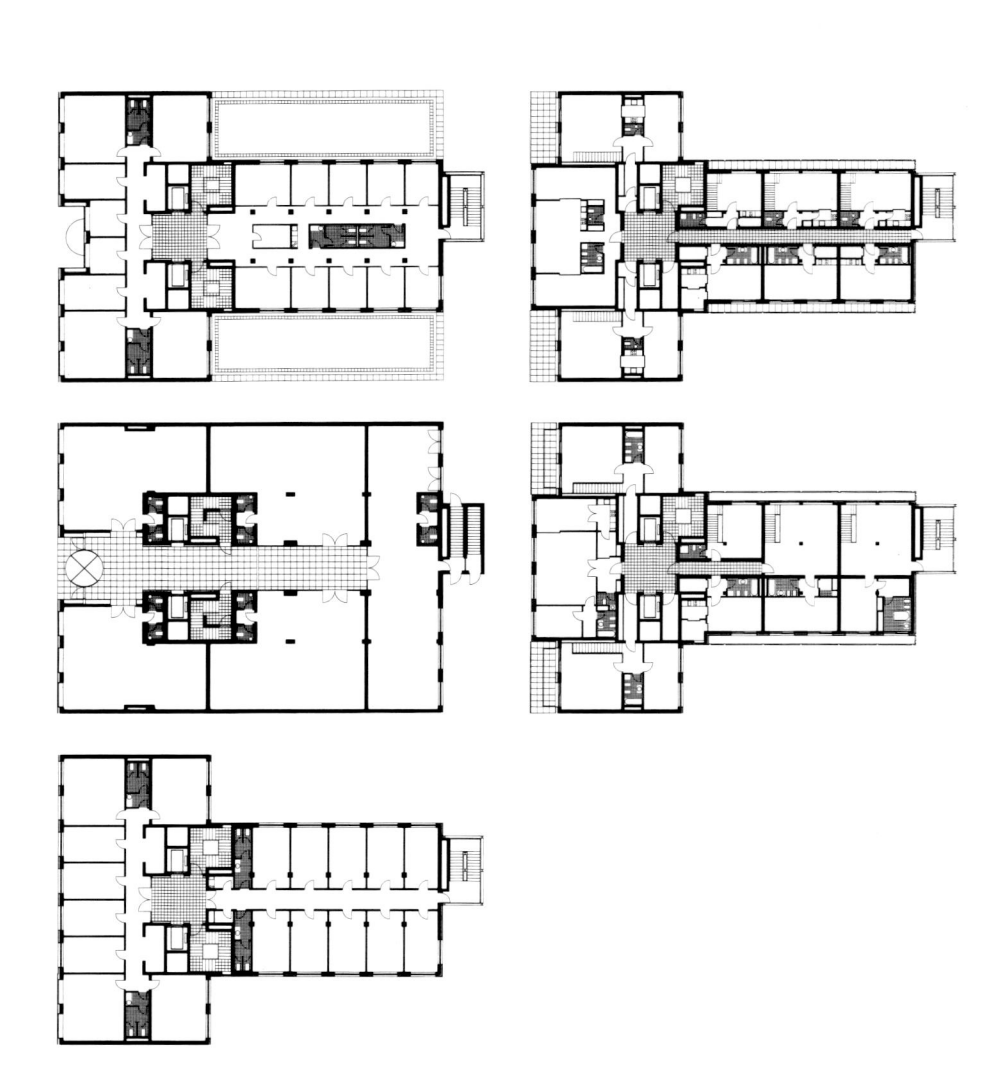

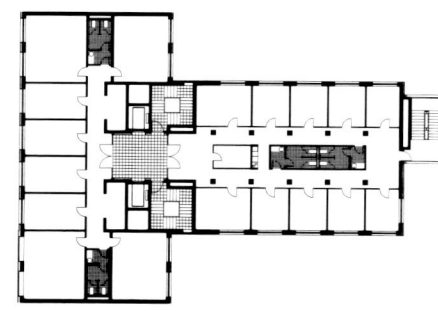

Grundriß Erdgeschoß
mit Ladennutzung
Ground floor plan
retail

Grundriß 1. Obergeschoß
mit Büronutzung
1st floor plan
offices

Grundriß 3. Obergeschoß
mit Büronutzung
3rd floor plan
offices

Grundriß 4. Obergeschoß
mit Büronutzung
4th floor plan
offices

Grundriß 6. Obergeschoß
mit Wohnungen
6th floor plan
apartments

Grundriß 7. Obergeschoß
mit Wohnungen
7th floor plan
apartments

1:750

1:750

Projektadresse:
Location:
**Markgrafenstrasse 35
in
10117 Berlin-Mitte**

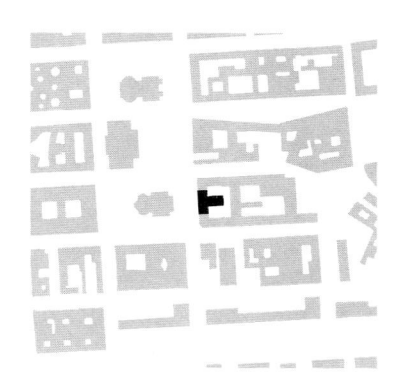

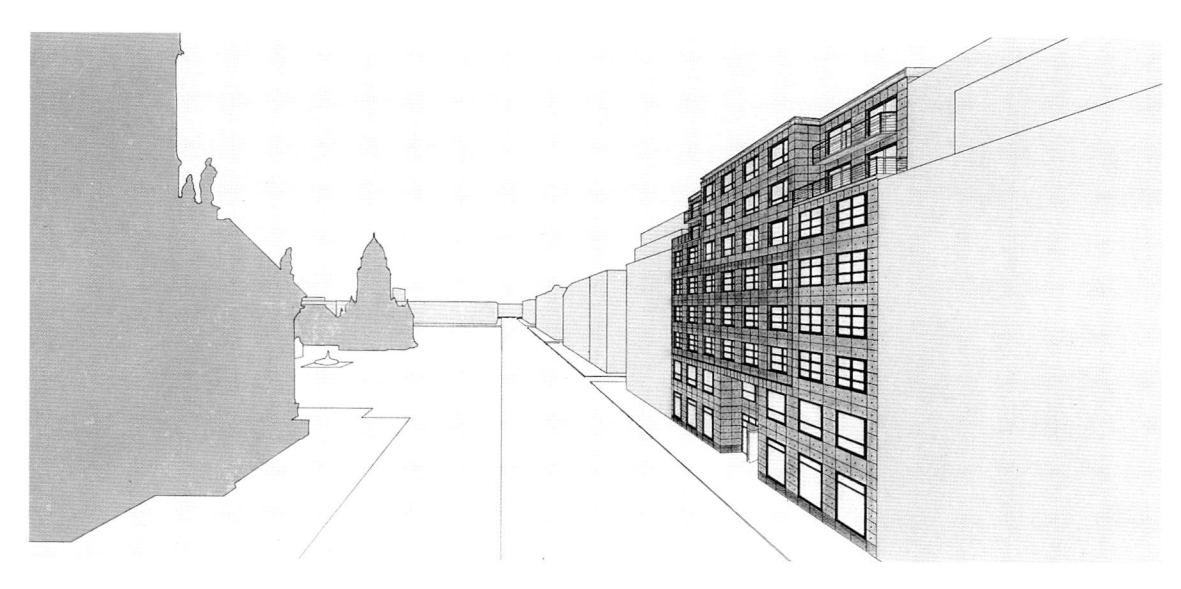

Client:
Berliner Kraft- und Licht
(Bewag)-AG
Berlin

Project Stages:
Appraisal 1993
Design development from 1993
Start of construction middle 1994
Expected completion end 1995

Building Use:
5 shops totalling
750 m²
5 office floors
à 838 m²
(a total of 4190 m²)
11 apartments totalling
1060 m²

Upper Floors (VIII):
Ground floor shops
1st-5th floor offices
6th and 7th floor apartments
Basement Floors (II):
1st basement car park, building services
2nd basement car park

Site Area:
1466 m²

Built Area:
1146 m²

Gross Floor Area:
9980 m²

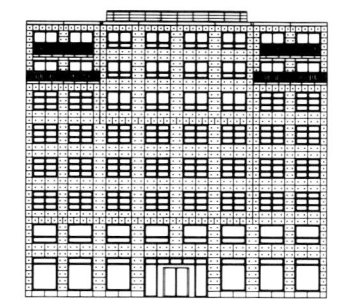

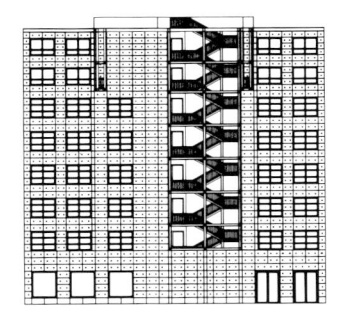

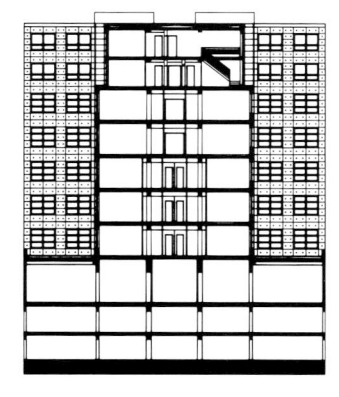

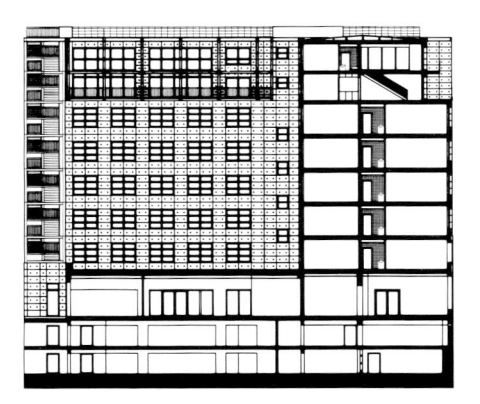

**Perspektivische Ansicht
Markgrafenstraße von Südwesten
Computersimulation**
Perspective elevation
Markgrafenstrasse
from the southwest
Computer simulation

Ansicht Markgrafenstraße von Westen
West elevation Markgrafenstrasse

**Gebäudequerschnitt durch den
Hofflügel mit Hofansicht des
Hauptgebäudes von Osten**
Cross section through courtyard
wing with courtyard east elevation
of main building

1:750

**Hofansicht mit offener Stahltreppe
von Osten**
East elevation of courtyard
with open steel staircase

**Querschnitt durch das Hauptgebäude
mit Ansicht des Hofflügels von Norden**
Section through main building with
north elevation of courtyard wing

1:750

**BEWAG-Geschäftssitz
Büro-, Wohn- und
Geschäftshaus**
Office and Apartment
Building of BEWAG

Gendarmenmarkt

Mit dem Bau dieses Hauses kehrt die BEWAG an einen Ort ihrer Geschichte zurück. Auf dem Grundstück, vis-à-vis dem Deutschen Dom am Gendarmenmarkt, wurde Ende des 19. Jahrhunderts das erste öffentliche Kraftwerk in Deutschland errichtet. Der neue Geschäftssitz der BEWAG greift die Erinnerung an die Geschichte des Ortes auf. In der Tradition der historischen Bebauung wird die Fassade des Neubaus symmetrisch aufgebaut und auf die Hauptachse des Deutschen Doms bezogen.

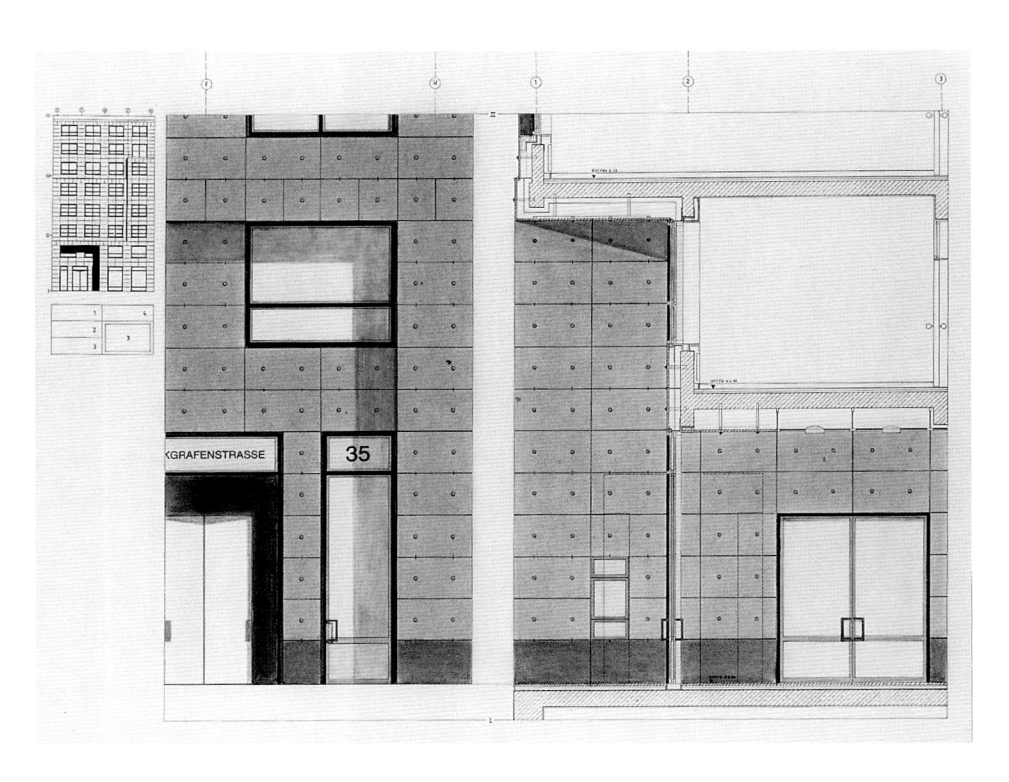

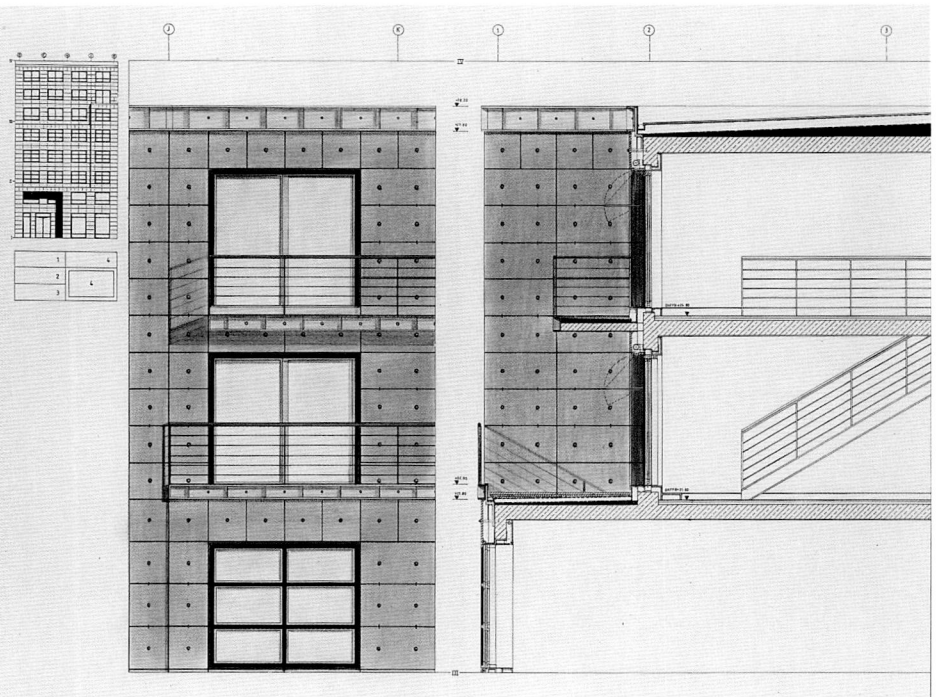

Fassadenstudien
Façade studies

**Ansicht und Schnitt
der Eingangssituation**
Elevation and section
of entrance situation

**Ansicht und Schnitt der
Attikageschosse
(6. und 7. Obergeschoß) mit
Maisonette-Wohnungen**
Elevation and section of the attic
floors (6th and 7th floors) with
maisonette apartments

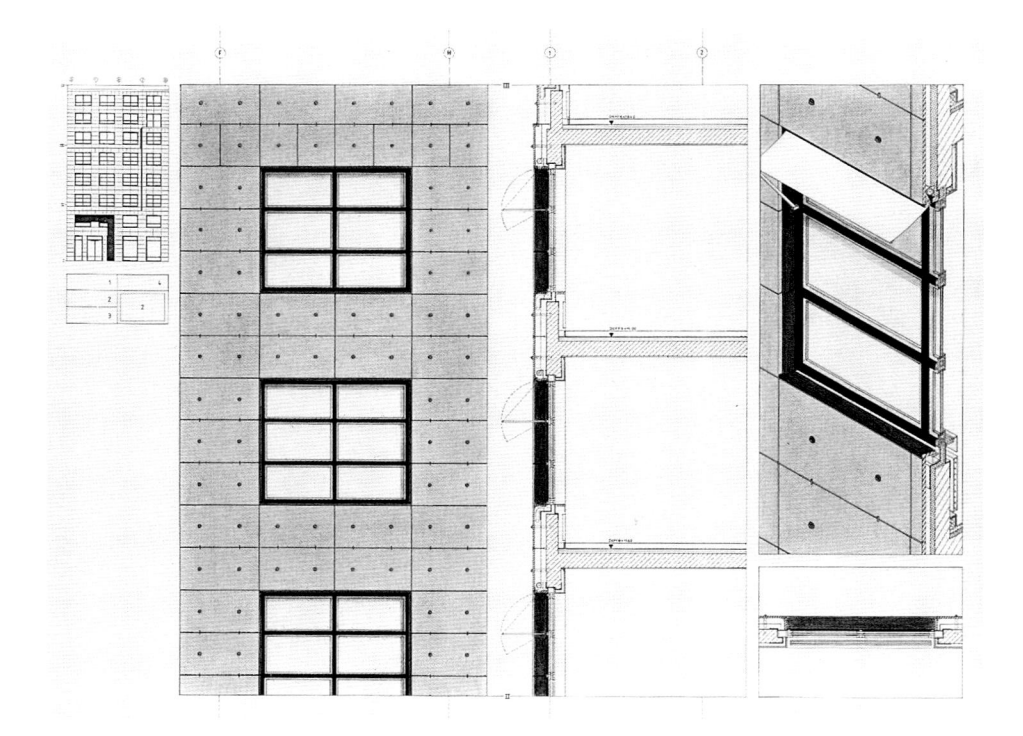

This building marks the return of BEWAG to a part of its history. At the end of the 19th century the first public-owned power station in Germany was erected here, opposite the Deutscher Dom at Gendarmenmarkt. The presence today of BEWAG's new headquarters here is a reminder of the history of the site. Following historical building tradition the façade of the new building is symmetrical and aligns with the main axis of the Deutscher Dom.

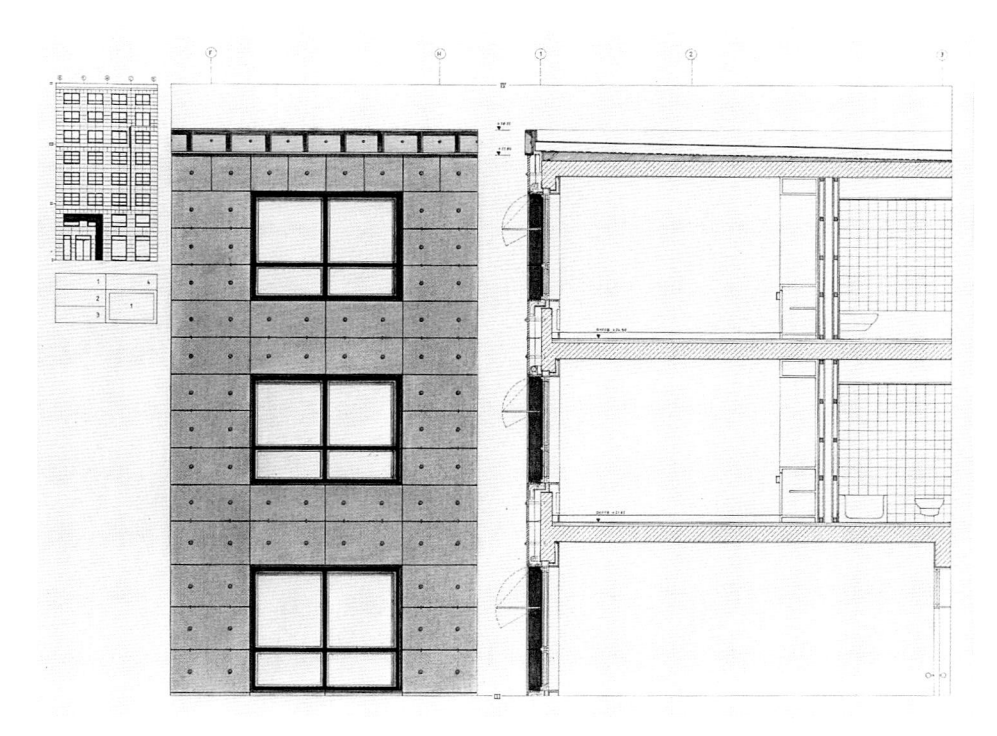

Fassadenstudien
Façade studies

**Ansicht und Schnitte
4. und 5. Obergeschoß
mit Büronutzung**
Elevation and sections
of 4th and 5th floors
offices

**Schnittisometrie
durch ein Fenster
mit Sonnenschutz**
Isometric section
through a window
with solar shading

**Ansicht und Schnitt der Attikageschosse
(6. und 7. Obergeschoß)
mit Wohnungen**
Elevation and section of attic floors
(6th and 7th floors)
apartments

| Büro-, Wohn- und Geschäftshaus Office and Apartment Building | Gendarmenmarkt | Josef Paul Kleihues Berlin mit with Peter Bastian (Projektleitung project manager) Norbert Hensel Andreas Heupel Roland Fritz Claudia Schulz Michael Alshut |

Bauherr:
Aufbaugesellschaft GbR
Berlin
ein Unternehmen
der Unternehmensgruppe
Roland Ernst

Planungstermine:
Entwurfsplanung seit 1992
Baubeginn 1994
Voraussichtlicher Bezug 1995

Nutzung:
Läden mit
ca. 591 m² Ladenfläche
80 Büros
(35 à 18 m², 35 à 25-30 m²,
10 à 35 m²)
9 Wohneinheiten mit
57-128 m²

Geschosse (VIII):
EG Läden
1.-5. OG Büros
6.-7. OG Wohnungen

Untergeschosse (II):
1.+2. UG
(à 1.256 m² Brutto-
geschoßfläche)
mit Tiefgarage, Technik, Lager

Grundstücksgröße:
954 m²

Überbaute Fläche:
944 m²

Bruttogeschoßfläche:
5.665,7 m²

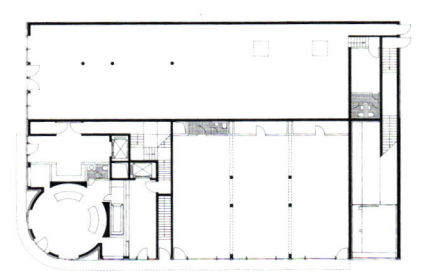

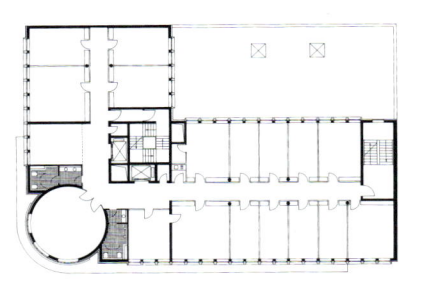

Angrenzend an das Geschäftshaus der BEWAG schließt das Gebäude die Blockecke zur Mohrenstraße. Vorhandene Traufhöhen und Gebäudetiefen werden aufgegriffen. Das Gebäude erfährt eine deutliche Betonung durch den Eckturm, dessen geometrische Überlagerungen von Zylinder – Kubus – Zylinder mit dem Turm des Deutschen Doms kommunizieren.

Perspektive
Markgrafen-/Ecke Mohrenstraße
Perspective drawing of the corner of
Markgrafenstrasse and Mohrenstrasse

Grundriß Erdgeschoß mit Ladennutzung
Ground floor plan retail

Grundriß Normalgeschoß
(1. – 5. Obergeschoß) mit Büronutzung
Typical floor plan
(1st to 5th floors) offices

1:750

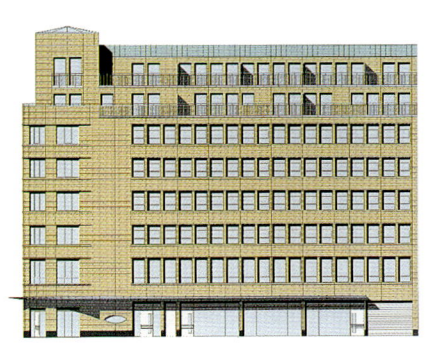

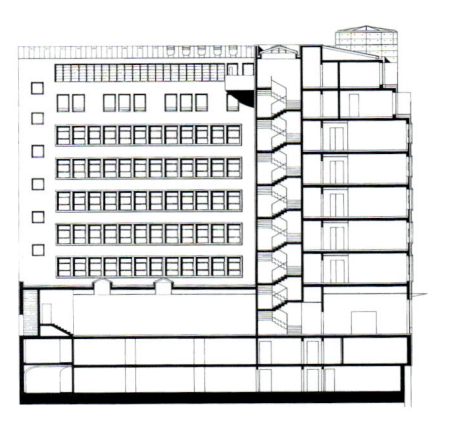

Ansicht Mohrenstraße
von Süden
South elevation
Mohrenstrasse

Querschnitt
im Bereich
des Treppenhauses
und Hofansicht
von Norden
Cross section
through stairwell
area
and north elevation
courtyard

1:750

Projektadresse:
Location:
Markgrafenstrasse 34
Mohrenstrasse 45
in
10117 Berlin-Mitte

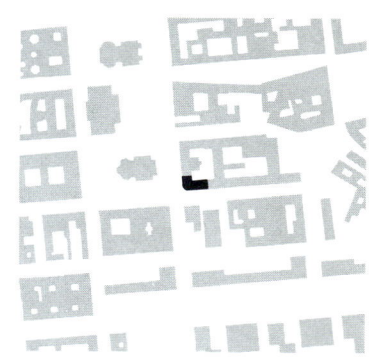

Client:
Aufbaugesellschaft GbR
Berlin
a company of
Unternehmensgruppe
Roland Ernst

Project Stages:
Design development from 1992
Start of construction 1994
Expected completion 1995

Building Use:
Shops with
ca. 591 m² sales area
80 offices
(35 à 18 m², 35 à 25-30 m²,
10 à 35 m²)
9 apartments
à 57-128 m²

Upper Floors (VIII):
Ground floor shops
1st-5th floor offices
6th and 7th floor apartments

Basement Floors (II):
1st and 2nd basement
(à 1256 m² gross floor area)
with car parks, services,
storeroom

Site Area:
954 m²

Built Area:
944 m²

Gross Floor Area:
5665.7 m²

Ansicht Markgrafenstraße
von Westen
West elevation
Markgrafenstrasse

1:200

Bordering directly on the BEWAG house, this building forms the corner of the block at the junction with Mohrenstrasse. Existing eaves height levels and building depths have been respected in its design. The corner tower sets a distinctive note, its geometric composition of cylinder – cube – cylinder echoing the tower of the Deutscher Dom.

Wohn- und Geschäftshaus
Apartment and Office Building

Gendarmenmarkt

Hilmer & Sattler Architekten
München
Heinz Hilmer
Christoph Sattler

Mitarbeit staff
Friedrich Treugut
Christian Winter
Barbara Schelle
Ulrich Greiler

Bauherr:
Aufbaugesellschaft GbR
Berlin
ein Unternehmen der
Unternehmensgruppe
Roland Ernst

Planungstermine:
Entwurfsplanung seit März 1993
Baubeginn Oktober 1994
Voraussichtlicher Bezug
Februar 1996

Nutzung:
3 Läden mit
615 m²
5-10 Büros mit
2.150 m²
8 Wohnungen mit
550 m²

Geschosse (VIII):
EG Läden
1.-5. OG Büros
6.-7. OG Wohnungen

Untergeschosse (II):
1.+2. UG (à 758 m²)
Tiefgarage, Lager, Technik

Grundstücksgröße:
909 m²

Überbaute Fläche:
909 m²

Bruttogeschoßfläche:
6.738,12 m²

Angrenzend an das Geschäftshaus der BEWAG schließt das Gebäude die Blockecke zur Taubenstraße. Ebenso wie der Nachbarbau verzichtet es auf architektonische Gesten. Die Fassadengestaltung ist klar und zurückhaltend strukturiert. Die kleinteilige vertikale Gliederung der Obergeschoßfassaden tritt dabei in ein Spannungsverhältnis zu den großen Spannweiten im Erdgeschoß, die technisch durch den Verlauf der U-Bahn-Trasse bedingt sind.

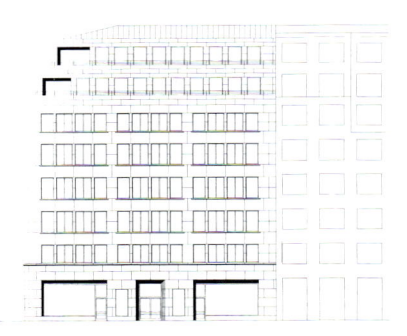

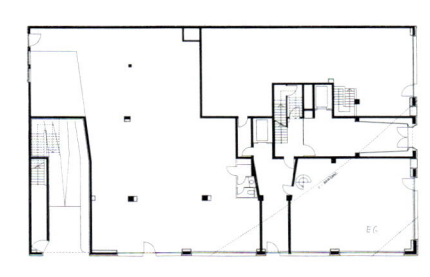

Ansicht Markgrafenstraße
von Westen
West elevation
Markgrafenstrasse

Ansicht Taubenstraße
von Norden
North elevation
Taubenstrasse

1:750

Grundriß Erdgeschoß
mit Ladennutzung
Ground floor plan retail

Grundriß Normalgeschoß
mit Büronutzung
Typical floor plan
offices

Grundriß 6. und 7. Obergeschoß
mit Wohnungen
Plan of 6th and 7th floors
apartments

1:750

Perspektive des Gebäudes
aus der Taubenstraße
von Osten
Perspective drawing
Taubenstrasse from the east

Projektadresse:
Location:
Markgrafenstrasse 36
in
10117 Berlin-Mitte

Schnitt durch den Gebäudeteil Markgrafenstraße mit Hofansicht von Süden
Section through the building on Markgrafenstrasse with courtyard south elevation

1:750

Perspektive des Gebäudes Taubenstraße/Ecke Markgrafenstraße
Perspective drawing, corner of Taubenstrasse and Markgrafenstrasse

1:750

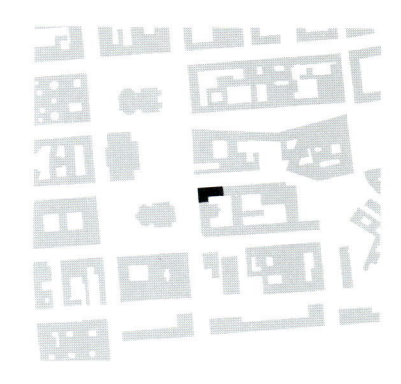

Client:
Aufbaugesellschaft GbR
Berlin
a company of
Unternehmengruppe
Roland Ernst

Project Stages:
Design development from
March 1993
Start of construction
October 1994
Expected completion
February 1996

Building Use:
3 shops totalling
615 m²
5-10 offices totalling
2150 m²
8 apartments totalling
550 m²

Upper Floors (VIII):
Ground floor shops
1st-5th floor offices
6th-7th floor apartments

Basement Floors (II):
1st and 2nd basement (à 758 m²)
car park, storeroom, building services

Site Area:
909 m²

Built Area:
909 m²

Gross Floor Area:
6738.12 m²

Bordering directly on the BEWAG headquarters, this building forms the corner of the block at the junction with Taubenstrasse. Like its neighbour, it avoids architectural gesture. The façade structure is clear and restrained and the vertical sectioning of the upper part of the façade sets up a contrast with the large spans at ground floor level, a feature which was governed by technical considerations concerned with the path of the U-Bahn below this point.

Büro-, Wohn- und
Geschäftshaus
Office and
Apartment Building

Triangel

Josef Paul Kleihues
Berlin
mit with
Peter Bastian
(**Projektleitung** project manager)
Norbert Hensel
Marco Angelini
Roland Fritz

Bauherr:
TCHA-Grundstücke Berlin GbR
Berlin

Planungstermine:
Entwurfsplanung seit 1992
Baubeginn 1994
Voraussichtlicher Bezug 1996

Nutzung:
4 Läden mit
44–83 m²
94 Büros
(80 à 10–20 m², 12 à 20–30 m²,
2 à 50 m²)
9 Studios mit jeweils ca. 20 m²
2 Wohnungen mit 100–130 m²

Geschosse (IX):
EG Läden
1.–4. OG Büros
5.+6. OG Büros, Wohnungen
7. OG Wohnungen
8. OG Technik/Lager, Archiv

Untergeschoß (I):
1. UG (484 m²)
automatisches Parksystem,
Technik, Lager

Grundstücksgröße:
489 m²

Überbaute Fläche:
484 m²

Bruttogeschoßfläche:
4.138,4 m²

Das Grundstück hat durch den Verlauf der ehemaligen Zollmauer als westlicher Begrenzung der Friedrichstadt einen dreieckigen Zuschnitt. Seine Überbauung folgt exakt den historischen Baufluchten und der heutigen Traufhöhe von 22 m. Oberhalb dieser Traufhöhe liegt ein zurückspringendes Attikageschoß mit Wohnungen, die über eigene Dachterrassen verfügen. Die nach Südwesten orientierte Fassade an der Mauerstraße ist im Bereich der Bürogeschosse voll verglast; die beiden kürzeren Fassaden erhalten eine Travertinverkleidung und horizontale Fensterbänder.

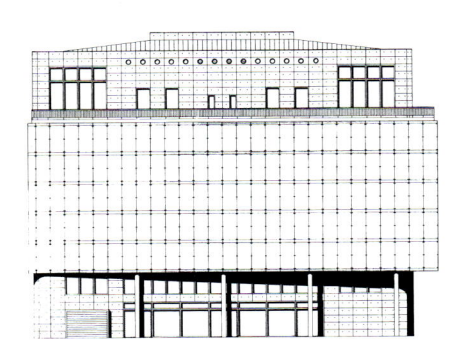

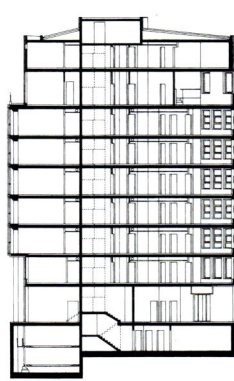

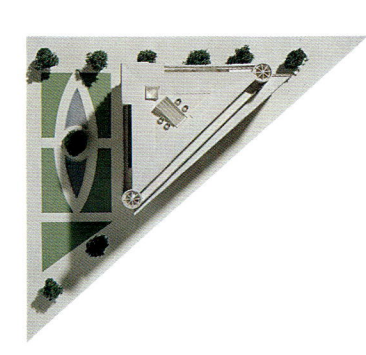

oben above
**Ansicht Mauerstraße
von Südwesten**
Southwest elevation
Mauerstrasse

Gebäudeschnitt
Section

1:750

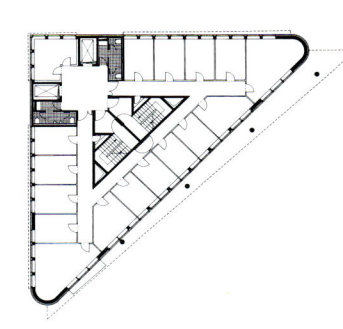

unten below
Modellaufsicht 1993
Top view of model 1993

**Grundriß 1. Obergeschoß
mit Büronutzung**
1st floor plan
offices

**Grundriß 2. – 4. Obergeschoß
mit Büronutzung**
Plan of 2nd to 4th floors
offices

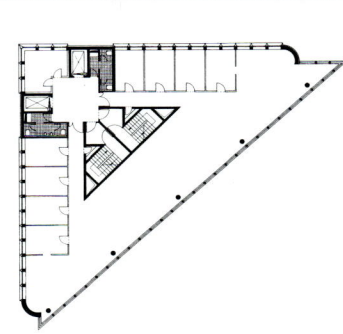

1:750

oben above
**Blick von der Friedrichstraße
von Süden
Modellaufnahme 1993**
View of Friedrichstrasse
from the south
Model photo 1993

Projektadresse:
Location:
Friedrichstrasse 204
in
10117 Berlin-Mitte

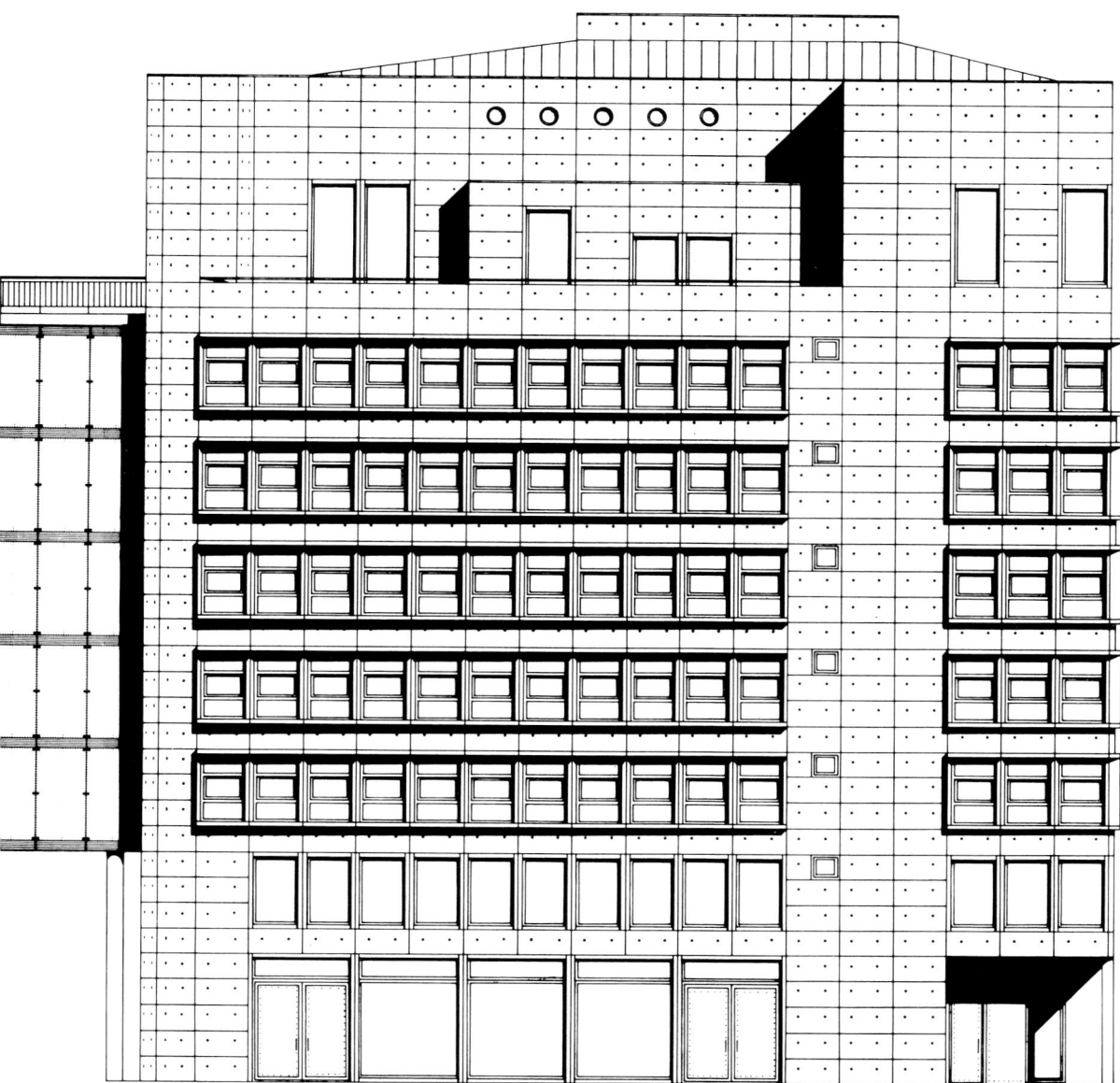

Client:
TCHA-Grundstücke Berlin GbR
Berlin

Project Stages:
Design development from 1992
Start of construction 1994
Expected completion 1996

Building Use:
4 shops
à 44-83 m²
94 offices
(80 à 10-20 m², 12 à 20-30 m²,
2 à 50 m²)
9 studios à ca. 20 m²
2 apartments à 100-130 m²

Upper Floors (IX):
Ground floor shops
1st-4th floor offices
5th and 6th floor offices,
apartments
7th floor apartments
8th floor services/storeroom,
archive

Basement Floor (I):
1st basement (484 m²)
with automatic parking system,
services, storeroom

Site Area:
489 m²

Built Area:
484 m²

Gross Floor Area:
4138.4 m²

The former customs wall at this point marking the western edge of Friedrichstadt has given rise to a triangular-shaped lot for this building. The new structure exactly corresponds to the lines of surrounding development, and adheres to the general eaves height of 22 m. Above the eaves and set back from the façade plane is an attic storey reserved for apartments, each one with its own roof terrace. The southwest-facing Mauerstrasse façade is fully glazed at the office levels; the two shorter façades are clad with travertine stone and have horizontal bands of windows.

**Ansicht Friedrichstraße
von Osten**
View of Friedrichstrasse
from the east

1:200

II
Blockergänzung

Kurt Berndt, Zollernhof Unter den Linden, 1910/11, Ansicht der Fassade von Bruno Paul, historische Aufnahme
Kurt Berndt, Zollernhof Unter den Linden, 1910/11, elevation of façade by Bruno Paul, contemporary photograph

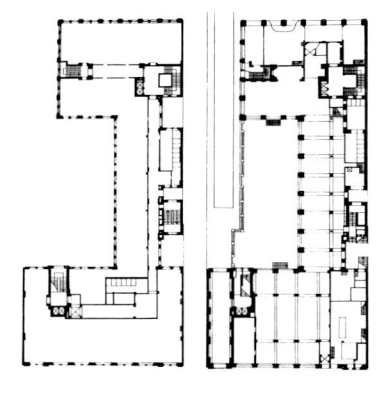

Kurt Berndt, Zollernhof Unter den Linden, 1910/11, Grundrisse Erdgeschoß und 2. Obergeschoß
Kurt Berndt, Zollernhof Unter den Linden, 1910/11, plans of ground floor and 2nd floor

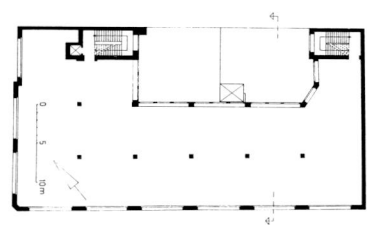

Otto Rudolf Salvisberg, Lindenhaus, 1912/13 (1965 abgerissen), historische Aufnahme und Grundriß Normalgeschoß
Otto Rudolf Salvisberg, Lindenhaus, 1912/13 (demolished in 1965), contemporary photograph and typical floor plan

Die Komplettierung zentral gelegener Blöcke ist Mitte der 90er Jahre ein wichtiger Beitrag zur Verdichtung und Rekonstruktion der Innenstadt. Während die zuvor besprochenen Architekturen für Situationen entworfen wurden, bei denen die Stadtbrache dominierte, geht es hier um eine punktuelle Ergänzung bestehender zusammenhängender Gebäudestrukturen. Das Spektrum der Eingriffe reicht vom Schließen einfacher Baulücken und der Neudefinition von Blockecken bis zur Wiedereinfassung kompletter Blockränder und zur Überbauung mit Teilblöcken. Insbesondere gehört zu dieser Gruppe von Projekten auch jene Vielzahl kleinerer innerstädtischer Bauvorhaben, die in ihrer Maßstäblichkeit dem Parzellencharakter der Vorkriegszeit am nächsten kommen.

Die Rekonstruktion wichtiger Ecksituationen folgt in der Dorotheen- und Friedrichstadt, je nach Grundstückszuschnitt und Bauaufgabe, sehr unterschiedlichen Gebäudetypologien. Deutlich wird dies an den auf den folgenden Seiten dargestellten Bauten von Jürgen Sawade, von Miroslav Volf und von Modersohn / Freiesleben.

Das Haus Pietzsch von Jürgen Sawade ist in Grundriß und Schnitt für ein Bürogebäude eher atypisch. Das architektonische Konzept definiert ein Gebäude mit einhüftigem Aufbau und mit einem schmalen haushohen Atrium, das sich zwischen die massive Brandwand des benachbarten Altbaus und die Büros des Neubaus schiebt. Der Ladenbereich im Erdgeschoß ist über eingehängte interne Treppen mit dem darüberliegenden Galeriegeschoß und dem 1. Untergeschoß verbunden, so daß sich im Gebäudeaufbau eine dreigeschossige Ladennutzung ergibt.

Das Haus Dussmann von Miroslav Volf hatte auf eine grundlegend andere Blocksituation zu reagieren. Der Abriß des Rückgebäudes Clara-Zetkin-Straße 41 ermöglichte eine T-förmige Grundrißfigur, die mit den beiden angrenzenden Altbauten zu einer Winkelform verschmilzt. Der sich ins Blockinnere erstreckende Gebäudeflügel integriert einen Lichthof, der von beiden Straßen aus über schmale Erdgeschoßpassagen zugänglich ist. Die Verwaltungseingänge werden durch deutliche Zäsuren im Baukörper markiert. Durch diese Zäsuren und die zurückgestaffelten Attikageschosse erhält das Gebäude Plastizität zur Straße hin.

Im Vergleich dazu verhält sich das Bibliotheksinstitut von Modersohn / Freiesleben mit seinen glatten, einem strengen Raster folgenden Lochfassaden zum Straßenraum hin bewußt anonym und zurückhaltend. Mittelpunkt ist ein kleiner Hof, der durch das konsequente Zurückstaffeln der Obergeschosse Weite gewinnt und eine nach innen gerichtete Plastizität entwickelt. Durch den Kon-

II
Block Completion

The completion of inner-city blocks is an important part in the increase in development density and the reconstruction of the city centre. While the types of architecture discussed previously were designed to be built on mostly empty inner-city expanses, this type of development concentrates on adding new buildings to existing structures. The range of such interventions stretches from the simple infill of building gaps and the redefinition of block corners through to a complete rebuilding of the block edges and subdivision into smaller blocks. One particular type included in this group is the many smaller inner-city projects which, in scale, most resemble the pre-war lot structure.

Depending on the shape of the lot and the nature of the project, very different types of building are being used in the reconstruction of important corner situations in Dorotheenstadt and Friedrichstadt. This can be seen clearly in the examples illustrated on the following pages – buildings by Jürgen Sawade, Miroslav Volf and Modersohn/Freiesleben.

The »Haus Pietzsch« by Jürgen Sawade is a somewhat atypical office block, both in ground plan and cross section. The design has a circulation corridor down one side and a narrow, full-height atrium reaching up between on the one side the monolithic fire wall of an existing building and on the other the offices of the new building. The shops on the ground floor are connected to the gallery level above and the first basement level via a suspended internal staircase; thus the sales area comprises three floors.

The Dussmann building by Miroslav Volf was faced with a completely different block situation. The demolition of an old building at the back of no. 41 Clara-Zetkin-Strasse opened up possibilities for a T-shaped building plan, which would blend with both neighbouring buildings to form an angled shape. The wing stretching into the interior of the block has an open courtyard which can be reached from both streets via narrow ground floor passageways. The entrances to the offices and administration levels are marked by distinct breaks in the building. This, together with the stepped attic storeys, adds an overall sculptural touch to the building's street façade.

In contrast the library institute building by Modersohn/Freiesleben presents a consciously restrained, anonymous face, with its smooth, regular punctuated street façade. In the centre is a small courtyard which gains width as a result of the tiered upper levels. The tiers give sculptural definition to the inner appearance of the building. Through its contrasting »stone«

Bruno Schmitz, Geschäftshaus als Blockrandschließung, Friedrichstraße 167/168, 1904/05, historische Aufnahme und Grundrisse
Bruno Schmitz, office building as completion of block edge, Friedrichstrasse 167/168, 1904/05, contemporary photograph and ground plans

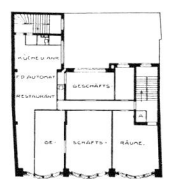

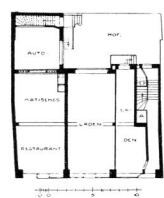

trast von »steinernen« Fassaden zur Straße und »gläsernen« Fassaden zum Hof konzentriert es sich introvertiert auf seine Mitte.
Während diese drei Projekte die Blockecken bewußt nicht architektonisch ausformen oder betonen, sondern zugunsten der Kontinuität des Straßenraumes eine hart geschnittene Ecke ausbilden, verleiht Josef Paul Kleihues bei seinen Geschäftshäusern Friedrichstadt der Gestaltung der Ecken besondere Bedeutung. Der symmetrische Bau schließt eine komplette Blockseite mit der langgestreckten Randbebauung an der Zimmerstraße und bindet über kurze Gebäudeflügel an die Nachbarbebauungen in der Charlotten- und der Friedrichstraße an. Diese Grundrißform ermöglicht es, die bauliche Verankerung des Blockes durch Markieren der Eckbaukörper zu betonen. Dabei bedient sich der Architekt, neben Überhöhungen und Zäsuren, der zu seinem Repertoire gehörenden schlanken Ship-Shape-Formen, die wie Pflöcke diagonal in den Eckbaukörpern sitzen. Zwischen ihnen spannt sich eine ruhige, ganz auf die Struktur zurückgenommene Fassade.

Das »duale Prinzip« eines zum Straßenraum durch strenge Lochfassaden zurückhaltenden und auf einen inneren Hof konzentrierten Gebäudes findet sich als Intention, in größerem Maßstab als beim Bibliotheksinstitut von Modersohn / Freiesleben, auch beim Gebäude des Deutschen Industrie- und Handelstages der Architekten Schweger + Partner. Die Straßenfassaden sind »steinern« und bilden einen geschlossenen Ecktypus, die Hoffassaden präsentieren sich verglast. Der einen Teilblock umfassende Komplex verzichtet auf absolut verstandene Geschlossenheit und Uniformität zugunsten von aufgebrochenen, den Hof öffentlich zugänglich machenden Strukturen und zugunsten von Variationen des gestalterischen Leitmotives, die aus der Beantwortung der angrenzenden, sehr unterschiedlichen urbanen Situationen und der verschiedenen Funktionsbereiche entwickelt sind. Die Lage an der Spree wird für ein dem Schwung des Ufers folgendes eigenes Wohngebäude genutzt. Der vor die benachbarte, unregelmäßig verlaufende Brandwand gesetzte Gebäudeflügel organisiert die Büroräume einhüftig und integriert – ähnlich dem Haus Pietzsch – die Brandwand in einen haushohen Luftraum, in dem auch Treppen und Aufzüge liegen.

Mit dem Rosmarin Karree in der Dorotheenstadt wird ebenfalls eine vorhandene Blockbebauung durch einen neuen Teilblock ergänzt. Die geforderten Wohnungen sind in einem von Kahlfeldt Architekten entworfenen linearen Baukörper konzentriert, der – zwischen Altbau und Bürogebäude – als über die Trauflinie hinausgezogene Scheibe quer durch den Block gesteckt ist. Die Büroflügel der Architekten Böge + Lindner komplettieren den Neubau zu einem Rechteckblock mit zwei innenliegenden Höfen. Das Quergebäude zwischen beiden Höfen dient als zentrale, geschoßbezogene Empfangszone für die zweihüftig angeordneten Büros. Die Hauptlobby im ersten Obergeschoß wird vom Haupteingang mit prominenter Adresse an der Friedrichstraße erschlossen.

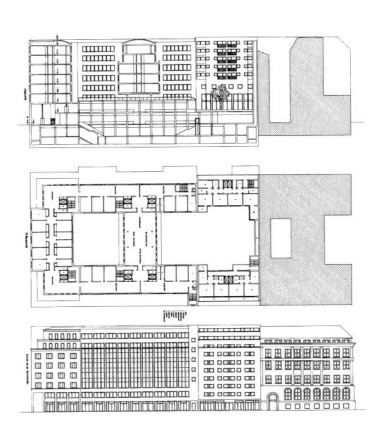

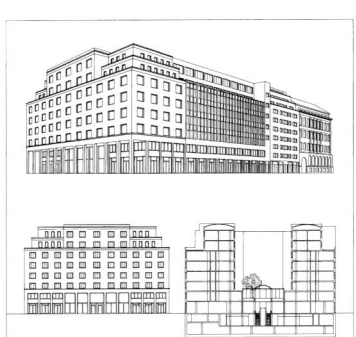

Kahlfeldt Architekten, Rosmarin Karree, Ansichten und Grundrisse, Wettbewerbsentwurf 1993/94
Kahlfeldt Architects, Rosmarin Karree, elevations and ground plans, competition design 1993/94

street façades and the »glass« façades facing the courtyard the building seems introverted, focussing on its own centre.

While these three projects consciously avoid any architectural emphasis for the corner of the block, tracing instead a precise definite angle which is in keeping with the continuity of the urban space, Josef Paul Kleihues' Office Buildings Friedrichstadt give particular emphasis to the corner situation. The symmetrical building completes an entire side of a block, joining up with a long block edge along Zimmerstrasse, and via short building wings to the neighbouring buildings on Charlottenstrasse and Friedrichstrasse. This base plan opened up the possibility for the architect to give demarcation to the whole block by emphasising the corners. To do this he used a variety of forms, including arches and breaks, and the slender pointed forms well known from his architectural repertoire – forms such as pegs inserted diagonally into the corners. Between the corner sections the façade design is much calmer, and reduced back to the structure of the building.

The »dual principle« of a building presenting a reserved, regular punctuated face to the street and centring internally around a courtyard, can be seen on a larger scale than Modersohn/Freiesleben's Library Institute, in the offices of the Association German Chambers of Industry and Commerce designed by the architects Schweger + Partner. The street façades are »stonelike« and form a closed corner type block, the courtyard façades are glazed. However, this complex, comprising part of a block, does not offer a completely closed, uniform structure in the traditional style, favouring instead a more broken-up arrangement which allows access from the outside to the public courtyard inside; design variations on the leitmotif are a response to the different urban situations bordering on the site and a result of the different functional zones of the **Association** building. The Spree-side location is exploited in a separate accommodation block following the curve of the riverbank. The offices in the wing bordering the irregular fire wall of existing buildings branch off along one side of a corridor; here, as in the »Haus Pietzsch« building, the situation has been used to incorporate the fire wall as part of a full height air space, which also contains stairs and lifts.

The Rosmarin Karree in Dorotheenstadt is also an example of an extension to an existing block, by addition of a new partial block. The requisite apartment space is concentrated in a linear building designed by Kahlfeldt Architects; this section is wedged through the centre of the block, between the existing building and the office building, and projects up beyond the eaves line. The office building, designed by Böge + Lindner Architects, completes this rectangular block with two interior courtyards. The transverse section between the two courtyards

Schweger + Partner, Deutscher Industrie- und Handelstag, Modellfoto, Wettbewerb 1994
Schweger + Partner, Association German Chambers of Industry and Commerce, model photo, competition 1994

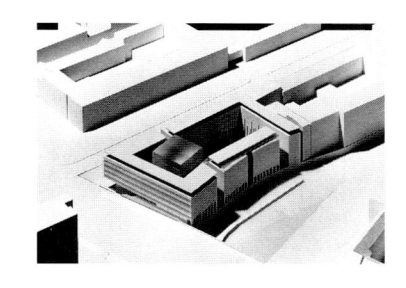

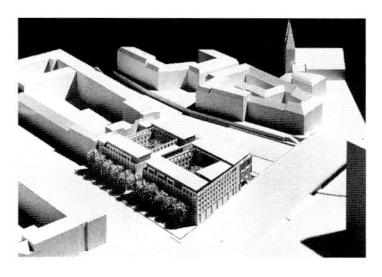

Brandt & Böttcher, Deutscher Industrie- und Handelstag, Modellfoto, Wettbewerb 1994
Brandt & Böttcher, Association German Chambers of Industry and Commerce, model photo, competition 1994

Gebäude des ehemaligen Ministeriums der DDR für Außer- und Innerdeutschen Handel, Aufnahme vor Beginn der Umbaumaßnahmen zum Abgeordnetenhaus des Deutschen Bundestages
Former GDR Ministry for Foreign and Inner German Trade, photograph of building before conversion to Bundestag parliamentary office building

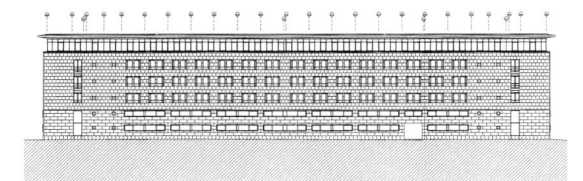

Brands Kolbe Wernik, Bürogebäude Deutscher Bundestag, Unter den Linden 44-60, Ansicht Mittelstraße
Brands Kolbe Wernik, Bundestag parliamentary office building, Unter den Linden 44-60, Mittelstrasse elevation

Klaus Theo Brenner, Büro-, Wohn- und Geschäftshaus Unter den Linden, perspektivische Ansicht
Klaus Theo Brenner, office and apartment building Unter den Linden, perspective elevation

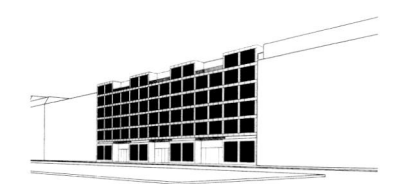

Einen auf den ersten Blick ähnlichen Hoftypus mit ebenfalls zweihüftig angeordneten Büroräumen zeigt das Gebäude des Deutschen Bundestages von Brands Kolbe Wernik Architekten. Hier handelt es sich nicht um einen Neubau, sondern – wie bei dem Geschäftshaus von Klaus Theo Brenner auf der gegenüberliegenden Straßenseite der Linden – um die vollständige Entkernung und Erneuerung eines zu DDR-Zeiten errichteten Gebäudes. Interessant ist der unterschiedliche Umgang mit der in beiden Fällen ähnlichen, durch die erhaltene Stahlbeton-Skelettkonstruktion vorgegebenen gerasterten Bauwerkstruktur. Durch sie werden Grundriß und Raumorganisation deutlich geprägt, bei der Gestaltung der Fassaden folgen die Architekten jedoch unterschiedlichen Ansätzen.

Für Brands Kolbe Wernik hängt die »Disposition der neuen Fassaden (...) zwar konstruktiv vom Raster ab, dennoch wird ihre Gestaltung in erster Linie durch ausgewogene proportionale Verhältnisse zwischen offenen und geschlossenen Flächen und die zeitgemäße Integration historischer Strukturelemente des Straßenzuges Unter den Linden bestimmt«.[1] In Anlehnung an die Gestaltungsmerkmale und Proportionen der Bebauungen der Linden wird das Gebäude aufgestockt, erhält einen klaren Fassadenaufbau in Sockel-, Haupt- und Attikazone und eine Natursteinverkleidung. Für Klaus Theo Brenner hingegen sollte das zu einem Büro-, Wohn- und Geschäftshaus umgebaute Gebäude »transparent gegenüber den wesentlichen strukturellen Gegebenheiten der vorgefundenen Architektur bleiben«.[2] Eine Verkleidung mit einer steinernen Lochfassade sowie jegliche Annäherung an den Charakter der historischen Lindenfassaden werden abgelehnt. Statt dessen zeigt Brenner das Rechteckraster der nackten Skelettstruktur mit absoluter Strenge: Die horizontalen und vertikalen Elemente des Tragwerks werden mit gelblichem Muschelkalk verkleidet, alle Öffnungen außenbündig vollflächig verglast.

Hinter dem linearen Gebäude von Brenner liegt im selben Block der Gebäudekomplex der Komischen Oper. Durch den Rückbau der Glinkastraße auf ihr altes Profil wurde hier ein Grundstück frei, das die Ergänzung des Blockes nach Westen durch ein Gebäude des Architekten Jürgen Sawade ermöglicht. Die Grundform entspricht jener der Geschäftshäuser Friedrichstadt an der Zimmerstraße: Ein in sich symmetrischer Bau schließt eine komplette Blockseite mit einer langgestreckten Randbebauung und bindet über kurze Gebäudeflügel an die Nachbarbebauung der Querstraßen an; damit werden auch die Blockecken definiert. Während jedoch Kleihues in der Zimmerstraße die Symmetrie seines Gebäudes mittels Betonung und Überhöhung der beiden Blockecken aufbaut, schneidet Sawade die Ecken scharfkantig und schafft Symmetrie durch risalitartige Ausbildung und Überhöhung eines Mittelbaus.

1 Brands Kolbe Wernick, Erläuterungen zum Bürohaus des Deutschen Bundestages.
2 Klaus Theo Brenner, Erläuterungen zum Büro-, Wohn- und Geschäftshaus Unter den Linden.

serves as a central reception zone for offices which branch off either side of central corridors. The main lobby on the first floor is accessed from Friedrichstrasse, thus giving the building a prestigious address.

A building which would at first glance appear to be a similar type of courtyard block, also with offices branching off central corridors, is the German Bundestag building designed by Brands Kolbe Wernik Architects. It is not a completely new structure, but – as with the office block by Klaus Theo Brenner on the opposite side of the »Linden« – an old GDR building, which has been stripped to the shell and completely renovated. An interesting aspect is the differing treatments in both cases of what are similar reinforced concrete skeletons with predefined basic grid structures. These factors leave their distinct mark on the ground plan and spatial organisation, but the façade designs of the two buildings take very different lines.

In the case of the building by Brands Kolbe Wernik the »disposition of the new façades (...) is indeed determined by the structural grid, but its design primarily represents a balanced proportional relationship between open and closed surfaces and a contemporary integration of historic structural elements typical for Unter den Linden.«[1] To harmonise with the design characteristics and proportions of existing development on Unter den Linden the height of the building is increased, and the base, main section and attic storey display a clear façade treatment with natural stone cladding. For Klaus Theo Brenner, on the other hand, his conversion to an apartment and office block is to »remain transparent in regard of the main structural terms of the existing architecture.«[2] He declines to introduce a punctuated stone façade or to adapt to the character of the historic structures along Unter den Linden. Instead Brenner opts to uncompromisingly reveal the rectangular grid of the bare skeleton frame; only the horizontal and vertical elements in the support structure are clad with yellowish limestone, all openings being fully glazed.

Behind Brenner's linear building, and in the same block, is the Komische Oper complex. As a result of reducing the Glinkastrasse width back to its former dimension, a building lot became available for an extension of the block to the west. This new building, designed by Jürgen Sawade, has a basic form similar to the office Buildings Friedrichstadt on Zimmerstrasse, i.e. a symmetrical structure closing one complete side of a block by means of linear block development, and forming a link to the buildings on the transverse streets via short wing sections; this entails, too, a definition of the block corners. While Kleihues in Zimmerstrasse establishes the symmetry of his building by emphasising and heightening the two corners of the block, Sawade cuts the corners at a sharp angle and creates symmetry with protruding façade bays and a heightened central section.

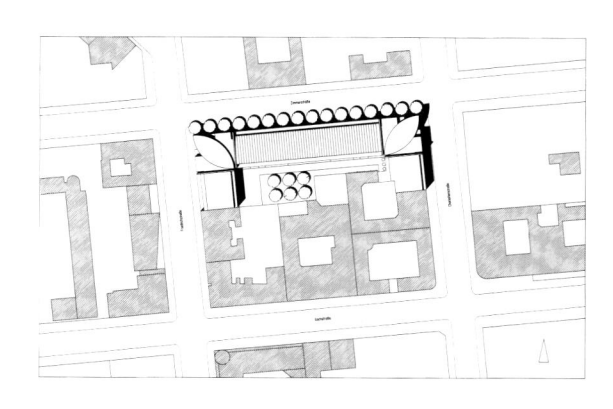

Josef Paul Kleihues, Geschäftshäuser Friedrichstadt, Lageplan
Josef Paul Kleihues, Geschäftshäuser Friedrichstadt buildings, site plan

Josef Paul Kleihues, Geschäftshäuser Friedrichstadt, Modellfoto
Josef Paul Kleihues, Geschäftshäuser Friedrichstadt buildings, model photo

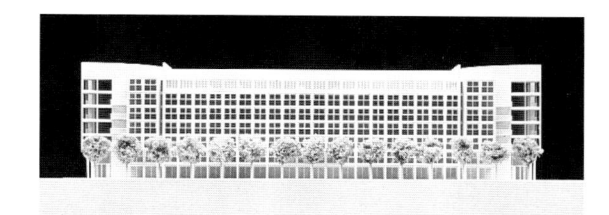

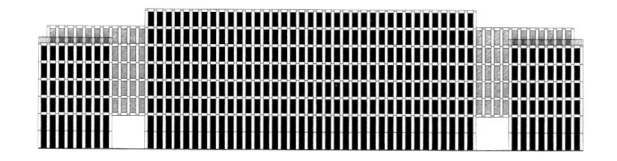

Jürgen Sawade, Büro-, Wohn- und Geschäftshaus an der Komischen Oper, Ansicht Glinkastraße
Jürgen Sawade, office and apartment building at the Komische Oper, Glinkastrasse elevation

1 Brands Kolbe Wernick, Explanatory notes Office Building Deutscher Bundestag.
2 Klaus Theo Brenner, Explanatory notes Office and Apartment Building Unter den Linden.

Büro- und
Geschäftshaus
Unter den Linden
Office Building
Unter den Linden

Haus Pietzsch

Jürgen Sawade
Berlin

Mitarbeit staff
Christine Hahner
(**Projektleitung** project manager)
Stephan Eich
Frank Hassenewert
Jürgen Ochernal

Bauherr:
Unter den Linden 42 GbR
vertreten durch
Wert-Konzept GmbH, Berlin

Planungstermine:
Entwurfsplanung seit 1991
Baubeginn 1992
Fertigstellung Ende 1994

Nutzung:
Läden mit
780 m²
Büros mit
3.320 m²

Geschosse (VII):
EG Läden
1.-6. OG Büros

Untergeschosse (II):
1. UG Läden
2. UG Technik und Tiefgarage
(36 Pkw-Stellplätze)

Grundstücksgröße:
783 m²

Überbaute Fläche:
759 m²

Bruttogeschoßfläche:
6.825,51 m²
(inclusive UG)

Das Haus schließt auf einem schmalen Grundstück von ca. 16 m Breite die Bebauung des Straßenzuges Unter den Linden an der Kreuzung mit der Neustädtischen Kirchstraße. Die Erschließung erfolgt, vom prominenteren Straßenzug her, über die schmale Kopffassade an den »Linden«. Zum angrenzenden Altbau entsteht ein schmales Atrium, das sich über die gesamte Gebäudehöhe erstreckt; hier wird die große vorhandene Brandwand als Gemäldegalerie genutzt.

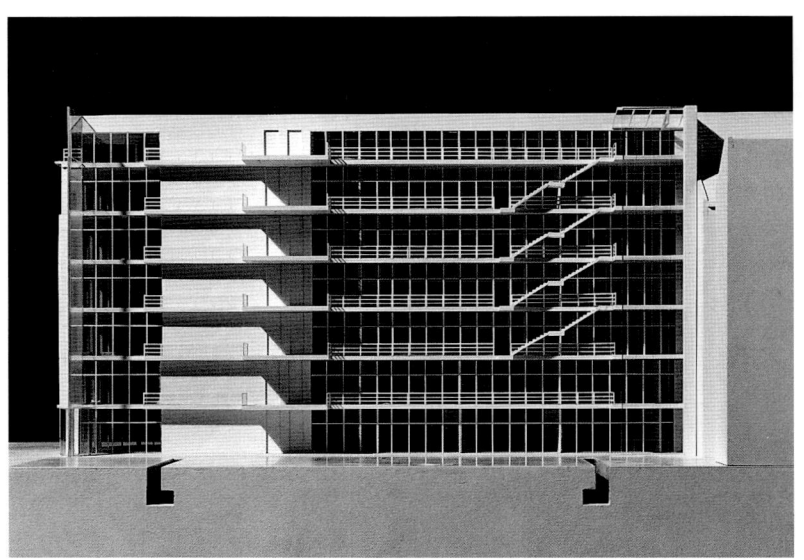

Ansicht des Gebäudes
Neustädtische Kirchstraße/
Unter den Linden
Modellaufnahme
View of the corner of
Neustädtische Kirchstrasse and
Unter den Linden
Model photo

Gebäudelängsschnitt
Modellaufnahme
Longitudinal section
Model photo

Projektadresse:
Location:
Unter den Linden 42
in
10117 Berlin-Mitte

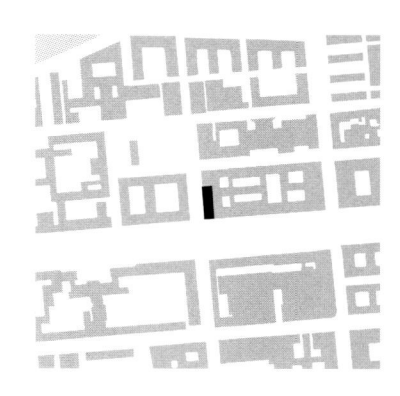

Client:
Unter den Linden 42 GbR
represented by
Wert-Konzept GmbH, Berlin

Project Stages:
Design development from 1991
Start of construction 1992
Completion end 1994

Building Use:
Shops totalling
780 m^2
Offices totalling
3320 m^2

Upper Floors (VII):
Ground floor shops
1st-6th floor offices

Basement Floors (II):
1st basement shops
2nd basement services and
parking (36 cars)

Site Area:
783 m^2

Built Area:
759 m^2

Gross Floor Area:
6825.51 m^2
(including basement)

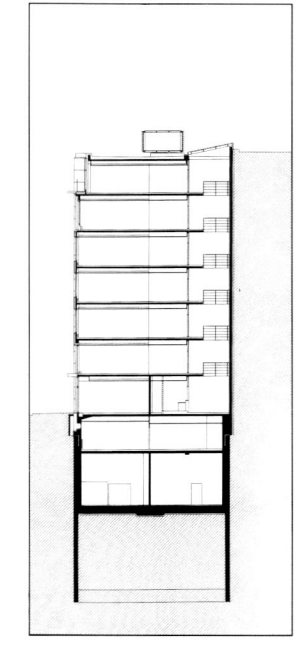

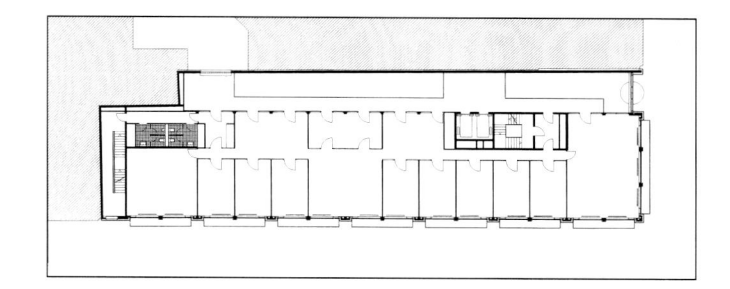

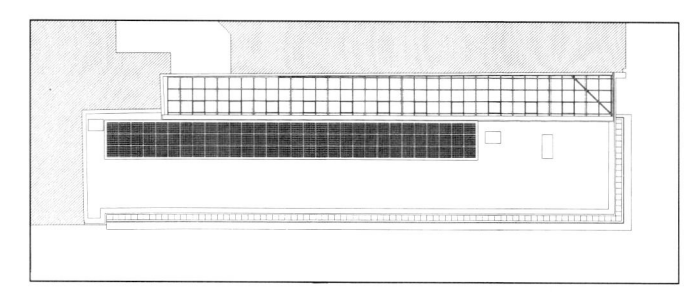

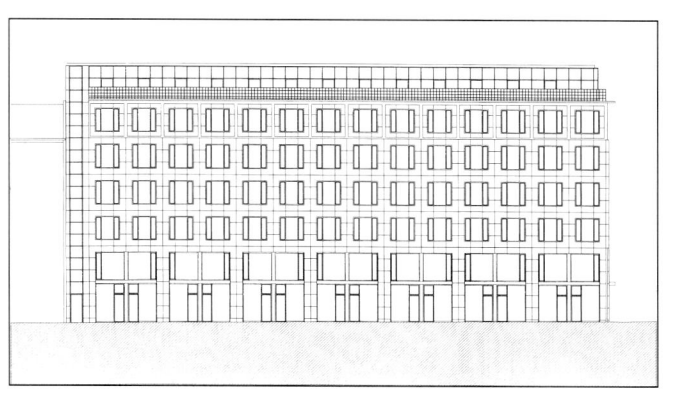

Grundriß Erdgeschoß mit Ladennutzung
Ground floor plan
retail

Grundriß 1. Obergeschoß mit Büronutzung
1st floor plan
offices

Dachaufsicht
Top view of roof

1:750

Ansicht Neustädtische Kirchstraße von Westen
West elevation
Neustädtische Kirchstrasse

rechts right
Gebäudequerschnitt
Cross section

1:750

The building spans a 16 m wide plot along Unter den Linden at the corner of Neustädtische Kirchstrasse. The main entrance is located in the narrow façade on the prestigious »Linden«. A narrow atrium stretching the entire height of the building forms the link with the existing building; here the large, preexisting fire wall is used as an art gallery.

Büro-, Wohn- und
Geschäftshaus
Office Building

Haus Dussmann

Miroslav Volf
Saarbrücken

Mitarbeit staff
Oliver Brünjes
Palo Panak

Statik statics
F. W. Tobien, Saarbrücken
Brandl, München
Haustechnik building services
Ingenieurbüro Werner
Kasprowski, Grünwald
Lichtplanung lighting planning
Christian Bartenbach,
Aldrans/Österreich

Bauherr:
Peter Dussmann
München

Planungstermine:
Wettbewerb 1994, 1. Preis
Entwurfsplanung seit 1994
Baubeginn 1995
Voraussichtlicher Bezug 1996

Nutzung:
Läden mit
2.000 m²
Büros mit
3.540 m²
36 Wohneinheiten mit
1.135 m² Gesamtfläche

Geschosse:
Neubau Haupthaus (VIII):
EG + 1. OG Läden
2.-6. OG Büros
7. OG Wohnungen
Neubau Clara-Zetkin-Straße (VI):
EG + 1. OG Läden
2.-6. OG Wohnungen
(Boardinghouse)

Untergeschosse (II):
Läden, Technik, Tiefgarage

Grundstücksgröße:
1.890 m²

Überbaute Fläche:
1.717 m²

Bruttogeschoßfläche:
11.928 m²

Unter Einbeziehung der zwei Altbauten an der Clara-Zetkin-Straße wird mit dem Gebäudekomplex die östliche Blockkante zur Friedrichstraße neu definiert. Die Hauptfassade wird durch 2-geschossige Arkaden mit dahinterliegender Ladennutzung betont; hier liegt auch der Eingang zum Foyer des Verwaltungsgebäudes. Über schmale Passagen wird von der Clara-Zetkin-Straße und der Friedrichstraße aus ein kleiner Lichthof im Inneren des Gebäudekomplexes erschlossen.

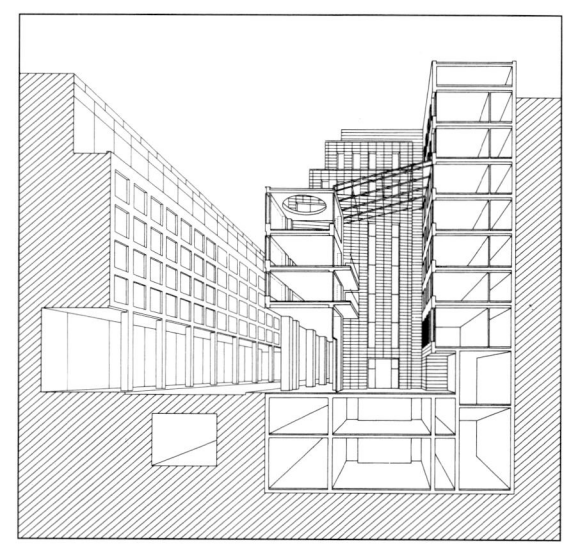

Perspektive des Gebäudes
Friedrichstraße / Mittelstraße
von Südwesten
Perspective drawing
of the corner of Friedrichstrasse and
Mittelstrasse from the southwest

Perspektivischer Gebäudequerschnitt
im Bereich des Lichthofes
Perspective cross section
through the inner courtyard area

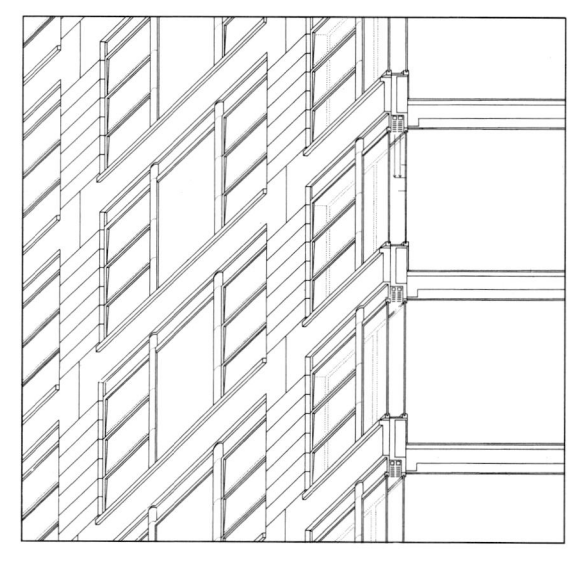

Ansicht Clara-Zetkin-Straße
von Norden
North elevation
Clara-Zetkin-Strasse

1:750

Fassadenschnitt/-ansicht
Isometrische Darstellung
Section/view of façade
Isometric projection

Projektadresse:
Location:
**Friedrichstrasse/
Clara-Zetkin-Strasse/
Mittelstrasse
in
10117 Berlin-Mitte**

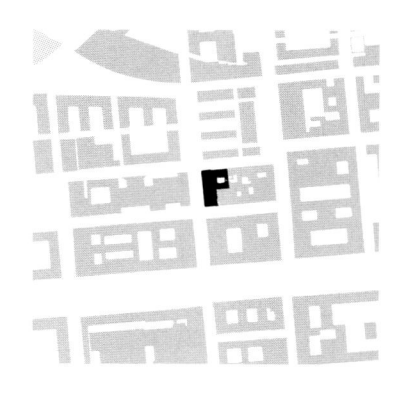

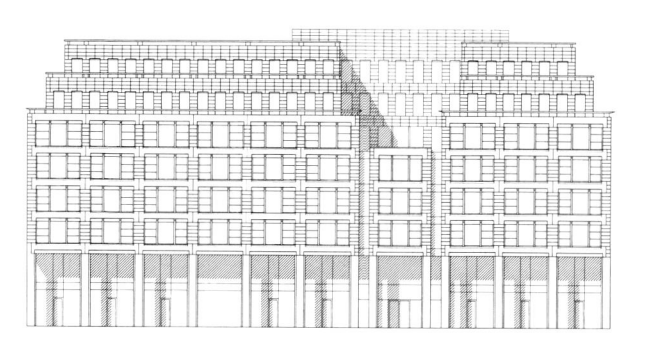

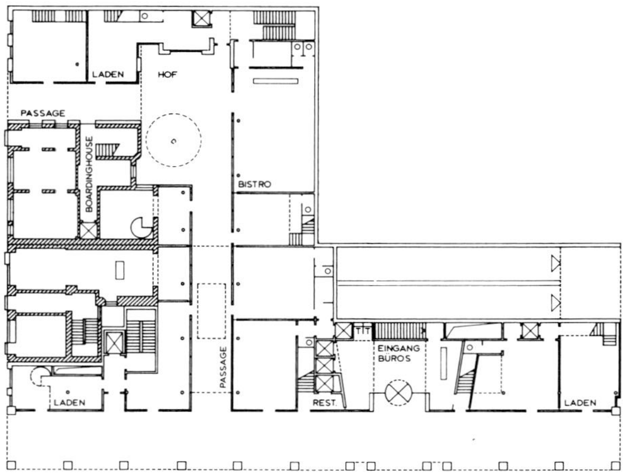

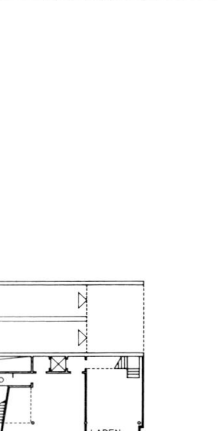

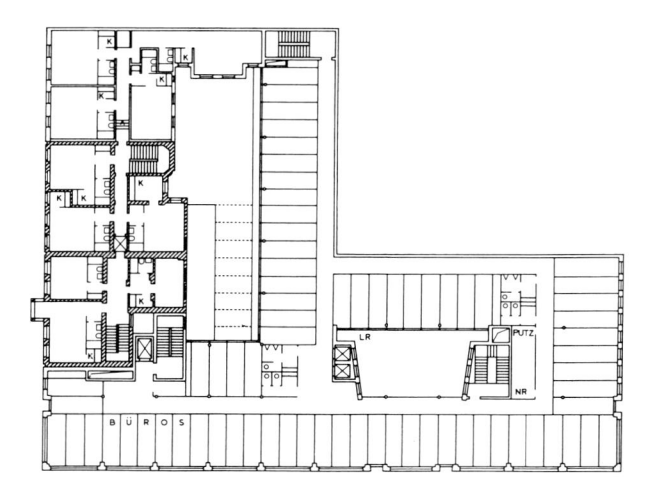

Client:
Peter Dussmann
München

Project Stages:
Competition 1994, 1st prize
Design development from 1994
Start of construction 1995
Expected completion 1996

Building Use:
Shops totalling
2000 m²
Offices totalling
3540 m²
36 apartment units with a total area of
1135 m²

Upper Floors:
New main building (VIII):
Ground floor and 1st floor shops
2nd-6th floor offices
7th floor apartments
New building
Clara-Zetkin-Strasse (VI):
Ground floor – 1st floor shops
2nd-6th floor apartments
(Boardinghouse)

Basement Floors (II):
Shops, services, car park

Site Area:
1890 m²

Built Area:
1717 m²

Gross Floor Area:
11928 m²

This new building complex incorporates two existing structures on Clara-Zetkin-Strasse in a reinterpretation of the eastern edge of the block towards Friedrichstrasse. The main façade consists of 2-floor arcades with retail premises behind; here also is located the entrance to the foyer of the administration building. Narrow passages lead from Clara-Zetkin-Strasse and Friedrichstrasse into a small open courtyard enclosed within the complex.

**Ansicht Friedrichstraße
von Westen**
West elevation
Friedrichstrasse

1:750

**Grundriß Erdgeschoß
mit Ladennutzung
und Gastronomie**
Ground floor plan
shops and restaurants

**Grundriß Normalgeschoß
mit Büronutzung (Achsraster)**
Typical floor plan
offices (grid plan)

1:750

**Ansicht Mittelstraße
von Süden**
South elevation
Mittelstrasse

1:750

Neubau für das Deutsche
Bibliotheksinstitut DBI
New Building for the German
Library Institute

Modersohn und Freiesleben
Berlin
Johannes Modersohn
Antje Freiesleben

Mitarbeit staff
Tobias Zepter
Lutz Artmann
Jens-Oliver Kempf

Bauherr:
Deutsches Bibliotheksinstitut
in Verbindung mit
der Senatsverwaltung für
Kulturelle Angelegenheiten,
Berlin

Planungstermine:
Wettbewerb 1994, 1. Rang
Baubeginn voraussichtlich 1995

Nutzung:
1 Laden mit
80 m²
ca. 110 Büroräume mit
10-24 m²

Geschosse (VII):
EG Läden, Büros
1.-6.OG Büros

Untergeschoß (I):
Technik, Lagerräume

Grundstücksgröße:
974,4 m²

Überbaute Fläche:
866 m²

Bruttogeschoßfläche:
6.450 m²

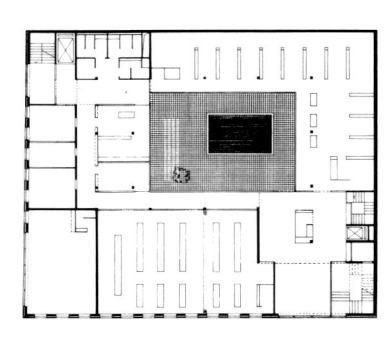

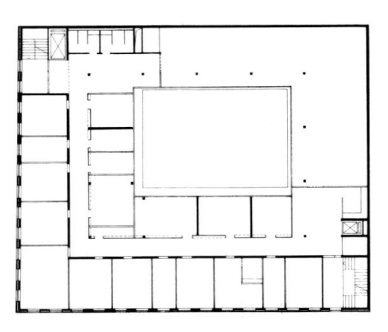

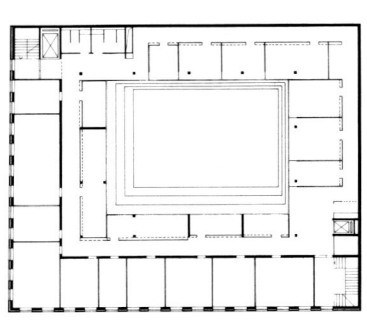

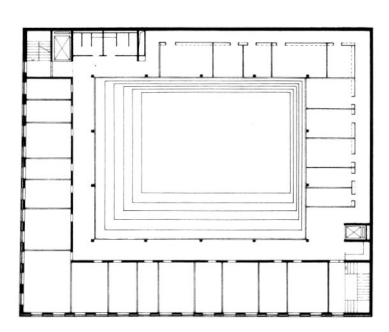

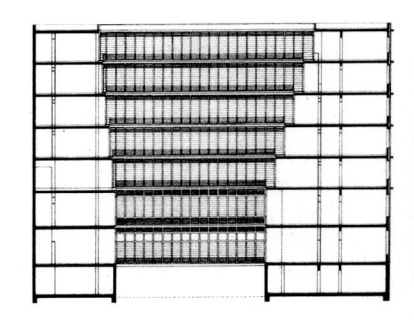

Grundriß Erdgeschoß
mit Laden- und
Bibliotheksnutzung
Ground floor plan
retail and library

Grundriß 2. Obergeschoß
mit Büronutzung
2nd floor plan
offices

Grundriß 4. Obergeschoß
mit Büronutzung
4th floor plan
offices

Grundriß 6. Obergeschoß
mit Büronutzung
6th floor plan
offices

1:750

Gebäudeschnitt
A-A
Section
A-A

1:750

In der Lage gegenüber der stadträumlich und funktional dominierenden Staatsbibliothek erhält das Verwaltungsgebäude des Bibliotheksinstitutes zum Straßenraum bewußt reduzierte Fassaden. Mit ihrer Bebauungsflucht und Traufhöhe integrieren sie sich zurückhaltend in die Bebauung der Dorotheenstadt. Durch die zum Innenhof hin abgetreppten Staffelgeschosse und die vollflächige Verglasung der Hoffassaden erhält das Gebäude einen introvertierten Charakter.

Projektadresse:
Location:
**Clara-Zetkin-Strasse/
Charlottenstrasse
in
10117 Berlin-Mitte**

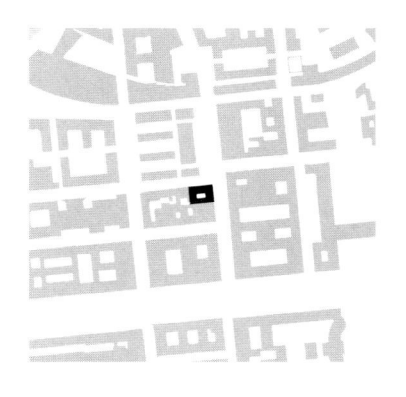

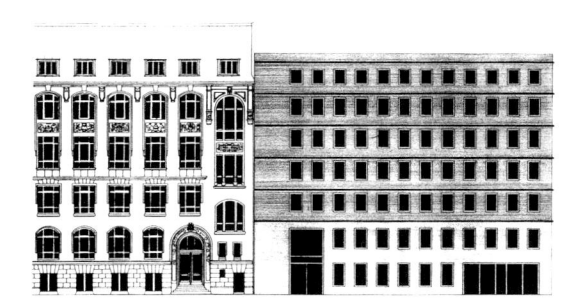

Client:
Deutsches Bibliotheksinstitut
in conjunction with the
Senatsverwaltung für Kulturelle
Angelegenheiten, Berlin

Project Stages:
Competition 1994, 1st stage
Start of construction expected
1995

Building Use:
1 shop
of 80 m^2
ca. 110 office rooms
à 10-24 m^2

Upper Floors (VII):
Ground floor shops, offices
1st-6th floor offices

Basement Floor (I):
Services, storerooms

Site Area:
974.4 m^2

Built Area:
866 m^2

Gross Floor Area:
6450 m^2

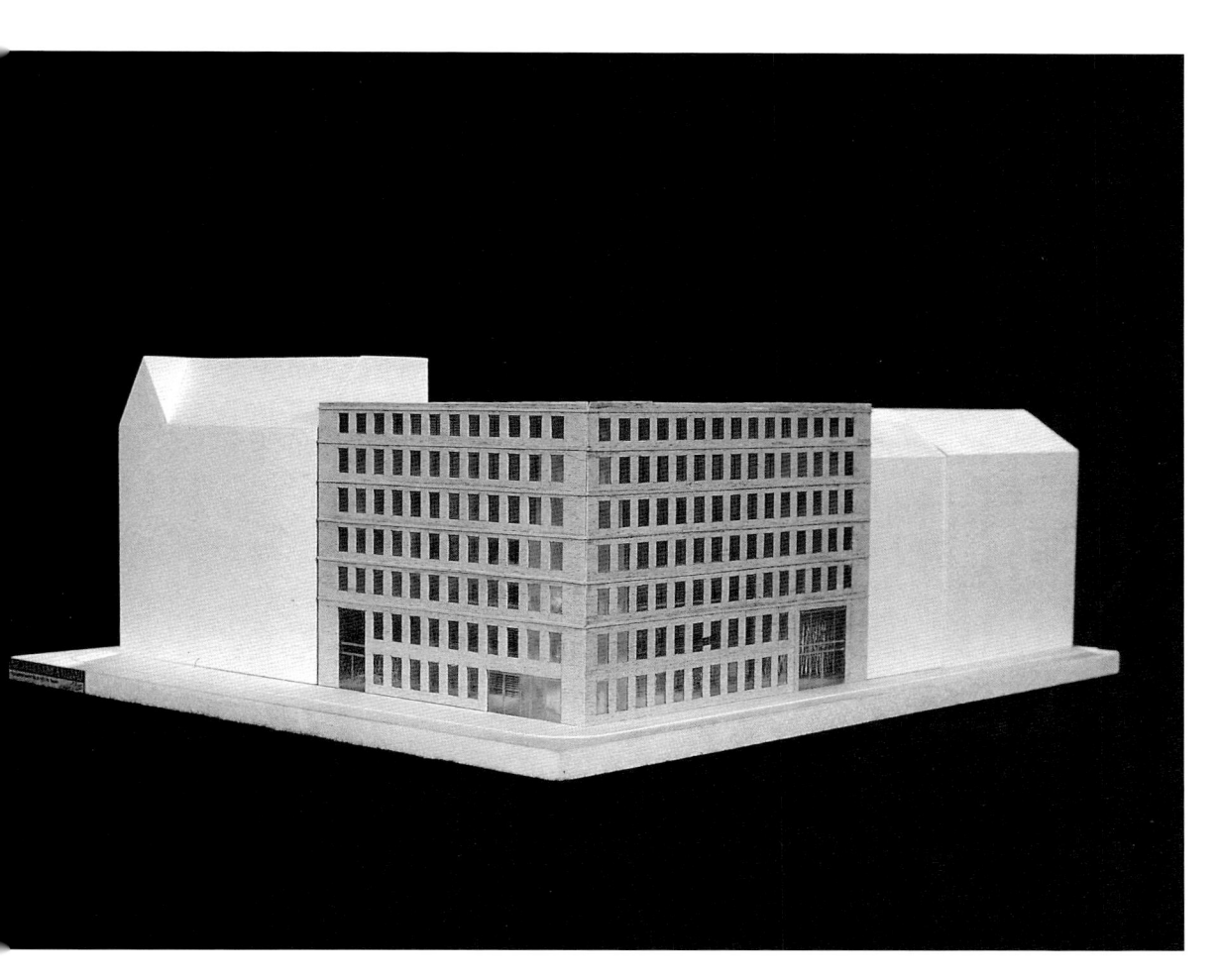

**Ansicht Charlottenstraße
von Osten**
East elevation
Charlottenstrasse

1:750

**Perspektive des Gebäudes
Charlottenstraße / Ecke
Clara-Zetkin-Straße
Modellaufnahme**
Perspective drawing of
the corner of
Charlottenstrasse and
Clara-Zetkin-Strasse
Model photo

**Ansicht
Clara-Zetkin-Straße
von Norden**
North elevation
Clara-Zetkin-Strasse

1:750

In its position opposite the dominating urban and functional structure of the State Library, the block housing the library's administration presents a deliberately restrained façade towards the street. The line of the building along the street and the eaves height carefully integrate it into the development along Dorotheenstrasse. Storeys stepped back towards the inner courtyard and the glazed courtyard façades lend the building an overall introspective character.

Büro-, Wohn- und
Geschäftshäuser
Zimmerstraße
Office and
Apartment Buildings

Geschäftshäuser Friedrichstadt

Josef Paul Kleihues
Berlin
mit with
Andre Santer
(Projektleitung project manager)
Dirk Blomeyer
Claudia Reinermann
Robin Foster
Helmuth Homm

Bauherr:
GSW Gemeinnützige
Siedlungs- und
Wohnungsbaugesellschaft mbH
Berlin
KAPHAG Unternehmensgruppe
Berlin
Württembergische
Hypothekenbank, Stuttgart

Planungstermine:
Entwurfsplanung seit 1991
Baubeginn 1994
Voraussichtlicher Bezug 1995

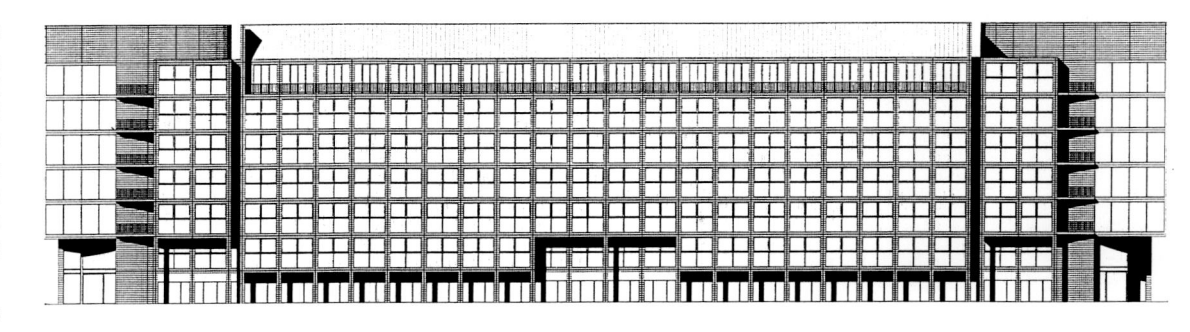

Nutzung:
12 Läden
(5 à 140 m², 2 à 110 m²,
4 à 80 m², 1 à 40 m²)
320 Büroräume
(240 à 20 m², 80 à 14 m²)
22 Konferenzräume
(10 à 35 m², 8 à 90 m², 4 à 60 m²)
30 Wohnungen
(6 à 60 m², 4 à 100 m², 20 à 45 m²)

Geschosse (VIII):
EG Läden
1.-5. OG Büros
6. OG Wohnen
7. OG Abstell-/Archivräume
Technik

Untergeschosse (IV):
Tiefgarage
(7.500 m², 232 Stellplätze)
und Technik (1.000 m²)

Grundstücksgröße:
3.822 m²

Überbaute Fläche:
2.709 m²

Bruttogeschoßfläche:
20.000 m²

Das Projekt komplettiert den Blockrand zur Zimmerstraße und schließt an der Friedrichstraße – hinter dem ehemaligen Sektorenübergang Checkpoint Charlie – als auch an der Charlottenstraße an die vorhandenen historischen Gebäude an. Die Strenge und Einfachheit der Fassaden wird durch Ship-Shape-Elemente in den Ecksituationen durchbrochen; sie dienen in den Obergeschossen als Konferenzräume.

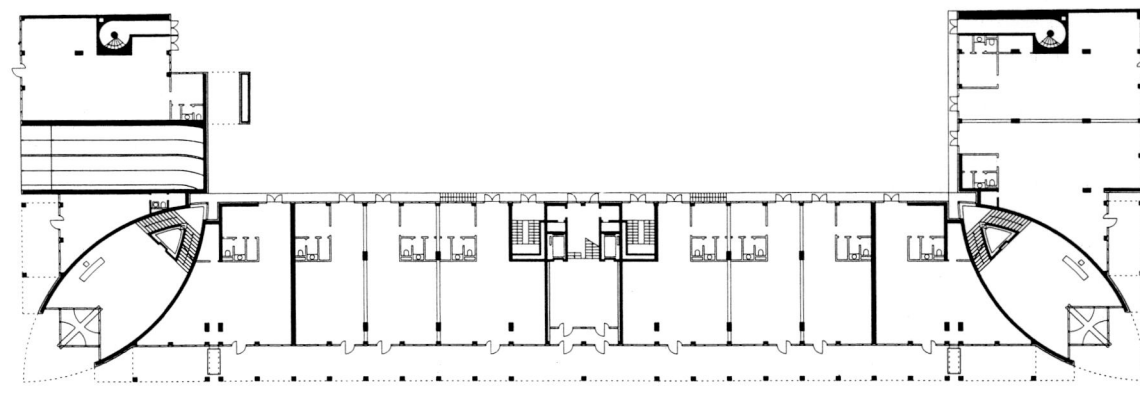

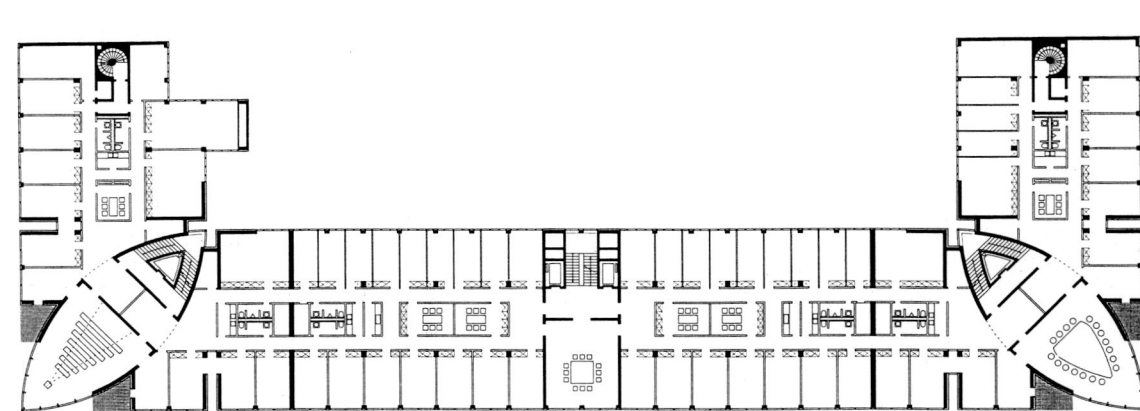

Ansicht Zimmerstraße
von Norden
North elevation
Zimmerstrasse

1:750

Grundriß Erdgeschoß
mit Ladennutzung
Ground floor plan retail

Grundriß Normalgeschoß
(1.-5. Obergeschoß)
mit Büronutzung
Typical floor plan
(1st to 5th floors) offices

1:750

Projektadresse:
Location:
**Friedrichstrasse 45–46/
Zimmerstrasse 20–25/
Charlottenstrasse 81
in
10969 Berlin-Mitte**

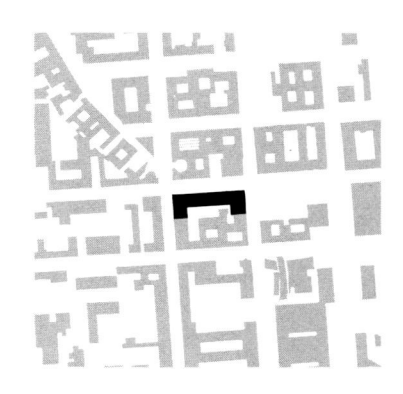

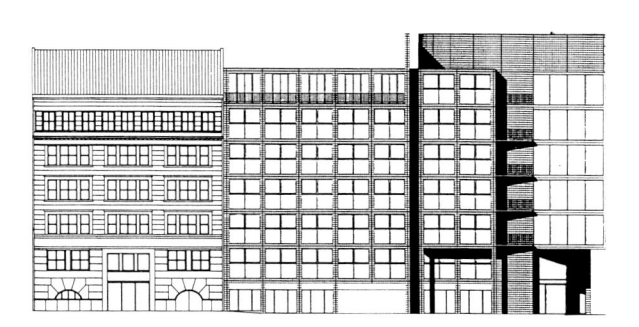

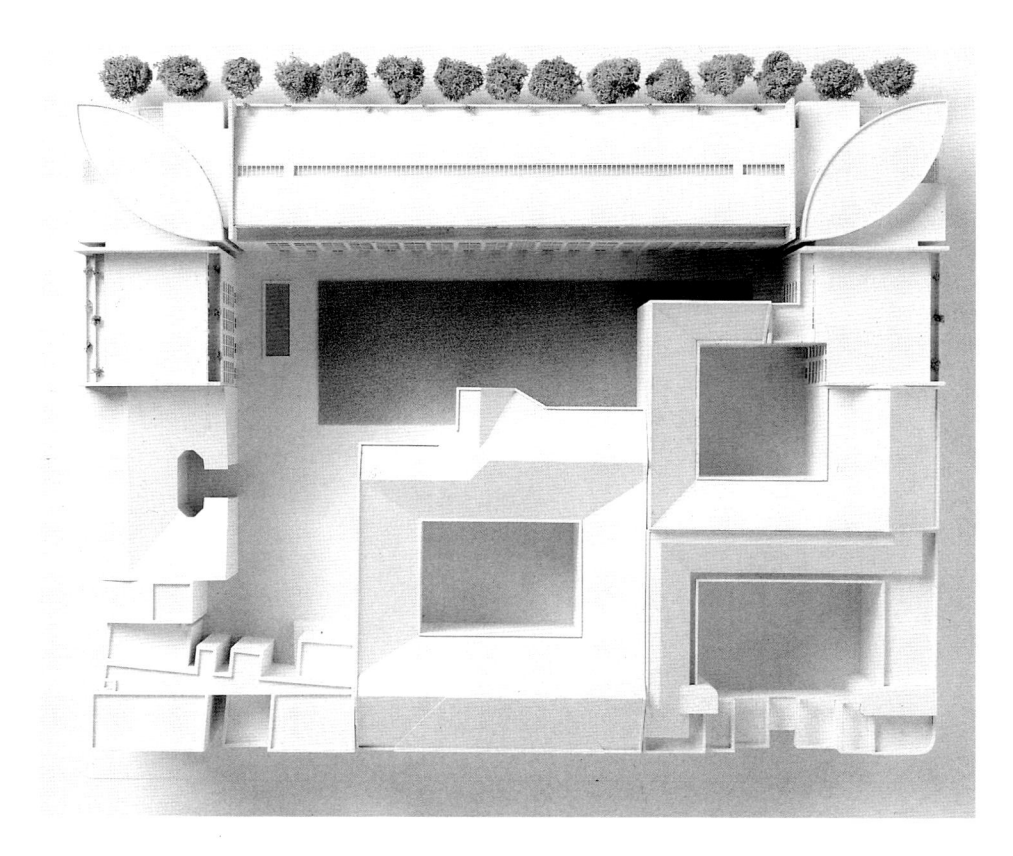

Client:
GSW Gemeinnützige
Siedlungs- und Wohnungs-
baugesellschaft mbH
Berlin
KAPHAG Unternehmensgruppe
Berlin
Württembergische
Hypothekenbank
Stuttgart

Project Stages:
Design development from 1991
Start of construction 1994
Expected completion 1995

Building Use:
12 shops (5 à 140 m², 2 à 110 m², 4 à 80 m², 1 à 40 m²)
320 officerooms (240 à 20 m², 80 à 14 m²)
22 Conference rooms (10 à 35 m², 8 à 90 m², 4 à 60 m²)
30 apartments (6 à 60 m², 4 à 100 m², 20 à 45 m²)

Upper Floors (VIII):
Ground floor shops
1st–5th floor offices
6th floor apartments
7th floor storerooms/
archives, services

Basement Floors (IV):
Car park
(7500 m², 232 parking spaces)
and services (1000 m²)

Site Area:
3822 m²

Built Area:
2709 m²

Gross Floor Area:
20000 m²

**Ansicht Charlottenstraße
von Osten**
East elevation
Charlottenstrasse

1:750

Modellaufsicht
Top view of model

The project completes the northern block edge on Zimmerstrasse and links with the existing older buildings on both Friedrichstrasse – near to the former Checkpoint Charlie crossing point – and Charlottenstrasse. The rigour and simplicity of the façades is interrupted at the corners of the building by projecting sections which serve as conference rooms in the upper floors.

Deutscher Industrie- und Handelstag DIHT Association German Chambers of Industry and Commerce		Architekten Schweger + Partner Hamburg Peter P. Schweger Franz Wöhler Hartmut H. Reifenstein Bernhard Kohl Wolfgang Schneider	Mitarbeit staff Mathis Tröster Yong Sun Feldmeyer Norbert Barstat Paul Schüler Roland Sommerer Anke Huss Ulrike Andreas Landschaftsarchitekt Landscape architect Gustav Lange Hamburg

Bauherr:
Industrie- und Wohnbau
Groth + Graalfs GmbH
Berlin

Planungstermine:
Wettbewerb 1994, 1. Preis
Entwurfsplanung seit 1994
Baubeginn 1995
Voraussichtlicher Bezug 1998

Nutzung:
Verbandsgebäude
Läden und Büros mit
insgesamt 10.300 m²
Wohnungen mit
5.200 m²

Geschosse:
Hauptgebäude
(Verbandsgebäude) (VII):
EG Empfang, Casino, Post
1.OG Konferenzsaal, Foyer
1.-6. OG Büros, Sitzungssäle
Bürogebäude (VII):
EG Läden, Restaurant, Café,
Buchladen
1.-6. OG Büros
Wohngebäude (VII):
EG Bar, Restaurant
1.-6. OG Wohnungen

Untergeschosse (II):
Technik, Tiefgarage,
Lager, Nebenräume

Grundstücksgröße:
ca. 6.850 m²

Überbaute Fläche:
ca. 4.100 m²

Bruttogeschoßfläche:
28.000 m²

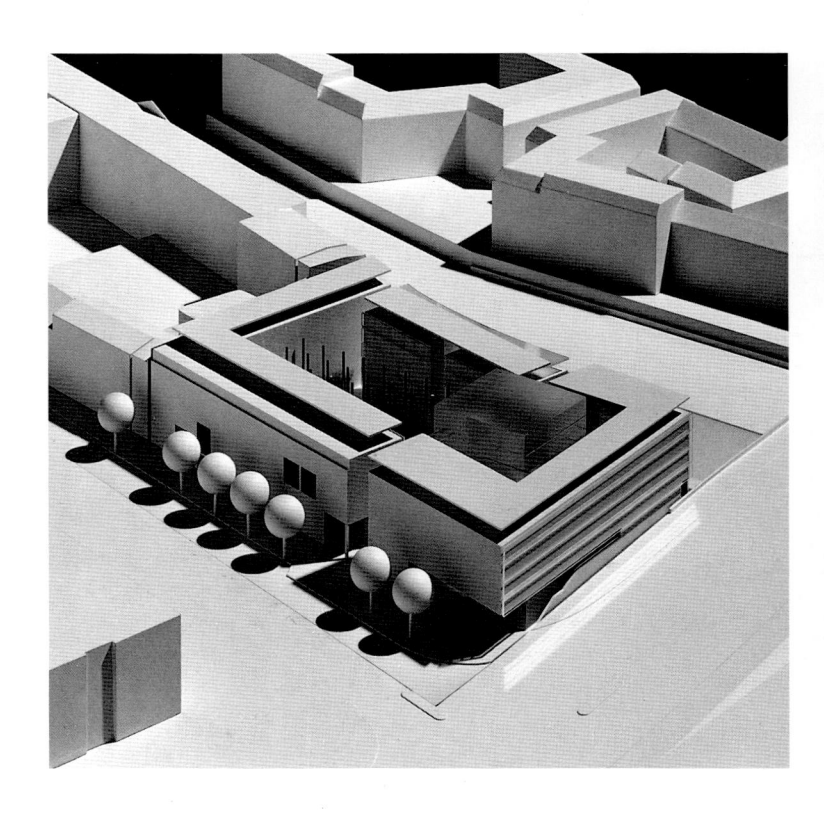

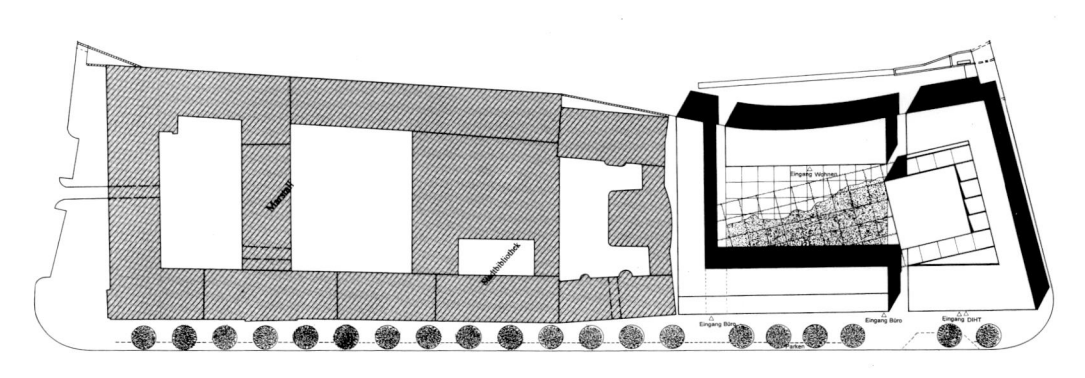

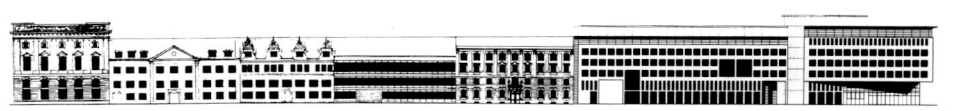

Lageplan
Wettbewerb
Site plan
Competition

Fassadenabwicklung
Breite Straße
Wettbewerb
Façade development,
Breite Strasse
Competition

1:2000

Blick auf den Gesamtkomplex
von Süden
Modellaufnahme
View of whole complex
from the south
Model photo

Projektadresse:
Location:
Breite Strasse/Ecke
Corner of
Mühlendammbrücke
in
10178 Berlin-Mitte

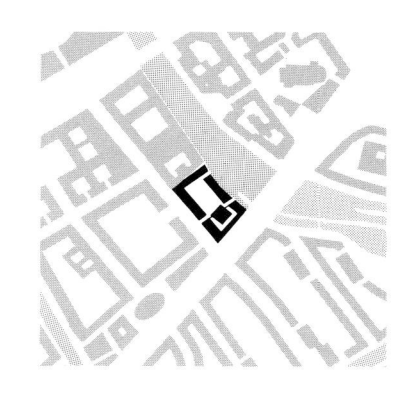

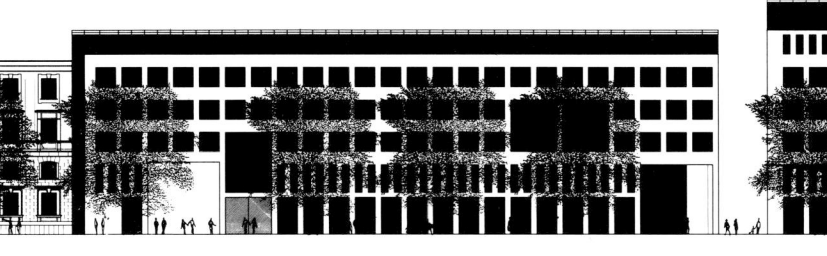

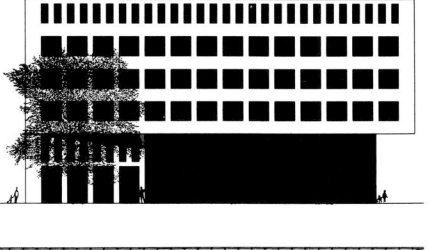

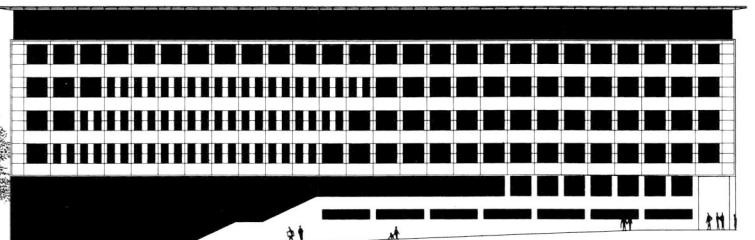

Client:
Industrie- und Wohnbau
Groth + Graalfs GmbH
Berlin

Project Stages:
Competition 1994, 1st prize
Design development from 1994
Start of construction 1995
Expected completion 1998

Building Use:
Association building
Shops and offices totalling
10300 m²
Apartments totalling
5200 m²

Upper Floors:
Main building (Association building) (VII):
Ground floor reception, casino, post office
1st floor conference hall, foyer
1st-6th floor offices, meeting rooms
Office building (VII):
Ground floor shops, restaurant, café, book shop
1st-6th floor offices
Apartment building (VII):
Ground floor bar, restaurant
1st-6th floor apartments

Basement Floors (II):
Services, car park, storeroom, ancillary rooms

Site Area:
ca. 6850 m²

Built Area:
ca. 4100 m²

Gross Floor Area:
28000 m²

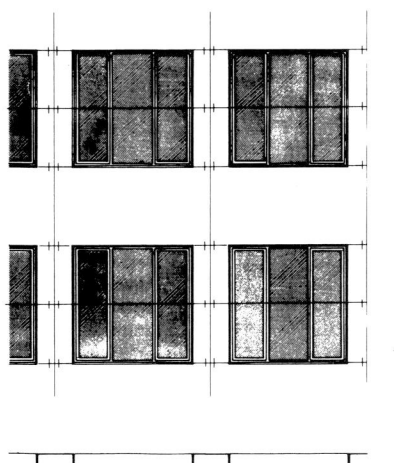

Fassadenstudie Mühlendammbrücke
Façade study
Mühlendammbrücke

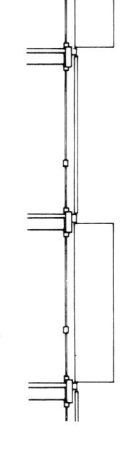

Fassadenstudie Innenhof
Façade study
inner courtyard

oben above
Ansicht Breite Straße von Südwesten Wettbewerb
Southwest elevation
Breite Strasse
Competition

Ansicht Mühlendammbrücke von Südosten Wettbewerb
Southeast elevation
Mühlendammbrücke
Competition

1:750

Deutscher Industrie- und Handelstag   **DIHT**
Association German
Chambers of Industry
and Commerce

Unmittelbar an der Mühlendammbrücke, zwischen Breiter Straße und Spreekanal, findet der Deutsche Industrie- und Handelstag seinen Sitz; die neue Niederlassung wird durch weitere Büros, Läden und Wohnungen ergänzt.

Die Komplettierung des Blocks ist den traditionellen Themen der Berliner Baukultur verpflichtet. Die Straßenfassaden mit ihrem Öffentlichkeitsanspruch sollen städtebauliche Konventionen und urbane Kontinuität reflektieren; sie sind steinern ausgebildet. Im Kontrast dazu wirkt der Hof offen gegliedert, lichtdurchflutet und »wie ein Kristall«. Nach außen will das Gebäude Angemessenheit und Zurückhaltung, nach innen die Offenheit des Handels und der Interaktion demonstrieren. Wichtiges architektonisches Prinzip ist daher im Gebäudeinneren der Ausdruck der Vielfalt von Begegnungen in Bewegungsräumen, Treppen, Rampen, Lufträumen und den Sichtbezügen zwischen ihnen.

Alle Gebäudebereiche sind entsprechend den jeweilgen Nutzungen differenziert und individualisiert. Büros, Sonderräume für Tagungen, Repräsentation und wissenschaftliches Arbeiten besitzen ihr jeweils spezifisches Ambiente.

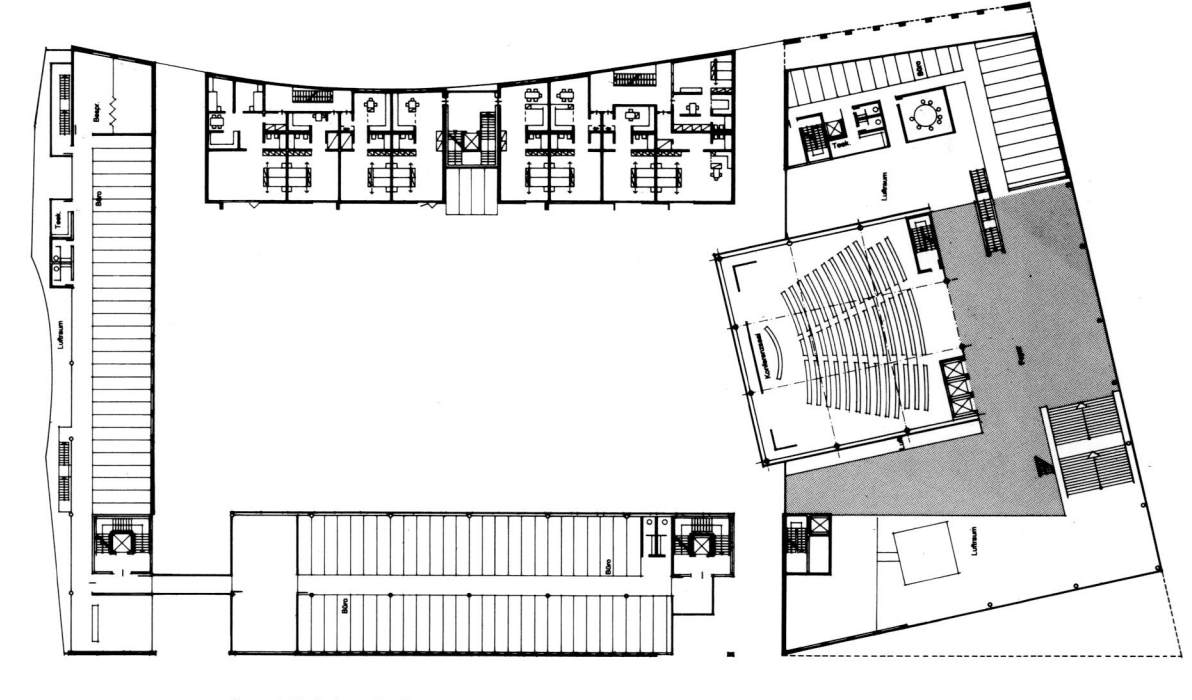

Grundriß Erdgeschoß
mit Foyer, Ladennutzung,
Gastronomie und Post
Ground floor plan
foyer, retail,
restaurants, post office

Grundriß 1. Obergeschoß
mit Foyer, Konferenzsaal,
Büronutzung und Wohnungen
1st floor plan
foyer, conference hall,
offices, apartments

1:750

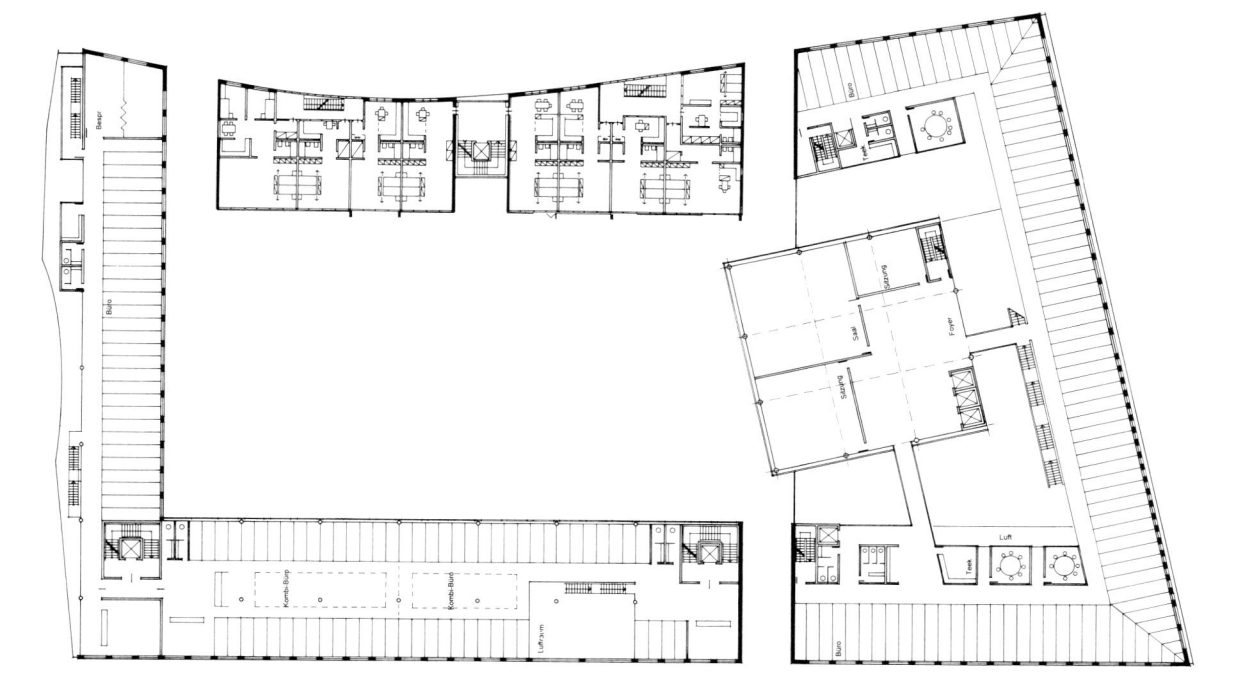

Close by the Mühlendamm-brücke between Breite Strasse and the Spreekanal are the offices of the Association German Chambers of Industry and Trade; the new headquarters is also to contain other offices, shops and apartments.

The completion of the block is indebted to the traditional themes in Berlin architecture. The public nature of the street façades is to reflect urban conventions and continuity; they have a solid, stone-like appearance. In contrast the courtyard side is more open, flooded with light and »like a crystal«. The outward face of the building is intended to display an appropriate reserved image while the openness of trade is reflected in its interior. An important architectural principle at work in the interior is that of expressing the multiplicity of encounters, in spaces for meeting and movement, stairs, ramps, open halls, all with visual links between them.

The different uses of parts of the building are reflected in the design. Offices, special conference rooms, reception and functions rooms and areas for study and research each have their own particular atmosphere.

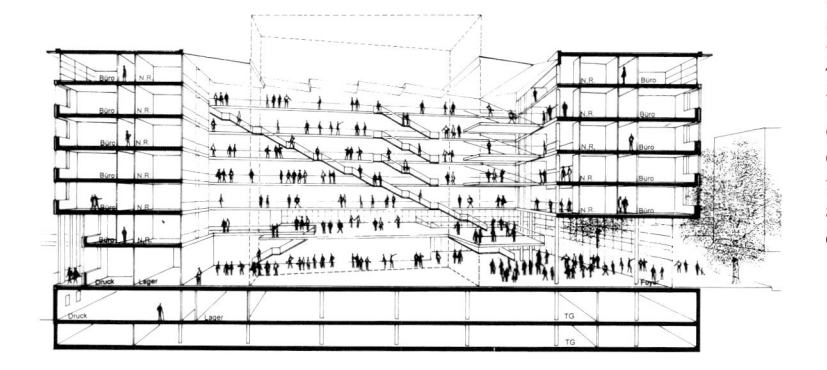

Grundriß 3. Obergeschoß
mit Büronutzung und Wohnungen
3rd floor plan
offices and apartments

1:750

Perspektivischer Gebäudequerschnitt
im Bereich des Verbandsgebäudes
Perspective cross section
through association building area

Gebäudelängsschnitt
im Bereich des Hofes
Longitudinal section
through courtyard area

1:750

Büro-, Wohn- und
Geschäftshaus
Unter den Linden 41
Office and
Apartment Building

Komische Oper

Klaus Theo Brenner
Berlin

Mitarbeit staff
Stefano Rigoni

Bauherr:
Wert-Konzept GmbH
Berlin
und Hanseatica
Hamburg, Berlin

Planungstermine:
Investorenauswahlverfahren
1992-1994
Entwurfsplanung seit 1994

Nutzung:
Läden mit
970 m² Bruttogeschoßfläche
Büros mit
4.100 m² Bruttogeschoßfläche
Wohnungen mit
970 m² Bruttogeschoßfläche

Geschosse (VI):
EG Läden
1.-4. OG Büros
5. OG Wohnungen

Untergeschoß (I):
Kellerräume

Grundstücksgröße:
ca. 1.000 m²

Überbaute Fläche:
ca. 970 m²

Bruttogeschoßfläche:
ca. 6.000 m²

Das bestehende Gebäude wird in seiner konstruktiven Struktur erhalten, ansonsten aber vollständig umgebaut. Dabei soll der heute anonym und ohne Bezug zum Straßenraum erscheinende Bau eine architektonische Transformation hin zu einem Haus mit ausgeprägt städtischem Charakter erfahren. Die Skelettstruktur der Stahlbeton-Konstruktion wird bewußt sichtbar gelassen; ein Verblenden des Tragwerks mit einer an die historischen Fassaden der Linden angelehnten Lochfassade soll kategorisch vermieden werden.

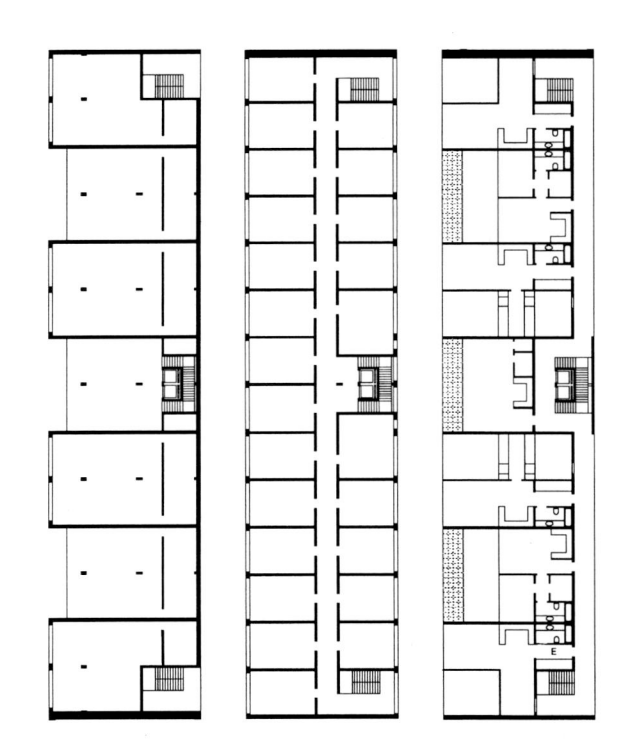

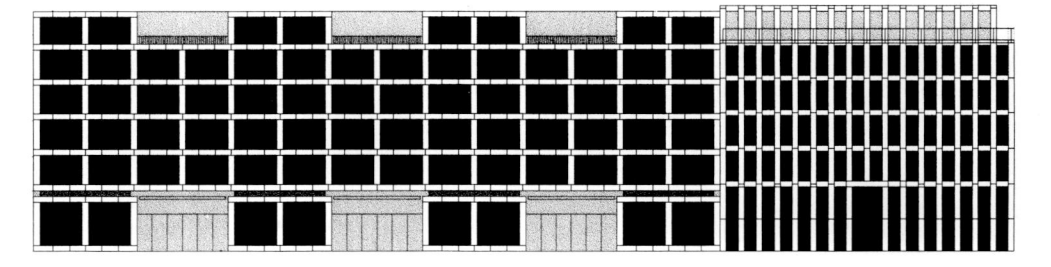

Ansicht Unter den Linden
von Norden
North elevation
Unter den Linden

1:750

Grundriß Erdgeschoß
mit Ladennutzung
Ground floor plan
retail

Grundriß 2./3. Obergeschoß
mit Büronutzung
Plan of 2nd/3rd floors
offices

Grundriß 5. Obergeschoß
mit Wohnungen
6th floor plan
apartments

1:750

Projektadresse:
Location:
**Unter den Linden 41
in
10117 Berlin-Mitte**

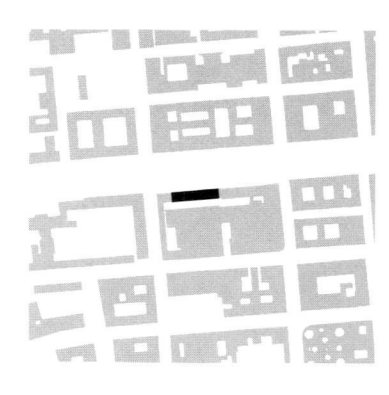

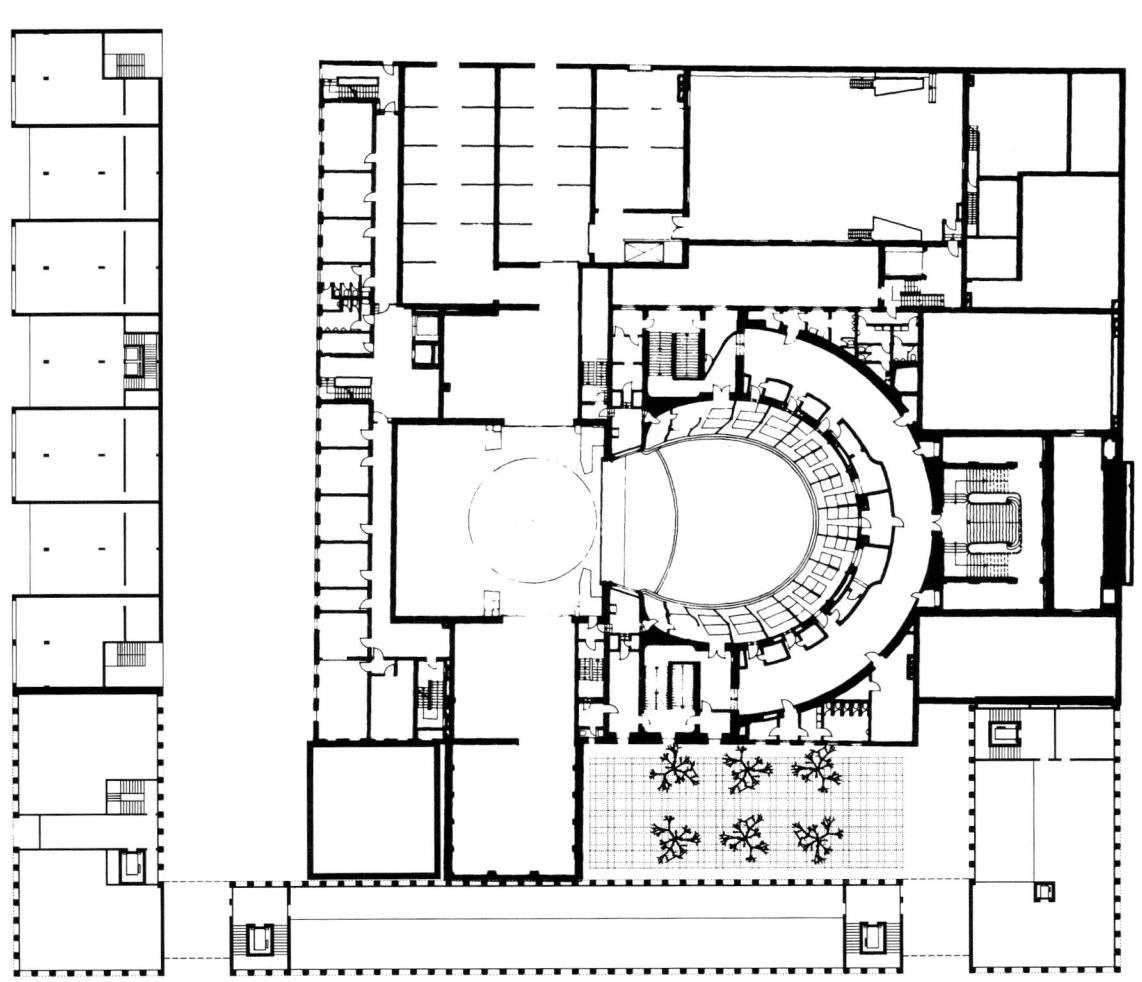

Client:
Wert-Konzept GmbH, Berlin
und Hanseatica Hamburg, Berlin

Project Stages:
Investors selection procedure
1992-1994
Design development from 1994

Building Use:
Shops totalling
970 m² gross floor area
Offices totalling
4100 m² gross floor area
Apartments totalling
970 m² gross floor area

Upper Floors (VI):
Ground floor shops
1st-4th floor offices
5th floor apartments

Basement Floor (I):
1 basement

Site Area:
ca. 1000 m²

Built Area:
ca. 970 m²

Gross Floor Area:
ca. 6000 m²

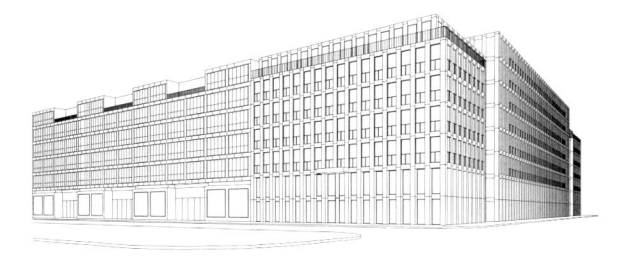

**Blockgrundriß
1. Obergeschoß
mit Büro- und
Ladennutzung**
1st floor plan of block
offices and retail

1:750

**Perspektivische Ansicht
Unter den Linden /
Ecke Glinkastraße**
Perspective elevation
at the corner
of Unter den Linden
and Glinkastrasse

The basic frame of the existing apartment and office building will remain the same, but all else is to be completely renovated. The aim is to architecturally transform the present anonymous structure with its lack of reference to the street into a building with a positive urban character. The reinforced concrete skeleton will be left visible; any attempt to conceal the support structure behind a punctuated façade of the kind typical for Unter den Linden is categorically rejected.

Büro-, Wohn- und
Geschäftshaus
Glinkastraße
Office and
Apartment Building
Glinkastraße

Komische Oper

Jürgen Sawade
Berlin

Mitarbeit staff
Joachim Kleine Allekotte
(**Projektleitung** project manager)
Ingo Schürmann

Bauherr:
Hanseatica, Pietzsch,
Wert-Konzept GmbH
Berlin

Planungstermine:
Gutachten 1992
Entwurfsplanung seit 1992

Nutzung:
Läden
Büros
Wohnungen

Geschosse (IX):
EG + Galerie (1. OG) Läden
2.-6. OG Büros
7. + 8. OG Wohnungen

Untergeschoß (I):
Nebenräume, Technik,
automatisches Parksystem
(88 Pkw-Stellplätze)

Grundstücksgröße:
2.777 m²

Überbaute Fläche:
1.806 m²

Bruttogeschoßfläche:
12.941 m²

Das Gebäude ergänzt die lückenhafte Blockstruktur westlich der Komischen Oper zur Glinkastraße hin. Durch Aufnahme der Bauflucht des südlichen Abschnitts der Glinkastraße werden die Grundstückstiefe vergrößert und der Straßenraum zurückgebaut. Durch diesen Neubau und das bestehende Grand Hotel an der Friedrichstraße wird das Gebäude der Komischen Oper symmetrisch eingefaßt. Über die Gesimshöhe von ca. 25 m hinaus wird der mittlere Baukörper an der Glinkastraße um ein Geschoß auf ca. 29 m erhöht und damit in Korrespondenz zum Bühnenturm der Komischen Oper und zur Dachlandschaft des Grand Hotels gestellt.

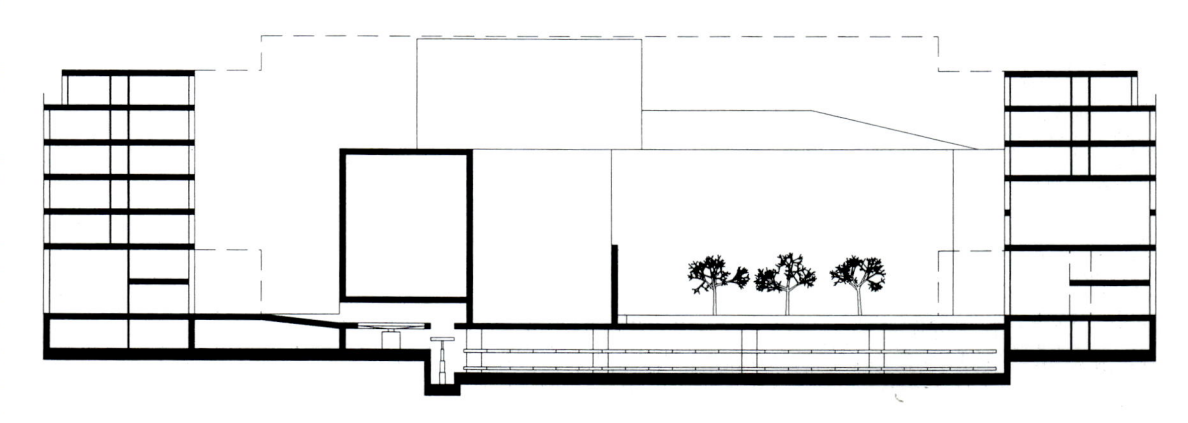

Perspektive des Gebäudes
Unter den Linden/
Glinkastraße
Persective drawing
Unter den Linden
and Glinkastrasse

Gebäudeschnitt
Section

1:750

Projektadresse:
Location:
**Unter den Linden/
Glinkastrasse/
Behrenstrasse
in
10117 Berlin-Mitte**

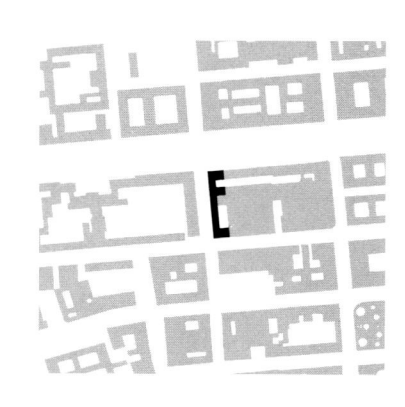

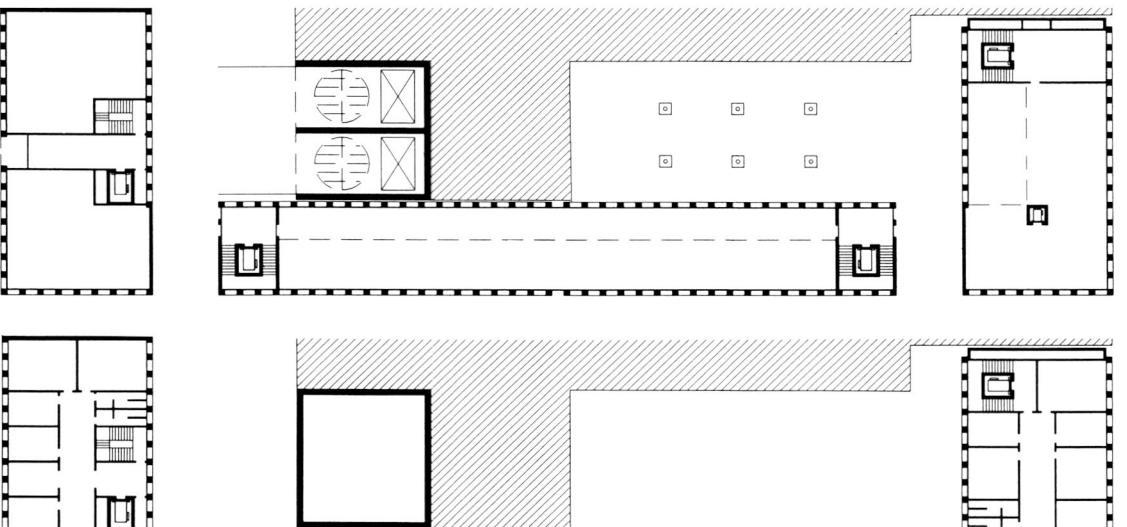

Client:
Hanseatica, Pietzsch,
Wert-Konzept GmbH
Berlin

Project Stages:
Appraisal 1992
Design development from 1992

Building Use:
Shops, offices, apartments

Upper Floors (IX):
Ground floor and 1st floor shops
2nd-6th floor offices
7th-8th floor apartments

Basement Floor (I):
ancillary rooms and services
automatic parking system with
space for 88 cars

Site Area:
2777 m^2

Built Area:
1806 m^2

Gross Floor Area:
12941 m^2

The building occupies one of the vacant plots in the incomplete block structure to the west of the Komische Oper towards Glinkastrasse. By following the line of buildings along the southern section of Glinkastrasse the depth of the plot is increased, and the street area thus reduced to its historic width. This new building and the existing Grand Hotel on the Friedrichstrasse form a kind of symmetrical frame around the Komische Oper. The centre section of the Glinkastrasse façade extends one storey above the general eaves height of 25 m, and at 29 m it thus corresponds to the stage tower of the Komische Oper and the general roof height of the Grand Hotel.

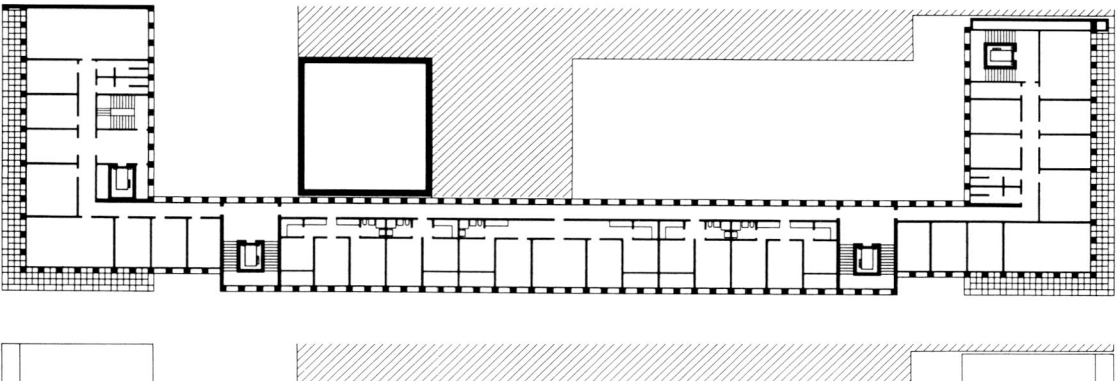

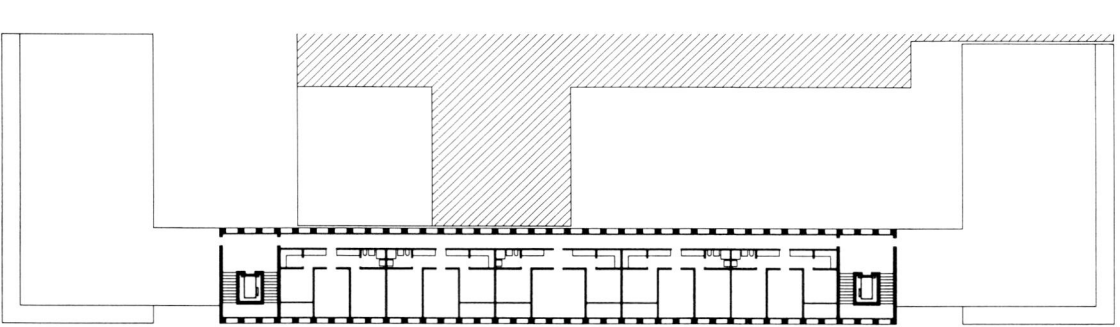

**Grundriß Erdgeschoß
mit Ladennutzung**
Ground floor plan
retail

**Grundriß 4./5. Obergeschoß
mit Büronutzung**
Plan of 4th/5th floors
offices

1:750

**Grundriß 6. Obergeschoß
mit Büronutzung**
6th floor plan
offices

**Grundriß 7. Obergeschoß
mit Wohnungen**
7th floor plan
apartments

1:750

Bürohaus für Parlamentarier
Office Building for delegates

Deutscher Bundestag

Brands Kolbe Wernik Architekten
Berlin
Ludger Brands
Alexander Kolbe
Siegfried Wernik

Mitarbeit staff
Chris Davies
Maria Grotthoff
Nico Johannsen
Irene Kemmel
Miriam Kiesel
Peter Nørgaard
Angelika Rehe
Dominic Seah
Gesamtplanung general plan
Argeplan GmbH Berlin

Bauherr:
Bundesrepublik Deutschland
vertreten durch das
Bundesministerium für
Raumordnung,
Bauwesen und Städtebau
Gesamtleitung:
Bundesbaudirektion Berlin

Planungstermine:
Entwurfsplanung seit 1992
Baubeginn 1994
Voraussichtlicher Bezug
Frühjahr 1997

Nutzung:
ca. 410 Büroräume für
Abgeordnete mit
jeweils ca. 16-36 m^2
(7.380 m^2 NF)
ca. 90 Büroräumes für den
Fraktionsbereich
(1.620 m^2 NF)
21 Sekretariate
(635 m^2 NF)
4 Läden
mit insgesamt 960 m^2 NF

Geschosse (VI):
EG + 1. OG Läden
2.-4. OG Büros
5. OG Büros, Technik

Untergeschoß (I):
Lager, Technik

Grundstücksgröße:
8.231 m^2

Überbaute Fläche:
4.980 m^2

Bruttogeschoßfläche:
33.713 m

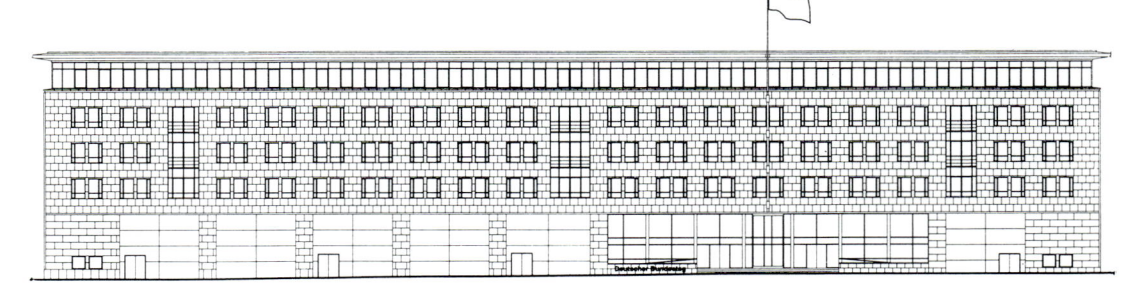

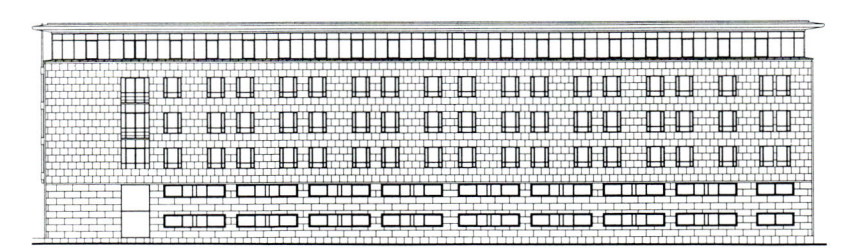

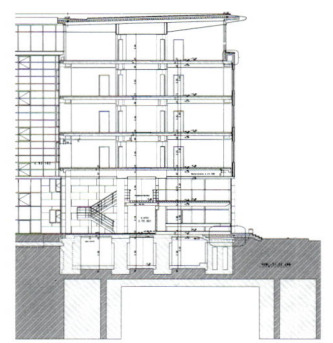

Ansicht Unter den Linden
von Süden
South elevation
Unter den Linden

Ansicht Neustädtische Kirchstraße
von Osten
East elevation
Neustädtische Kirchstrasse

1:750

Gebäudequerschnitt
im Bereich der Eingangshalle
Cross section
near the entrance hall

1:750

Perspektive des Gebäudes
Unter den Linden / Neustädtische
Kirchstraße
Computersimulation
Perspective drawing
of the corner Unter den Linden
and Neustädtische Kirchstrasse
Computer simulation

Projektadresse:
Location:
**Unter den Linden 44-60
in
10117 Berlin-Mitte**

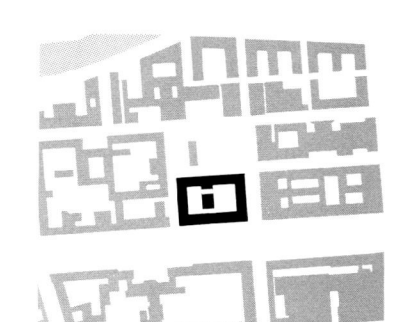

Client:
The Federal Republic of Germany
represented by the Ministry for
Regional Planning, Building and
 Urban Development
Overall management: Federal
Board of Construction, Berlin

Project Stages:
Design development from 1992
Start of construction 1994
Expected completion
spring 1997

Building Use:
ca. 410 office rooms
à ca. 16-36 m^2
(7380 m^2 floor area)
for members of parliament
ca. 90 party office rooms
1620 m^2 floor area
21 secretariats
635 m^2 floor area
4 shops totalling
960 m^2

Upper Floors (VI):
Ground floor and 1st floor shops
2nd-4th floor offices
5th floor offices, services

Basement Floor (I):
Storeroom, services

Site Area:
8231 m^2

Built Area:
4980 m^2

Gross Floor Area:
33713 m^2

**Grundriß 1. Obergeschoß
mit Büronutzung, Ladengalerien
Bauteil Unter den Linden**
1st floor plan
offices, retail galleries
wing Unter den Linden

**Grundriß 3. Obergeschoß
mit Büronutzung
Bauteil Unter den Linden**
3rd floor plan
offices
wing Unter den Linden

1:750

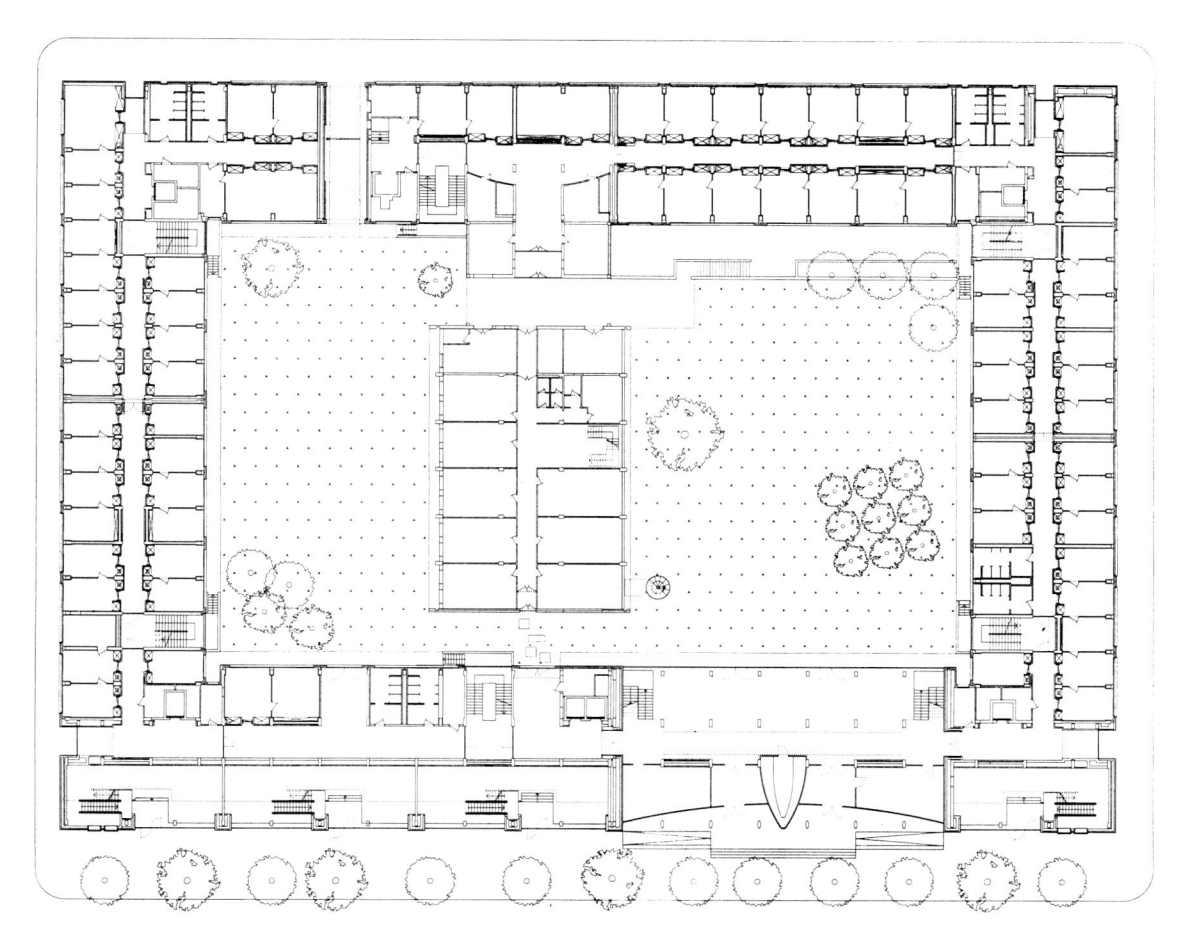

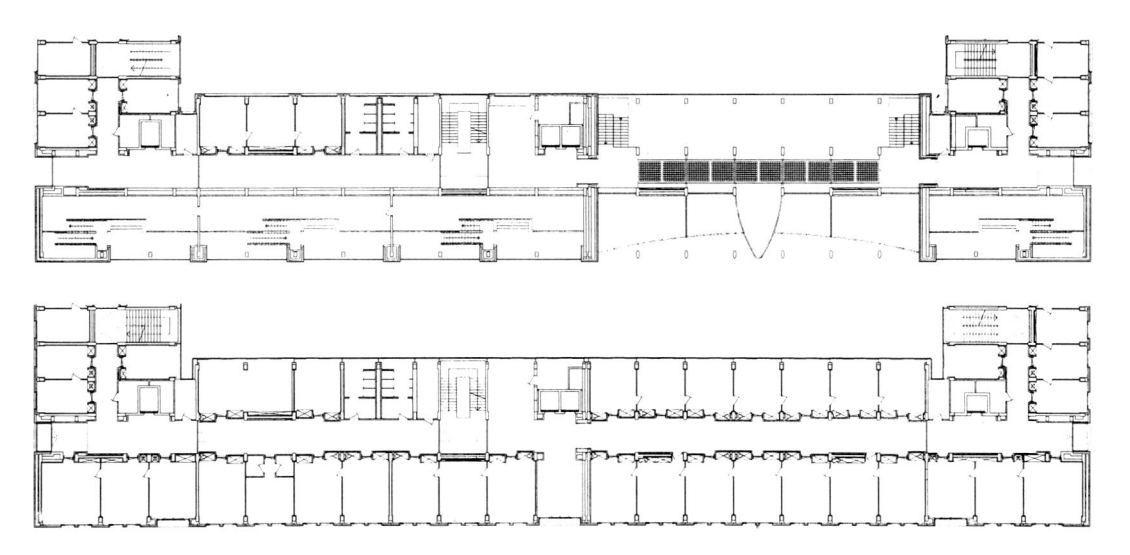

**Grundriß Erdgeschoß
mit Eingangshalle, Läden
und Büronutzung**
Ground floor plan
entrance hall, retail
and offices

1:750

**Bürohaus
für Parlamentarier** **Deutscher Bundestag**
Office Building
for delegates

Das ehemalige Ministerium der DDR für Außer- und Innerdeutschen Handel wird bis auf das Tragwerk entkernt. Es erfolgen eine vollständige Erneuerung des gesamten Aufbaus und eine architektonische Neudefinition der Fassaden. Durch den Ersatz des vorhandenen Dachgeschosses durch ein weiteres Vollgeschoß wird die Traufhöhe der Nachbargebäude aufgenommen. Trotz der Bindung der neuen Fassaden an die Rasterstruktur der vorhandenen Stahlbetonskelett-Konstruktion werden sie bewußt gestaltet: durch die Ausgewogenheit zwischen offenen und geschlossenen Flächen und durch die Aufnahme und Interpretation prägender Gestalt- und Strukturelemente der Fassaden des Straßenzuges Unter den Linden.

**Blick in die Eingangshalle
Unter den Linden
Computersimulation**
View of entrance hall
Unter den Linden
Computer simulation

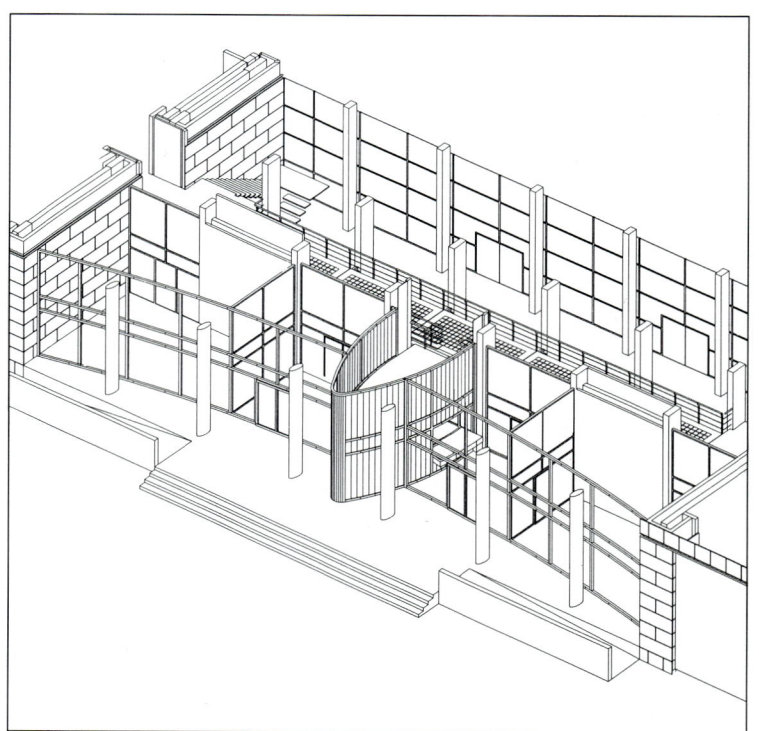

**Eingangshalle
Isometrische Darstellung**
Entrance hall
Isometric projection

The former GDR Ministry for Foreign and Inner German Trade is to be stripped down to its support structure, the construction completely renovated and the façades redesigned. The existing attic storey is to be replaced by a further full storey to bring the building on a level with the eaves height of surrounding buildings. Despite the restricting factor of the need to adhere to the grid of the building's original reinforced concrete frame, its façade design is a careful, conscious balance of open and closed areas blended with a reinterpretation of general façade-defining elements typical of Unter den Linden.

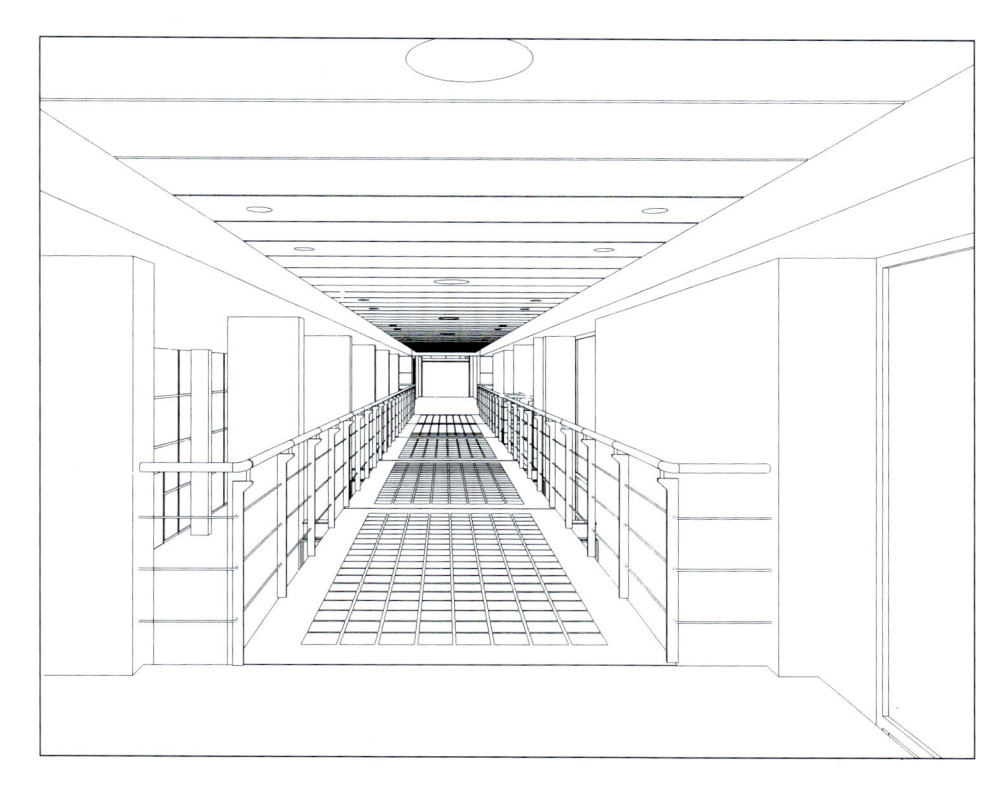

**Detailstudie Markisenanlage
Computersimulation**
Detail of awnings
Computer simulation

**Detailstudie Fensterbank
Computersimulation**
Detail of window seat
Computer simulation

**Perspektivische Darstellung
der Brücke durch die Eingangshalle**
Perspective drawing
of the bridge
through the entrance hall

Büro-, Wohn- und
Geschäftshäuser
Office and
Apartment Buildings

Rosmarin Karree

Büro- und Geschäftshaus
Offices and commercial
premises:
Böge + Lindner
Hamburg
Jürgen Böge
Ingeborg Lindner-Böge

Mitarbeit Wettbewerb
Staff competition
Peter Lehmann
Detlev Kozian
Morten Winding
Arend Buchholz-Berger
Mitarbeit Planung
Staff planning
Volker Fuchs
Thomas Haupt
Swantje Kuhr
Tilmann Grube
Stefan Wirth

Bauherr:
Rosmarin Karree
Grundstücks GmbH & Co.
Berlin

Planungstermine:
Wettbewerb 1993/94
(1. Preis first prize
Böge + Lindner;
2. Preis second prize
Kahlfeldt Architekten)
Entwurfsplanung seit 1994
Baubeginn Herbst 1994
Voraussichtlicher Bezug
Herbst 1996

Nutzung:
Läden und Restaurants mit
ca. 3.400 m²
Büros mit
ca. 15.000 m²
70 Wohnungen mit
ca. 4.600 m²

Geschosse:
Büro- und Geschäftshaus (VIII):
EG – 1. OG Läden,
Gastronomie, Büros
2.-7. OG Büros
Wohnhaus (X):
EG + 1. OG Läden
2.-9. OG Wohnungen

Untergeschosse (II):
1. UG Läden, Tiefgarage
2. UG Tiefgarage
(ca. 140 PkwStellplätze),
Lager, Technik

Grundstücksgröße:
ca. 3.500 m²

Überbaute Fläche:
ca. 3.500 m²

Bruttogeschoßfläche:
ca. 23.000 m²

Ansicht Rosmarinstraße
von Norden
North elevation
Rosmarinstrasse

Ansicht Friedrichstraße
von Westen
West elevation
Friedrichstrasse

1:750

Fassadenstudie
Computersimulation
Façade study
Computer simulation

Wohnhaus apartment block:
**Kahlfeldt Architekten
Berlin
Petra Kahlfeldt
Paul Kahlfeldt
Mitarbeit Wettbewerb**
Staff competition
**Anne Kuhlmey
Jörn Pötting
Mitarbeit Planung**
Staff planning
**Kurt Bauer
(Projektleiter** project manager)

Projektadresse:
Location:
**Friedrichstrasse 82/83
Rosmarinstrasse 7–8
Behrenstrasse 47–48
in
10117 Berlin-Mitte**

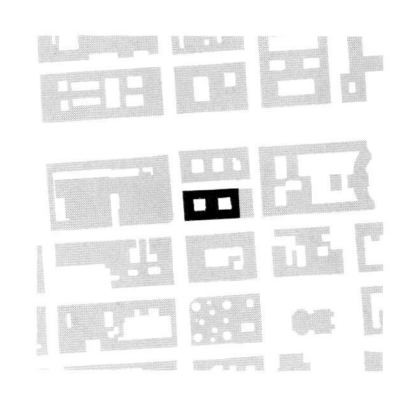

Client:
Rosmarin Karree Grundstücks
GmbH & Co.
Berlin

Project Stages:
Competition 1993/94
Design development from 1994
Start of construction
autumn 1994
Expected completion
autumn 1996

Building Use:
Shops and restaurants totalling
ca. 3400 m^2
Offices totalling
ca. 15000 m^2
70 apartments totalling
ca. 4600 m^2

Upper Floors:
Offices and commercial premises
(VIII):
Ground floor – 1st floor shops,
restaurants, offices
2nd-7th floor offices
Apartment block (X):
Ground floor – 1st floor shops
2nd-9th floor apartments

Basement Floors (II):
1st basement shops, car park
2nd basement car park
(ca. 140 parking spaces),
storeroom, services

Site Area:
ca. 3500 m^2

Built Area:
ca. 3500 m^2

Gross Floor Area:
ca. 23000 m^2

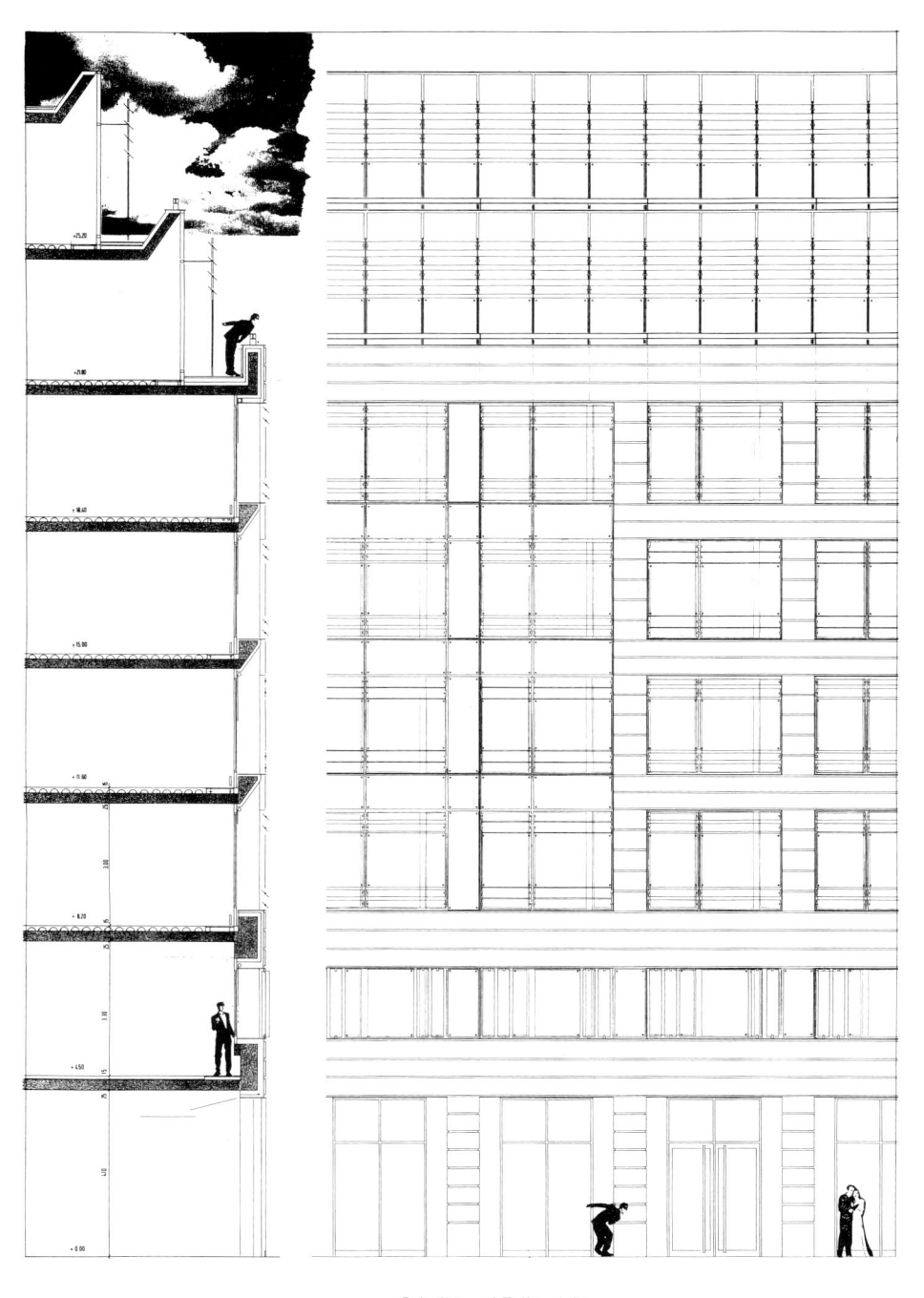

**Schnitt und Teilansicht
der Fassade
Behrenstraße**
Section and façade detail
Behrenstrasse

Büro-, Wohn- und
Geschäftshaus Rosmarin Karree
Office and
Apartment Buildings

Das Rosmarin Karree liegt am Südrand der alten Dorotheenstadt auf einem Block zwischen Lindencorso und Hofgarten. Es muß sich einerseits gegen das große Bauvolumen des Lindencorso behaupten, andererseits den Übergang zum Maßstab der historischen Häuser der Friedrichstadt herstellen. Wichtiger Bezug sind dabei die denkmalgeschützten Gebäude der ehemaligen Commerz- und Privatbank, die östlich angrenzen.

Der neue Gebäudekomplex greift mit dem Büro- und Geschäftshaus an der Friedrichstraße die Blockstruktur als Thema der Dorotheen- und Friedrichstadt auf. Gleichzeitig grenzt er sich durch das Zwischenschieben einer höheren Scheibenbebauung mit reiner Wohnnutzung gegen die historischen Häuser ab und behauptet seine eigene architektonische Identität.

Das Rosmarin Karree wird in der Erdgeschoßzone durch Arkaden mit dahinter liegenden Läden bestimmt. Die Büroetagen werden durch eine Empfangslobby im 1. Obergeschoß erschlossen.

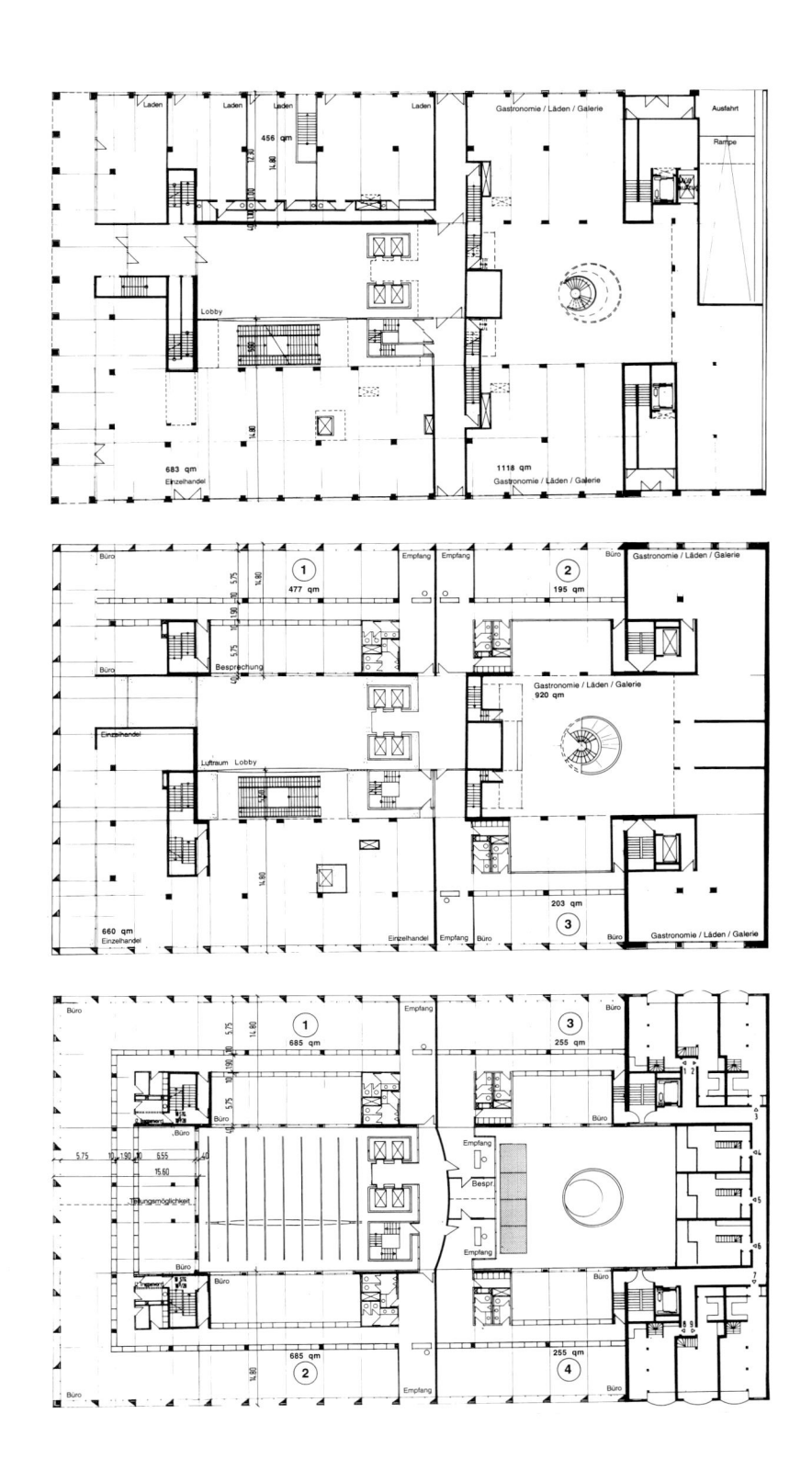

Grundriß Erdgeschoß
mit Ladennutzung
Ground floor plan
retail

Grundriß 1. Obergeschoß
mit Ladennutzung
1st floor plan
retail

Grundriß 2.-5. Obergeschoß
mit Büronutzung und Wohnungen
Plan of 2nd to 5th floors
offices and apartments

1:750

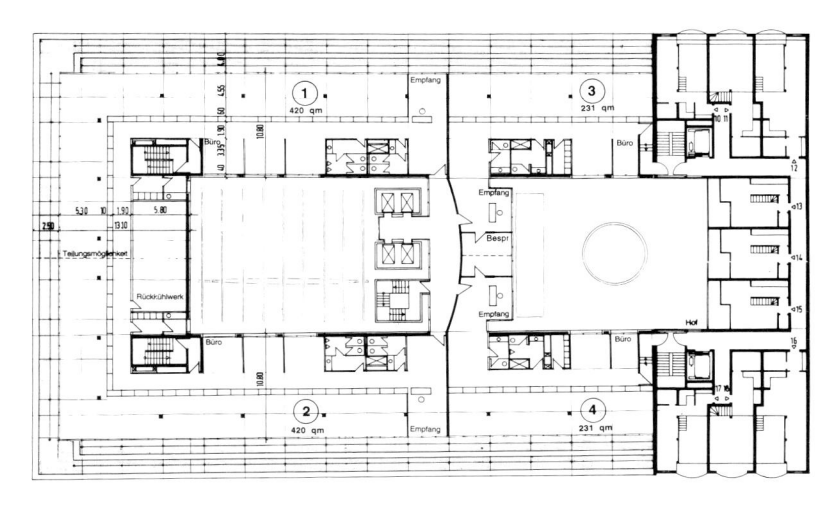

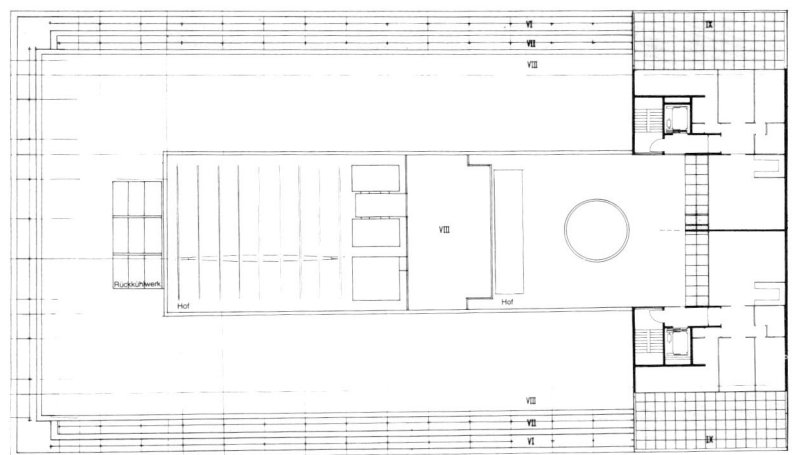

The Rosmarin Karree is situated on a block between Lindencorso and Hofgarten, on the southern edge of the old Dorotheenstadt. It must assert its own identity on the one side against the large building structure of Lindencorso while on the other mastering the transition to the scale of the historic houses along Friedrichstrasse. An important point of reference here are the listed buildings of the former Commerz- and Privatbank, bordering on the east.

The office and commercial building on the Friedrichstrasse side of the new complex echoes the block structure typical of Dorotheenstrasse and Friedrichstadt. An architecturally distinct, higher slab structure, used exclusively for residential purposes, marks the border to the older development and gives the complex its own distinctive architectural stamp.

At street level the Rosmarin Karree has arcades leading to shops; the offices are reached via a reception lobby at 1st floor level.

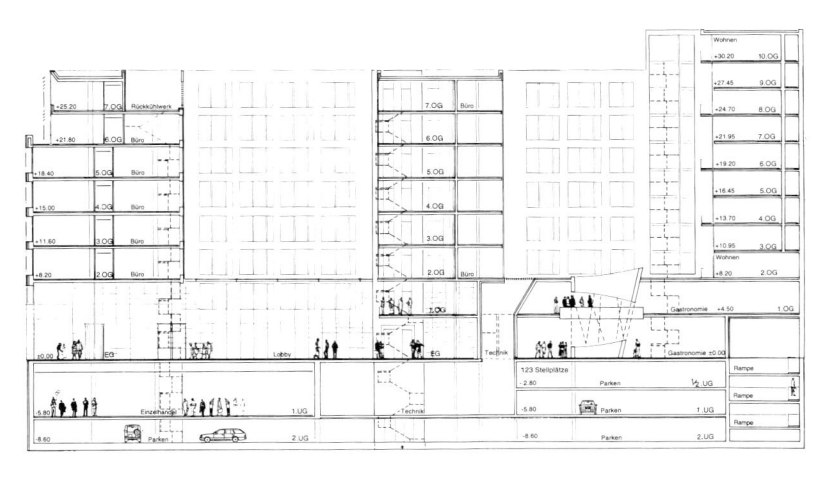

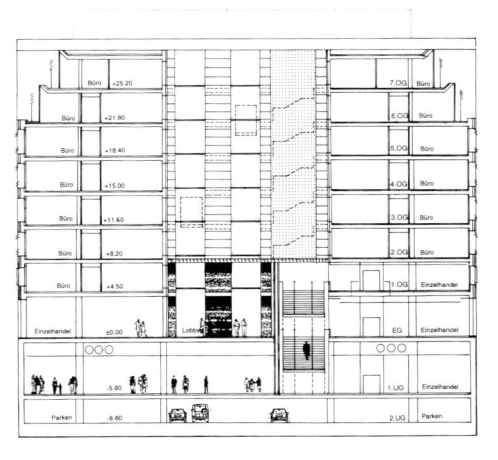

Grundriß 7. Obergeschoß
mit Büronutzung und Wohnungen
7th floor plan
offices and apartments

Grundriß 10. Obergeschoß
mit Wohnungen/
Dachaufsicht
10th floor plan
apartments/
top view of roof

Gebäudelängsschnitt
Longitudinal section

1:750

Gebäudequerschnitt
durch Lobby und Lichthof
des Geschäftshauses
Cross section through lobby
and inner courtyard
of office block

1:750

III
Großblock

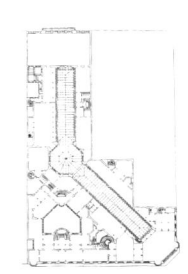

Kaisergalerie, 1871-73, Grundriß Erdgeschoß
Kaisergalerie, 1871-73, ground floor plan

Kaisergalerie, 1871-73, historische Aufnahme des Innenraumes
Kaisergalerie, 1871-73, contemporary photograph of interior

Friedrichstraßenpassage, Grundriß Erdgeschoß
Friedrichstrassenpassage, ground floor plan

Friedrichstraßenpassage, historische Aufnahme des Innenraumes
Friedrichstrassenpassage, contemporary photograph of interior

Die Auflösung der ursprünglichen Besitzverhältnisse und Parzellenstrukturen in der DDR hat vielerorts zu großen zusammenhängenden Grundstücken geführt. Hierdurch wurde nach der Wende die Bebauung mit den von vielen Investoren bevorzugten Großformen befördert, die einen Block ganz oder großenteils besetzen. Dabei sind die unteren Geschosse in der Regel zu einer vollflächigen Überbauung zusammengefaßt, in der Passagen oder Atrien als überdachte Ladenstraßen und -plätze untergebracht sind. Mit der Erschließung der Überbauung bis in die Tiefe des Blockes und bis in die Untergeschosse hinein wird auf eine Maximierung der Ausnutzung der teuren innerstädtischen Grundstücke gezielt. In der Regel sind mindestens das Erdgeschoß und 1. Obergeschoß sowie ein bis zwei Untergeschosse für kommerzielle Zwecke genutzt. Darüber liegen Büros, und in den Attikageschossen oder – aus Gründen der getrennten und einfacheren Erschließung – in einem eigenen Baukörper oder Teilbereich des Gebäudes wird die Auflage des 20-prozentigen Wohnanteils erfüllt.

Insbesondere für die Friedrichstraße, die eine alte Tradition von Passagen und Galerien hat, wurden Gebäude mit Ladenpassagen konzipiert. Das größte und international am meisten beachtete Bauvorhaben sind die Friedrichstadt Passagen, drei Blöcke zwischen der Friedrichstraße und der Rückseite des Schauspielhauses und der Dome des Gendarmenmarkts. Hier sind die Grundstücke nicht nur oberirdisch mindestens in den unteren, zum Teil in allen Geschossen vollflächig überbaut, sondern darüber hinaus sind drei von insgesamt vier Untergeschossen zusammengefaßt; sie bilden ein großes unterirdisches Bauwerk, das alle drei Blöcke einschließlich des dazwischenliegenden Straßenlandes unterbaut und die zentrale und namengebende Ladenpassage sowie Tiefgaragen aufnimmt. Die drei Bauten sind in ihrer architektonischen Konzeption und in ihrem Bezug zur Großstadt trotz gleicher Standort- und Rahmenbedingungen so unterschiedlich wie ihre Architekten: Jean Nouvel/Paris, Pei Cobb Freed & Partners/New York und O. M. Ungers & Partner/Berlin.

Das Gebäude von Jean Nouvel bildet entlang der Friedrichstraße, auf dem Weg von den Linden nach Süden, mit dem kraftvollen Schwung der Blockecke zur Französischen Straße den Auftakt zum Gesamtkomplex. Seine ganze Hülle, die Fassaden ebenso wie das schräg verlaufende Dach, ist gläsern und transparent. Das Tragwerk tritt hinter die Hülle zurück, läßt aber in deren Rasterung die Gebäudestruktur erahnen. Insbesondere werden die Horizontalen betont: Ein Bandraster zeichnet die Stirnflächen der Geschoßdecken nach und dient der Aufnahme von Reklame-

III
The Large Block Form

The disintegration of the original land ownership structures in the GDR and the disappearance of the traditional fragmented lot structure has given rise in many places to large continuous tracts of land in the urban area. After the fall of the wall this circumstance played a role in the preference on the part of many investors for creating large buildings on these sites, such that a whole block or most of it would be taken up by a single building. Generally the lower floors of these buildings form one continuous development, containing within them arcades or atria which are used as covered shopping streets or as public open space. By opening up the insides of the buildings in this way, including access through to the lower levels, the potential of expensive inner-city sites is exploited to the full. In most cases the ground floor and first upper storey as well as one or two basement levels are used for retail. Above them are offices and in the attic storey is the requisite 20 % residential allocation. Alternatively, the apartments are found in a separate building or as a section of the main building – separate access is sometimes found to be simpler and more desirable.

Particularly in Friedrichstrasse, a street where arcades and galleries have a long tradition, we see buildings with shopping arcades. The biggest and most internationally renowned project is the Friedrichstadt Passagen, covering three blocks between Friedrichstrasse and the back of the Schauspielhaus and the churches on Gendarmenmarkt. Here development is very dense, with extensive building not only above ground, particularly in the lower storeys, but also below street level where three of the four basement levels are joined together across the whole site, including the streets, to form one large underground »building«. In this subterranean area are the underground car parks and the central shopping arcade which gives the complex its name. Despite their shared location and identical circumstances, in terms of their design and relationship to the city the three buildings making up the complex are as different as their architects: Jean Nouvel/Paris, Pei Cobb Freed & Partners/New York and O. M. Ungers & Partner/Berlin.

Along Friedrichstrasse leading south from Unter den Linden, Jean Nouvel's building, with its powerful swing around the corner of the block to Französische Strasse, forms the introduction to the whole complex. Its entire skin, façades as well as sloping roof, is clad with glass and transparent. The load-bearing framework retreats behind the skin, but can still be detected in the divisions on the façade. Horizontal lines in particular are

Oswald Mathias Ungers, Friedrichstadt Passagen, Quartier 205, perspektivische Ansicht vom Gendarmenmarkt aus gesehen, Computer-simulation, Entwurfsplanung

Oswald Mathias Ungers, Friedrichstadt Passagen, Block 205, perspective elevation viewed from Gendarmen-markt, computer simulation, design planning

Oswald Mathias Ungers, Friedrichstadt Passagen, Quartier 205, perspektivische Ansicht der inneren Halle am Kreuzungspunkt der Passagen, Computer-simulation

Oswald Mathias Ungers, Friedrichstadt Passagen, Block 205, perspective elevation of the inner hall at the meeting point of the Passagen, computer simulation

**Jean Nouvel,
Friedrichstadt
Passagen,
Quartier 207,
Blick in den
inneren
Lichtkegel,
Computer-
simulation**
Jean Nouvel,
Friedrichstadt
Passagen,
Block 207, view
into the inner
light cone,
computer
simulation

**Pei Cobb Freed &
Partners,
Friedrichstadt
Passagen,
Quartier 206,
Modellfoto,
Wettbewerbs-
planung 1991**
Pei Cobb Freed
& Partners,
Friedrichstadt
Passagen,
Block 206,
model photo,
competition
planning 1991

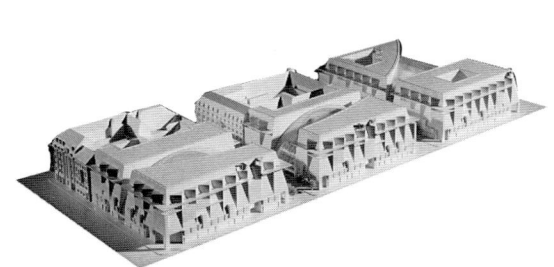

**Pei Cobb Freed &
Partners,
Friedrichstadt
Passagen,
Quartier 206,
Innenansicht,
Computer-
simulation,
Wettbewerbs-
planung 1991**
Pei Cobb Freed
& Partners,
Friedrichstadt
Passagen, Block
206, interior
view, computer
simulation,
competition
planning 1991

schriftzügen, die hinter die Verglasung geschoben werden. Auch die inneren Fassaden des Bauwerks sind gläsern und umschließen Belichtungskegel und -zylinder, die das Gebäudevolumen durchdringen und ebenfalls dem konzeptionellen Spiel von Reklame und künstlichem wie natürlichem Licht dienen. So leicht und elegant sich die Fassaden geben, sie umhüllen dennoch eine hochkompakte Baumasse und ein sehr vielfältiges Spektrum unterschiedlichster Nutzungen, vom zentralen mehrgeschossigen Modehaus Galeries Lafayette, über Läden und kulturelle Einrichtungen bis zu Büros und den in einem Teil des Gebäudes an der Jägerstraße untergebrachten, vertikal geschichteten Wohnungen. Während sich das Gebäude von Nouvel seiner massiven Materialität zu entziehen und in Bewegung, Licht und Transparenz aufzugehen sucht, scheint der massiv und hart geschnitten wirkende, aber weniger kompakt überbaute Block von Oswald Mathias Ungers am anderen Ende der Friedrichstadt Passagen fest mit dem Boden verankert. Dieses »steinerne« Bauwerk sucht eine andere Art der Kommunikation und des Dialoges mit dem Straßenraum und der Stadt als sein »gläserner« Nachbar. Das Gebäude folgt einer Variante jener Typologie mit zweihüftig um zwei Innenhöfe angeordneten Büros, die man – neben den Beispielen im vorangegangenen Kapitel – bei den Projekten von Christoph Mäckler für den Lindencorso und von Thomas van den Valentyn für die Victoria-Versicherung finden kann. Jedoch sucht Ungers nicht den nach außen geschlossenen Blockcharakter dieser beiden Bauten, sondern verfolgt eine plastische und differenzierte Gestaltung der Gebäudemassen zum Straßenraum. Das Erdgeschoß und das 1. Obergeschoß, die den ganzen Block überbauen, sind als Ladenzone auch in der Fassade zusammengefaßt und geben mit ihren großen, in das Raster des Tragwerks gesetzten Verglasungen ihre Nutzung zu erkennen. Darüber liegen die Büroetagen, ganz oben die Wohnungen. Sechs Gebäudeeingänge befinden sich deutlich erkennbar in den Zäsuren zwischen den an die Straße gerückten Einzelbaukörpern.

In der Mitte zeigen die Architekten Pei Cobb Freed & Partners eine dritte Art des Umgangs mit dem Thema Großstadtblock. Mittelpunkt ist ein Atrium mit linsenförmigem Luftraum, von dem aus fünf Galeriearme zur Jäger-, Tauben- und Friedrichstraße strahlen; die so entstandenen Sektoren des Grundrisses definieren die Läden. Das 2-geschossige Atrium wird von einem darüber angeordneten Hof durch ein Glasdach belichtet, das als arabeskes Kristall der organisch geschwungenen Form des Hofes einbeschrieben ist. Zur Straße wird das Gebäude durch ein horizontales Bandraster und einen Rhythmus dreieckiger, erkerartiger Vertikalprismen geprägt, die oberhalb der Trauflinie das Schrägdach durchdringen. Sie verleihen der Fassade aus Aluminium, Glas und beigem Jura-Kalksandstein eine durch die Schattenwirkung betonte räumliche Tiefe.

emphasised: a banded grid traces the floor levels on the outside of the building and serves also as an advertising carrier, the wording being inserted just behind the glazing. The inner façades of the building are also of glass; they encompass light cones and light cylinders which penetrate the building and also conform to the conceptual play of advertising and artificial as well as natural light. Although the façades appear light and elegant, they do in fact enclose a highly compact building volume and a very varied spectrum of uses: from the central, multi-storey fashion house, Galeries Lafayette, shops and cultural facilities to offices and apartments, the latter arranged vertically in a part of the building on Jägerstrasse.

While Nouvel's building would seem to be trying to deny its massive materiality and turn it instead into movement, light and transparence, Oswald Mathias Ungers' solid, firmly contoured, but less compact building at the other end of the Friedrichstadt Passagen seems to be firmly anchored to the ground. This »stone« structure seeks a different kind of communication and dialogue with the street and the town than its »glass« neighbour. Its basic plan is a variant of the standard arrangement around two inner courtyards, with central corridors in each of the wings; this pattern can be found in Christoph Mäckler's Lindencorso project and in Thomas van den Valentyn's project for Victoria Versicherung, in addition to the examples mentioned in previous chapters. However, Ungers does not seek to present these two buildings as a block structure closed to the outside, but instead creates a much more sculptured building volume to project towards the street. Ground floor and first upper storey extend across the whole site area; with their large glazed fronts following the rhythm of the structural grid they form a unified and easily identifiable retail zone. Above this area are the office levels, and at the top the apartments. Six building entrances are easily found between the individual building sections which project towards the street.

Between these two blocks is a third type of approach to the subject of the large block, the contribution of the architects Pei Cobb Freed & Partners. The focus of the building is a lens-shaped atrium space from which five galleries radiate towards Jägerstrasse, Taubenstrasse and Friedrichstrasse; the shops are located in the sectors defined by these »arms«. The 2-floor height atrium is lit from above through an arabesque crystalline glass roof tracing the organic form of the space. The building's street façade has a horizontal grid pattern and a rhythmical sequence of triangular vertical prisms projecting towards the street and extending beyond the eaves line of the sloping roof. This gives spatial depth through light and shade effects on the aluminum, glass and beige sandstone face of the building.

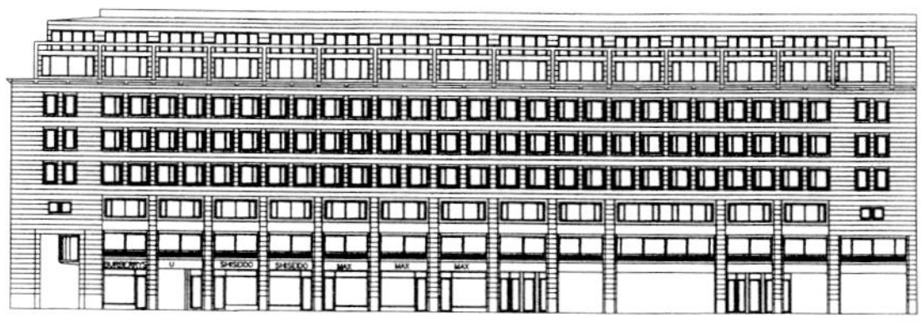

Christoph Mäckler, Lindencorso, Ansicht Rosmarinstraße
Christoph Mäckler, Lindencorso, Rosmarinstrasse elevation

Christoph Mäckler, Lindencorso, Grundriß 1. Untergeschoß
Christoph Mäckler, Lindencorso, plan of 1st basement level

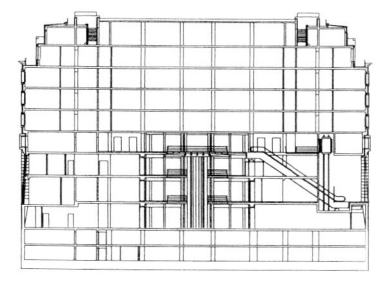

Christoph Mäckler, Lindencorso, Querschnitt
Christoph Mäckler, Lindencorso, cross section

Thomas van den Valentyn, Büro- und Geschäftshaus der VICTORIA, perspektivische Ansicht, Computersimulation
Thomas van den Valentyn, VICTORIA office and commercial building, perspective elevation, computer simulation

Die beiden bereits erwähnten Geschäftshausblöcke von Christoph Mäckler für den Lindencorso und von Thomas van den Valentyn für die Victoria-Versicherung liegen ebenfalls in zentraler Lage an der Friedrichstraße. Beide tragen zum Rückbau der Straße auf ihr historisches Profil an den Kreuzungen mit bedeutenden Querstraßen bei: die Victoria-Versicherung an der Leipziger Straße, der Lindencorso Unter den Linden. Beide Bauten ordnen die oberen Geschosse um zwei rechteckige Innenhöfe und besitzen darunter eine vollflächige Grundstücksüberbauung. In diesem unteren Bereich, der Erdgeschoß und 1. Untergeschoß sowie beim Lindencorso zusätzlich zwei weitere Obergeschosse (mit insgesamt 4-geschossiger Halle) umfaßt, liegen Läden, Gastronomie und kulturelle Einrichtungen. Wohnungen liegen beim Lindencorso im obersten der beiden Attikageschosse; das ein Geschoß höhere Victoria-Gebäude hingegen verfügt über Wohnungen in insgesamt drei Attikageschossen, die in gleichmäßigen Sprüngen von der Straße zurückgestaffelt sind. Dieses Thema wird – als Abtreppung – auch im Inneren des schmalen und langgestreckten Hofes umgesetzt, der an die Nachbarbebauung grenzt.

Außerhalb der strengen Blockstruktur von Dorotheen- und Friedrichstadt gibt es große Geschäftshäuser mit Hallen oder Passagen, die sich mit völlig anderen Blocksituationen auseinandersetzen. Hierzu gehören – bei grundsätzlich unterschiedlichen Architekturauffassungen – die Bauten von Claude Vasconi für das Centre Paris-Berlin an der Mollstraße in Friedrichshain und von Nicolas Grimshaw & Partners für das Ludwig Erhard Haus an der Fasanenstraße in Charlottenburg. Beide Bauten integrieren eine innere überdachte Straße mit Läden bzw. Gastronomie und kulturellen Einrichtungen.

Grundlegend verschieden ist, neben dem architektonischen Ausdruck, der Dialog der Gebäude mit der Stadt. Beim Centre Paris-Berlin werden lineare Baukörper um Atrium und Passage wie um einen überdachten Innenhof organisiert und reflektieren die Auseinandersetzung mit den umliegenden Plattenbauten. Sie sollen zur städtebaulichen Neuordnung des Quartiers mit klaren Baufluchten, abgestimmten Gebäudehöhen und einer sinnvollen Verdichtung beitragen. Die Passage wird an ihren beiden Zugängen durch die Baukörper der Blockrandbebauung eindeutig definiert.

Das Ludwig Erhard Haus dagegen wird dem unregelmäßigen Grundstück als ausgesprochen eigenwillige gestalterische Großform einbeschrieben und paßt sich der durch den angrenzenden Gebäudebestand schwierigen Situation im Blockinneren organisch an. Große Stahlbögen überspannen das gesamte Grundstück und bilden eine mit Schuppenstrukturen verkleidete Außenhaut; von den Bögen sind die einzelnen Geschosse abgehängt. Die Fußgängerpassage ist zur Fasanenstraße raumhoch verglast; sie ist das konzeptionelle Rückgrat des Gebäudes, über das alle Bereiche erschlossen werden und das Einblick von der Straße ins Innere gibt. Bauwerk und Stadtraum verschmelzen zu einer komplexen Einheit.

The two office blocks mentioned above – the Lindencorso by Christoph Mäckler and Thomas van den Valentyn's Victoria Versicherung building – are also in a central location near Friedrichstrasse. Both contribute to the reinstatement of the street's historic profile at the junctions with important roads: Victoria Versicherung on the corner of Leipziger Strasse and Lindencorso on Unter den Linden. In both buildings the upper floors are arranged around central square courtyards, while the lower levels completely extend across the whole site area. In these lower sections, the ground floor and first floor in the Victoria Versicherung, plus the second and third upper storeys in Lindencorso (to create a 4-storey height hall), are shops, restaurants, cafés and cultural facilities. In Lindencorso the apartments are located in the uppermost of the two attic storeys; the Victoria building has apartments on three attic levels, each set back in equal measure from the main façade plane. This »stepped« arrangement is echoed also in the narrow linear courtyard which borders on the neighbouring building.

Beyond the strictly regular block structure of Dorotheenstadt and Friedrichstadt are a number of large office blocks also with halls and passageways but in a totally different type of block situation. Included here are Claude Vasconi's Paris-Berlin Centre on Mollstrasse in Friedrichshain and Nicholas Grimshaw & Partners' Ludwig Erhard Building on Fasanenstrasse in Charlottenburg. Although fundamentally different in architectural design both buildings have an integrated, covered inner street with shops, restaurants, cafés and cultural facilities.

In addition to the differing architectures, there is a considerable distinction in the way each building relates to the urban environment. In the Paris-Berlin Centre linear building structures are arranged around atria, passageways and an inner covered courtyard, as a response to the nearby slab buildings. These features are intended to contribute to the urban renewal of the district with their clear **lines**, aligned building heights and appropriate level of development density. The entrances at either end of the internal street are clearly defined by the volumes of the corner blocks.

The Ludwig Erhard Building on the other hand occupies its irregular-shaped site with a distinctly idiosyncratic building form, adapting itself organically inside the block to the difficult situation bordering on existing development. Great steel arches span the whole site, a scaled cladding forming the building's outer skin; the floors are suspended from these arches. On the Fasanenstrasse front the pedestrian passageway is fully glazed; this constitutes the conceptual backbone of the whole building – from here all other areas within the building can be reached and from the street people can see right into the interior. Building space and street space become one integrated unit.

Claude Vasconi, Centre Paris-Berlin, Ansicht Mollstraße und Ansicht Barnimstraße, Querschnitte, Wettbewerbsplanung 1992
Claude Vasconi, Centre Paris-Berlin, Mollstrasse elevation and Barnimstrasse elevation, cross sections, competition planning 1992

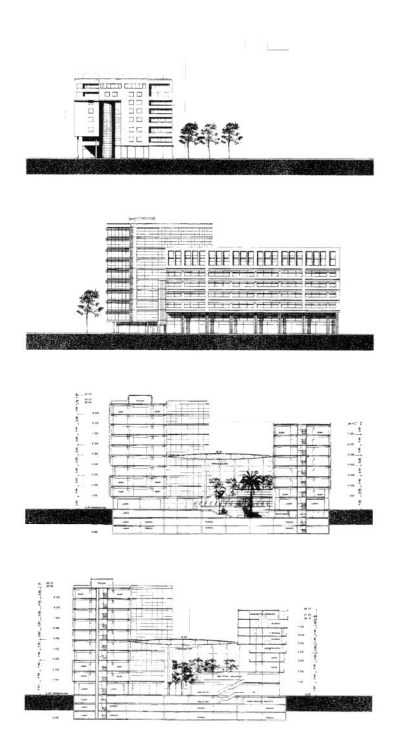

Büro-, Wohn- und Geschäftshaus Quartier 207 Office and Apartment Building Block 207	Friedrichstadt Passagen	AJN Architectures Jean Nouvel Paris

Mitarbeit Wettbewerb
Staff competition
Laurence Daude
Judith Simon
Nicole Weber
Wolfgang Kruse

Mitarbeit Planung
Staff planning
Laurence Daude
Judith Simon
Vivianne Morteau
Matthias Raasch

Bauherr:
Euro-Projektentwicklungs GmbH

Planungstermine:
Wettbewerb 1991, 1. Preis
Entwurfsplanung
August 1991 – Juli 1992
Baubeginn September 1993
Voraussichtlicher Bezug
Frühjahr 1995

Nutzung:
Läden mit
3.888 m² Bruttogeschoßfläche
Büros mit
23.953 m² Bruttogeschoßfläche
Modehaus mit
11.095 m² Bruttogeschoßfläche
Wohnungen mit
1.614 m² Bruttogeschoßfläche

Geschosse (VIII):
EG Modehaus, Läden
1.–3. OG Modehaus, Büros, Wohnungen
4.+5. OG Büros, Wohnungen
6.+7. OG Büros

Untergeschosse (IV):
1. UG (Zwischengeschoß) Technik
2. UG Modehaus, Passage
3.+4. UG Tiefgarage

Grundstücksgröße:
5.139 m²

Überbaute Fläche:
5.094,57 m²

Bruttogeschoßfläche:
56.442 m²

Perspektive
Französische Straße /
Ecke Friedrichstraße von Westen
Computersimulation
Perspective view at the corner of Französische Strasse and Friedrichstrasse from the west
Computer simulation

Projektadresse:
Location:
**Französische Strasse/
Friedrichstrasse/
Jägerstrasse
in
10117 Berlin-Mitte**

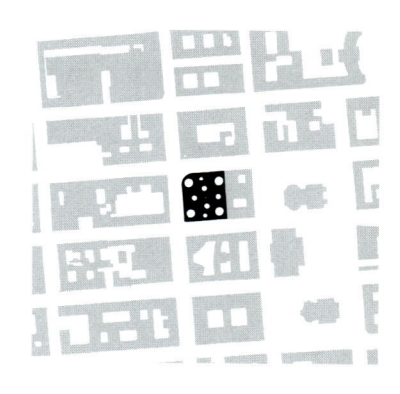

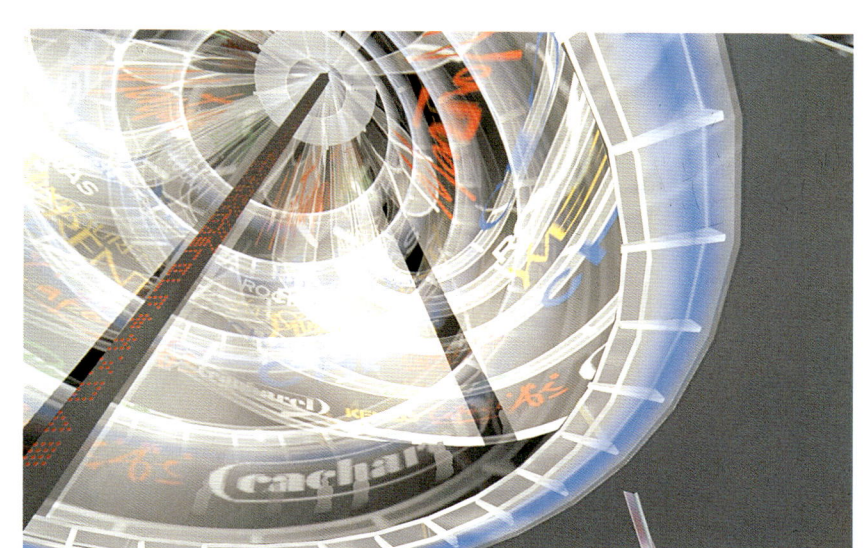

Client:
Euro-Projektentwicklungs GmbH

Project Stages:
Competition 1991, 1. prize
Design development
August 1991 – July 1992
Start of construction
September 1993
Expected occupation date
Spring 1995

Building Use:
Shops totalling
3888 m² gross floor area
Offices totalling
23953 m² gross floor area
Fashion store with
11095 m² gross floor area
Apartments totalling
1614 m² gross floor area

Upper Floors (VIII):
Ground floor fashion store
1st-3rd floor fashion store,
offices, apartments
4th and 5th floor offices,
apartments
6th and 7th floor offices

Basement Floors (IV):
1st basement (intermediate level)
building services
2nd basement fashion store,
arcade
3rd and 4th basement car park

Site Area:
5139 m²

Built Area:
5094.57 m²

Gross Floor Area:
56442 m²

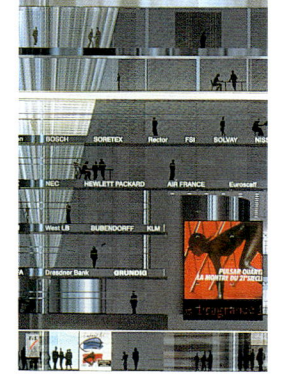

**Fassadenausschnitt
Friedrichstraße
Computersimulation**
Façade detail
Friedrichstrasse
Computer simulation

**Blicke in die mittleren Lichtkegel
Computersimulationen**
Views to central light cones
Computer simulations

Büro-, Wohn- und
Geschäftshaus
Quartier 207   Friedrichstadt Passagen
Office and
Apartment Building
Block 207

Ansicht des Gebäudes
Französische Straße /
Ecke Friedrichstraße
von Nordwesten
Modellaufnahme
View of the building
Französische Strasse /
corner of Friedrichstrasse
from the northwest
Model photo

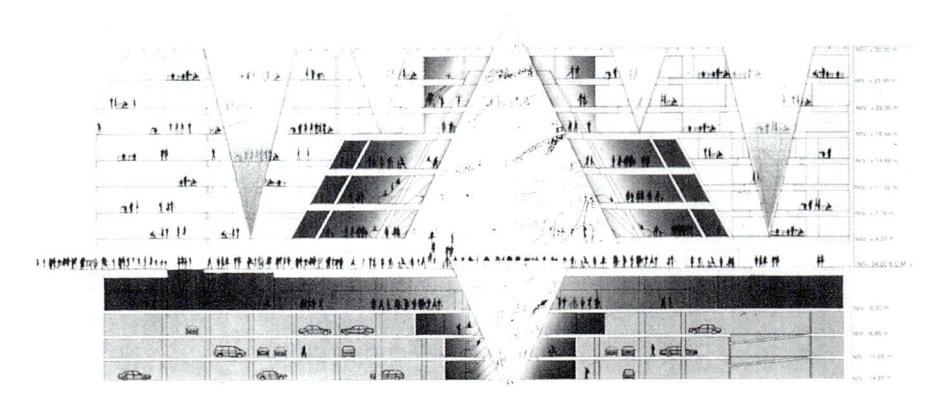

Diagonalschnitt
im Bereich der Kegel
Diagonal section through
cone area

1:750

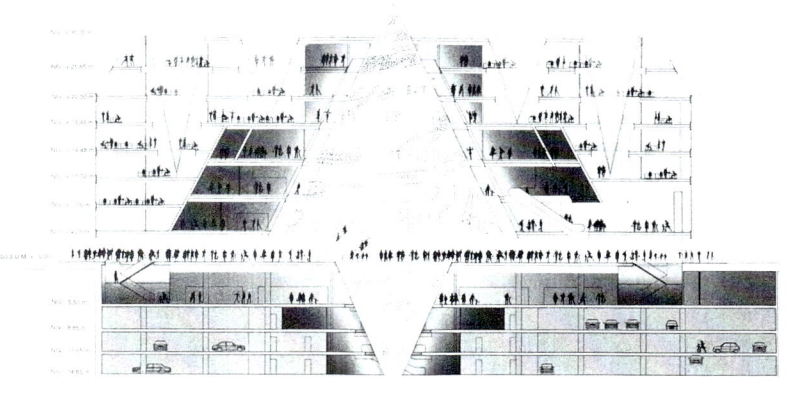

**Längsschnitt
im Bereich der Kegel**
Longitudinal section
through cone area

1:750

Schnitt
Section

Büro-, Wohn- und
Geschäftshaus
Quartier 207
Office and
Apartment Building
Block 207

Friedrichstadt Passagen

Das Gebäude bildet eine vollständige Überbauung des nördlichen Blockes der Friedrichstadt Passagen. Zur Belichtung der inneren Nutzungsbereiche wird es von Lichtkegeln und Lichtzylindern durchdrungen, in denen sich Leuchtreklamen spiegeln. Die gleiche Thematik des Spiels von künstlichem und natürlichem Licht, von Reklameschriftzügen und vollflächiger Verglasung findet sich auch in den Fassaden, die sich in drei horizontale Bereiche gliedern: das zurückspringende Erdgeschoß, mit markantem umlaufenden Vordach; die Mittelzone bis zur Traufhöhe von 22,55 m; die oberhalb der Traufe unter 60° nach innen geneigte Attikazone.

An der Kreuzung Friedrichstraße / Französische Straße ist der Baukörper abgerundet und bildet zur Friedrichstraße den formalen Abschluß der Friedrichstadt Passagen. Im Zentrum des Gebäudes wird dieser Abschluß durch ein Modehaus gebildet, das im Erdgeschoß von Läden umgeben ist. Auf der 3. Obergeschoßebene des Modehauses und – zugänglich von der Passage – im 1. Untergeschoß werden kulturelle Nutzungen wie Kabarett-Theater, Galerien oder ähnliches untergebracht. An der Jägerstraße liegen vom 1. bis 5. Obergeschoß insgesamt 15 Wohnungen, mit einem eigenen repräsentativen Entrée. Alle weiteren Nutzflächen werden von Büros eingenommen.

oben above
Grundriß 2. Obergeschoß
mit dem Modehaus
»Galeries Lafayette«
und Wohnungen
2nd floor plan
with Galeries Lafayette
department store
and apartments

1:750

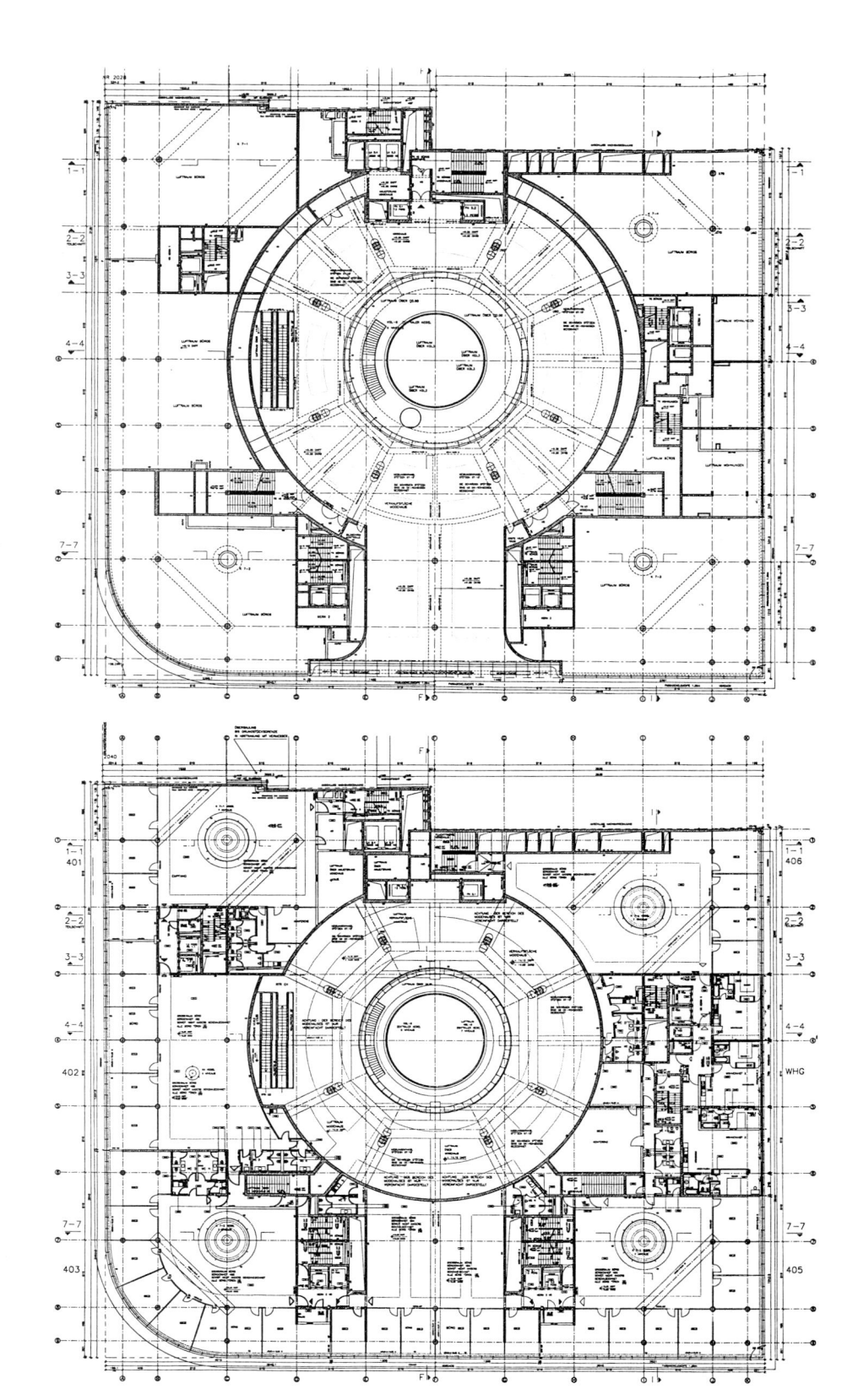

Grundriß 4. Obergeschoß
mit Büronutzung und Wohnungen
4th floor plan
offices and apartments

1:750

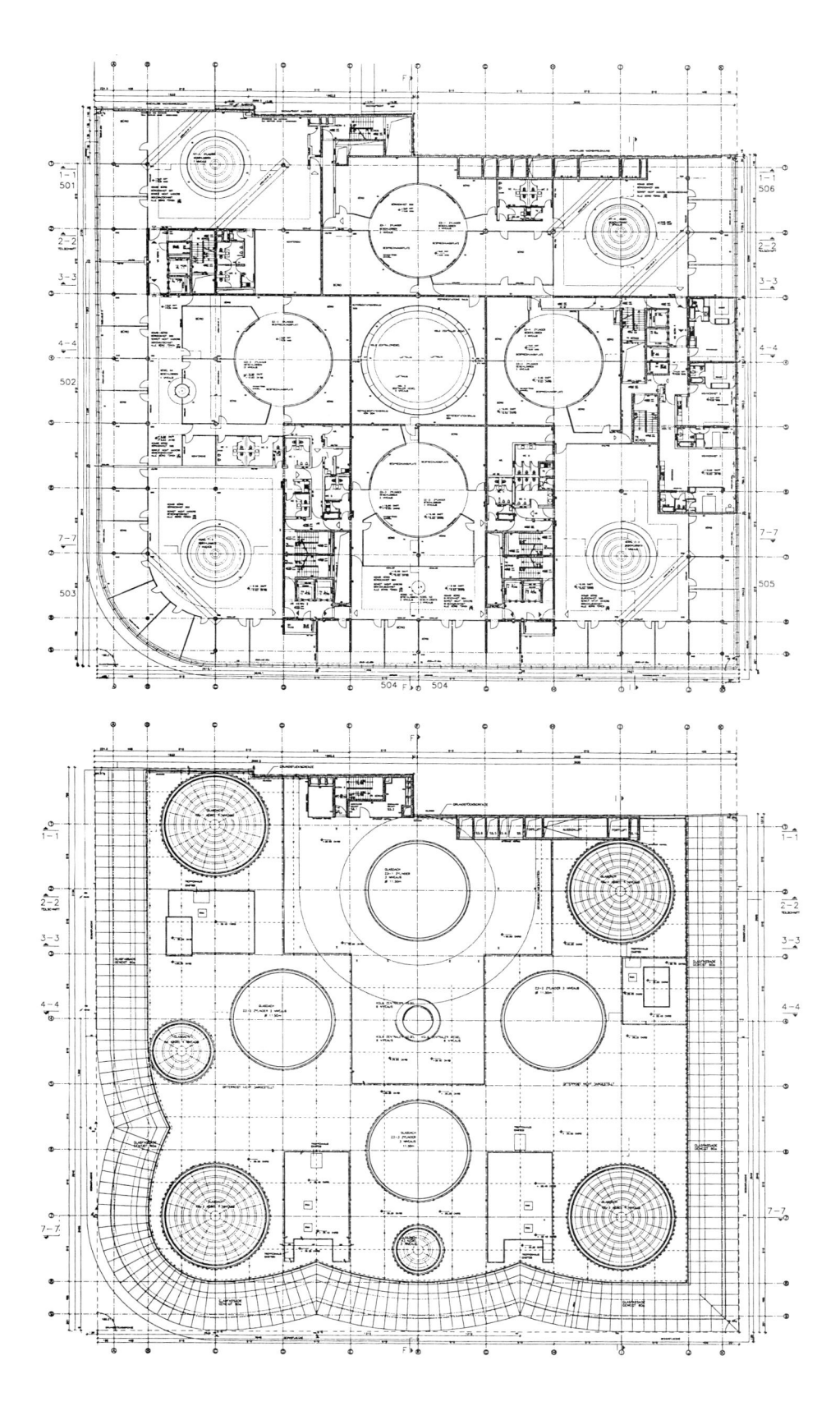

The building occupies the entire northern block of the Friedrichstadt Passagen development. The internal areas are lit by light cones and light cylinders displaying illuminated advertisements. The same theme of an interplay of artificial and natural light, of advertising and floor-to-ceiling glazing is repeated in the façades which are divided into three horizontal zones: set back slightly, the ground floor with its distinctive roof canopy; the 22.55 m high central zone up to the eaves; the roof parapet zone angled at 60° back from the eaves line.

At the junction of Friedrichstrasse and Französische Strasse the building is rounded, thus indicating with its form the end of the Passagen complex. In the centre of this front is a fashion store, flanked at ground floor level by other shops. On the 3rd floor of the fashion store, and, accessed via the arcade, on the 1st basement level, are areas for cultural uses such as a cabaret theatre, galleries etc. Between the 1st and 5th floors facing Jägerstrasse are a total of 15 apartments, which share a common entrance hall. All remaining usable floor space in the building is given over to offices.

Grundriß 5. Obergeschoß mit Büronutzung und Wohnungen
5th floor plan
offices and apartments

1:750

Dachaufsicht
Top view of roof

1:750

Büro-, Wohn- und Geschäftshaus Quartier 206 Office and Apartment Building Block 206	Friedrichstadt Passagen	Pei Cobb Freed & Partners Architects New York

Henry N. Cobb
(Entwurfspartner design partner)
George H. Miller
(Leitender Partner
Managing partner)
Theodore J. Musho
(Leitender Architekt
Senior designer)
Brian P. McNally
(Projektleitung project manager)

Bauherr:
Jagdfeld Friedrichstadt Passagen
Quartier 206
Vermögensverwaltungs KG
Berlin

Planungstermine:
Wettbewerb 1991, 1. Preis
Entwurfsplanung seit 1991
Baubeginn 1992
Voraussichtlicher Bezug 1995

Nutzung:
Läden (variable Größe) mit
6.855 m² Hauptnutzfläche
Büros (variable Größe) mit
11.760 m² Hauptnutzfläche
Wohnungen (variable Größe) mit
1.051,25 m²
Öffentliche Flächen mit
1.516 m²

Geschosse (VIII):
EG – 1. OG Läden,
öffentliche Flächen
1.-7. OG Büros, Wohnungen

Untergeschosse (IV):
1. UG (Zwischengeschoß)
Lager/Technik
2. UG (5.574,55 m²)
Läden, Passage, öffentliche
Flächen
3.-4. UG (10.609 m²)
Tiefgarage

Grundstücksgröße:
ca. 4.900 m²

Überbaute Fläche:
ca. 4.900 m²

Bruttogeschoßfläche:
48.592,29 m²

Perspektive
Jägerstraße / Ecke Friedrichstraße
von Nordwesten
Computersimulation
Perspective view
of the corner of
Jägerstrasse and Friedrichstraße
from the northwest
Computer simulation

Fritz Sulzer
(**Vorhangfassade** curtain wall)
Georg Jell
(**Projektarchitekt**
Project architect)

Kontaktarchitekt:
ARGE Friedrichstadt Passagen
Berlin
Rolf Niedballa
Uwe Grahl
Gottfried Hein

Projektadresse:
Location:
Friedrichstrasse 71-74
in
10117 Berlin-Mitte

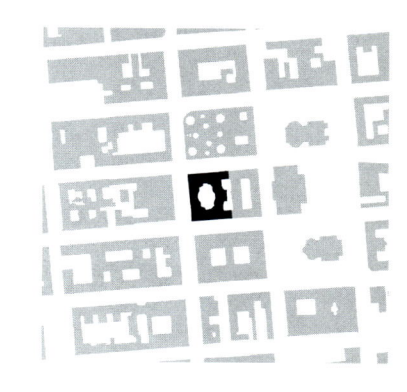

Client:
Jagdfeld Friedrichstadt Passagen
Quartier 206 Vermögens-
verwaltungs KG
Berlin

Project Stages:
Competition 1991, 1st prize
Design development from 1991
Start of construction 1992
Expected completion 1995

Building Use:
Shops (variable size) totalling
6855 m² main floor space
Offices (variable size) totalling
11760 m² main floor space
Apartments (variable size)
totalling
1051.25 m²
Public areas covering
1516 m²

Upper Floors (VIII):
Ground floor and 1st floor
shops, public areas
1st-7th floor offices, apartments

Basement Floors (IV):
1st basement (intermediate level)
storeroom/services
2nd basement (5574.55 m²)
shops/arcade, public areas
3rd basement – 4th basement
(10609 m²) car park

Site Area:
ca. 4900 m²

Built Area:
ca. 4900 m²

Gross Floor Area:
48592.29 m²

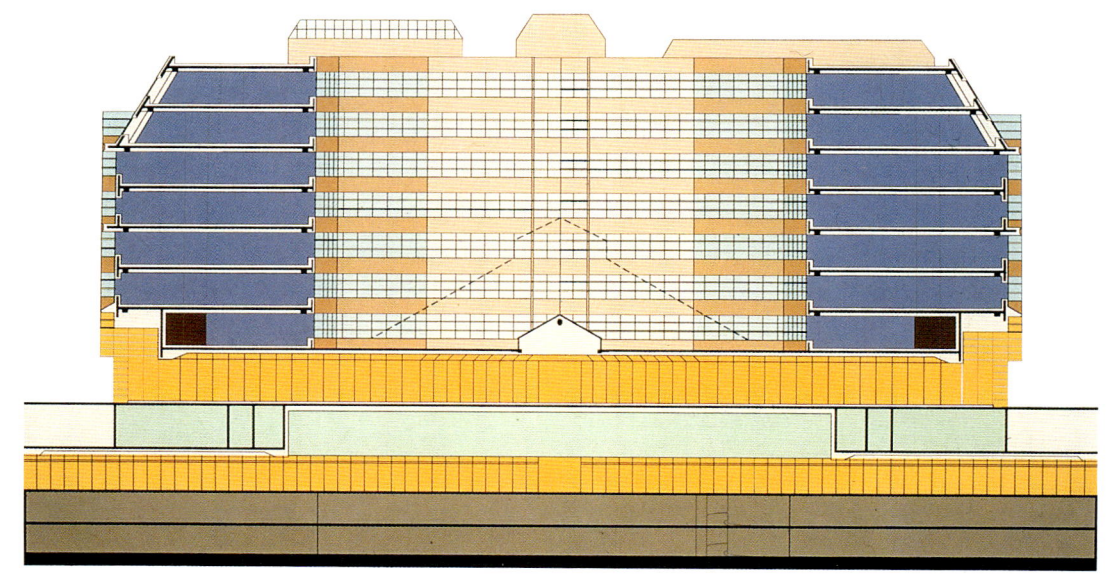

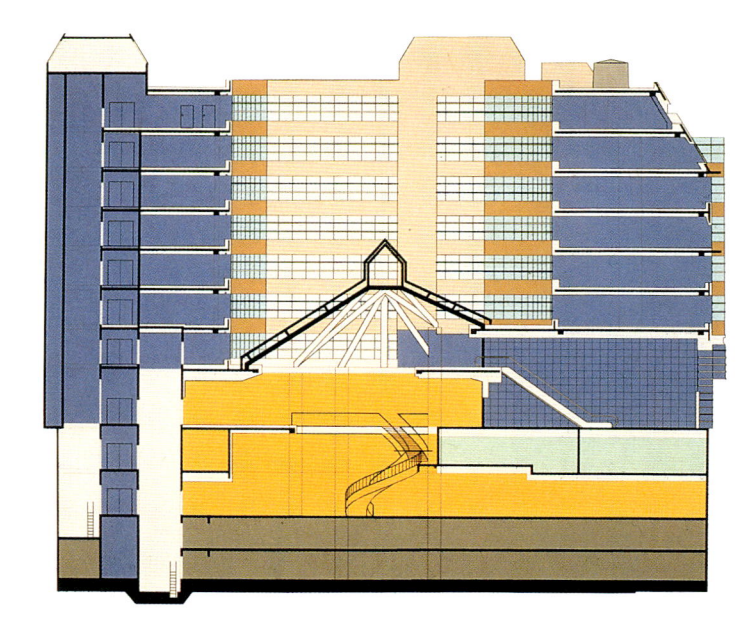

**Eingangssituation
Skizze**
Entrance situation
Sketch

Gebäudelängsschnitt
Longitudinal section

**Gebäudequerschnitt
im Bereich der Lichtkuppel**
Cross section through
light dome area

1:750

Büro-, Wohn- und
Geschäftshaus
Quartier 206
Office and
Apartment Building
Block 206

Friedrichstadt Passagen

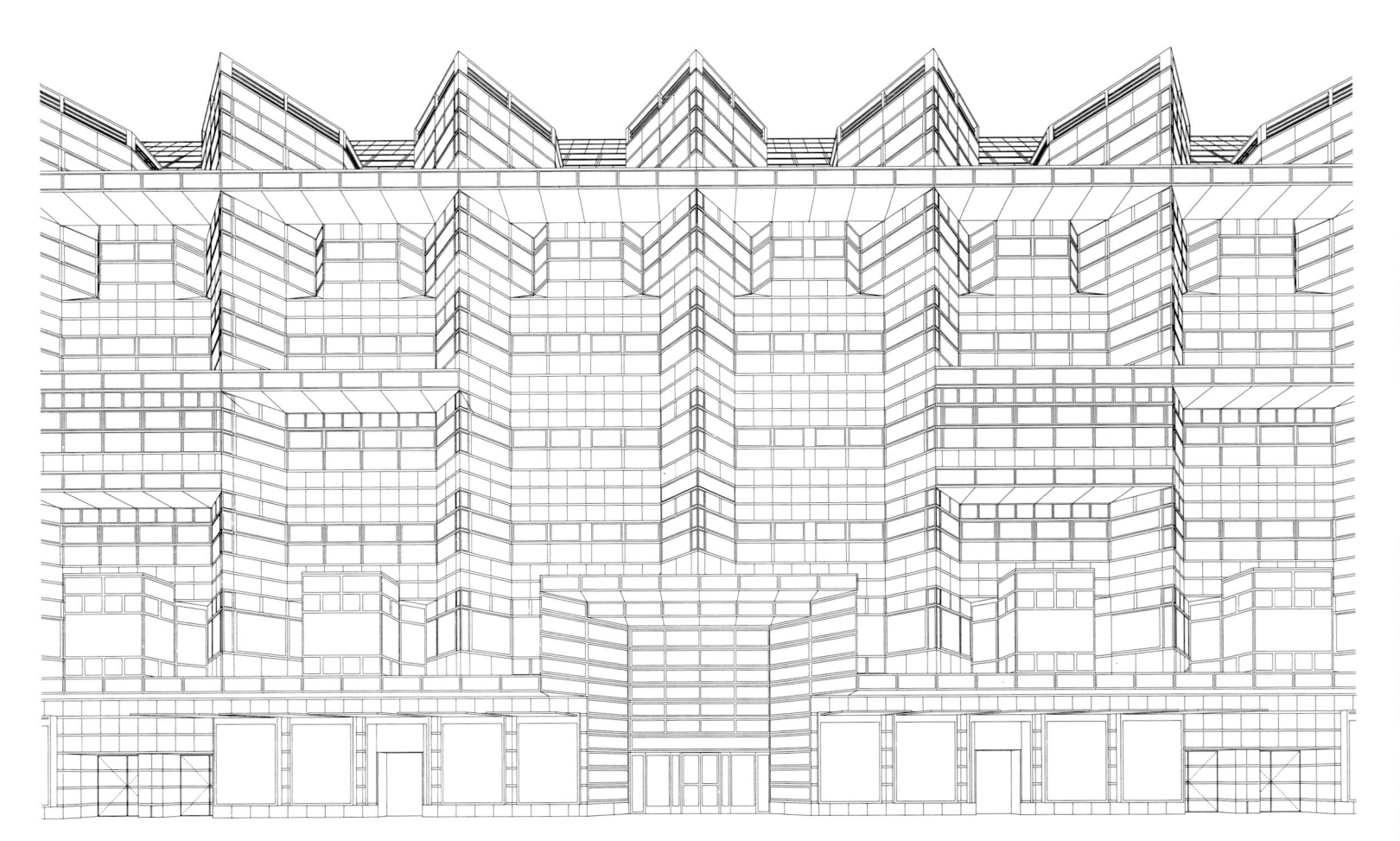

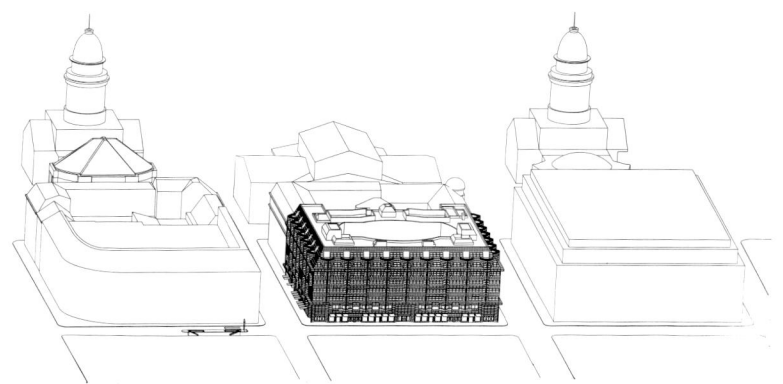

**Fassadenausschnitt
mit Eingangssituation
Perspektive**
Façade detail
with entrance situation
Perspective drawing

**Städtebaulicher
Zusammenhang aus
der Vogelflugperspektive
von Westen**
Bird's-eye view
from the west
of urban context

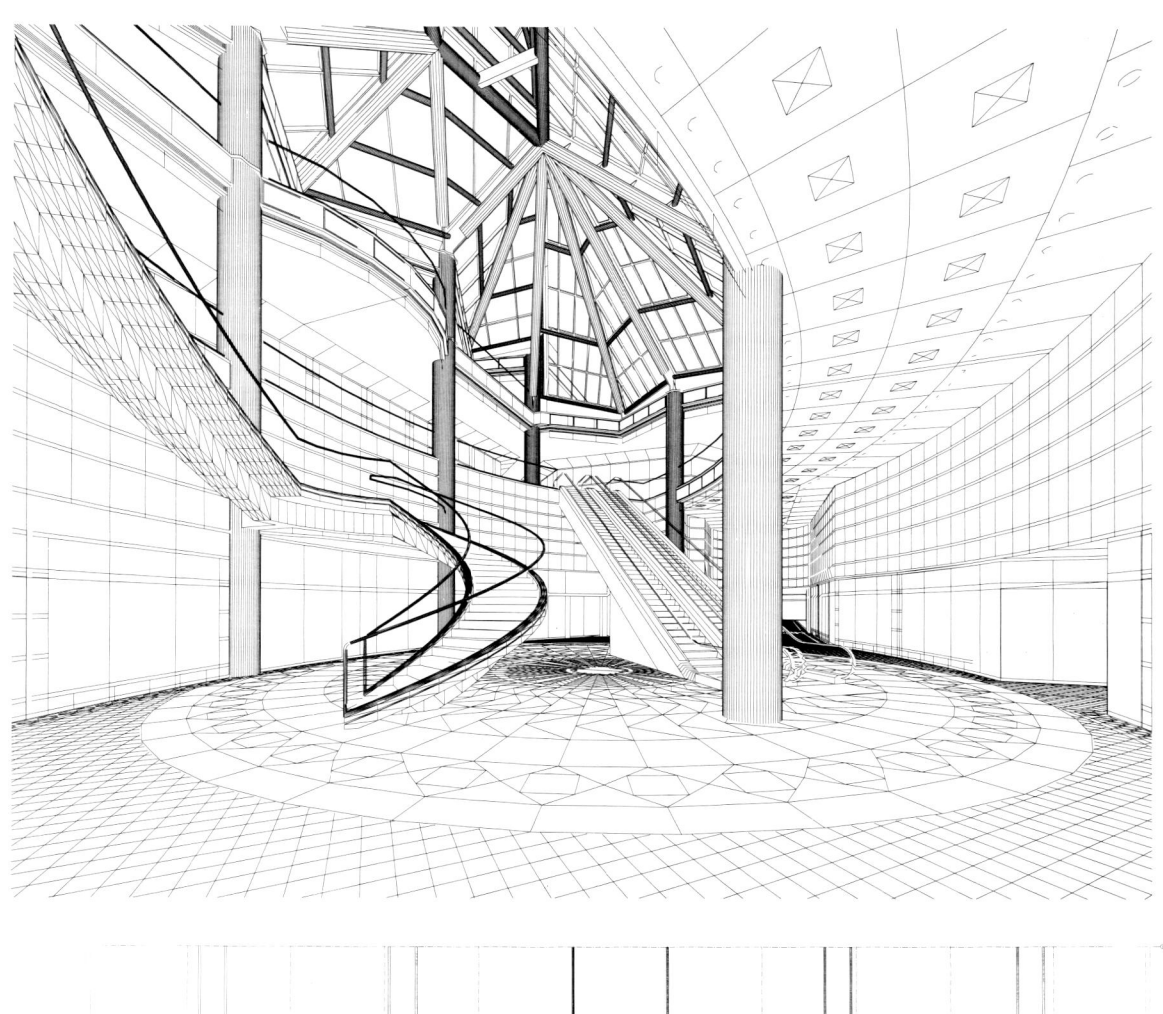

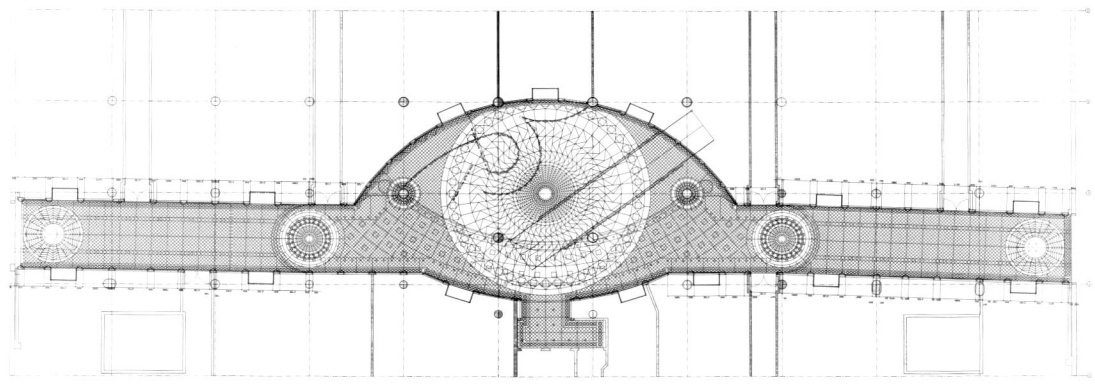

**Perspektive der Ladenpassage
im Bereich des Atriums**
Perspective of shopping arcade
at atrium

**Fliesenplan der die Friedrichstadt-
Blöcke verbindenden Ladenpassage
im Untergeschoß**
Plan of tiled floor in basement
arcade in Friedrichstadt Blocks

Büro-, Wohn- und
Geschäftshaus
Quartier 206   Friedrichstadt Passagen
Office and
Apartment Building
Block 206

Das Bauwerk komplettiert den Block in Ergänzung der Altbauten an der Charlottenstraße. Es ist zugleich zentrales Glied der Friedrichstadt Passagen.

Der stark plastische Ausdruck des Wettbewerbsentwurfes mit seinen schräg zurückfliehenden Fassaden wurde bei der Entwurfsbearbeitung verhaltener. Dennoch bleibt das Gebäude, nicht zuletzt durch die Strukturierung mit vertikalen, spitzwinklig Fassade und Dach durchdringenden Vorsprüngen, von expressivem Charakter. Dieser Ausdruck verstärkt sich durch die über das Bauwerk gelegte netzartige Rasterstruktur.

Die vertikale Rhythmisierung der Fassade durch im Grundriß dreieckige, erkerähnliche Elemente versteht sich als zeitgemäße Interpretation der als visuelle Vielfalt erlebbaren Abfolge von Einzelgebäuden im historischen Block. Sie berücksichtigt das Erleben der Straßenwand als Sequenz und die Wahrnehmung der Fassade aus schräger statt frontaler Ansicht.

Mittelpunkt des Quartiers 206 ist ein linsenförmiges Atrium mit umlaufenden Galerien. Das Atrium wird über sternförmig angeordnete Passagen betreten und erschließt die auf mehreren Ebenen angegliederten Ladenbereiche.

**Grundriß Erdgeschoß
mit Ladennutzung**
Ground floor plan
retail

**Grundriß 1. Obergeschoß
mit Ladennutzung, Büronutzung,
Wohnungen**
1st floor plan
shops, offices and apartments

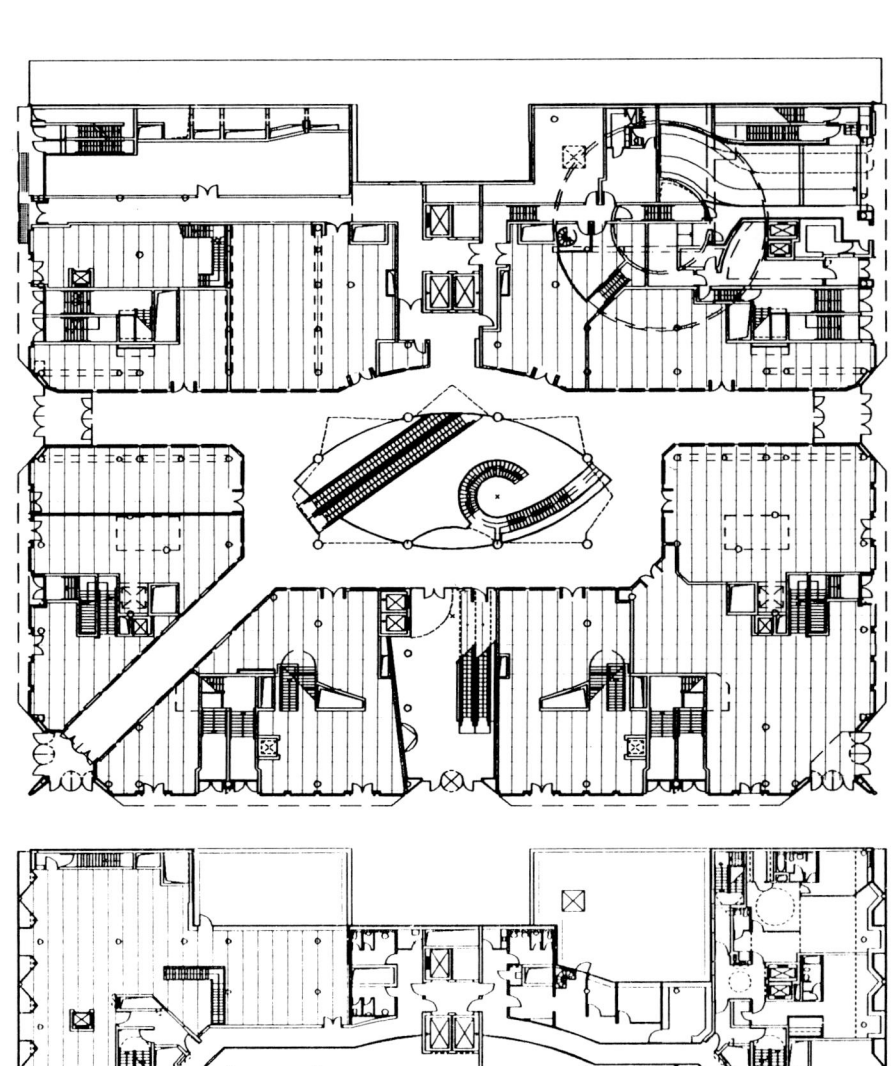

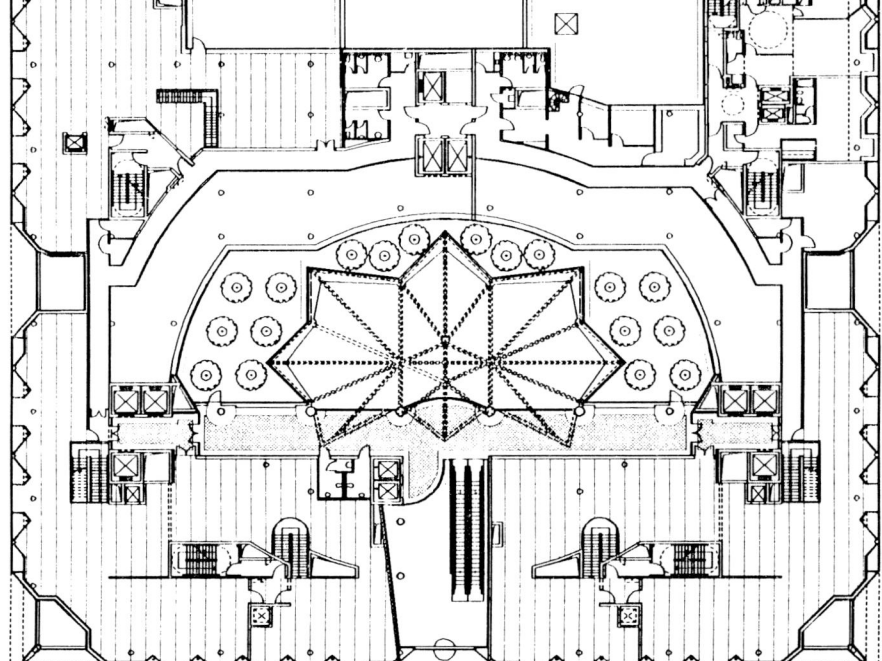

1:750

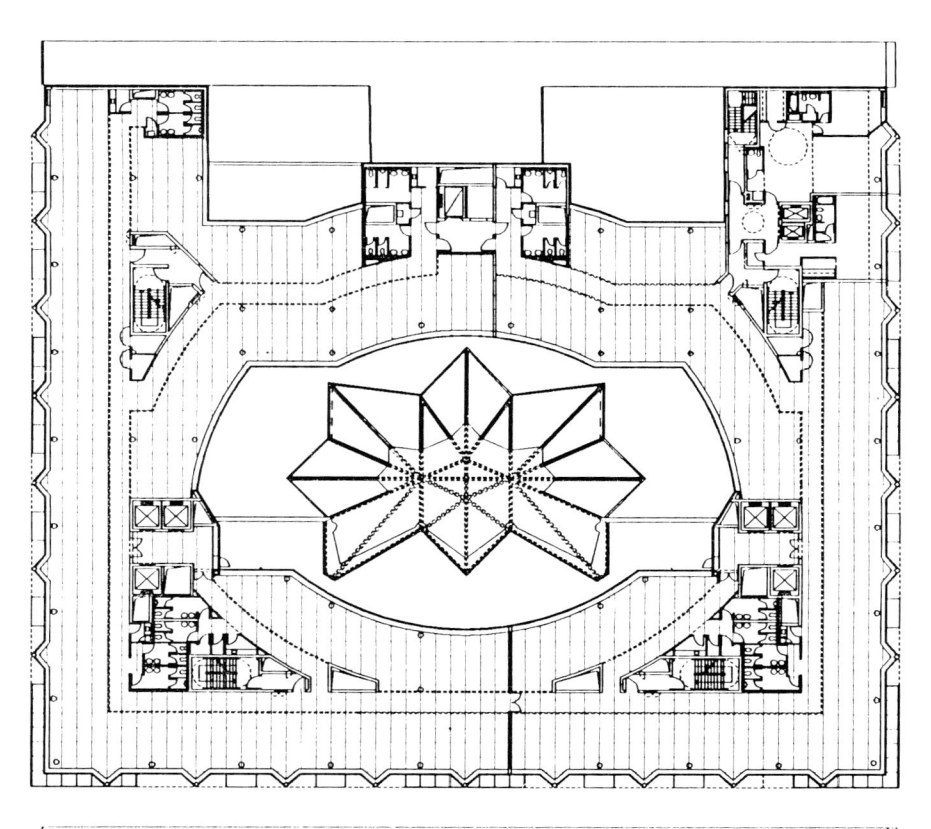

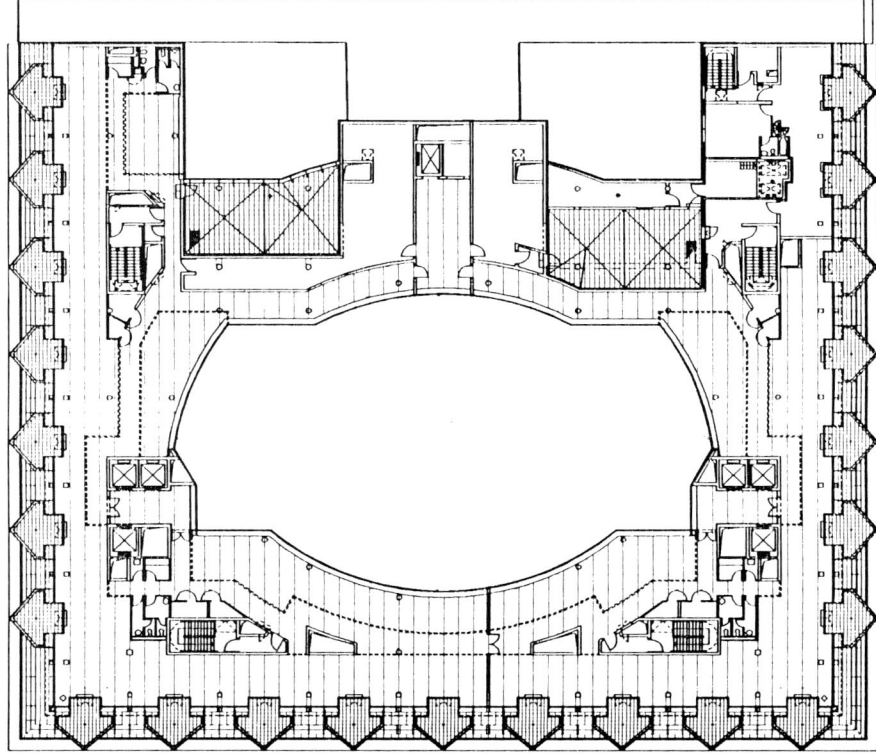

The building completes the block, adding on to the existing buildings on Charlottenstrasse. It also represents the central section of the Friedrichstadt Passagen.

The strongly sculptural expression of the competition design with its diagonally retreating façades became more reserved in the design development stage. Nevertheless it retains an expressive character, revealed in the form of the vertical sections projecting sharply through façade and roof. This impression is intensified by the net-like grid structure overlaying the building.

The vertical rhythm of the façade, achieved by bay-like projections triangular in plan, is meant as a contemporary interpretation of a range of individual buildings in the historic block structure with their typical visual variety. It takes up the idea of experiencing the street front as a sequence, with the façade being perceived at an angle rather than frontally.

At the centre of block 206 is a lens-shaped atrium rimmed with galleries. Passageways radiate from here, giving access to the associated shopping areas on several levels.

**Grundriß 2. Obergeschoß
mit Büronutzung und Wohnungen**
2nd floor plan
offices and apartments

**Grundriß 7. Obergeschoß
mit Büronutzung und Wohnungen**
7th floor plan
offices and apartments

1:750

Büro-, Wohn- und Geschäftshaus Quartier 205 Office and Apartment Building Block 205	Friedrichstadt Passagen	O.M. Ungers & Partner Berlin Oswald Mathias Ungers Projektleiter project manager: Karl-Heinz Winkens Sebastian Klatt	Mitarbeit staff Robert Beyer Chase Mc Carthy Hugo Daiber Guido Funke-Kaiser Angela Leonhardt Barbara Lutz Jarno Nillesen Tobias Scheel Birgit Schindler Nicoletta Zarattini

Bauherr:
Tishman Speyer Berlin GmbH & Co Friedrichstraße KG
Berlin

Planungstermine:
Wettbewerb 1991, 1. Preis
Entwurfsplanung seit 1991
Baubeginn 1992
Voraussichtlicher Bezug 1995

Nutzung:
Läden mit
16.000 m²
Büros mit
33.000 m²
36 Wohnungen
à 60–110 m²

Geschosse (IX):
EG und 1. OG Läden
2.–7. OG Büros
8. OG Wohnungen

Untergeschosse (IV):
1. UG (Zwischengeschoß) Technik
2. UG Läden, Passage
3.+4. UG Tiefgarage
(510 Pkw-Stellplätze)

Grundstücksgröße:
8.325 m²

Überbaute Fläche:
8.315 m²

Bruttogeschoßfläche:
94.600 m²

Perspektive
vom Gendarmenmarkt
von Nordosten
Computersimulation
Perspective view
of Gendarmenmarkt
from the northeast
Computer simulation

Projektadresse:
Location:
Friedrichstrasse 66-70/
Charlottenstrasse 57-59/
Mohrenstrasse 46-50
Taubenstrasse 14-15, 18
in
10117 Berlin-Mitte

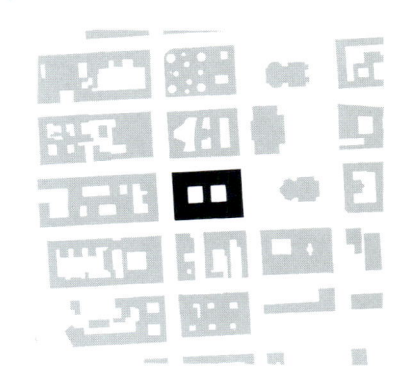

Client:
Tishman Speyer Berlin
GmbH & Co
Friedrichstrasse KG
Berlin

Project Stages:
Competition 1991, 1st prize
Design development from 1991
Start of construction 1992
Expected completion 1995

Building Use:
Shops totalling
16000 m²
Offices totalling
33000 m²
36 apartments
à 60-110 m²

Upper Floors (IX):
Ground floor and 1st floor shops
2nd-7th floor offices
8th floor apartments

Basement Floors (IV):
1st basement (intermediate level)
services
2nd basement shops, arcade
3rd-4th basement car park with
510 car spaces

Site Area:
8325 m²

Built Area:
8315 m²

Gross Floor Area:
94600 m²

**Eingang Friedrichstraße
von Westen
Computersimulation**
Friedrichstrasse entrance
from the west
Computer simulation

**Perspektive
Friedrichstraße / Ecke Mohrenstraße
von Süden
Computersimulation**
Perspective view
from the south
of the corner of Friedrichstrasse
and Mohrenstrasse
Computer simulation

Büro-, Wohn- und
Geschäftshaus
Quartier 205
Office and
Apartment Building
Block 205

Friedrichstadt Passagen

Das Bauwerk liegt auf dem südlichen Grundstück der Friedrichstadt Passagen. Es thematisiert den »Berliner Block« mit der Überlagerung von zwei unterschiedlichen Motiven: Von der Straßenkante zurückgesetzt entsteht ein 8-geschossiger, massiv wirkender Baublock mit zwei Innenhöfen oder Atrien; um diesen Kernbau gruppieren sich sechs »Einzelhäuser«, die die Fluchtlinie und Traufhöhe der Nachbarbebauung aufnehmen. Die quadratischen Grundrisse der Einzelhäuser überschneiden sich mit der Grundrißform des Kernblockes. Auch in den Materialien der Fassadenverblendungen – Klinker und Elbsandstein – heben sich diese beiden Elemente voneinander ab.

In den obersten drei Geschossen durchstoßen die Gebäudeflügel des Kernblocks die zurückspringende Attikafassade und zeichnen sich zur Straße hin als Kopfbauten ab. Insgesamt entsteht eine starke Differenzierung der Volumina des Großstadtblockes.

Im Bereich der Fassadeneinschnitte zwischen den »Einzelhäusern« liegen die Eingänge zu den Friedrichstadt Passagen und den im Erdgeschoß angrenzenden Läden. Vom 2. bis 7. Obergeschoß sieht der Entwurf eine reine Büronutzung, im 8. Obergeschoß Appartments und größere, um einen offenen Patio angelegte Wohnungen vor.

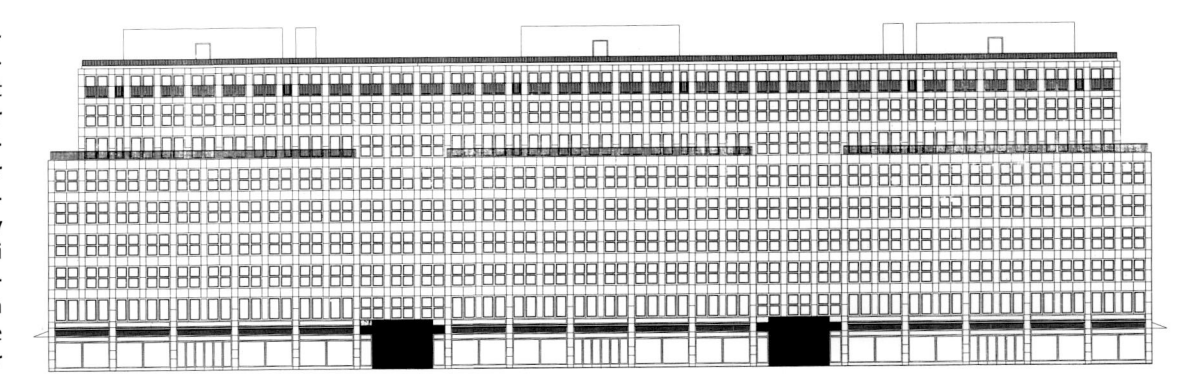

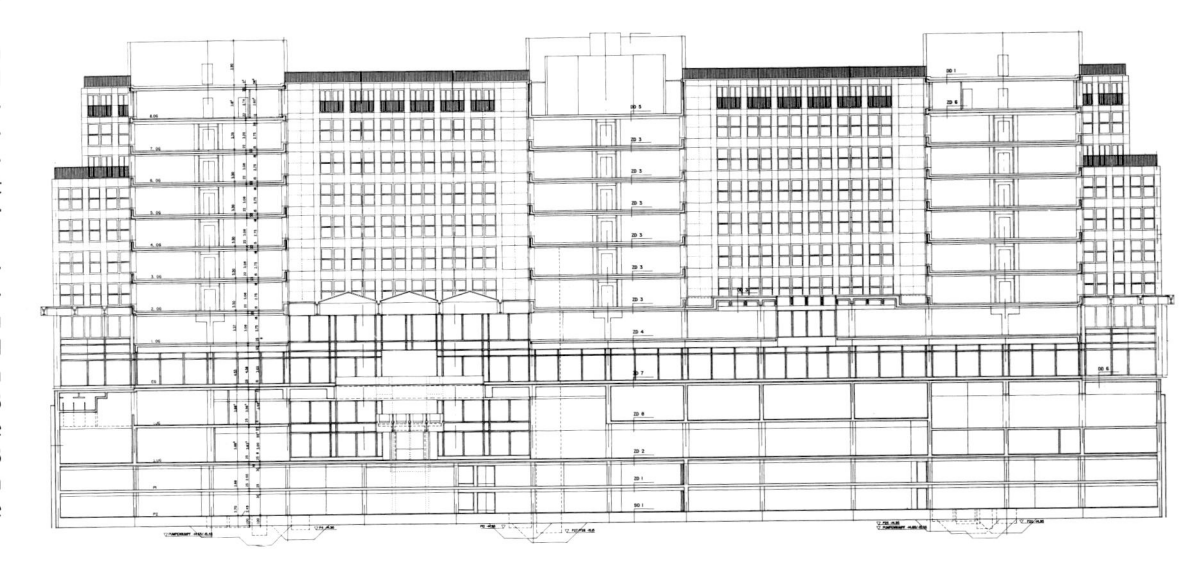

Ansicht Mohrenstraße
von Süden
South elevation
Mohrenstrasse

Gebäudelängsschnitt
in der Mittelachse
Central longitudinal section
of the building

1:750

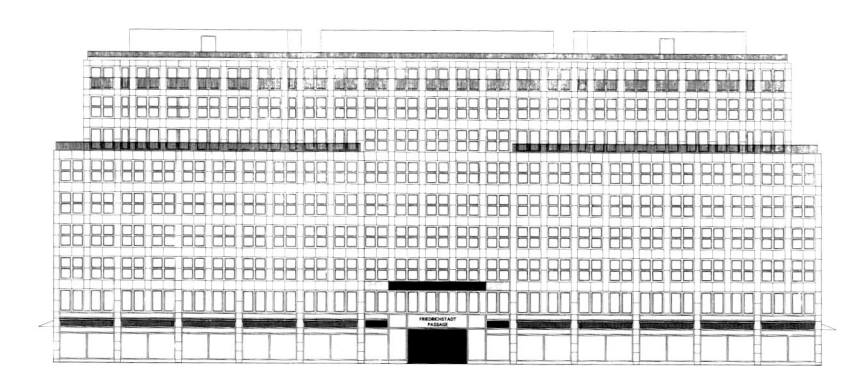

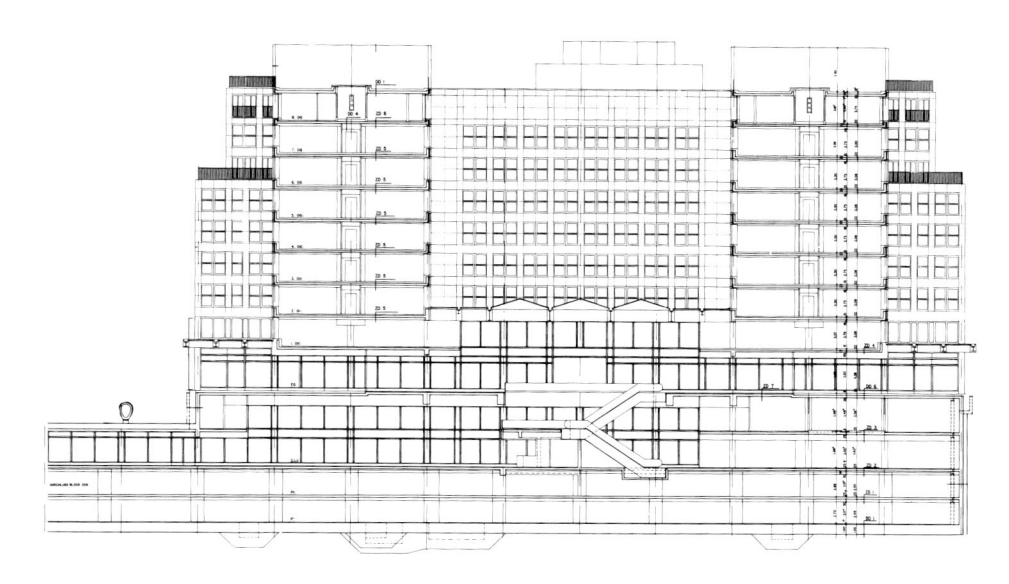

This building is situated on the southern part of the Friedrichstadt Passagen. It takes up the theme of the »Berlin Block« by overlapping two differing motifs. Set back from the street is an 8-storey block of monolithic appearance, with two inner courtyards or atria; grouped around this core structure are six »individual buildings« which echo the lines and eaves heights of surrounding development. The square ground plans of the individual buildings overlap with the ground plan of the core block. Differing facing materials – clinker brick and Elbe sandstone – further distinguish the two elements.

In the uppermost three floors the wings of the core block pierce the roof parapet which is set back slightly. The general impression is a great differentiation in the volume of this city block.

The entrances to the Friedrichstadt Passagen and the ground floor shops are located in the gap between the two »individual buildings«. The 2nd to 7th floors are intended for office use, with apartments of varying sizes on the top floor, the larger ones grouped around an open patio.

Ansicht Friedrichstraße von Westen
West elevation
Friedrichstrasse

Gebäudequerschnitt
Cross section

1:750

Büro-, Wohn- und Geschäftshaus Quartier 205
Office and Apartment Building Block 205

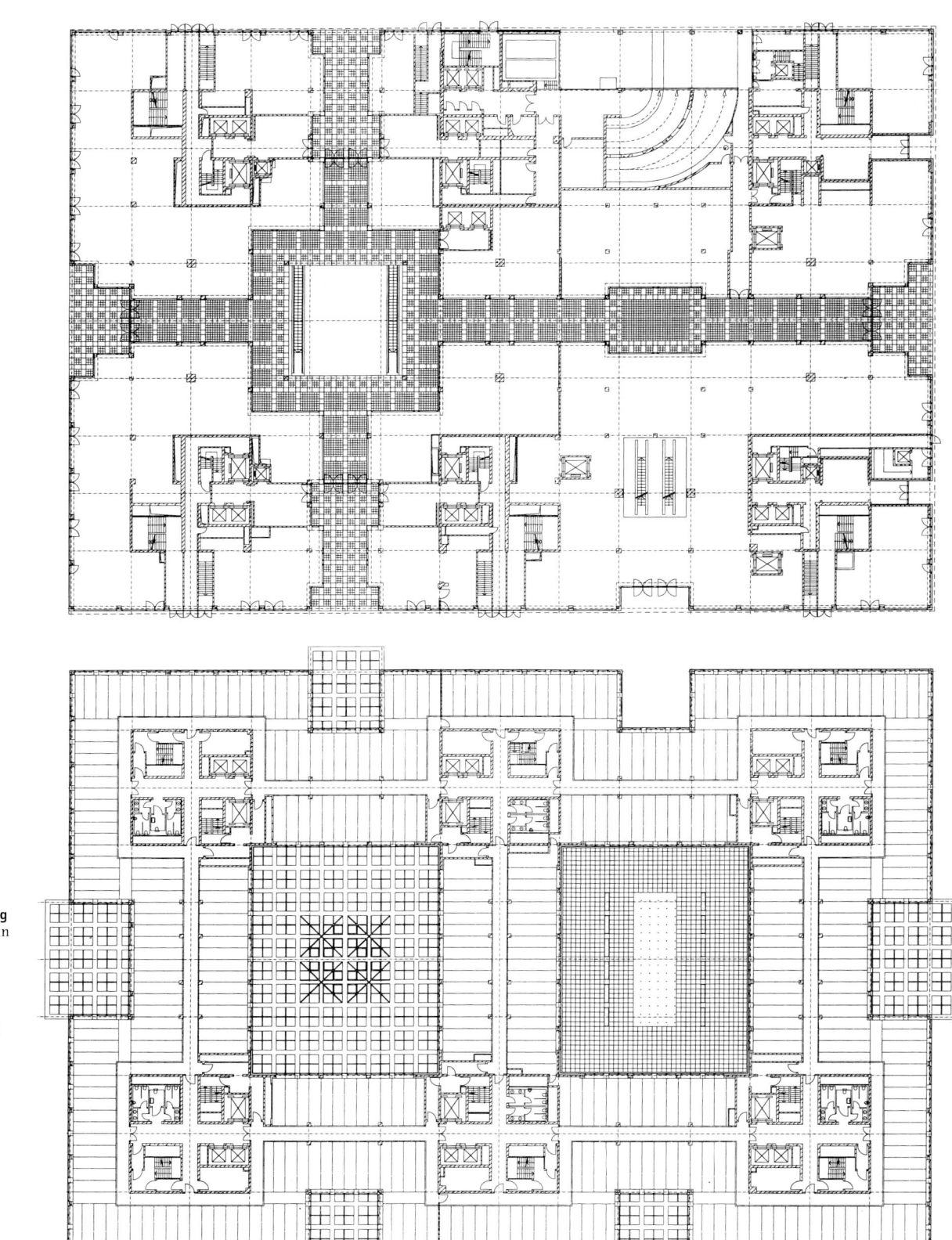

Friedrichstadt Passagen

Grundriß Erdgeschoß mit Ladennutzung
Ground floor plan retail

Grundriß 3. Obergeschoß mit Büronutzung
3rd floor plan offices

1:750

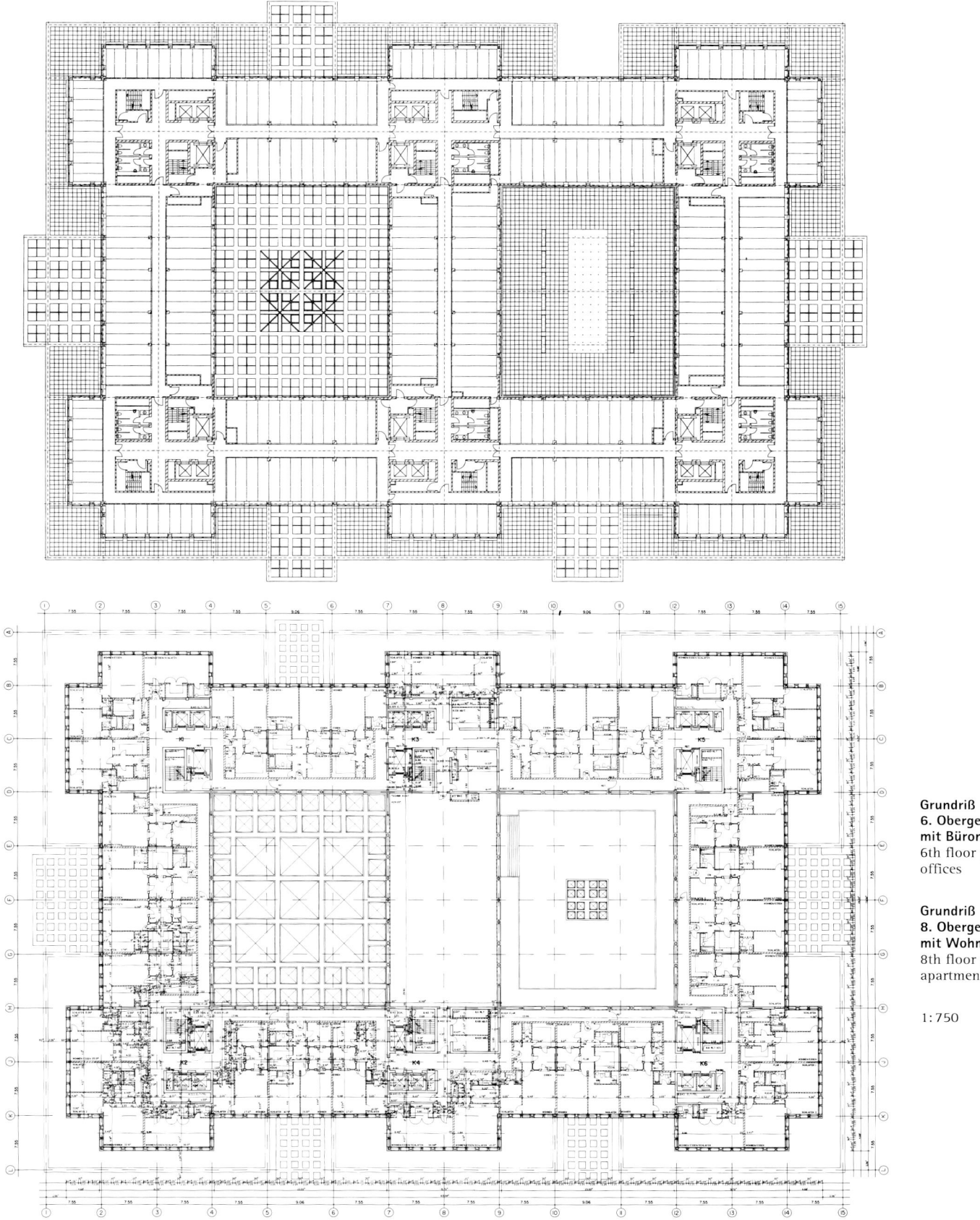

Grundriß
6. Obergeschoß
mit Büronutzung
6th floor plan
offices

Grundriß
8. Obergeschoß
mit Wohnungen
8th floor plan
apartments

1:750

Büro-, Wohn- und
Geschäftshaus
Quartier 108
Office and
Apartment Building
Block 108

VICTORIA

Thomas van den Valentyn
Köln
mit with
Norbert Kostka

Mitarbeit staff
Bernd Driessen
Benedikt Baumewerd
Lukas Baumewerd
Angela Ader
Axel Schoth
Christoph Merten

Bauherr:
VICTORIA Lebensversicherung AG
Düsseldorf

Planungstermine:
Entwurfsplanung seit 1993
Baubeginn 1995
Voraussichtlicher Bezug 1996

Nutzung:
7 Läden mit
3.745 m² Hauptnutzfläche
390 Büros mit
9.365 m² Hauptnutzfläche
34 Wohnungen mit
2.790 m² Hauptnutzfläche

Geschosse (IX):
EG Läden
1.-5. OG Büros
6.-8. OG Büros, Wohnungen

Untergeschosse (II):
1. UG (3.700 m²
Bruttogeschoßfläche)
mit Läden, Anlieferung, Technik
2. UG (3.700 m² Brutto-
geschoßfläche)
mit Tiefgarage, Lager, Technik

Grundstücksgröße:
3.679 m²

Überbaute Fläche:
3.679 m²

Bruttogeschoßfläche:
25.284 m²

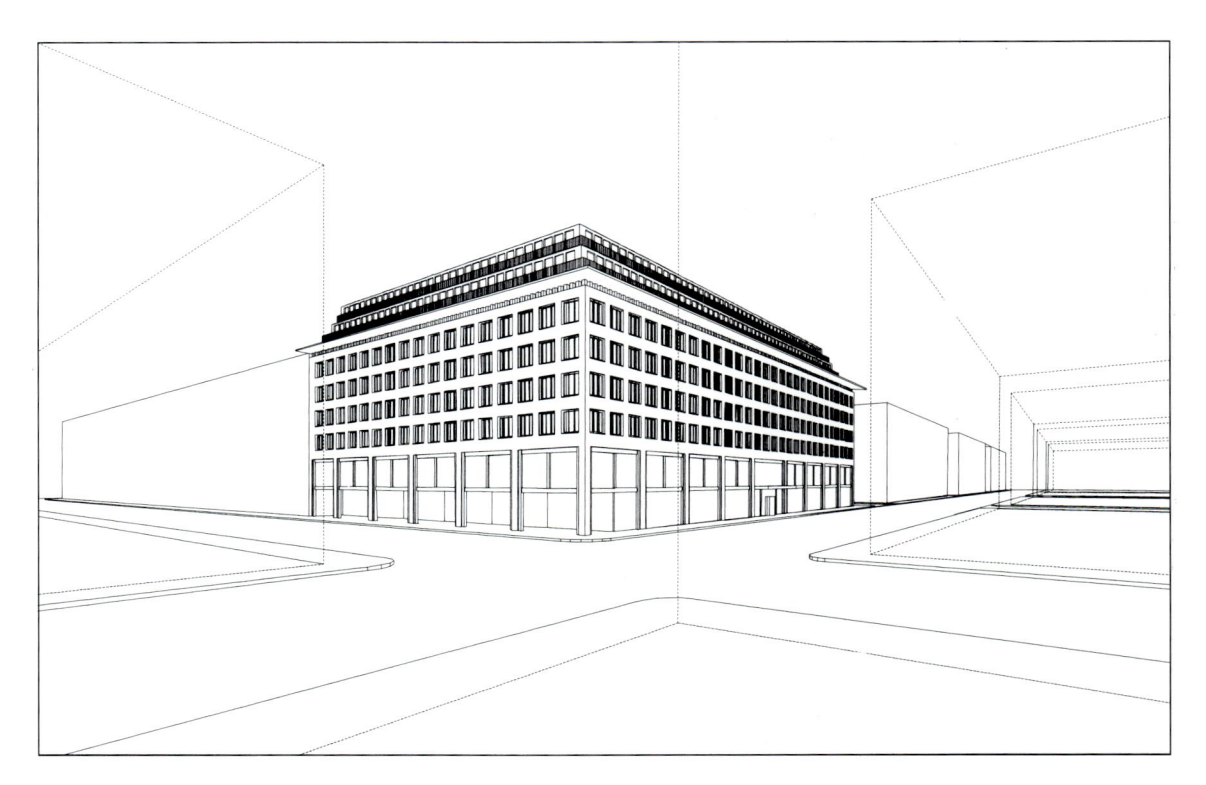

Perspektive des Gebäudes an
der Kreuzung Leipziger Straße /
Friedrichstraße
Perspective drawing of the building
on the junction of Leipziger Strasse
and Friedrichstrasse

Arkade an der Leipziger Straße
Computersimulation
Arcade on Leipziger Strasse
Computer simulation

Projektadresse:
Location:
**Friedrichstrasse 192-193/
Leipziger Strasse 103-105/
Kronenstrasse 12-14**
in
10969 Berlin-Mitte

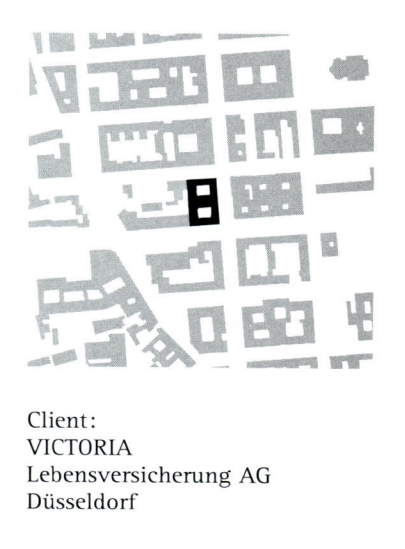

Client:
VICTORIA
Lebensversicherung AG
Düsseldorf

Project Stages:
Design development from 1993
Start of construction 1995
Expected completion 1996

Building Use:
7 shops totalling
3745 m² main floor space
390 offices totalling
9365 m² main floor space
34 apartments totalling
2790 m² main floor space

Upper Floors (IX):
Ground floor shops
1st-5th floor offices
6th-8th floor offices, apartments

Basement Floors (II):
1st basement
(3700 m² gross floor area)
shops, delivery, services
2nd basement
(3700 m² gross floor area)
car park, storeroom, services

Site Area:
3679 m²

Built Area:
3679 m²

Gross Floor Area:
25284 m²

**Traufgesims und Staffelgeschosse
an der Leipziger Straße
Computersimulation**
Eaves cornice and storeys
stepped back from the façade
plane on Leipziger Strasse
Computer simulation

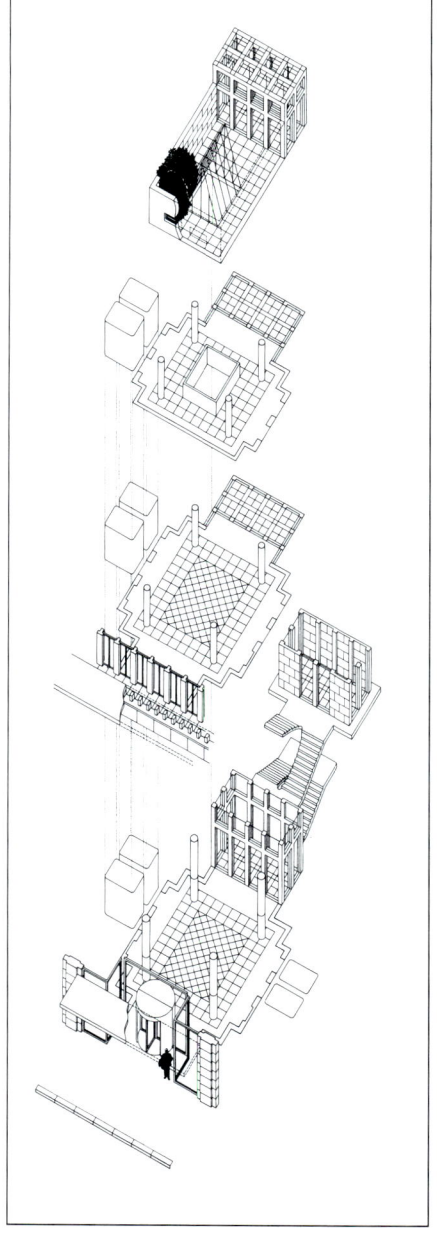

**Eingangshalle, Foyer
und Vertikalerschließung
Isometrische Darstellung**
Entrance hall, foyer
and vertical circulation
Isometric projection

Büro-, Wohn- und
Geschäftshaus
Quartier 108   VICTORIA
Office and
Apartment Building
Block 108

Das Haus nimmt als großstädtischer 9-geschossiger Block die Fluchtlinien des historischen Stadtgrundrisses auf. Als monolithischer Baukörper ergänzt und definiert es die Blockbebauung nach Osten hin; Friedrichstraße und Leipziger Straße werden dabei auf ihre historische Breite zurückgebaut. Der in den 80er Jahren an der Ecke Friedrichstraße/Leipziger Straße als Casino errichtete Plattenbau war aufgrund der angestrebten Straßenverbreiterungen deutlich hinter die historische Flucht zurückgesetzt. Da seine Grundstruktur und Bauweise keine Änderungen an Gestalt und Nutzungsart zulassen, weicht er dem Neubau des VICTORIA-Gebäudes.

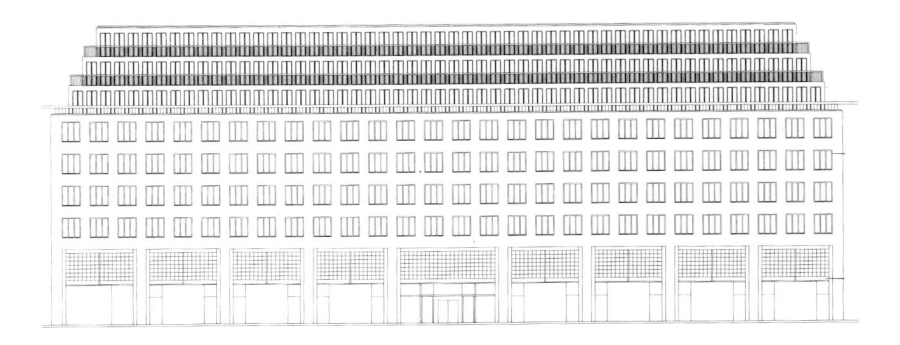

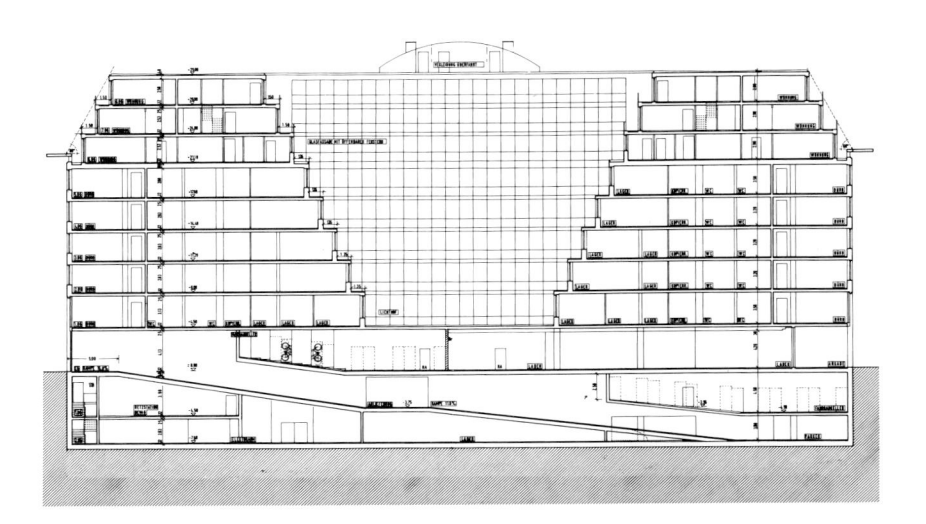

Ansicht Friedrichstraße
Friedrichstrasse elevation

Gebäudelängsschnitt im Bereich des Lichthofes an der Grundstücksgrenze zum Nachbarhaus
Longitudinal section through the inner courtyard area at the border to the adjacent building

Gebäudelängsschnitt im Bereich der Innenhöfe
Longitudinal section through the inner courtyards

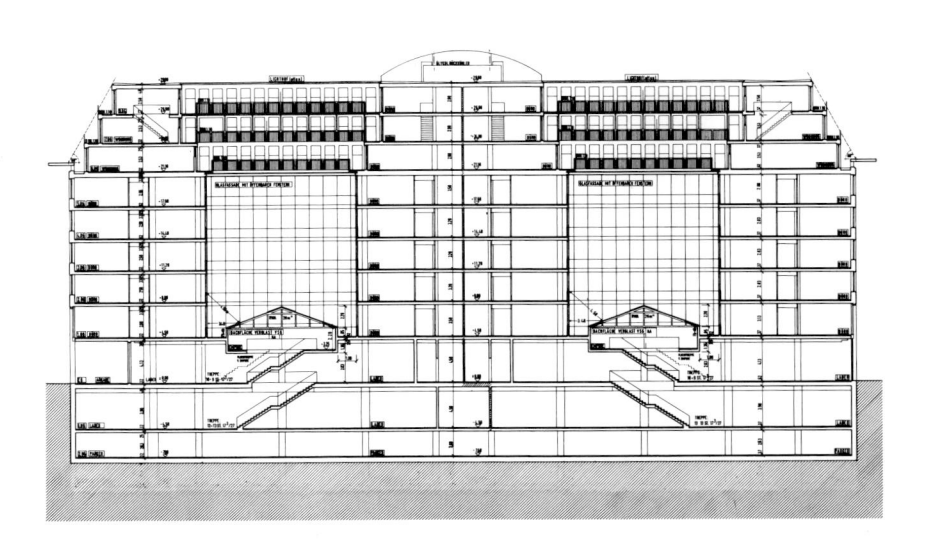

1:750

This large, 9-storey building follows the line of the historic structure of the city. Its monolithic form extends and defines the block development towards the east; Friedrichstrasse and Leipziger Strasse thus regain their former width. A slab-built casino, built on this spot in the 1980s, had been positioned considerably further back than the original line of the buildings, as part of the general plan at the time to widen street areas. Since, however, the basic structure and construction of the building did not allow for any changes of use or form, it is to be demolished to make way for the new VICTORIA building.

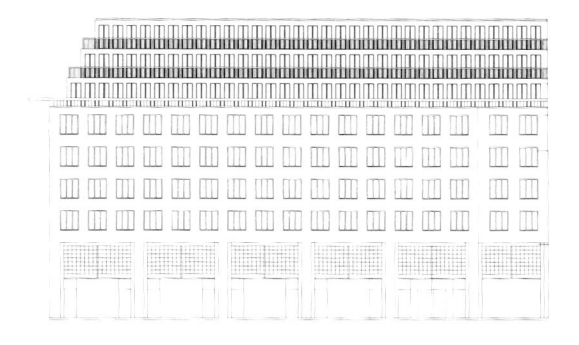

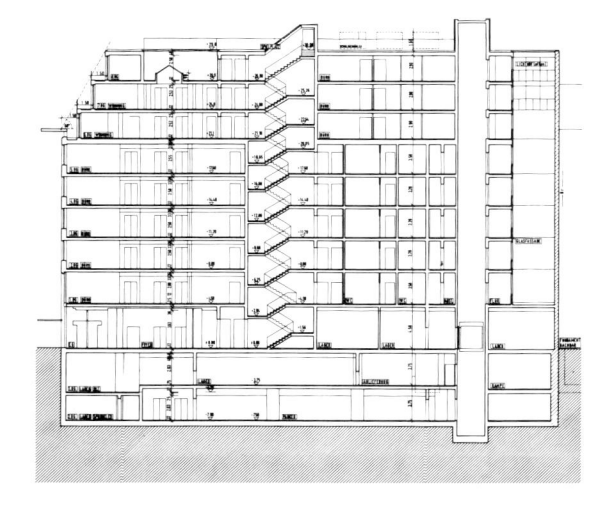

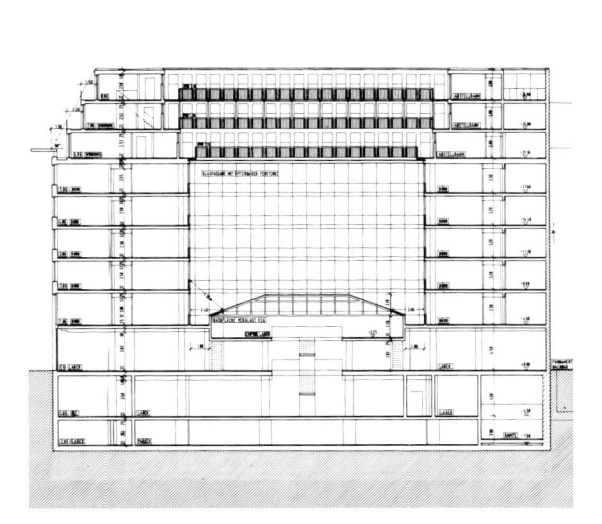

Ansicht Kronenstraße von Norden
North elevation
Kronenstrasse

Gebäudequerschnitt im Bereich des Haupterschließungskerns
Cross section
through the main communications core area

Gebäudequerschnitt im Bereich des südlichen Innenhofs
Cross section through
the southern inner
courtyard area

1:750

Büro-, Wohn- und
Geschäftshaus
Quartier 108   VICTORIA
Office and
Apartment Building
Block 108

Grundriß Erdgeschoß
mit Ladennutzung
Ground floor plan
retail

Grundriß Normalgeschoß
(2. – 5. Obergeschoß)
mit Büronutzung
Typical floor plan
(2nd to 5th upper floors)
offices

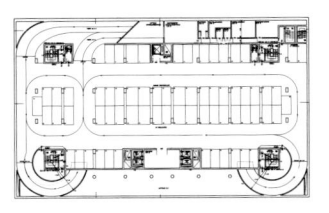

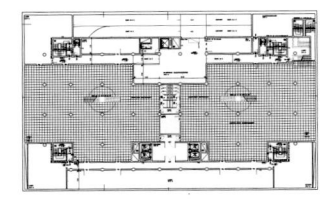

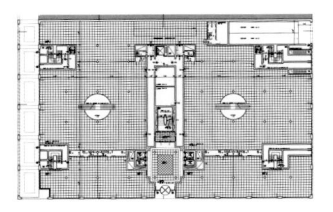

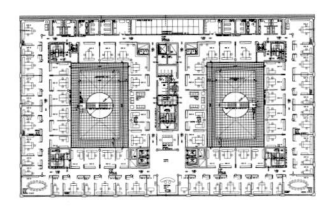

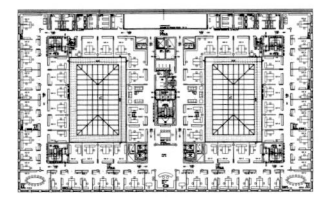

1:750

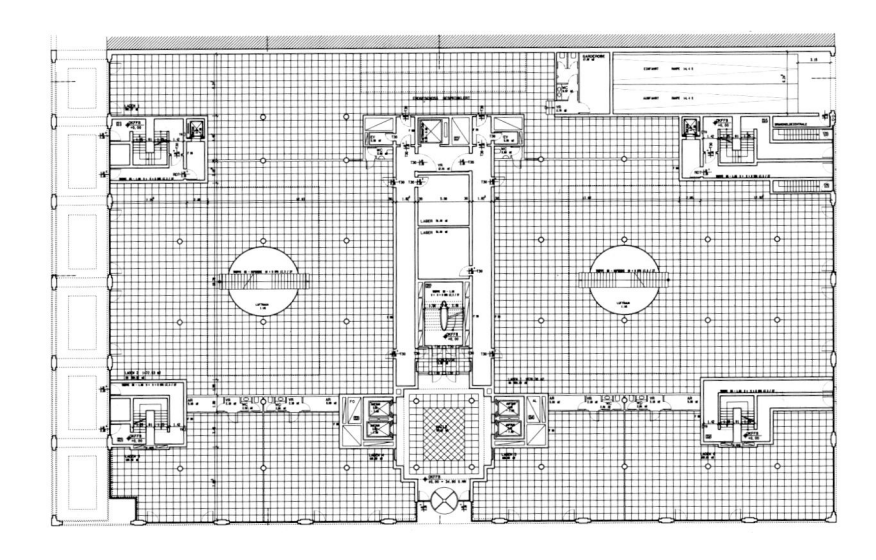

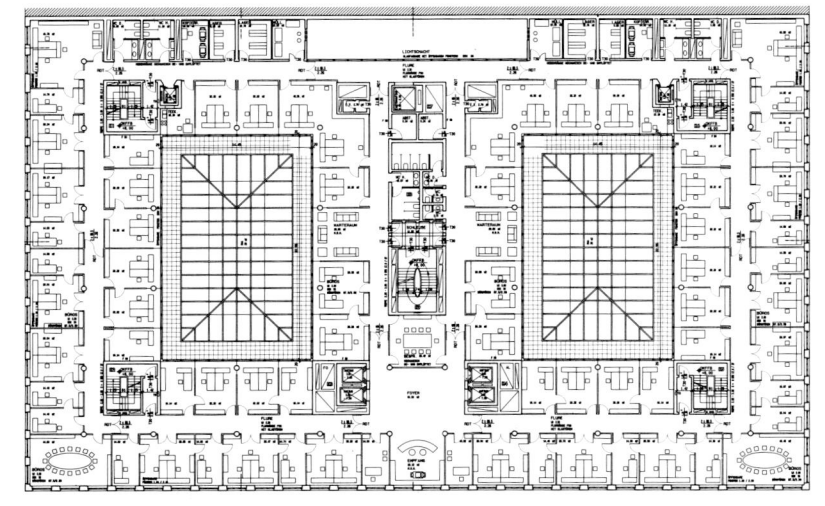

Grundrisse aller Geschosse
Plan of all floors

1:2000

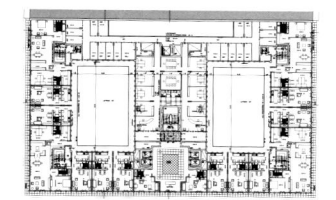

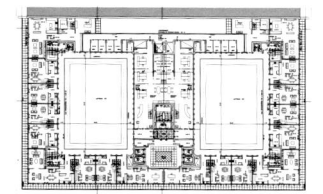

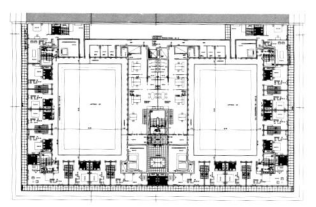

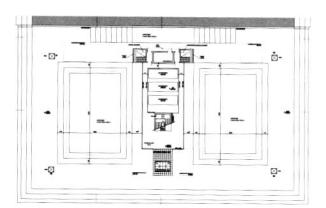

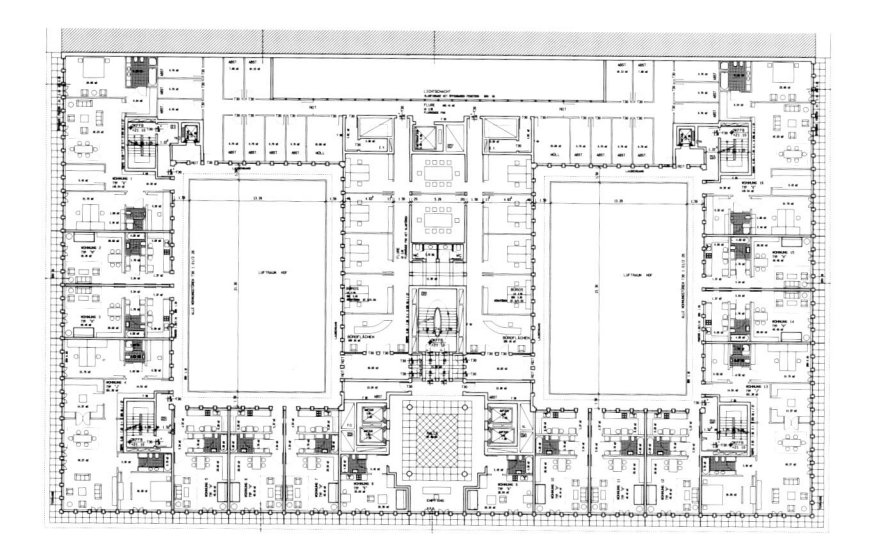

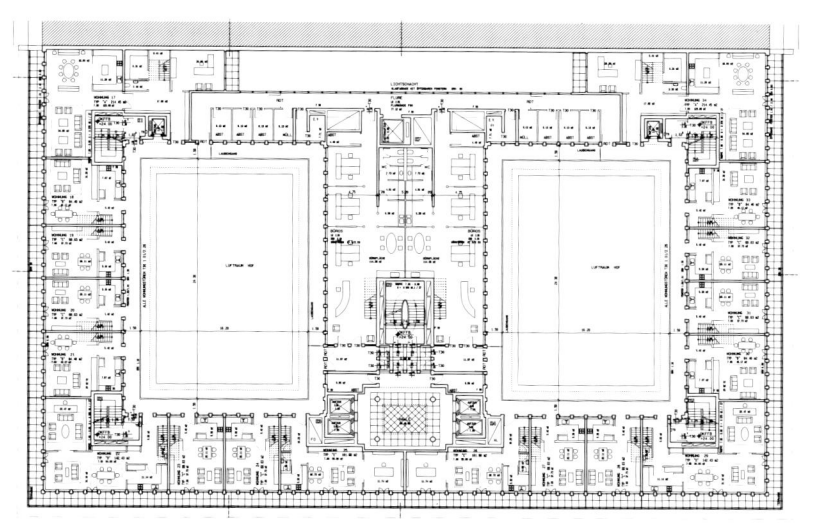

Grundrisse
der Attikageschosse
(6., 7. und 8. Obergeschoß)
mit Wohnungen und,
im Mittelflügel,
Büronutzung
Plans of attic floors
(6th, 7th and 8th floors)
with apartments and,
in the central section, offices

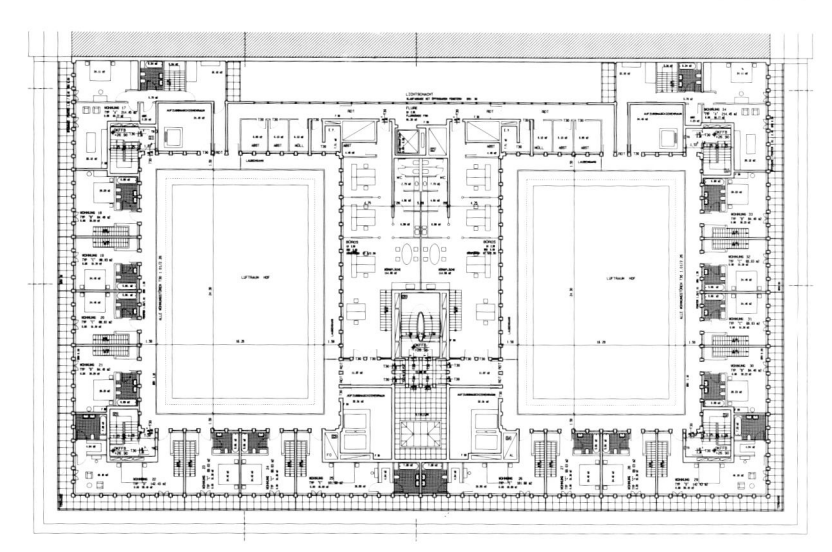

Büro-, Hotel- und Geschäftshaus
Office, Hotel and Apartment Building

Centre Paris-Berlin

Claude Vasconi
Paris
mit with
W. R. Borchardt, Berlin

Mitarbeit Wettbewerb
Staff competition
Guy Bez
Dagmar Gross
Margrith Hartmann
Jean-François Pasqualini
Katja Gäbel
Henrike Böhm

Bauherr:
EUWO Holding AG und Partner
Berlin

Planungstermine:
Wettbewerb 1992, 1. Preis
Entwurfsplanung seit 1993
Baubeginn voraussichtlich 1995
Voraussichtlicher Bezug 1996/1997

Nutzung:
Läden mit
1.100 m² Bruttogeschoßfläche
Büros mit
28.000 m² Bruttogeschoßfläche
126 Wohnungen
(96 à 1 1/2 Zimmer,
30 à 3 Zimmer)
76 Wohnungen à 1 1/2 Zimmer
(Appartments/Hotel)
Bibliothek mit 4.644 m²

Geschosse:
Gebäude A (XII):
EG Läden, Büros
1.-11. OG Büros
Gebäude B (X):
EG Läden, 1.-9. OG Büros
Gebäude C (X):
EG und 1. OG Bibliothek
2.-9. OG Hotel

Untergeschosse (II):
1. UG Atrium mit Restaurantbetrieben, Lager, Tiefgarage
2. UG Tiefgarage, Lager

Grundstücksgröße:
7.700 m²

Überbaute Fläche:
ca. 6.650 m²

Bruttogeschoßfläche:
45.600 m²

Blick nach Nordosten
von der Mollstraße
Modellaufnahme
Wettbewerb 1992
Looking northeast from Mollstrasse
Model photo
Competition 1992

Ansicht Hans-Beimler-Straße
von Nordwesten
Northwest elevation
Hans-Beimler-Strasse

1:750

Das Centre Paris-Berlin entsteht auf einem Areal nördlich des Alexanderplatzes. Das Stadtbild ist an dieser Stelle durch die Plattenbauten der 60er Jahre geprägt. Ein auf dem Standort vorhandenes 18-geschossiges Wohngebäude wird aufgrund bautechnischer Mängel abgerissen.
Ziel des Entwurfs von Claude Vasconi ist die Neuordnung des Quartiers mit neudefinierten Baufluchten, abgestimmten Gebäudehöhen und einer verträglichen innerstädtischen Verdichtung. Die in der Nachkriegszeit zugunsten der Großblockform zerschlagene Parzellenstruktur wird durch ein als Stadtraum erfahrbares Viertel ersetzt.
Leitmotiv des architektonischen Entwurfes ist eine fiktive Diagonale zwischen Alexanderplatz und Volkspark Friedrichshain. Sie definiert den städtischen Block und bildet den Schlüssel zur inneren Organisation. Das Bürogebäude an der Ecke Mollstraße/Hans-Beimler-Straße bildet durch seine Gebäudehöhe und seine markante dreieckige Grundrißform einen wichtigen städtebauliche Akzent.

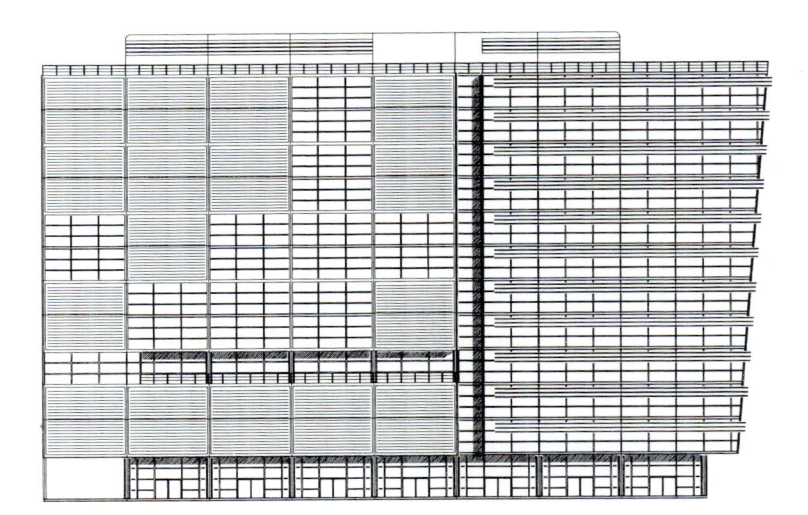

Mitarbeit Planung
Staff planning
Guido Loeckx
Dagmar Gross
Henrike Böhm

Projektadresse:
Location:
Mollstrasse 31
in
10249 Berlin-Friedrichshain

»Dreiecksgebäude« und Bürogebäude
an der Hans-Beimler-Straße/
Ecke Mollstraße
Computersimulation
»Triangle Building« and office building
on the corner of Hans-Beimler-Strasse
and Mollstrasse
Computer simulation

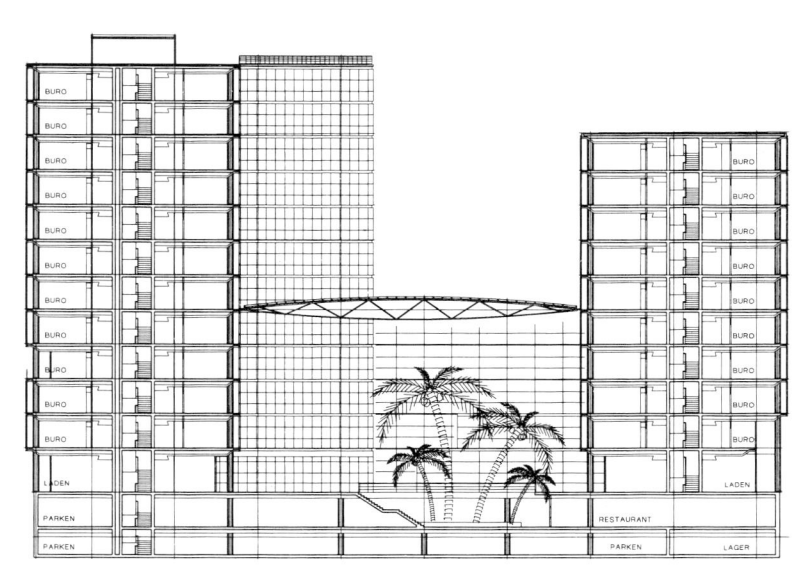

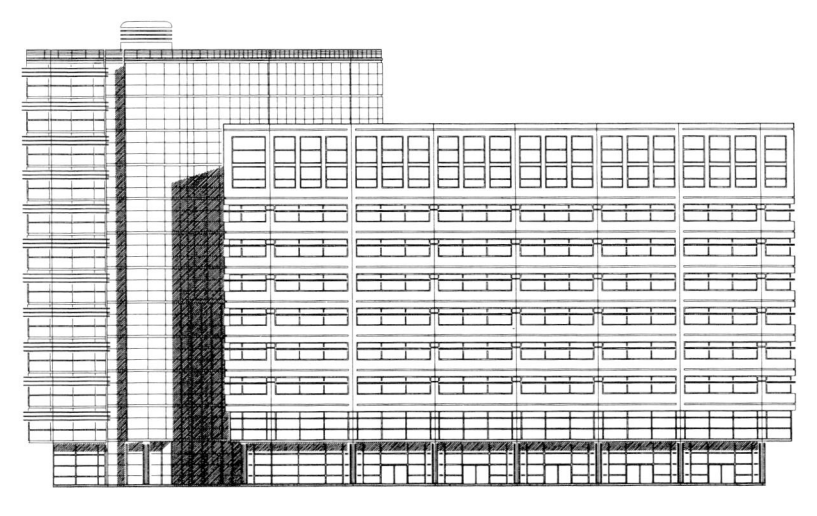

Gebäudeschnitt
im Bereich des Atriums
Section through atrium area

Ansicht Mollstraße
von Südwesten
Southwest elevation
Mollstrasse

1:750

Client:
EUWO Holding AG und Partner
Berlin

Project Stages:
Competition 1992, 1st prize
Design development from 1993
Start of construction expected 1995
Expected completion 1996/1997

Building Use:
Shops totalling
1100 m² gross floor area
Offices totalling
28000 m² gross floor area
126 apartments
(96 à 1 1/2 rooms, 30 à 3 rooms)
76 apartments
à 1 1/2 room (suites/hotel)
Library, 4644 m²

Upper Floors:
Building A (XII):
Ground floor shops, offices
1st-11th floor offices
Building B (X):
Ground floor shops
1st-9th floor offices
Building C (X):
Ground and 1st floor library
2nd-9th floor hotel

Basement Floors (II):
1st basement atrium with
restaurants storeroom, car park
2nd basement car park, storeroom

Site area:
7700 m²

Built Area:
ca. 6650 m²

Gross Floor Area:
45600 m²

The Paris-Berlin Centre occupies a site to the north of Alexanderplatz. In this area 1960's slab buildings dominate the urban scene. An 18-storey apartment block standing on the site is to be demolished because of structural defects.
Claude Vasconi's plan aims at reorganising the district and redefining building lines, aligning building heights and achieving an acceptable level of inner city development density. The tower block type of development which after the war replaced the former small city block structure is now to give way to a district with a distinct urban character.
A principle theme in the architectural design is an imaginary diagonal between Alexanderplatz and the Volkspark Friedrichshain. It gives definition to the urban block and is the key to its inner organisation. The office building on the corner of Mollstrasse and Hans-Beimler-Strasse sets a key urban accent through its height and its distinctive triangular ground plan.

Büro-, Hotel- und
Geschäftshaus Centre Paris-Berlin
Office, Hotel and
Apartment Building

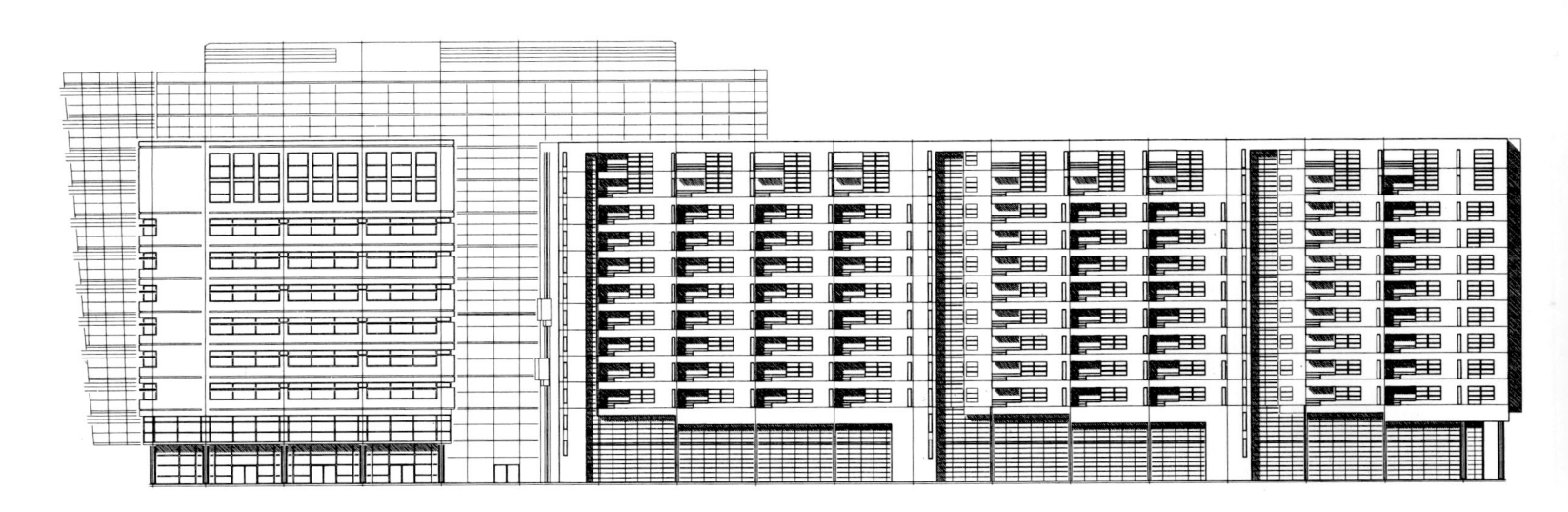

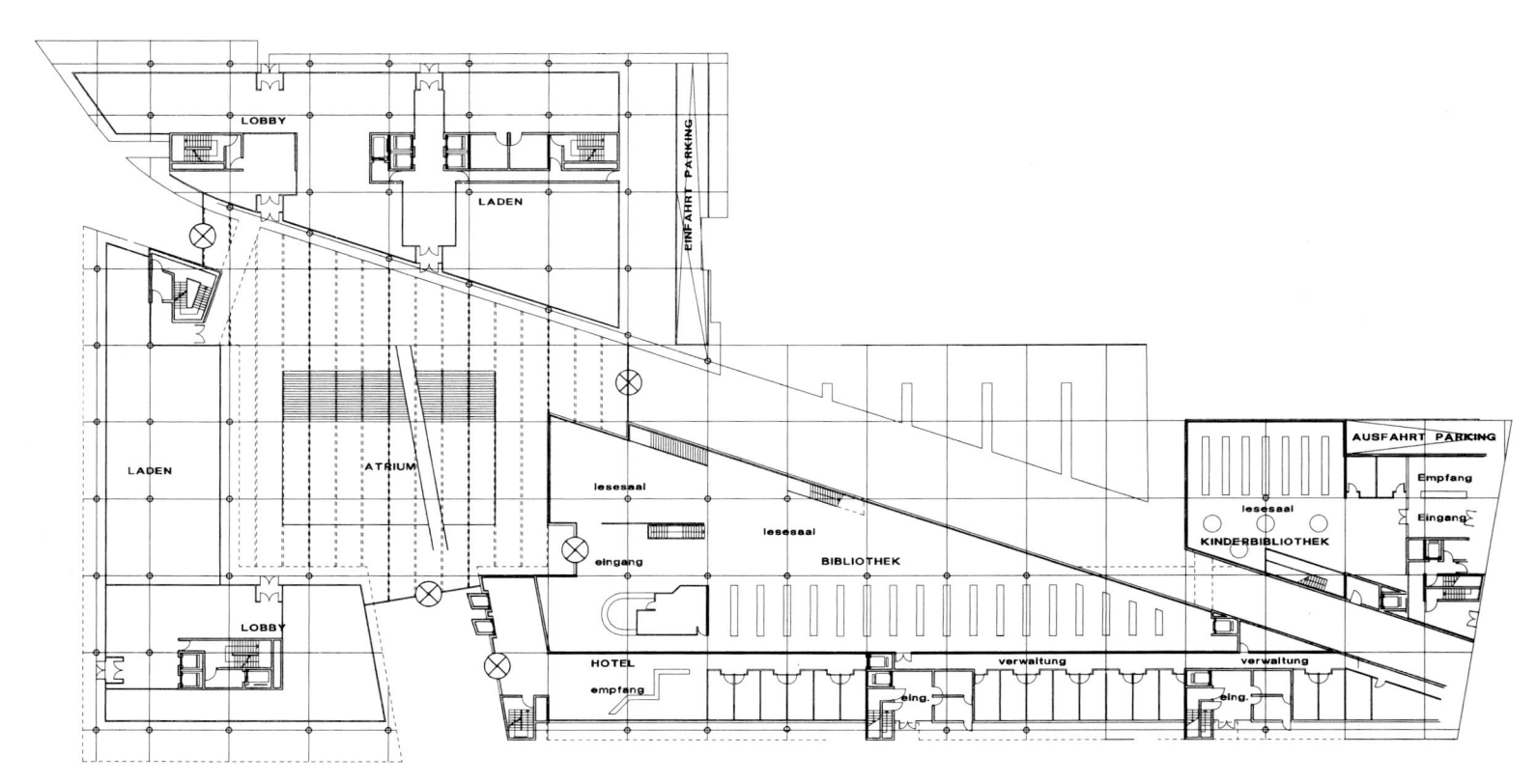

**Ansicht Georgenkirchstraße
von Südosten**
Southeast elevation
Georgenkirchstrasse

**Grundriß Erdgeschoß
mit Ladennutzung, Atrium,
Hotelempfang, Bibliothek**
Ground floor plan
retail, atrium, hotel reception, library

1:750

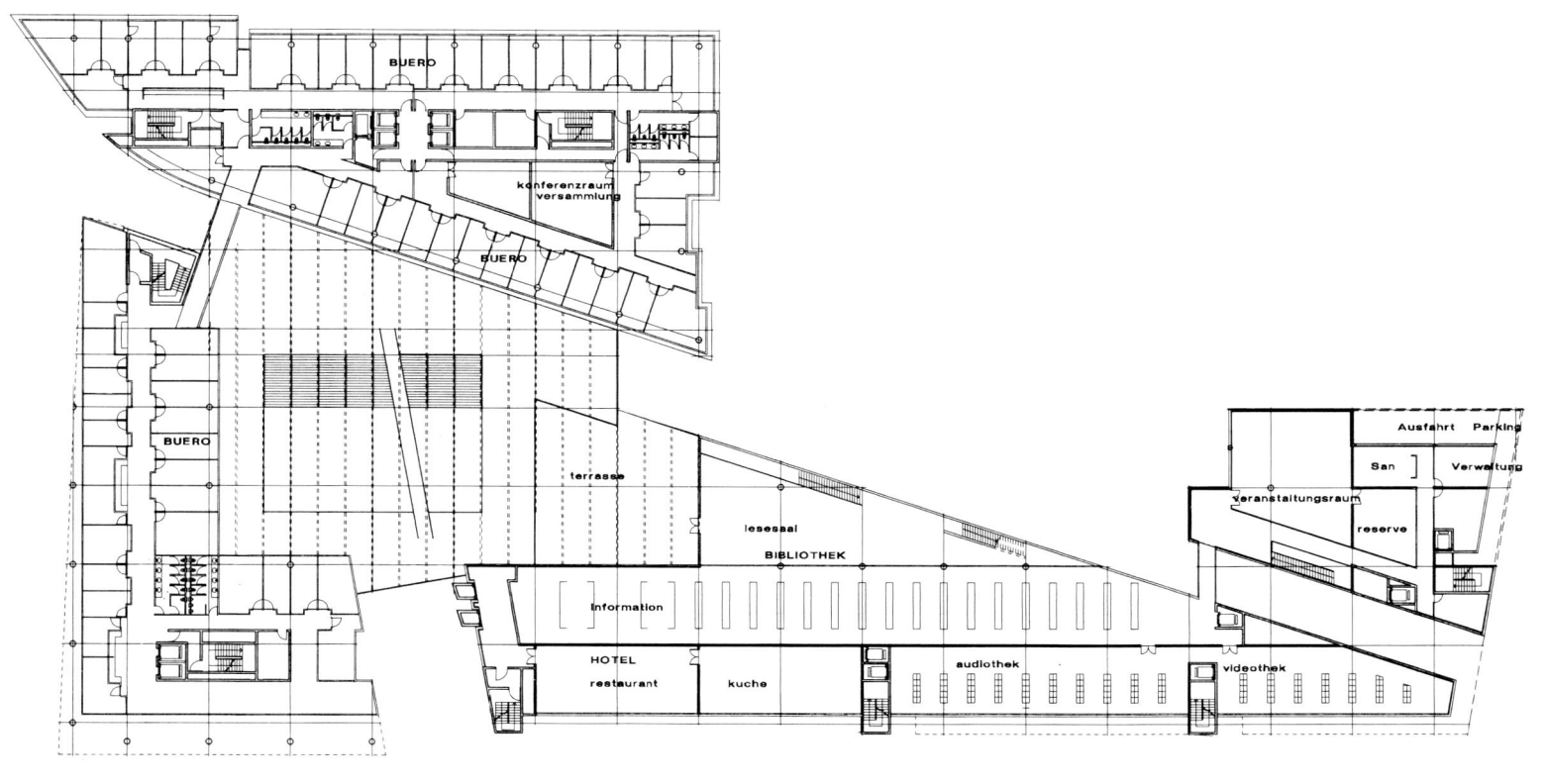

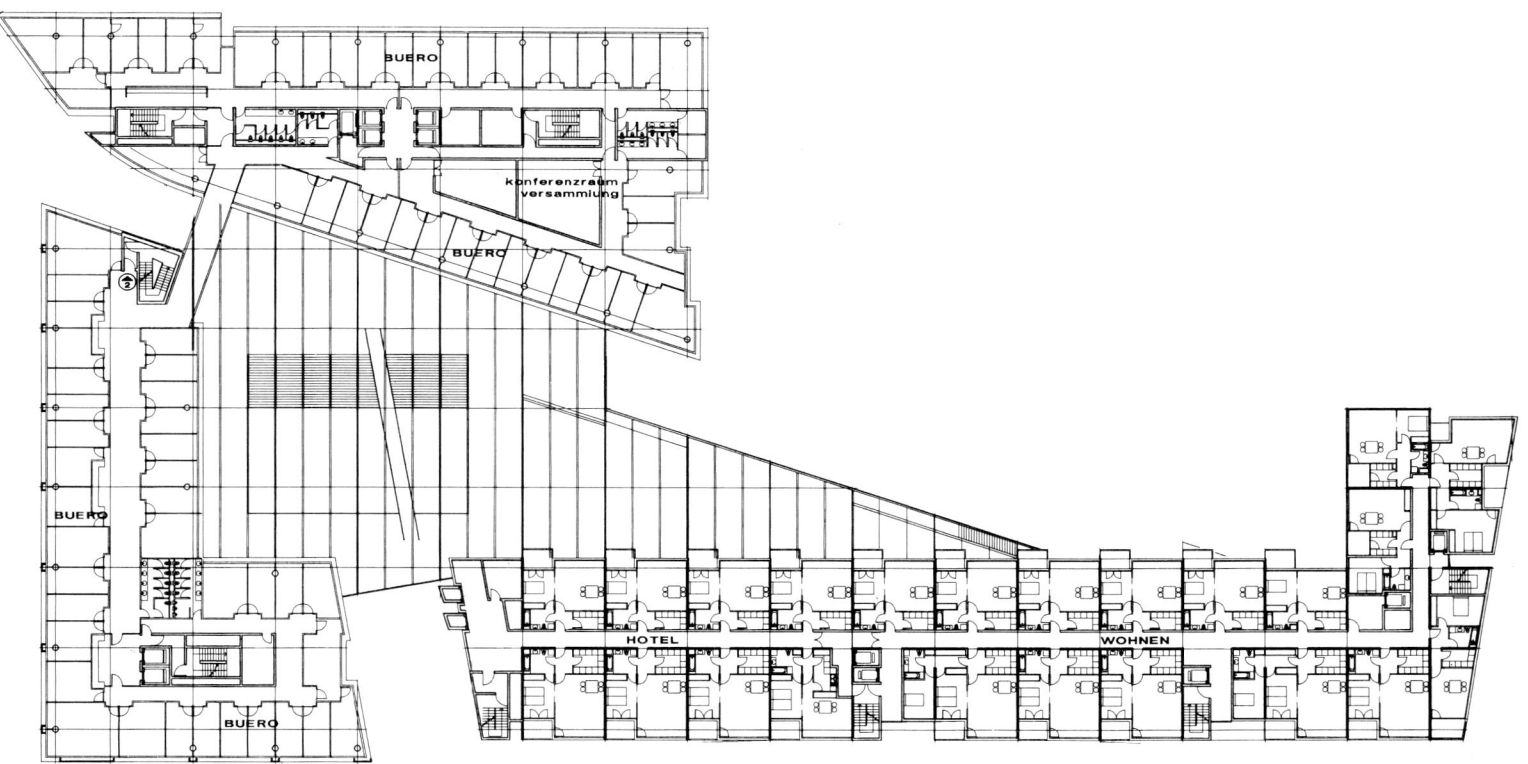

Grundriß 1. Obergeschoß
mit Büronutzung, Hotel, Bibliothek
1st floor plan
offices, hotel, library

1:750

Grundriß 5.-7. Obergeschoß
mit Büronutzung bzw.
6.-10. Obergeschoß mit
Hotel und Wohnungen
Plans of 5th to 7th floors
offices and 6th to 10th floors
hotel and apartments

1:750

Börse und
Dienstleistungszentrum
Stock Exchange and
Services Centre

Ludwig Erhard Haus

Grimshaw & Partners
London
Nicholas Grimshaw
Neven Sidor

Mitarbeit staff
Michael Pross
Paul Grayshon
Mathew Keeler
Stefan Camenzind
Ingrid Bille
Andrew Hall
David Kirkla
Garry Colligan
Will Stephens
John Lee
Martin Bauer
Philip Enklebrecht

Bauherr:
Industrie- und Handelskammer
zu Berlin

Planungstermine:
Wettbewerb 1991, 1. Preis
Entwurfsplanung seit 1991
Baubeginn Ende 1994
Voraussichtlicher Bezug 1997

Nutzung:
Service- und
Kommunikationszentrum
mit Börse
Büros mit
17.800 m²

Geschosse (X):
EG Börse (1.200 m²), Restaurant
(830 m²), »Innere Straße«
(1.450m²)
1. OG Büros, Verein Berliner
Kaufleute und Industrieller,
2.-9. OG Büros

Untergeschosse (II):
1. UG Konferenzzentrum (450
Plätze), Vortragssaal (100 Plätze)
mit Foyer, Tiefgarage
(101 Pkw-Stellplätze)
2. UG Tiefgarage
(147 Pkw-Stellplätze), Technik

Grundstücksgröße:
9.000 m²

Überbaute Fläche:
5.320 m²

Bruttogeschoßfläche:
30.713 m²

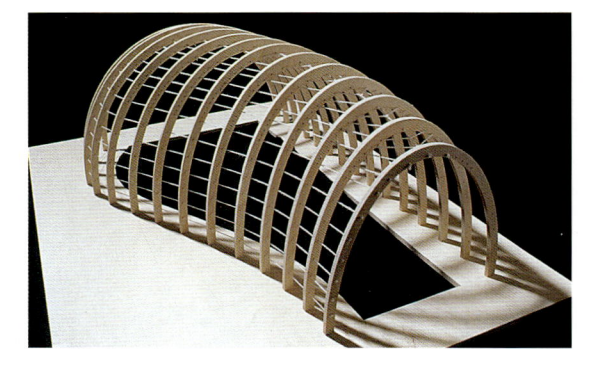

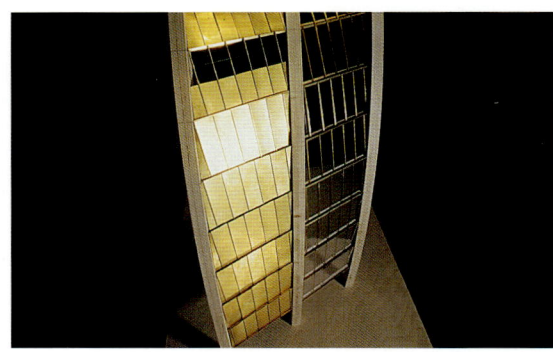

Blick von Südwesten
Modellaufnahme
View from the southwest
Model photo

Tragwerk,
Modellaufnahme
Support structure,
model photo

Fassadenstudie,
Modellaufnahme
Façade study,
model photo

Die Börse mit Kommunikations- und Dienstleistungszentrum entsteht in zentraler Lage der City West. Sie ist als kompakter, geschlossener Gebäudekomplex mit starker und eigenwilliger Formgebung konzipiert. Das Bauwerk soll auf dem unregelmäßig zugeschnittenen Gelände die angrenzende Teilbebauung des Blockes unter Einhaltung der Traufhöhe komplettieren. Die Komplexität der Nutzungen führte zur Kon-

Projektadresse:
Location:
Fasanenstrasse 83-84
in
10623 Berlin-Charlottenburg

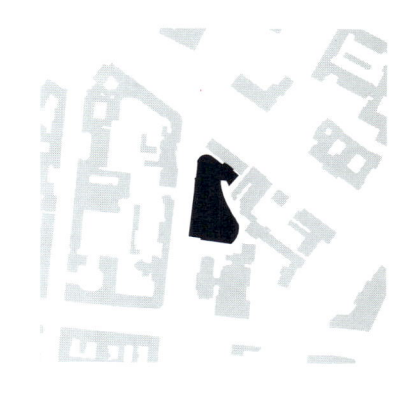

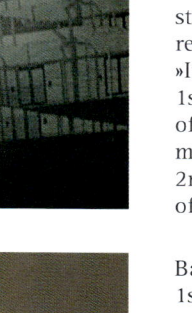

Client:
Chamber of Industry and
Commerce in Berlin

Project Stages:
Competition 1991, 1st prize
Design development from 1991
Start of construction end 1994
Expected completion 1997

Building Use:
Services and communications
centre with stock exchange
Offices totalling
17800 m^2

Upper Floors (X):
Ground floor
stock exchange (1200 m^2)
restaurant (830 m^2)
»Internal Street« (1450 m^2)
1st floor
offices, Association of Businessmen and Industrialists in Berlin
2nd-9th floor
offices

Basement Floors (II):
1st basement
conference centre (450 seats)
lecture hall (100 seats)
with foyer, car park
(101 parking spaces)
2nd basement
car park (147 parking spaces),
building services

Site Area:
9000 m^2

Built Area:
5320 m^2

Gross Floor Area:
30713 m^2

**Blick auf die Atriumfassade
mit Brücke und Aufgang
Computersimulation**
View of the atrium façade
with bridge and approach
Computer simulation

**Eingangshalle mit Konferenzsaal
Computersimulation**
Entrance hall with conference hall
Computer simulation

**Börsenparkett
Computersimulation**
Floor of stock exchange
Computer simulation

The stock exchange and communications and services centre is located in the centre of the City West. The compact, closed building complex has a strong individual design. On its irregularly sized plot it is intended to complement and link up with the neighbouring buildings, keeping the same eaves height. The many different functions of the building led to the idea of an »internal street«, from which one

**Börse und
Dienstleistungszentrum**
Stock Exchange and
Services Centre

Ludwig Erhard Haus

zeption einer öffentlich zugänglichen »internen Straße«, von der aus man Einblick in den Börsensaal und Zugang zu Konferenzzentrum, Restaurant und Büros erhält. Dieser zweigeschossige Raum ist zur Fasanenstraße in voller Höhe verglast; Stadtraum und Gebäudeinneres werden miteinander verwoben. Die komplexen Ansprüche an Nutzung, Raum und Technologie, wie sie mit einem modernen Kommunikations- und Dienstleistungszentrum verbunden werden, spiegeln sich in Gebäudetyp, Konstruktion und Materialwahl wider.

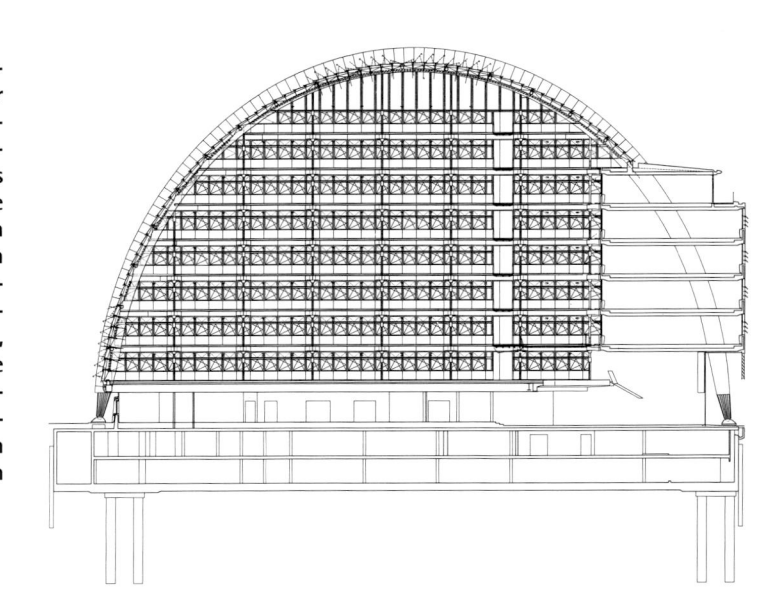

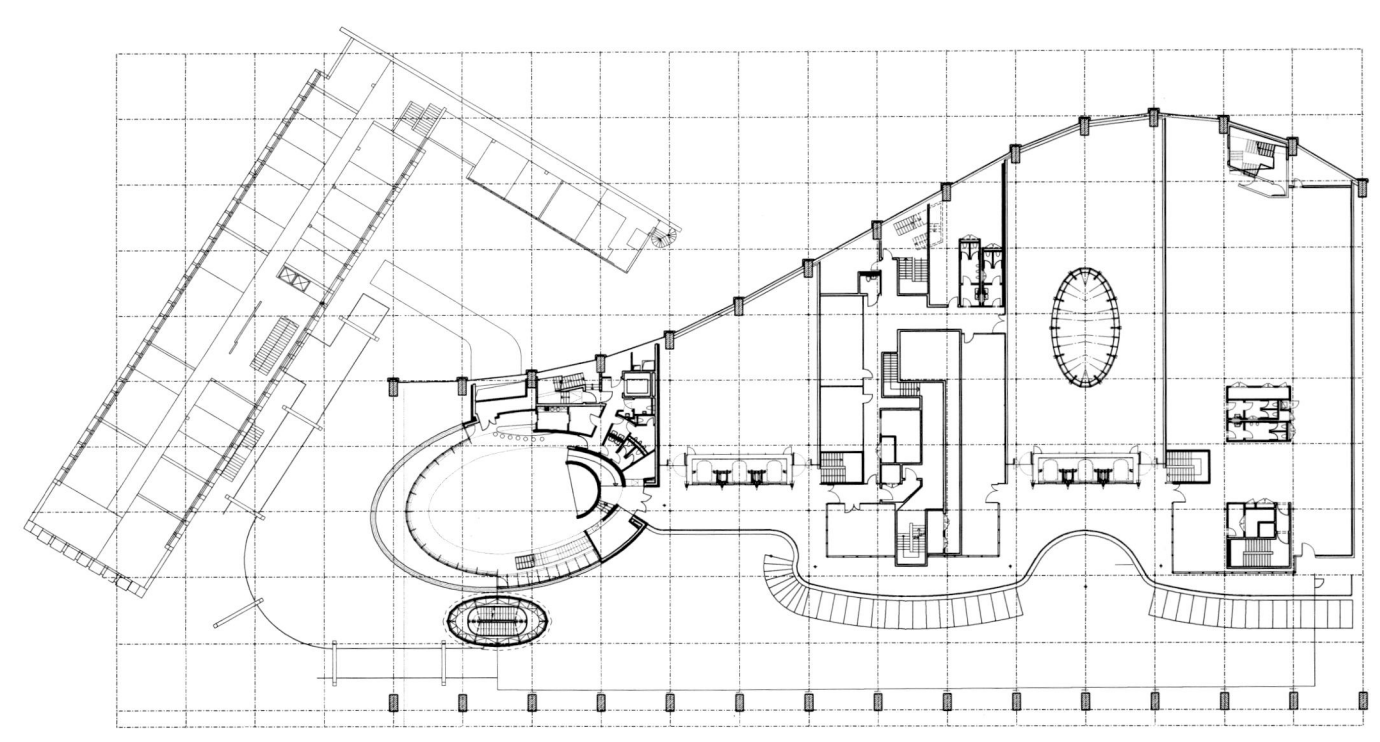

Gebäudequerschnitt
Cross section

**Grundriß 1. Obergeschoß
mit Büronutzung
und Konferenzräumen**
1st floor plan
with offices
and conference rooms

1:750

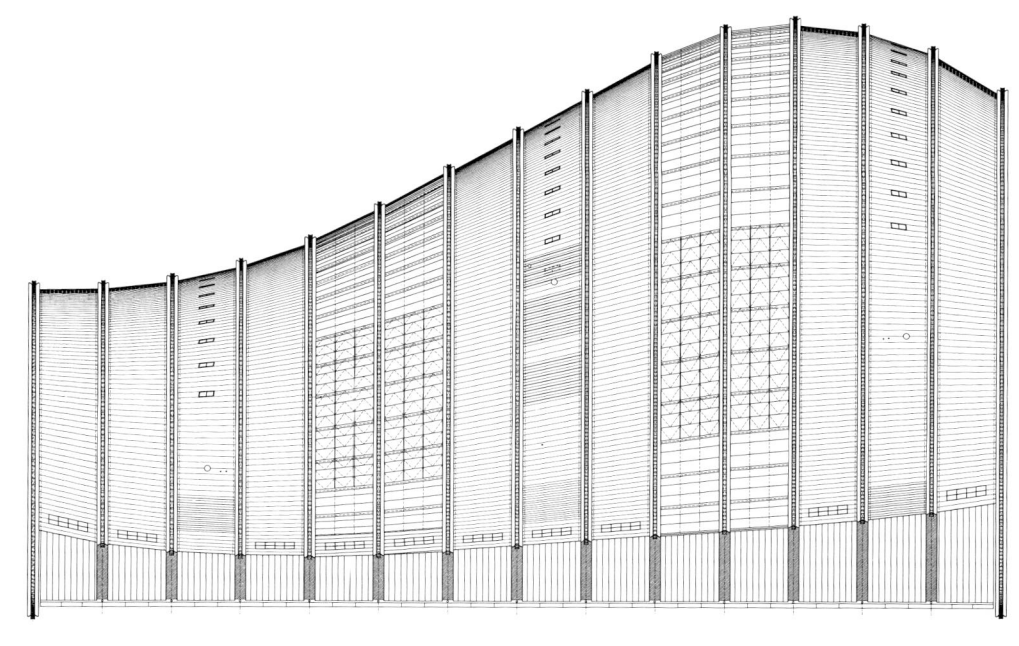

would be able to see into the main hall of the stock exchange, and have access to the conference centre, restaurant and offices. This double-height »street« area is fully glazed on the side facing Fasanenstrasse, thus creating an interaction between public urban space and the inside of the building. The complex requirements in terms of building use, space and technology, such as are found in a modern communications and services centre are reflected in the blend of building construction, form and material choice.

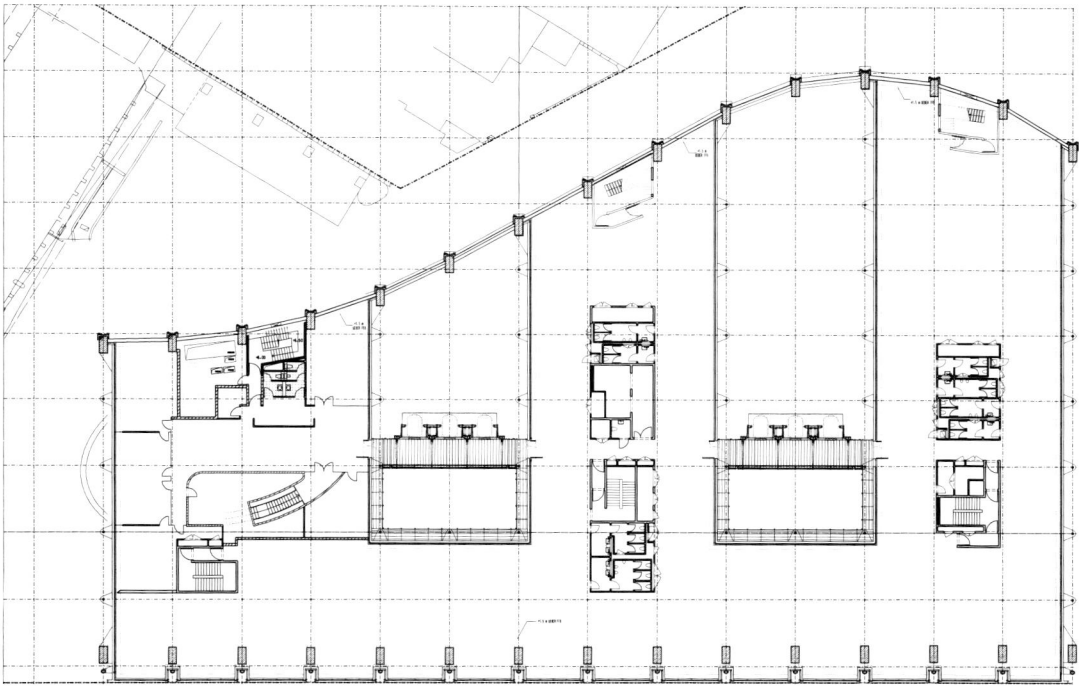

Dachaufsicht
Top view of roof

**Grundriß 2. Obergeschoß
mit Büronutzung**
2nd floor plan
offices

1:750

Deutsch-französisches
Kultur- und
Handelszentrum
German-French
Centre of
Culture
and Trade

Lindencorso

Christoph Mäckler
Berlin – Frankfurt a.M.

Mitarbeit Wettbewerb
Staff competition
Zlatka Damianova
Susanne Widmer
Klaus Elz
Georg Düx

Mitarbeit Planung
Staff planning
Beate Grimm
Jan Pieter Fraune
(Projektleitung project manager)
Birgitt Jaehne
Sergio Canton
Georg Düx
Thomas Mayer

Bauherr:
Lindencorso
Grundstücksgesellschaft mbH
Berlin

Planungstermine:
Wettbewerb November 1992,
1. Preis
Entwurfsplanung seit 1993
Baubeginn 1993
Voraussichtlicher Bezug 1996

Nutzung:
max. 46 Ladeneinheiten
(25-1.900 m²)
mit 10.508,18 m²
max. 34 Büroeinheiten
(300-600 m²)
mit 16.291,73 m²
23 Wohneinheiten
(45-128 m²)
mit 1.752,27 m²

Geschosse (VIII):
EG + 1. OG Läden
2. OG Ausstellungsräume
2.-6. OG Büros
7. OG Wohnungen

Untergeschosse (III):
1. UG (4.570,34 m² NGF)
Auditorium für 400 Personen
sowie Läden, Technik
2. UG (4.579,47 m² NGF) und
3.UG (4.637,03 m² NGF)
Tiefgarage (229 Pkw-Stellplätze)

Grundstücksgröße:
4.897 m²

Überbaute Fläche:
4.775,65 m²

Bruttogeschoßfläche:
46.759,99 m²

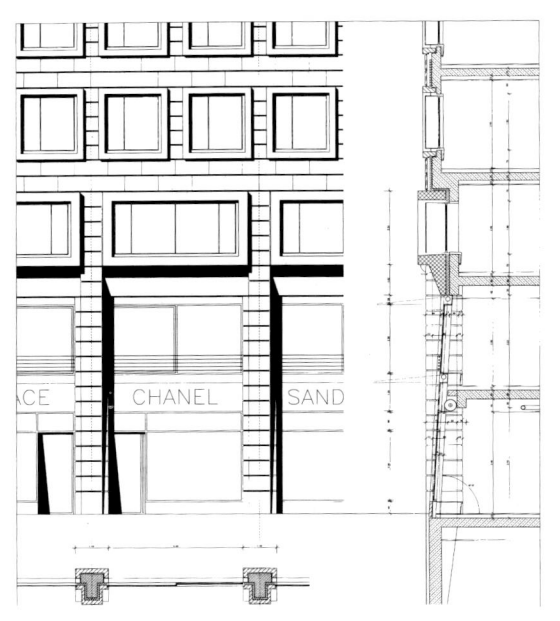

Ansicht Unter den Linden
von Norden
North elevation
Unter den Linden

1:750

Fassadenausschnitt im Bereich
Haupteingang
Unter den Linden
Façade detail
of main entrance
Unter den Linden

Fassadenstudie
Unter den Linden,
Ansicht und Schnitte
im Bereich der Schaufenster
Façade study
Unter den Linden
with elevation and sections
through shop windows area

Projektadresse:
Location:
**Unter den Linden 19
in
10117 Berlin-Mitte**

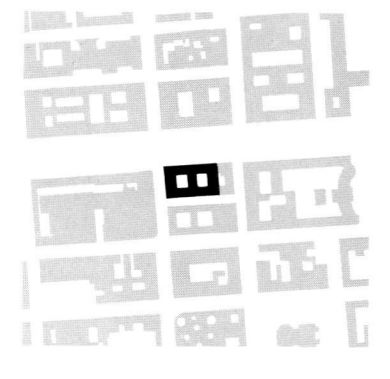

Client:
Lindencorso Grundstücks-
gesellschaft mbH, Berlin

Project Stages:
Competition November 1992,
1st prize
Design development from 1993
Start of construction 1993
Expected completion 1996

Building Use:
Max. 46 shop units
à 25-1900 m² totalling
10508.18 m²
Max. 34 office units
à 300-600 m² totalling
16291.73 m²
23 apartments
à 45-128 m² totalling
1752.27 m²

Upper Floors (VIII):
Ground floor and 1st floor shops
2nd floor exhibition areas
2nd-6th floor offices
7th floor apartments

Basement Floors (III):
1st basement
(4570.34 m² net floor area)
auditorium to seat 400, shops,
services
2nd basement
(4579.47 m² net floor area) and
3rd basement
(4637.03 m² net floor area)

Basement levels have parking
for 229 cars

Site Area:
4897 m²

Built Area:
4775.65 m²

Gross Floor Area:
46759.99 m²

**Ansicht Friedrichstraße
von Westen**
West elevation
Friedrichstrasse

1:750

**Haupteingang
Unter den Linden
mit Blick in die Eingangshalle
Computersimulation**
Main entrance
Unter den Linden
with view of entrance hall
Computer simulation

Deutsch-französisches Kultur- und Handelszentrum
German-French Centre of Culture and Trade

Lindencorso

Der große rechteckige Block baut die Friedrichstraße von 60 m Breite auf ihr historisches Maß von 22 m zurück. Damit ist die in der Nachkriegszeit angelegte platzartige Erweiterung beseitigt und die ursprüngliche Hierarchie des Straßennetzes mit Unter den Linden als Hauptmagistrale wieder hergestellt. Der in den 60er Jahren entstandene Restaurantkomplex Lindencorso wurde zu diesem Zweck abgerissen.

Das neue Gebäude besitzt eine komplexe Nutzungsstruktur. Es verfügt neben den Büro- und Wohngeschossen über ein Auditorium für 400 Personen, Ausstellungsräume, Vertretungen der französischen Regionen, Ladenlokale, Restaurants, einen Salon de Thé und das traditionsreiche Café Bauer.

Die Läden sind um eine viergeschossige Halle organisiert, die nicht das moderne Shopping-Center, sondern die großstädtische Ladenpassage zum Vorbild hat. Zugänge zu diesem Gebäudemittelpunkt liegen unterhalb der Arkaden an der Friedrichstraße und in der Achse der Fassade Unter den Linden.

Der Aufbau der Fassaden spiegelt die innere Nutzungsstruktur und folgt im wesentlichen den städtebaulichen Vorgaben: Sockelhöhe 8 m, Traufhöhe 22 m, Gesamtbauhöhe 30 m.

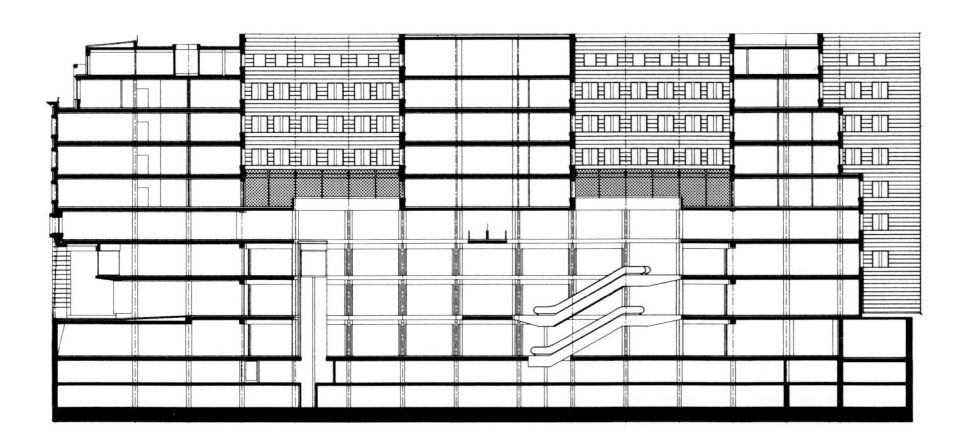

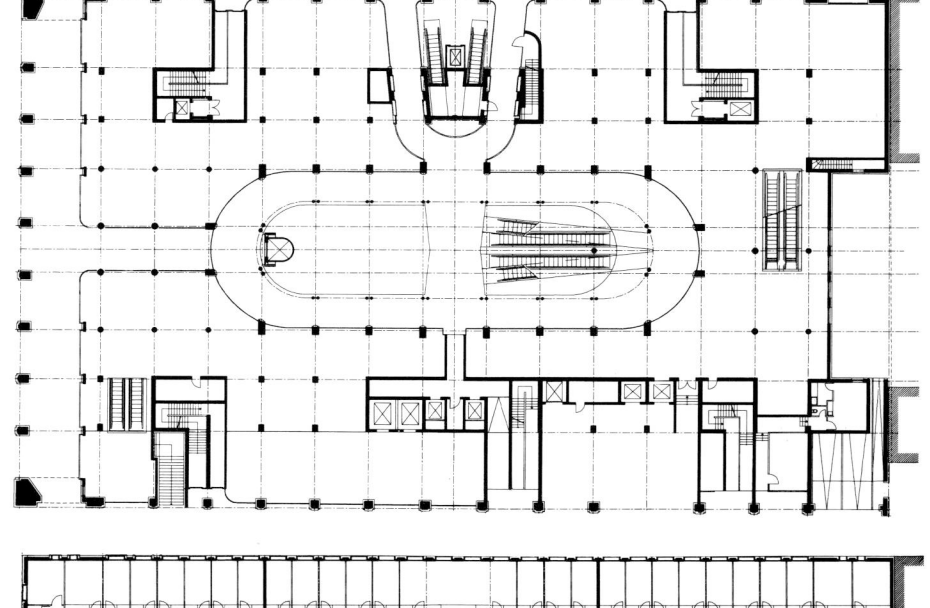

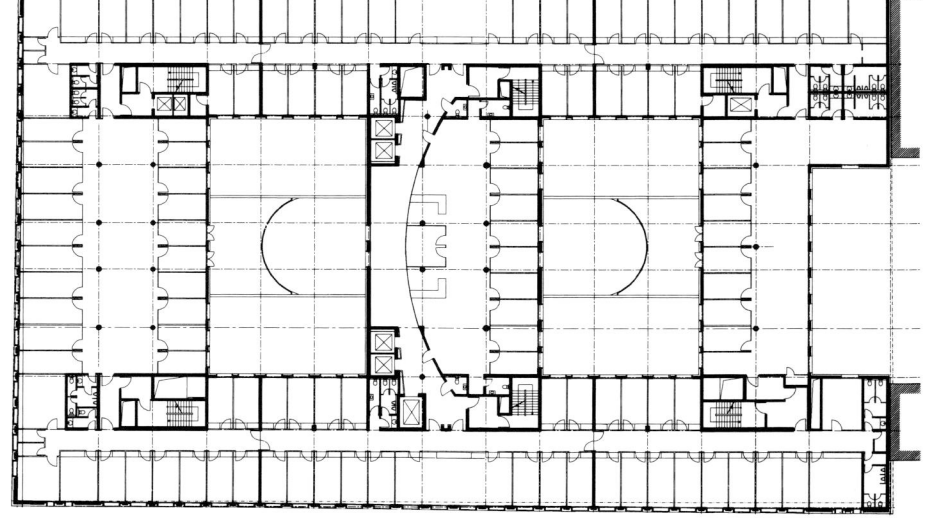

Gebäudelängsschnitt
Longitudinal section

Grundriß Erdgeschoß mit Ladennutzung
Ground floor plan retail

Grundriß Normalgeschoß mit Büronutzung
Typical floor plan offices

1:750

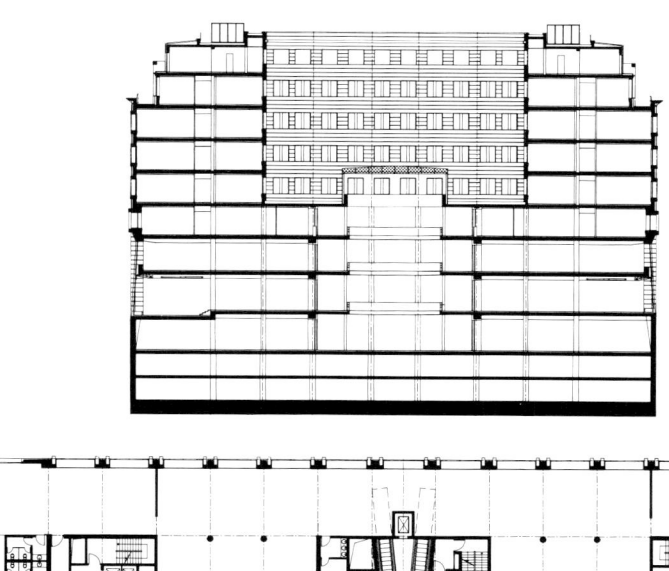

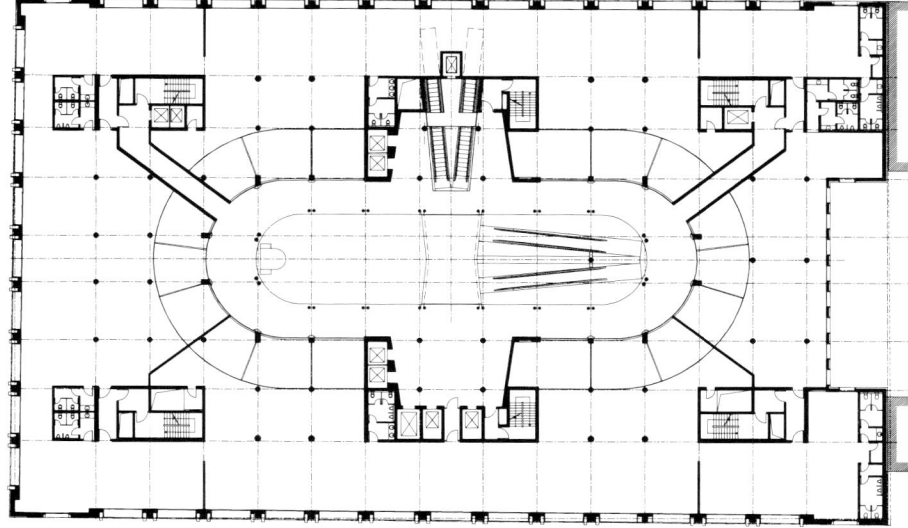

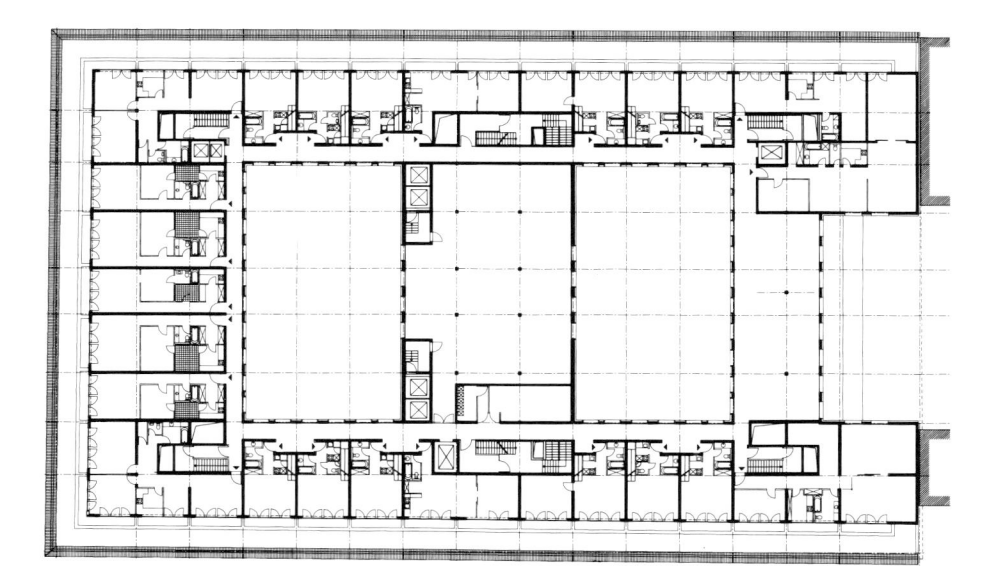

This large rectangular block achieves a reduction in the width of Friedrichstrasse from 60 m in recent times to its former dimension of 22 m. This effectively removes the square-like expansion of the street and reinstates the hierarchy of the local street network with the primacy of Unter den Linden as the main communications axis. The Lindencorso restaurant complex, built in the 60s, was demolished to make way for this development.

The new building has a complex structure of use. In addition to office and residential space it has an auditorium for 400 people, exhibition rooms, representative agencies for the French regions, shops, bars, restaurants, a tea salon and the famous Café Bauer.

The shops are arranged around a 4-storey high hall, modelled not on modern shopping centres, but on inner city shopping arcades. Access to the centre of the building is gained via the arcades on Friedrichstrasse and from Unter den Linden.

The façade construction reflects the internal structure of use and adheres generally to the city planning guidelines: 8 m high base, 22 m eaves height, total building height of 30 m.

Gebäudequerschnitt
Cross section

Grundriß 2. Obergeschoß mit Ausstellungsflächen
2nd floor plan
exhibition areas

Grundriß Attikageschoß (7. Obergeschoß) mit Wohnungen
Plan of attic floor (7th floor)
apartments

1:750

IV
Turm und Hochhaus:
Fixpunkte im Stadtbild

Ludwig Mies van der Rohe, Glashochhaus mit polygonaler Gliederung, 1920/21
Ludwig Mies van der Rohe, glass skyscraper with polygonal forms, 1920/21

Ludwig Mies van der Rohe, Glashochhaus mit prismatischer Gliederung am Bahnhof Friedrichstraße, Wettbewerbsentwurf 1919
Ludwig Mies van der Rohe, glass skyscraper with prismatic forms at Friedrichstrasse station, competition design 1919

Unmittelbar nach der Wende, als man in Berlin einen spontan einsetzenden Investitionsboom erwartete, gab es im Zusammenhang mit Überlegungen zur Verdichtung der Stadt auch einen ersten Boom von Hochhausprojekten. Viele dieser Entwürfe, die oft ganze Hochhauscluster nach amerikanischem Vorbild umfaßten, blieben auf dem Papier. Eine Reihe möglicher Standorte, die ganz gezielt in hocherschlossenen, zentral gelegenen Bereichen angesiedelt wurden, blieben aber auch nach Verklingen des ersten Gründerzeitfiebers für eine zumindest punktuelle Bebauung mit Hochhäusern aktuell. Dabei handelte es sich in erster Linie um Flächen am Bahnhof Zoo (City West), am Alexanderplatz (City Ost), am Potsdamer Platz (Zentraler Bereich) sowie am S-Bahn-Ring um die Innenstadt.

Mit den Standorten am S-Bahn-Ring wurde das Ende der achtziger Jahre angedachte Konzept einer »Ringstadt« um die Citykerne weiterverfolgt. Die Suche nach gut erschlossenen Flächen hatte gezeigt, daß brachliegende Areale am inneren S-Bahn-Ring, insbesondere in den Kreuzungspunkten mit den radial in die Stadt führenden Hauptstraßen, über hervorragende Verkehrsanbindungen verfügen. Sie zeichnen sich durch besonders gute Erreichbarkeit nicht nur von außen, sondern insbesondere auch untereinander aus. Daher schien das Konzept der »Ringstadt« geeignet, die berlintypische polyzentrische Struktur zu stärken und die Innenstadtbereiche zu entlasten, ohne die Investoren an den Stadtrand oder ins Umland zu drängen.

Die Ringbahn-Quartiere wurden als Dienstleistungszentren mit einer vielfältigen Nutzungsmischung konzipiert, deren Schwerpunkt jedoch eindeutig bei den Büroflächen liegt. Ein Großteil dieser Flächen wurde in Hochhäusern konzentriert, die visuell miteinander verknüpft sind und den Ring um die Innenstadt weithin sichtbar markieren. Diese aneinandergereihten Inseln mit hoher baulicher Dichte sollen dazu beitragen, die Abgrenzung des Stadtkörpers gegen eine noch nicht zersiedelte Landschaft so weit als möglich zu erhalten.

Auch unter stadträumlichen Gesichtspunkten eignet sich die Ringbahn für vertikale Dominanten. Durch ihre Führung als Hochbahn bzw. durch den Geländeeinschnitt der Bahntrasse definiert sie eine bereits heute räumlich erfahrbare Grenzsituation, die den Übergang unterschiedlicher Bebauungsstrukturen kennzeichnet. Am Kreuzungspunkt mit den radial in die Stadt führenden Magistralen entstehen darüber hinaus Torsituationen auf dem Weg zur Innenstadt. Einer der bekanntesten frühen Hochhausentwürfe für Berlin, das gläserne Hochhaus von Mies van der Rohe am Bahnhof

IV
Tower and Tower Block:
Fixed Points in the Urban Scene

Immediately after the fall of the Berlin wall plans began to emerge for a series of inner-city high-rise buildings intended to appeal to the first wave of investors. Many of these designs, often American-style high-rise clusters, remained on the drawing board. In some locations, specifically in central areas with high-density development, the proposals managed at least in part to assert themselves even after the initial wave of enthusiasm had passed. These areas centred around Bahnhof Zoo (City West), Alexanderplatz (City East), Potsdamer Platz (Central District) and on the inner-city S-Bahn (surburban railway) ring. The projects planned for locations around the S-Bahn ring are a continuation of an idea developed at the end of the 1980s for a circle of development around the city core. The search for good building locations had shown that the areas of wasteland on the inner S-Bahn ring, particularly at the junctions with main roads leading into the city, were very well placed for road and rail communications to areas both inside and outside the city. In addition links between these sites were also optimal. These considerations promoted the concept of an »urban ring«, as an intensification of the traditional polycentric structure of Berlin and as a zone which would counteract concentration in the inner city, without the need to push investors to the edge of the city or into the surrounding areas.

The districts in this outer ring area were conceived as services centres with a wide mix of activities, yet with the emphasis on office space. Much of this space was concentrated in high-rise buildings, which are visually linked with each other in a ring clearly marking the limits of the inner city. Like a chain of densely built-up islands encircling the city, their towers are also intended as far as possible to maintain the borders of the city against the surrounding countryside as yet largely unspoiled by development.

Also from the point of view of overall urban development the outer ring can easily accommodate vertical emphasis. The course of the S-Bahn already defines a physical feature on the face of the city; in places the tracks are raised, in others they run in cuttings, constituting a distinct spatial situation on the border between differing types of development. The intersection points between the S-Bahn and the main roads form a kind of threshold, or town gate, leading into the city. One of the most well known high-rise designs (not carried out) for Berlin, the highly visible glazed tower at Friedrichstrasse station designed by Mies van der Rohe, was intended for just such a »gateway« situation, albeit not on this outer ring.

Hermann Henselmann, Hochhaus am Strausberger Platz, Modellfoto 1953
Hermann Henselmann, high-rise on Strausberger Platz, model photo 1953

Brüder Luckhardt, Chicago Tribune Tower, Wettbewerbsentwurf 1922
Luckhardt Brothers, Chicago Tribune Tower, competition design 1922

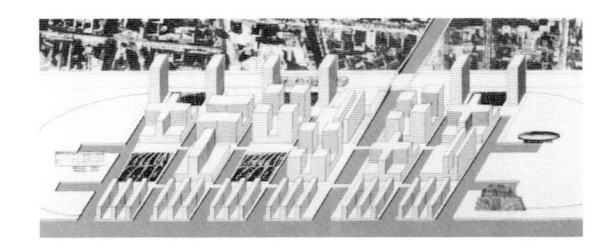

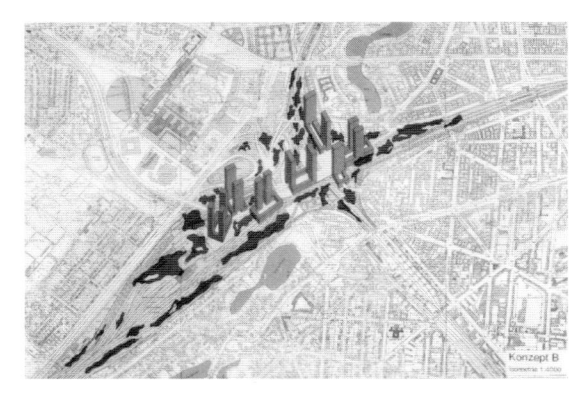

oben above
Klaus Theo
Brenner und
Benedict Tonon,
Ringstadtprojekt
Westhafen
Klaus Theo
Brenner and
Benedict Tonon,
Westhafen city
ring project

Mitte center
Christoph
Langhof,
Ringstadtprojekt
Ostkreuz,
Büropark an der
Spree
Christoph
Langhof,
Ostkreuz city
ring project,
Business park at
the Spree

Hans Kollhoff
mit Stephan
Höhne,
Ringstadtprojekt
Westkreuz,
Konzept B
Hans Kollhoff
with Stephan
Höhne,
Westkreuz city
ring project,
concept B

Friedrichstraße, war – wenngleich nicht an der Ringbahn – in einer ähnlichen Torsituation gedacht und schob sich weithin sichtbar in den Straßenraum.

Zu den Hochhausprojekten, die in Zusammenhang mit dem Ringstadtkonzept entstanden, gehören das Geschäftszentrum Frankfurter Allee der Architekturbüros HPP und SOM, die Zwillingshochhäuser von Klaus Theo Brenner für den Bereich Ostkreuz / Rummelsburger Bucht und der Büro- und Dienstleistungskomplex am Treptower Park von Gerhard Spangenberg sowie Kieferle & Partner.

Der Kreuzungspunkt der Frankfurter Allee mit dem S- und U-Bahn-Netz ist nahezu ein Idealfall für die beschriebene Verkehrserschließung. Das 33-geschossige Hochhaus ist die Dominante eines aus zwei Blöcken bestehenden Geschäftszentrums. Auf einem schiffsförmigen Grundriß, dessen Spitze stadtauswärts weist, erhebt sich ein schlanker Baukörper mit einer reinen Stahl-Glas-Fassade. Dem Hochhaus liegt die »Idee eines Stadtzeichens, eines visuellen Signals« zugrunde, das nicht nur ablesbarer Teil der Ringstadt ist, sondern zudem einen stadträumlichen »Brückenschlag vom Alexanderplatz über das Frankfurter Tor zur Berliner Ringbahn« herstellt. Als Bezugshöhe dient dabei das Hotel Stadt Berlin am Alexanderplatz. »Berlin« – so die Verfasser – »braucht solche Fixpunkte. Sie sind Orte, die Erinnerungen prägen in der ausufernden Stadt.«[1]

Die drei Zwillingshochhäuser von Klaus Theo Brenner sind 21-geschossig, mit 10-geschossigem verbindendem Mittelbau, und liegen südlich des Ostkreuzes zwischen dem Ufer des Rummelsburger Sees und dem Bahnkörper der S-Bahn. Aus den besonderen Bedingungen dieser Lage heraus ist das Gebäudevolumen entwickelt: ein zur Bahn hin glattes, zur Bucht plastisch ausgebildetes, linear der Bahntrasse folgendes »steinernes Hochhaus mit Mauerwerksfassade«. Das Prinzip der Reihung verbindet die drei Häuser zu einem städtebaulichen Ensemble, dessen »Prägnanz und Präsenz vergleichbar wäre mit den Bauten der Siemensstadt am Stadtring in Charlottenburg.«[2]

Nur eine S-Bahnstation vom Ostkreuz entfernt liegt der Standort des neuen Dienstleistungszentrums auf dem Gelände des ehemaligen DDR-Kombinats Elektro Apparate Werke (EAW). Das städtebauliche Gesamtkonzept von Gerhard Spangenberg versucht den Flußlauf der Spree als stadtbildprägendes Element und als öffentlich erlebbaren Stadtraum stärker als zuvor zur Geltung zu bringen. Entlang der Spree entsteht eine städtische Kante, die durch eine Reihung von Turmhäusern und Kopfbauten Betonung findet. Baulicher Höhepunkt der Anlage und »städtebauliche Dominante« ist ein 30-geschossiges Hochhaus, das als Brückenkopf an der Elsenbrücke steht. Es markiert den Übergang von der »Landschaftsspree« zur »Stadtspree«. Die Spreeufer im Bereich des Dienstleistungs- und Bürokomplexes sind dementsprechend als städtische Uferlandschaft mit Promenaden, Uferwegen und Parks konzipiert.

Examples of the high-rise projects designed as part of the outer ring concept are the Frankfurter Allee office centre by HPP and SOM architects, the twin towers by Klaus Theo Brenner for the Ostkreuz/Rummelsburger Bucht area and the office and services complex at Treptower Park by Gerhard Spangenberg and Kieferle & Partner.

The junction of Frankfurter Allee and the S-Bahn and underground lines represents practically the ideal case in terms of communcations as mentioned above. Here the 33-storey highrise by HPP and SOM is the dominating feature in an office centre consisting of two blocks. On a tear-drop shaped ground plan, with the pointed end directed out of the town, the slim building rises up, enclosed in an all steel and glass façade. The high-rise is based on the idea of creating »a visual signal, or urban marker« which is not only a clearly legible component of the outer ring but in addition forms an urban »bridge link from Alexanderplatz past Frankfurter Tor to the Berlin Ring.« »Berlin,« in the words of the architects, »needs fixed points like this. They are distinctive points of reference against the background of an expanding city.«[1]

Klaus Theo Brenner's three twin tower blocks are 21 storeys high and linked via a 10-storey central section; they are located south of the Ostkreuz between the banks of Lake Rummelsburger and the S-Bahn tracks. These locational considerations influenced the design of the building volume: a linear »stone high-rise with brick façade« along the line of the tracks, a smooth façade towards the railway and more sculptured towards the Bucht. By arranging the three towers in a line they become a single urban ensemble whose »concise, distinctive presence is similar to that of the Siemensstadt buildings on the outer Ring of Charlottenburg.«[2]

Only one S-Bahn station away from Ostkreuz is the site of the new services centre on land formerly occupied by the GDR state concern Elektro Apparate Werke (EAW). The overall urban concept by Gerhard Spangenberg attempts to emphasise the role of the course of the river Spree as a key urban element and to increase access to the river so that it becomes more public in character. Along the Spree an urban strip will develop marked by a series of towers. The focus of the complex and at the same time a key element in the general urban picture is a 30-storey high-rise, located in a bridgehead position at the Elsenbrücke. It marks the transition from the »riverlike« to the »townlike« part of the Spree. The banks near the services and offices complex are accordingly designed as an urban riverbank landscape with promenades, pathways and parks.

Based on this overall plan the individual projects were developed by various architectural offices, including Kieferle & Partner who designed in the western part one of the 18-storey twin

HPP und SOM, Hochhaus Frankfurter Allee, Modellfoto
HPP and SOM, Frankfurter Allee high-rise, model photo

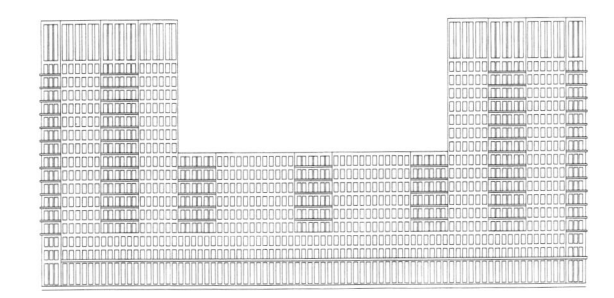

Klaus Theo Brenner, Zwillingshochhäuser Kynaststraße, Ansicht von der Rummelsburger Bucht
Klaus Theo Brenner, twin towers on Kynaststrasse, elevation from Rummelsburger Bucht

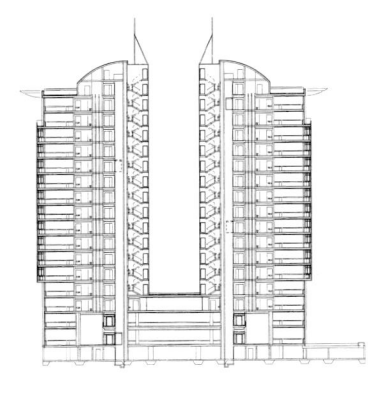

Kieferle & Partner, Zwillingshochhäuser Eichenstraße, Längsschnitt
Kieferle & Partner, Eichenstrasse twin towers, longitudinal section

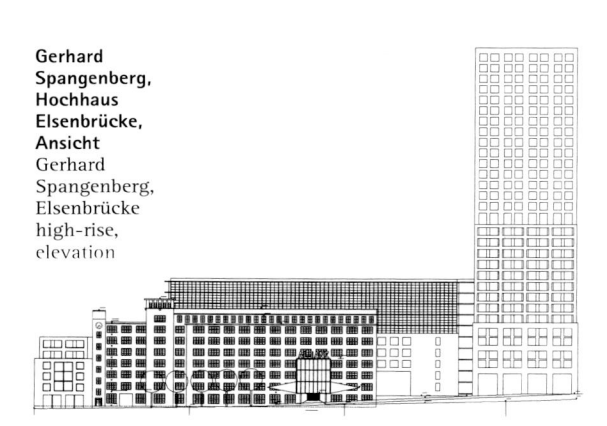

Gerhard Spangenberg, Hochhaus Elsenbrücke, Ansicht
Gerhard Spangenberg, Elsenbrücke high-rise, elevation

Die Ausarbeitung der architektonischen Projekte auf der Grundlage des städtebaulichen Wettbewerbs erfolgte durch verschiedene Architekturbüros, darunter Kieferle & Partner für den westlichen Teilbereich. Hierzu gehören eines der 18-geschossigen Zwillingshochhäuser an der Spree und die zwei U-förmigen 7-geschossigen Bürogebäude an der Eichenstraße. Alle drei Gebäude erhalten ausgeprägte »Dachlandschaften, die von der Fußgängerebene erlebbar sind, aber auch in der Fernwirkung den Gebäuden ihre eigene Identifikation im Stadtbild geben«[3]. Die Bauten werden zum Teil durch eine detaillierte Strukturierung und durch die Verwendung leichter, reflektierender oder transparenter Materialien wie Glas und Metall optisch aufgelöst und kontrastieren mit anderen, kubisch, massiv und »steinern« wirkenden Baukörpern. Die Kombination unterschiedlicher Materialien wird bewußt zur Gestaltung eingesetzt.

Das im Herzen der City West gelegene Hochhaus »Zoofenster« von Richard Rogers hingegen ist vollständig durch seine gläserne Haut und filigrane Struktur geprägt und stellt sich auch mit der starken Gliederung seiner Baukörper in Kontrast zu den Gebäuden seiner Umgebung. In seiner Lage am Bahnhof Zoo bietet es Ausblick auf die City, den Bahnhof und die Grünanlagen des Zoologischen Gartens. Auch dieses Hochhaus entsteht an einer durch ein Brückenbauwerk der Hochbahn geprägten Stelle der Stadt. Der Grundriß fügt sich als Addition einzelner Nutzungsbereiche in das dreieckige Grundstück zwischen Hardenbergstraße, Joachimstaler Straße und Kantstraße. Zur Kantstraße definiert eine 22-geschossige Hochhausscheibe den Straßenraum, während das Gebäude zur Hardenbergstraße durch die ihm vorgelagerten turmartigen Baukörper stark plastisch gegliedert wirkt. In diesen Türmen liegen die aus den Büroflächen ausgelagerten Treppen, Aufzüge und WC-Anlagen. Der höhere dieser beiden Türme – der zusätzlich zu der Aussichtsgalerie von einer Antennenanlage gekrönt wird – schiebt sich durch einen zwischengeschalteten zweiten Büroriegel weit an die Kreuzung der Hardenbergstraße mit der Joachimstaler Straße vor und dominiert von dieser Stelle den Hardenbergplatz vor dem Bahnhof Zoo.

Charakteristisch für alle dargestellten Hochhausprojekte ist, daß sie städtebaulich wichtige Situationen akzentuieren oder dominieren. Themen sind das Hochhaus als Markierung einer Stadttor-Situation (HPP/SOM), das Hochhaus als Aussichtsturm an der Grenze von offener und geschlossener Stadtstruktur (Rogers), das Hochhaus als Brückenkopf (Spangenberg) sowie das Zwillingshochhaus als gereihtes uferbegleitendes (Kieferle) bzw. auch die Bahntrasse begleitendes Element (Brenner).

1 Hentrich-Petschnigg & Partner, Skidmore, Owings & Merrill, Erläuterungen zum Hochhaus Frankfurter Allee.
2 Klaus Theo Brenner, Erläuterungen zu den Zwillingshochhäusern Kynaststraße.
3 Kieferle & Partner, Erläuterungen zum Bürozentrum Elsenstraße.

high-rises on the Spree and the two U-shaped, 7-storey office buildings on Eichenstrasse. All three buildings have a distinctive »roof landscape which is not only visible from pedestrian level but gives the buildings a unique identity also from a distance.«[3] Optically their mass is partly broken up by detailed structuring and through the use of lighter, reflecting or transparent materials such as glass and metal; this produces a contrast with other nearby buildings which are more cubic, solid and »stone-like« in appearance. The combination of materials is a deliberate feature of the design.

A characteristic feature of Richard Rogers' »Zoofenster« high-rise in the heart of the City West district is its all glass skin and filigree structure; its distinct structural divisions set up a contrast to the surrounding buildings. In its location at the Zoo station it overlooks the city, the station and the park areas of the Zoological Gardens. Here, as with other high-rises around the S-Bahn ring, the location is marked by a bridge situation, with S-Bahn tracks crossing a main road. »Zoofenster« is actually a configuration of several building sections on the triangular lot between Hardenbergstrasse, Joachimstaler Strasse and Kantstrasse. Facing Kantstrasse a 22-storey high rise slab shape gives urban definition, while the effect facing Hardenbergstrasse is altogether more sculptural as a result of the tower-like structures placed in front of it. The stairs, lifts and WCs for the office areas are located in these towers. The higher of the two towers – which is topped by a viewing gallery and antenna system – projects forward towards the junction of Hardenbergstrasse and Joachimstaler Strasse, thus dominating the Hardenbergplatz area in front of the Zoo station.

Typical for all the high-rises shown here is that they accentuate or dominate important urban locations. Different themes within this can be identified: the high-rise as a marker for a »towngate« situation (HPP/SOM), or the high-rise as a look-out tower on the border between open and closed urban structures (Rogers); the high-rise as a bridgehead (Spangenberg) or the twin high-rise as a series along a river bank (Kieferle) and also along rail tracks (Brenner).

1 Hentrich-Petschnigg & Partner, Skidmore, Owings & Merrill, Explanatory notes Frankfurter Allee High-Rise.
2 Klaus Theo Brenner, Explanatory notes Twin Towers Kynaststrasse.
3 Kieferle & Partner, Explanatory notes Office Centre Elsenstrasse.

Richard Rogers Partnership, Zoofenster, Modellfoto
Richard Rogers Partnership, Zoofenster building, model photo

Erwin Gutkind, Josty-Hochhaus am Potsdamer Platz, Projekt 1929
Erwin Gutkind, Josty high-rise on Potsdamer Platz, project 1929

Büro- und
Geschäftshaus
Frankfurter Allee
Office and
Commercial Centre
Frankfurter Allee

Bürohaus High-Rise

HPP
Hentrich-Petschnigg & Partner
Berlin
mit with
Skidmore, Owings & Merrill
Chicago

Städtebauliches
Rahmengutachten
General urban development
appraisal
Martin & Pächter
Berlin

Bauherr:
ECE Projektmanagement GmbH
Hamburg

Planungstermine:
Entwurfsplanung seit 1992
Baubeginn 1995
Voraussichtlicher Bezug 1998

Nutzung:
Büros mit
45.000 m² Bruttogeschoßfläche

Geschosse (XXXIII):
EG Lobby, Wintergarten
1.OG Luftraum, Technik
2.-32. OG Büros

Untergeschosse (II):
Technik, Archiv

Grundstücksgröße:
3.881 m²

Überbaute Fläche:
Hochhaus: 1.143 m²
Wintergarten: 770 m²

Bruttogeschoßfläche:
53.800 m² (incl. UG)

Das Geschäftszentrum befindet sich in einer wichtigen städtebaulichen Position am Rande der City Ost. Unmittelbar angrenzend liegt mit dem Bahnhof Frankfurter Allee ein wichtiger Verkehrsknotenpunkt. Mit seiner als Hochbahn über die Straße geführten Bahntrasse bildet er eine torähnliche Situation. Bis heute stadträumlich erfahrbar lag hier der Stadteingang nach Berlin. In dieser Schlüsselposition wird das Hochhaus als weithin sichtbares Stadtzeichen eingefügt. Vom Alexanderplatz erscheint seine Fassade auf einer Sichtachse zwischen den Türmen des Frankfurter Tores.
Das Hochhaus dominiert zwei angrenzende Baublöcke des Geschäftszentrums, ein Warenhaus östlich und ein Einkaufszentrum westlich der Bahntrasse. Beide Bereiche sind durch eine unterirdische Ladenstraße miteinander verbunden.

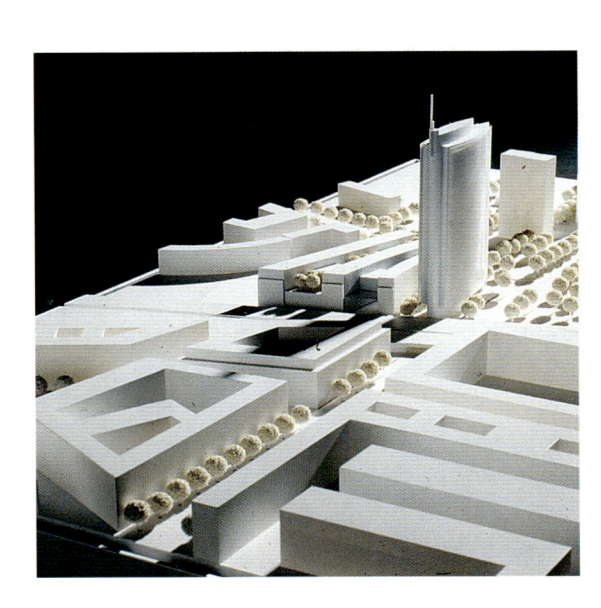

Blick vom Frankfurter Tor
auf die Gesamtanlage
Modellaufnahme
Model photo of the whole complex,
from Frankfurter Tor

Lageplan
Site plan

Bürohochhaus Frankfurter Allee/
Ecke Möllendorfstraße
von Südwesten
Modellaufnahme
Office high-rise at the corner of
Frankfurter Allee
and Möllendorfstrasse,
viewed from the southeast
Model photo

Projektadresse:
Location:
Frankfurter Allee 111
in
10247 Berlin-Friedrichshain

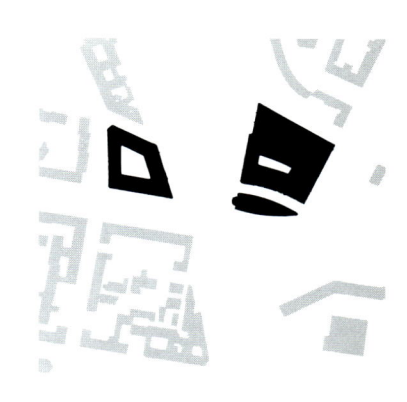

Client:
ECE Projektmanagement GmbH
Hamburg

Project Stages:
Design development from 1992
Start of construction 1995
Expected completion 1998

Building Use:
Offices totalling
45000 m² gross floor area

Upper Floors (XXXIII):
Ground floor lobby, winter garden
1st floor air space, services
2nd-32nd floor offices

Basement Floors (II):
Services, archives

Site Area:
3881 m²

Built Area:
High-rise: 1143 m²
Winter garden: 770 m²

Gross Floor Area:
53800 m² (incl. basement)

This business centre is located in a key urban location on the edge of the City East. The adjacent Frankfurter Allee station is a major traffic junction. Rail tracks cross on a bridge over the street, giving rise to a gate-like situation. Still today passing through here feels like entering the city gates of Berlin. This key position is the site for the new office tower, a highly visible urban symbol. Seen from Alexanderplatz its façade, pointed like a ship's prow, appears in the line of sight between the towers of Frankfurter Tor.
The high-rise dominates two neighbouring blocks of the business centre, a department store on the east and a shopping centre to the west of the railway tracks. Both areas are connected to each other via an underground shopping mall.

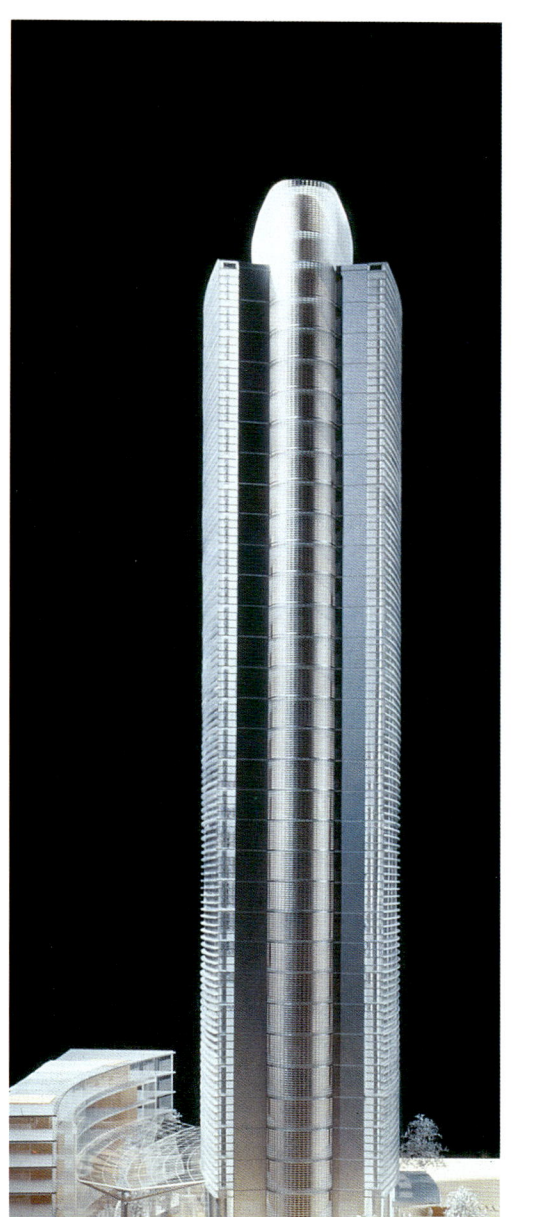

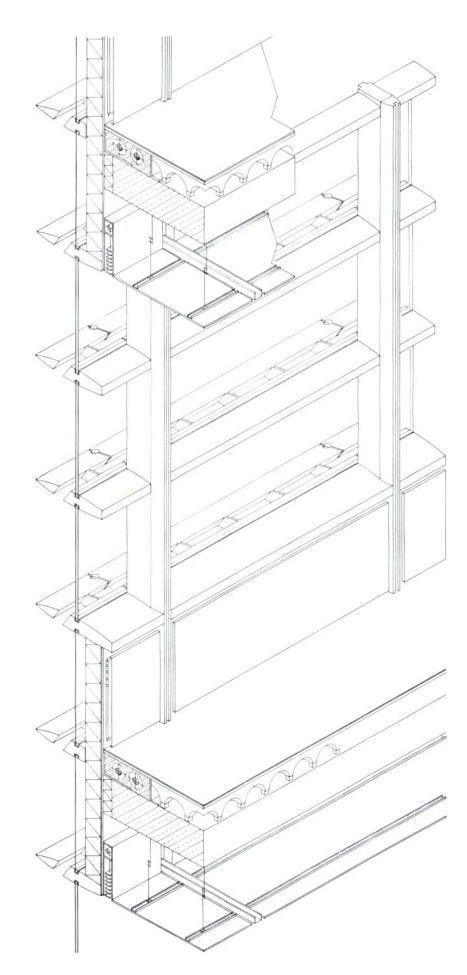

Ansicht von Westen
Modellaufnahme
West elevation
Model photo

Schnittisometrie der
Fassadenkonstruktion
Isometric section of
the façade structure

Blick in den Wintergarten
von Osten
Modellaufnahme
View of the winter garden
from the east
Model photo

Büro- und
Geschäftshaus
Frankfurter Allee
Office and
Commercial Centre
Frankfurter Allee

Bürohaus High-Rise

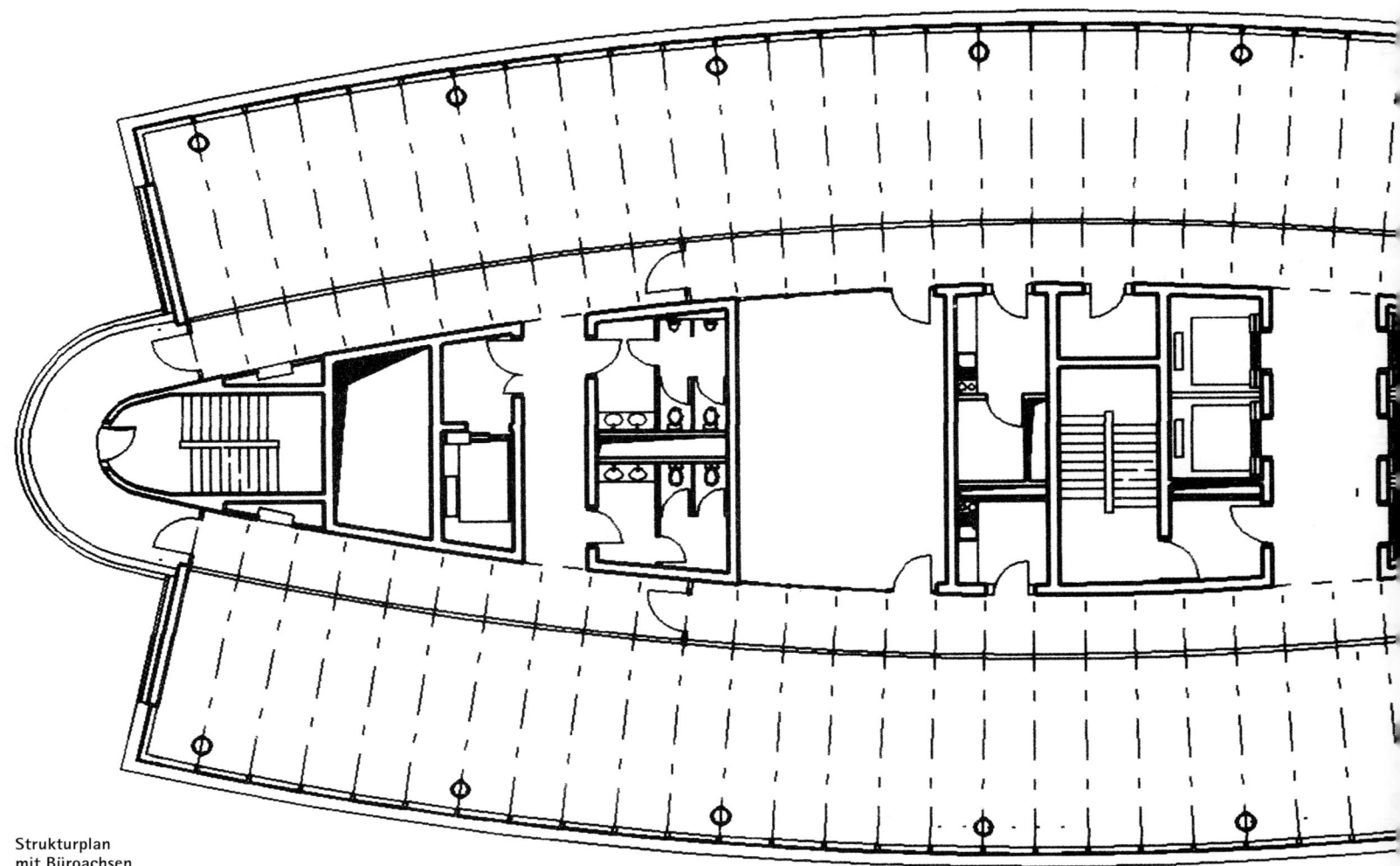

**Strukturplan
mit Büroachsen**
Plan of structure
with office grid

1:200

Grundriß Erdgeschoß
Ground floor plan

**Grundriß 3.–17. Obergeschoß
mit Büronutzung**
Plan of 3rd to 17th floors
offices

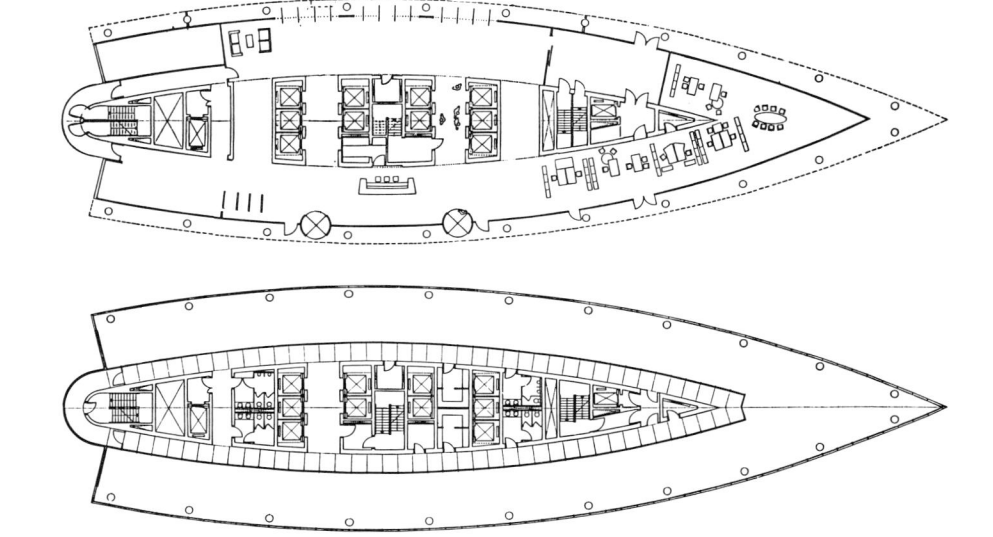

1:750

Grundriß 18. – 32. Obergeschoß mit Büronutzung
Plan of 18th to 32nd floors offices

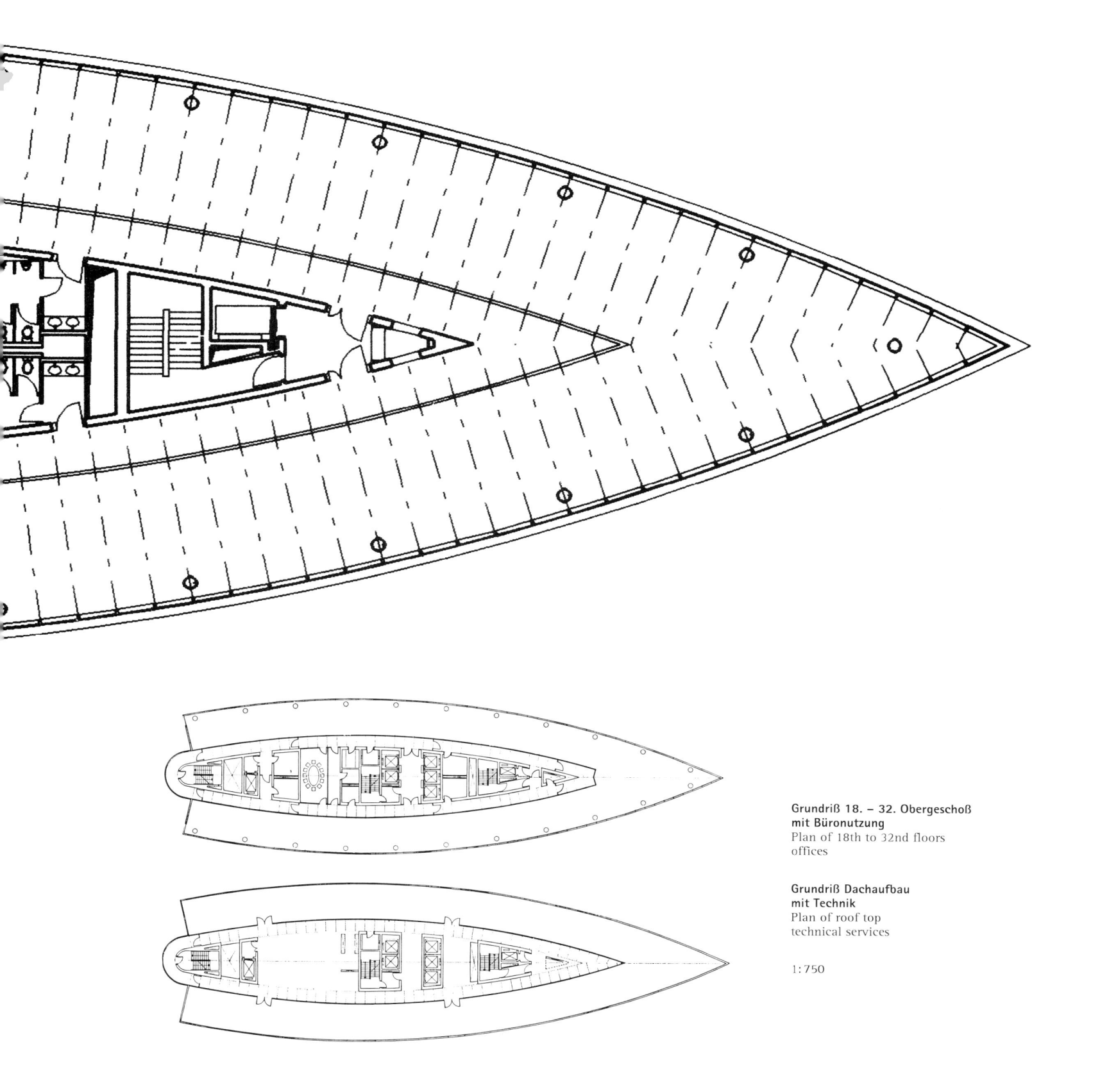

Grundriß Dachaufbau mit Technik
Plan of roof top technical services

1:750

Bürohochhaus
Brau und Brunnen
Office Building
Brau und Brunnen

Zoofenster

Richard Rogers Partnership
London

Mitarbeit staff
L. Abbott, P. Barber, P. Botschi,
H. Brunskill, O. Collignon,
P. Collins, S. Coldrey, T. Colquhoun,
J. Coward, M. Darbon, M. Davies,
K. Dzenus, K. Egge,
S. Forbes-Waller, P. Gibbons,
M. Goldschmied, L. Grut, J. Hands,
B. Haraldsdottir, J. Höpfner,

O. Kühn, S. Kühn, S. Light,
N. Kurishima, S. Martin,
A. Partridge, G. Patsalosavvis,
R. Peebles, C. Poole, R. Rogers,
A. Sasa, B. Schneppenseifen,
Y. Shinohara, S. Smithson,
K. Stallard, G. Stirk, T. Tezuka,
A. Vassiliades, A. Wada,
C. Wan, W. Wagener,
M. Williams, A. Wright,
J. Young

Bauherr:
Brau und Brunnen
Dortmund

Planungstermine:
Wettbewerb 1991
Entwurfsplanung 1991-1992

Nutzung:
Läden
Büros
Konferenzräume
Gastronomie

Geschosse (XXII):
EG + 1. OG Läden, Gastronomie
2.-21. OG Büros, Konferenzräume

Untergeschosse (II):
Tiefgarage

Grundstücksgröße:
2.200 m²

Überbaute Fläche:
1.650 m²

Bruttogeschoßfläche:
34.200 m²

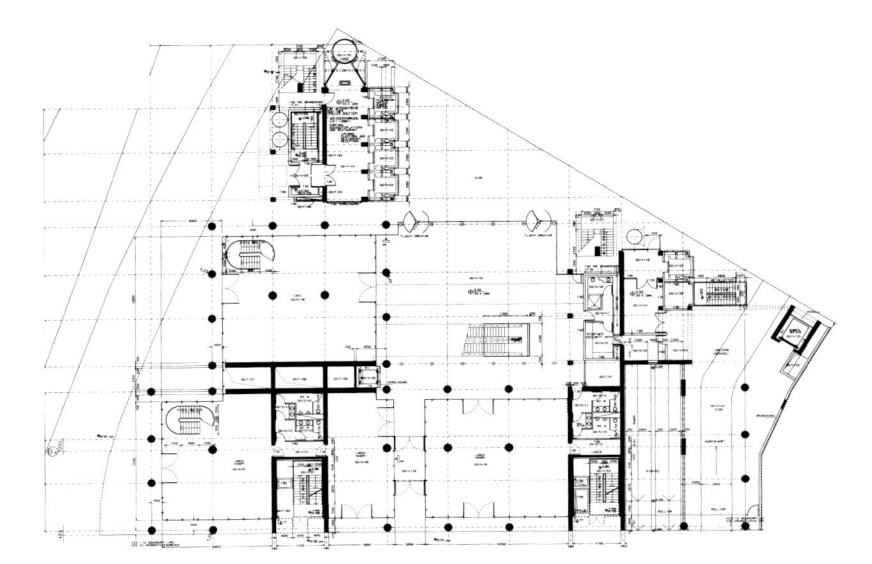

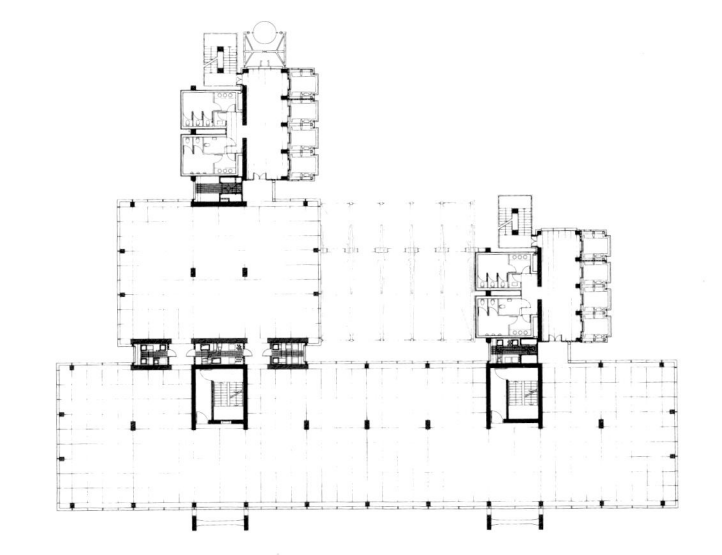

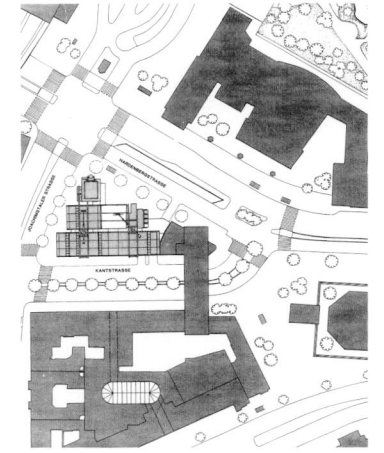

Grundriß Erdgeschoß
mit Ladennutzung, Gastronomie
Ground floor plan
retail, restaurants

Grundriß 17. Obergeschoß
mit Achsraster
Plan of 17th floor
with grid

1:750

Lageplan
Site plan

Tragwerksingenieure:
Structural Engineer:
Ove Arup & Partners/Pr. Nötzold
Haustechnik:
Service Engineer:
YRM Engineers/Schmidt Reuter
Baukostenkalkulation:
Quantity Surveyor:
ECE/Hanscomb
Modellbau:
Model Makers:
Michael Fairbrass, Jackie Hands

Projektadresse:
Location:
**Kantstrasse/
Joachimstaler Strasse/
Hardenbergstrasse
in
10623 Berlin-Charlottenburg**

Client:
Brau und Brunnen
Dortmund

Project Stages:
Competition 1991
Design planning 1991-1992

Building Use:
Offices
Shops
Conference rooms
Restaurants and cafés

Upper Floors (XXII):
Ground floor and 1st floor
shops, restaurants
2nd-21st floor offices,
conference rooms

Basement Floors (II):
Car park
Site Area:
2200 m²

Built Area:
1650 m²

Gross Floor Area:
34200 m²

Entwurfsskizze
Design sketch

**Ansicht Joachimstaler Straße/
Ecke Hardenbergstraße von Norden
Modellaufnahme**
North elevation at the corner
of Joachimstaler Strasse and
Hardenbergstrasse
Model photo

153

**Bürohochhaus
Brau und Brunnen**
Office Building
Brau und Brunnen

Zoofenster

Als Hauptverwaltung der Getränkefirma »Brau und Brunnen« wird das Hochhaus »Zoofenster« in zentralster Lage der City West entstehen. In der unmittelbaren Nachbarschaft liegen mit dem Bahnhof Zoo, dem Breitscheidplatz mit Gedächtniskirche und mit dem Kurfürstendamm wichtige Mittelpunkte innerstädtischen Lebens. Dieser Bereich ist wichtiger Knotenpunkt für Verkehr und Kommerz. Zugleich treffen mit den vorhandenen Bebauungsstrukturen und den Parkanlagen des Zoologischen Gartens sehr unterschiedliche stadträumliche Situationen aufeinander.

Der Entwurf basiert auf der Ausarbeitung dieser besonderen Schlüsselposition. Die Sockelzone mit öffentlichem Atrium und Läden (ergänzt durch die Aussichtsgalerie im obersten Geschoß) bildet einen Mittelpunkt für das Fußwegenetz der anliegenden Einkaufsstraßen; eine Teilnutzung als Hotel und Konferenzzentrum profitiert von der Nähe zum Bahnhof Zoo. Als höchstes Gebäude der Stadt soll das Hochhaus einen dominanten städtebaulichen Akzent setzen und als ›landmark‹ den Straßenraum und die Stadtsilhouette beherrschen.

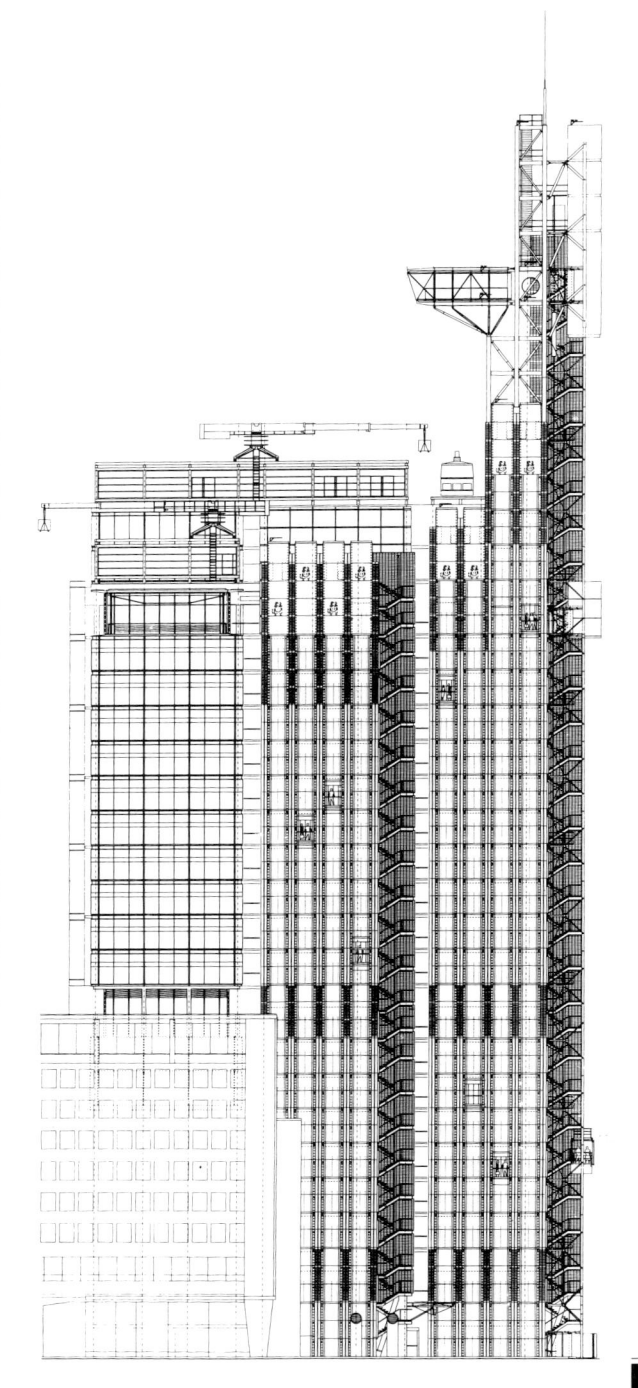

Ansicht Breitscheidplatz
von Osten
East elevation
Breitscheidplatz

1:750

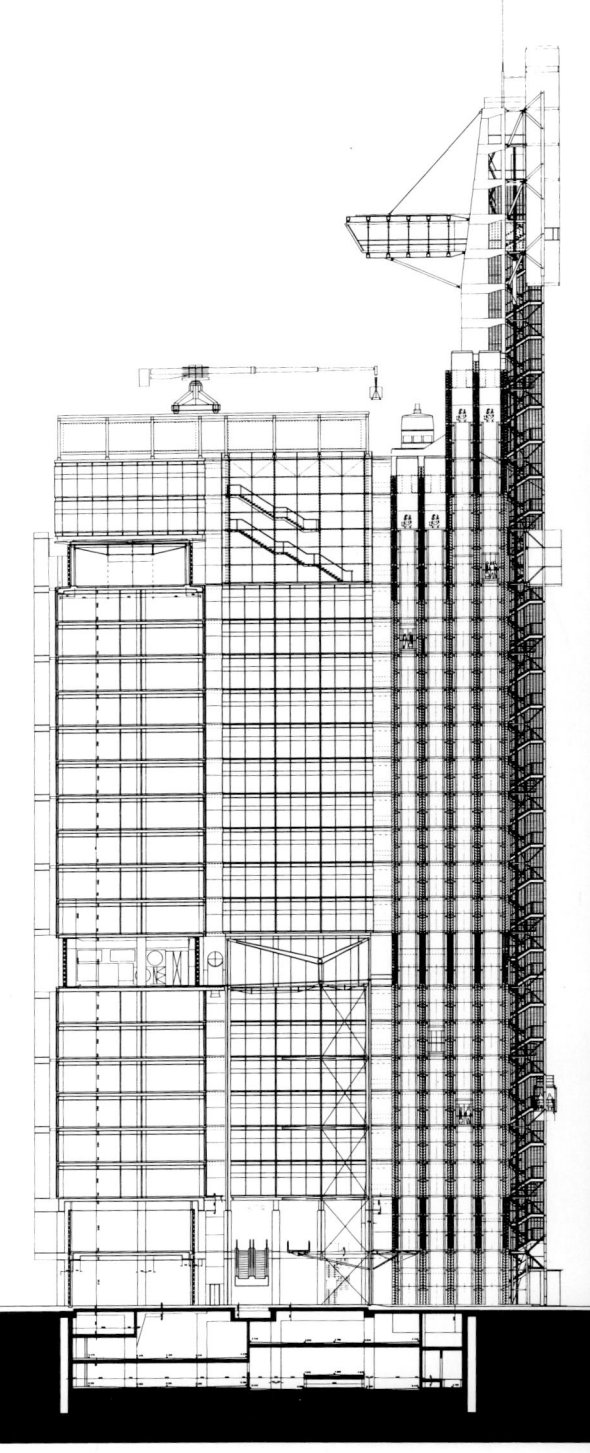

Gebäudequerschnitt
Nord/Süd
im Bereich des Atriums
North/south section
through atrium area

1:750

The »Zoofenster« high-rise, in the middle of the City West, is to be the headquarters of the drinks firm »Brau und Brunnen«. Key city landmarks are located very close by: the Zoo station, Breitscheidplatz with the Gedächtniskirche, and the Kurfürstendamm. This area is a centre of commerce and city transport. It also marks a junction of widely different urban landscapes with existing building structures and the park area of the Zoological Garden.

The design is a response to the circumstances of this special location. The base zone with public atrium and shops (supplemented by the viewing gallery on the top level) forms a centre point for the network of pedestrian routes in the neighbouring shopping streets; the inclusion of a hotel and conference centre here benefits from the proximity to the Zoo station. The »Zoofenster« will be the tallest building in the city.

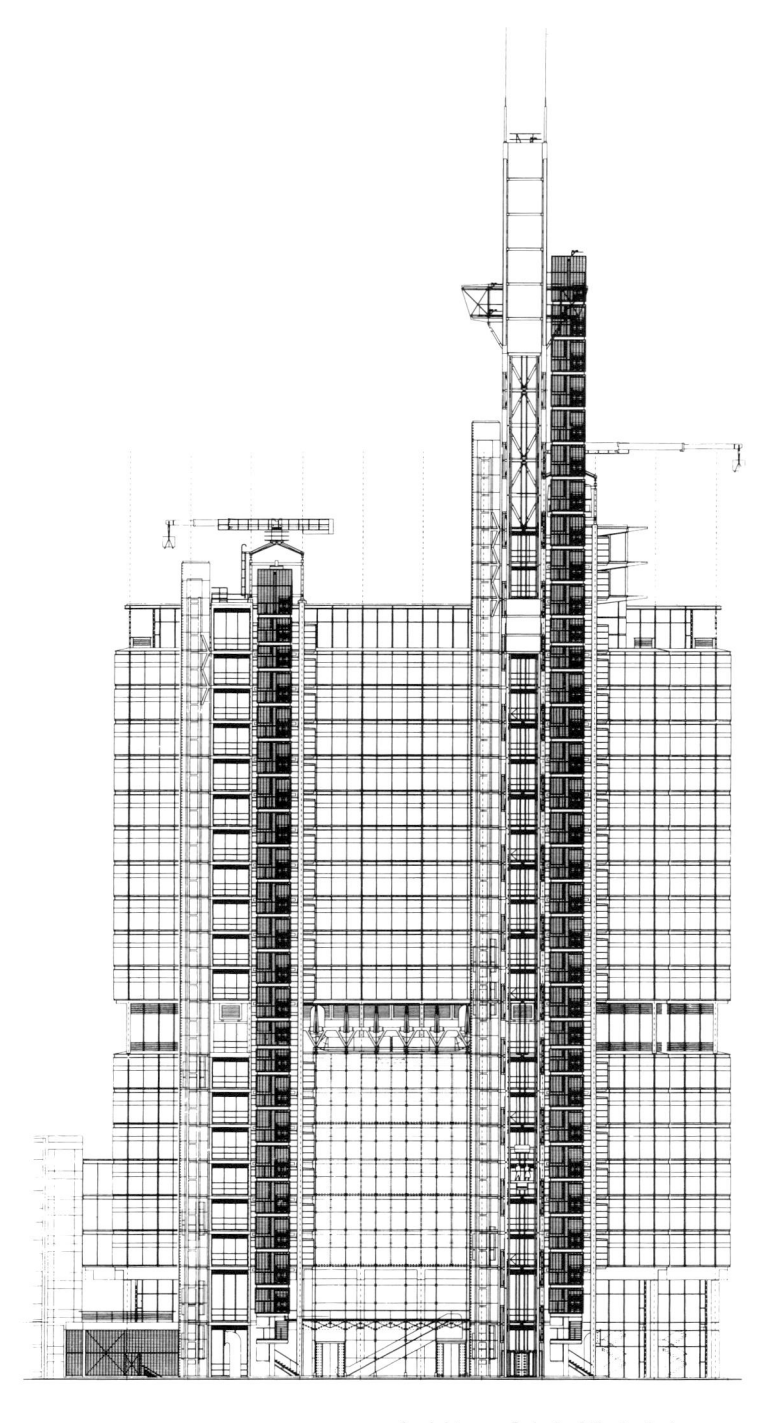

Ansicht vom Bahnhof Zoologischer Garten von Norden
North elevation facing Zoologischer Garten station

1:750

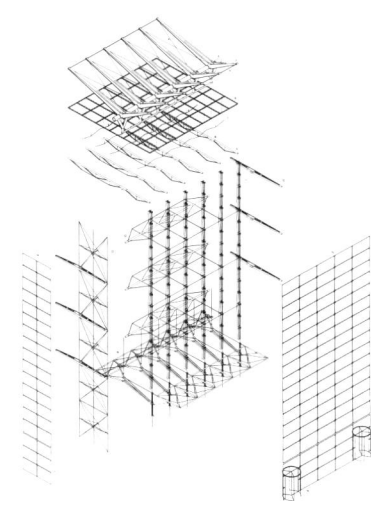

Konstruktion Atrium Sprengaxonometrie
Atrium structure
Exploded axonometric projection

Konstruktion Atrium Modellstudie
Atrium structure
Study model

Büro- und Dienstleistungskomplex am Treptower Park
Office and Services Complex at Treptower Park | Allianz-Standort, Berlin | Gerhard Spangenberg
Berlin
mit with
Brigitte Steinkilberg

Stadtplanung und Städtebau
Urban planning and development
Gerhard Spangenberg
und and Hannes Fehse
(Freie Planungsgruppe Berlin)
mit with Brigitte Steinkilberg | Konzeptplanung und Architektur
Concept and architecture
Gerhard Spangenberg
mit with Brigitte Steinkilberg

Realisierungsplanung
Project planning
Arbeitsgemeinschaft
Gerhard Spangenberg
Schweger + Partner
Reichel und Staudt |

Bauherr:
Grundstücksgesellschaft
Am Treptower Park
Berlin
ein Unternehmen der
Unternehmensgruppe
Roland Ernst

Planungstermine:
Wettbewerb 1993, 1. Preis
Entwurfsplanung seit 1993
Baubeginn 1995
Voraussichtlicher Bezug
1997-1998

Nutzung:
Ladenfläche mit
600 m²
3.300 Büroräume
à 19,5 m² (unterschiedliche
Büro-Raumtypen umgerechnet
auf Standardbüros)

Geschosse:
Hochhaus (XXX):
EG – 29. OG Büros
Bürohaus (V):
EG – 4. OG Büros und Praxen
9 Hofbebauungen (V):
EG – 4. OG Büros
3 Zeilenbebauungen (X):
EG – 9. OG Büros

Untergeschosse:
Hochhaus (II):
Technik, Lager
Bürohaus (I):
Technik, Mieterkeller
Hof- und Zeilenbebauungen (II):
Tiefgarage

Grundstücksgröße:
48.000 m²

Überbaute Fläche:
25.000 m²

Bruttogeschoßfläche:
180.000 m²

Perspektive der Gebäude
an der Spree von Nordosten
Schauzeichnung
Perspective drawing
of the buildings on the Spree
from the northeast
Presentation drawing

Projektadresse:
Location:
Hoffmannstrasse 15–26
in
12435 Berlin-Treptow

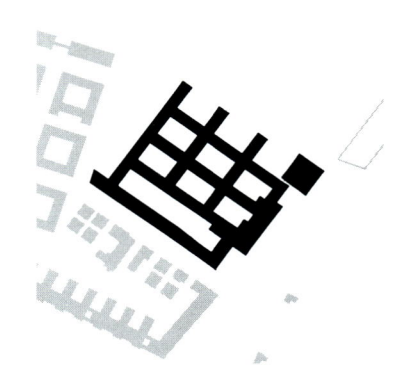

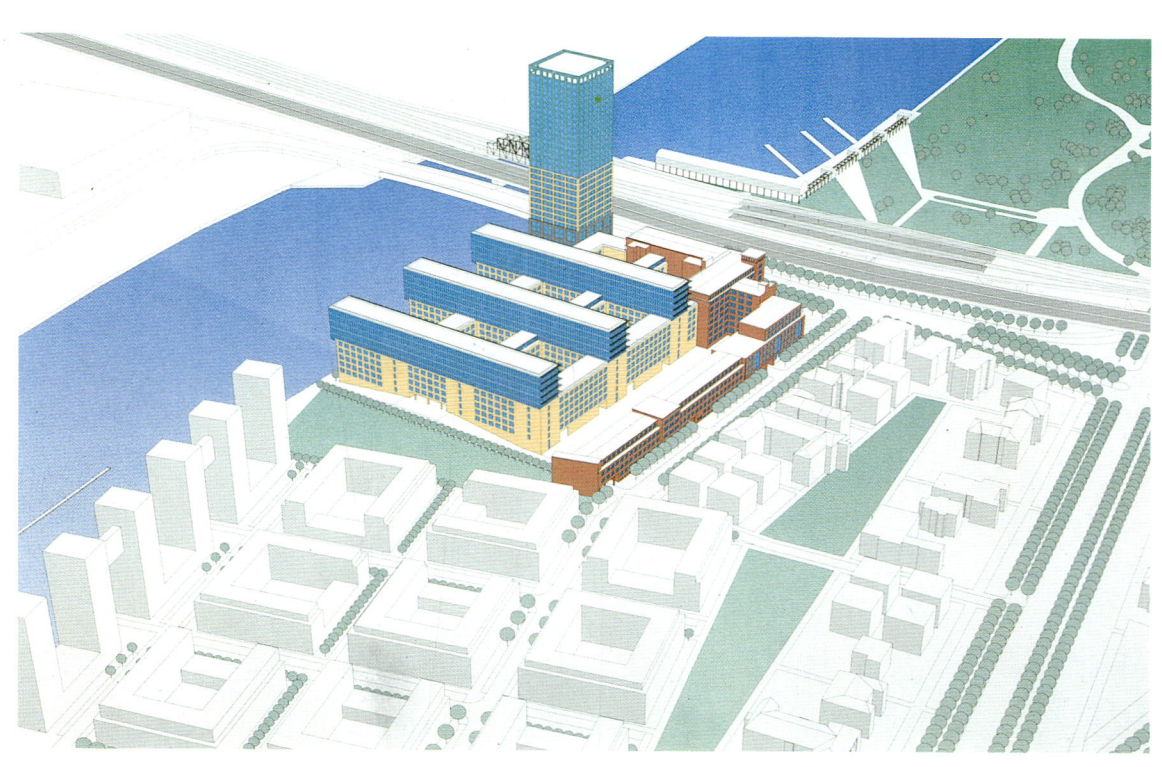

Client:
Grundstücksgesellschaft
Am Treptower Park
Berlin
a company of
Unternehmensgruppe
Roland Ernst

Project Stages:
Competition 1993, 1st prize
Design development from 1993
Start of construction 1995
Expected completion 1997-1998

Building Use:
Retail space of
600 m^2
3300 office rooms
à 19.5 m^2
(different types of offices calculated here as standard offices)

Upper Floors:
High-rise (XXX):
Ground floor – 29th floor offices
Office block (V):
Ground floor – 4th floor offices
and surgeries
9 courtyard blocks (V):
Ground floor – 4th floor offices
3 row buildings (X):
Ground floor – 9th floor offices

Basement Floors:
High-rise (II):
services, storeroom
Office block (I):
services, rented cellar space
Courtyard blocks and row
buildings (II):
car park

Site Area:
48000 m^2

Built Area:
25000 m^2

Gross Floor Area:
180000 m^2

Perspektive des Komplexes von Südwesten
Southwest perspective drawing of the complex

Lageplan
Site plan

**Büro- und
Dienstleistungskomplex
am Treptower Park**
Office and
Services Complex at
Treptower Park

Allianz-Standort, Berlin

Auf dem Gelände des ehemaligen DDR-Kombinats Elektro Apparate Werke (EAW) entsteht ein neues Dienstleistungs- und Gewerbeviertel, das auch Flächen für Wohnen und Gemeinbedarf umfaßt. Im Anschluß an einen internationalen Wettbewerb werden einzelne Bereiche des Komplexes auf der Grundlage des prämierten städtebaulichen Konzeptes des Büros Spangenberg von unterschiedlichen Architekturbüros realisiert. Auf dem östlichen Abschnitt des an die Spree grenzenden Grundstücks entsteht ein Bürozentrum der Allianz nach dem Architekturentwurf von Gerhard Spangenberg.

Bei Erhalt der stadtbildprägenden Klinkerbauten der 20er und 30er Jahre ist eine 5-geschossige Hofbebauung geplant. Ihr wird eine ebenfalls 5-geschossige Zeilenbebauung aufgesattelt, die durch ihre Südsüdwest-Nordnordost-Ausrichtung die Voraussetzung für gute Belichtungs- und Besonnungsverhältnisse schafft.

Als städtebauliche Dominante steht an der Elsenbrücke ein 30-geschossiges Hochhaus, das den Übergang vom naturnahen Landschaftsraum der Spreeufer zur urbanen Gestaltung markiert. Es wird zum Wahrzeichen des gesamten Bürokomplexes.

**Grundriß Erdgeschoß
Bürohochhaus
mit Eingangshalle und Café**
Ground floor plan
Office high-rise
with entrance hall and café

**Grundriß 2.-5. Obergeschoß
Bürohochhaus
mit Büronutzung
(Turmsockel)**
2nd to 5th floor plan
Office high-rise
offices (tower base)

**Grundriß 6.-14. Obergeschoß
Bürohochhaus
mit Büronutzung
(Turmschaft)**
6th to 14th floor plan
Office high-rise
offices (tower shaft)

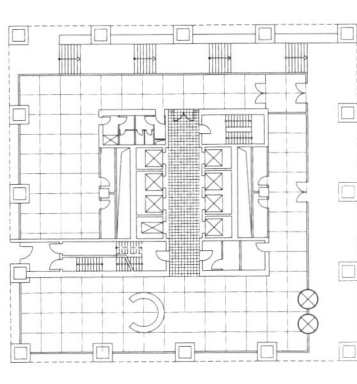

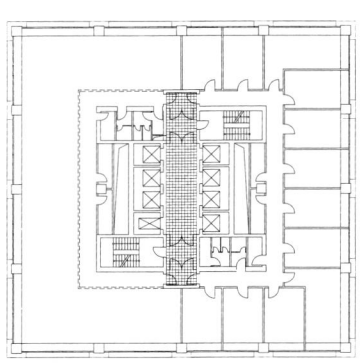

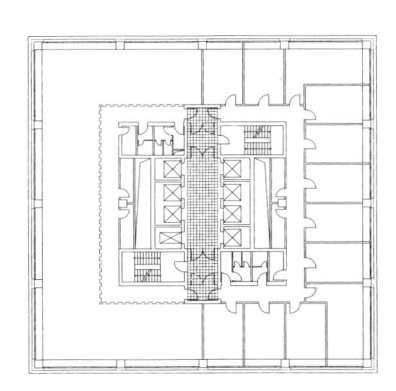

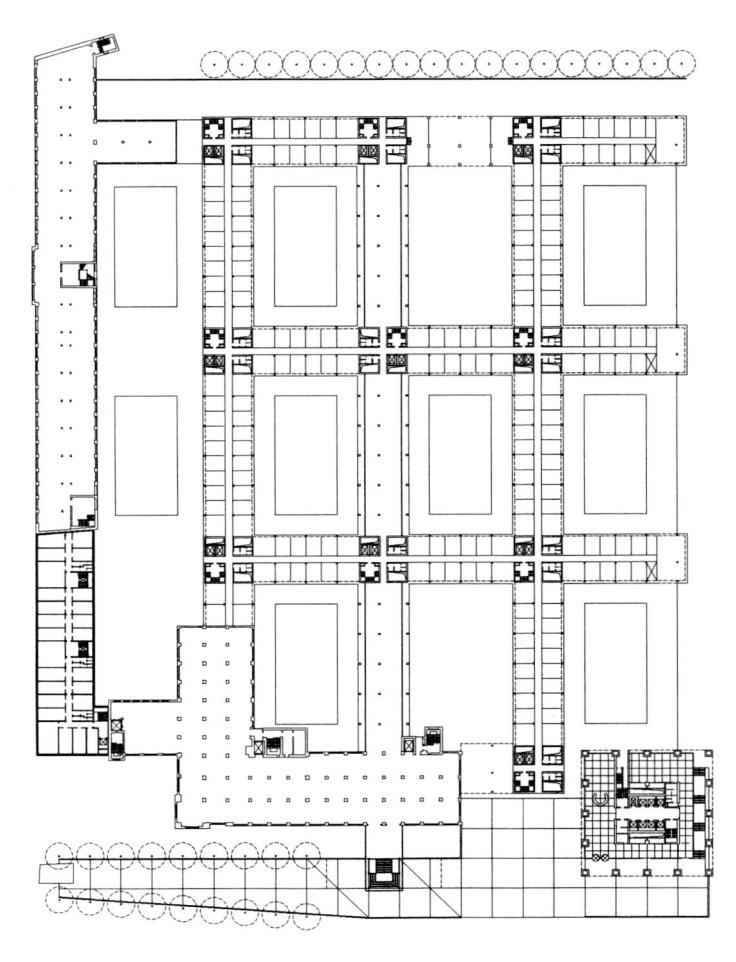

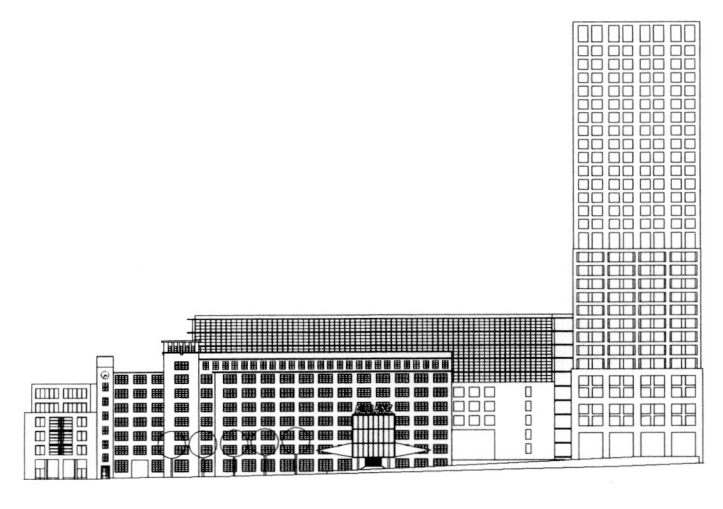

1:750

**Gesamtgrundriß Erdgeschoß
mit Erschließung der Büroetagen
durch den Altbau Elsenstraße**
Overall ground floor plan
with junction of office levels with
existing building on Elsenstrasse

**Ansicht Elsenstraße
von Südosten**
Southeast elevation
Elsenstrasse

1:2000

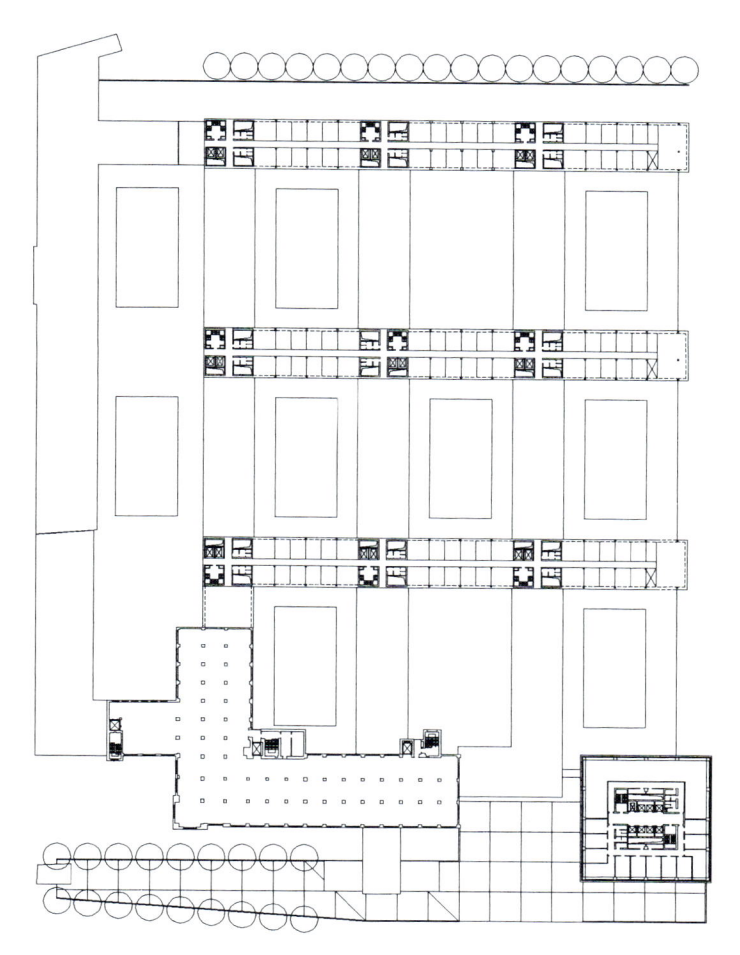

On the site of the former GDR Elektro Apparate Werke (EAW) a new services and business district is being developed. It is also to contain apartments and general purpose areas. Following an international competition individual areas of the complex are to be built by different architects, all of whom base their designs on the general urban concept worked out by Spangenberg. In the eastern section of the site bordering on the Spree is an office centre owned by the Allianz company and designed by Gerhard Spangenberg.

In keeping with the characteristic brick buildings of the 1920s and 1930s the proposal is for a 5-storey courtyard block.

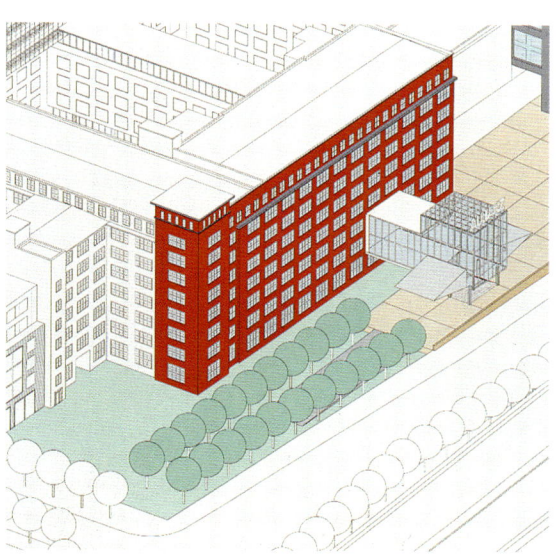

**Gesamtgrundriß
6. Obergeschoß
mit Büronutzung**
Overall 6th floor plan
offices

1:2000

**Eingang »Allianz«
an der Elsenstraße
von Südosten
Axonometrische Darstellung**
Entrance on Elsenstrasse
from the southeast
Axonometric projection

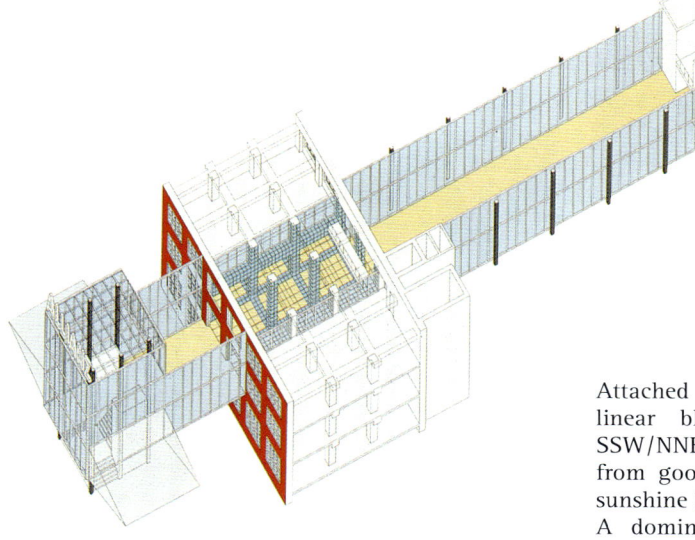

**Erschließungsachse
Eingang »Allianz«
an der Elsenstraße von Südosten
Innenraumaxonometrie**
Circulations axis,
entrance Elsenstrasse
from the southeast
Axonometric projection
of the interior

Attached to this is a 5-storey linear block which with its SSW/NNE alignment benefits from good natural lighting and sunshine levels.

A dominating 30-storey highrise is situated at Elsenbrücke, marking the transition between the natural landscape of the banks of the Spree and the urban fabric. This tower block becomes the symbol of the whole office complex.

Büro- und
Dienstleistungskomplex
am Treptower Park
Office and
Services Complex at
Teptower Park

Spreetürme und Karrees

Georg Kieferle & Partner
Stuttgart – Berlin
Georg Kieferle
Cornelia Kieferle-Nicklas
Eberhard Bender

Bauherr:
Grundstücksgesellschaft
Am Treptower Park
Berlin
ein Unternehmen der
Unternehmensgruppe
Roland Ernst

Planungstermine:
Wettbewerb 1993
(1. Preis Gerhard Spangenberg,
1. Ankauf Kieferle & Partner)
Entwurfsplanung
seit Dezember 1993
Baubeginn August 1994
Voraussichtlicher Bezug 1996

Nutzung:
Läden
Büros

Geschosse:
Hochhaus (XVIII):
EG Läden
1.-15. OG Büros
16.+17. OG Technik
2 Karrees (VII):
EG – 5.OG Büros
6. OG Technik

Untergeschoß (I):
Tiefgarage

Grundstücksgröße:
12.440 m²

Überbaute Fläche:
2 Karrees à 2.036 m²
Hochhaus 735 m²

Bruttogeschoßfläche:
(ohne Tiefgarage)
Hochhaus 11.187 m²
2 Karrees à 10.477 m²

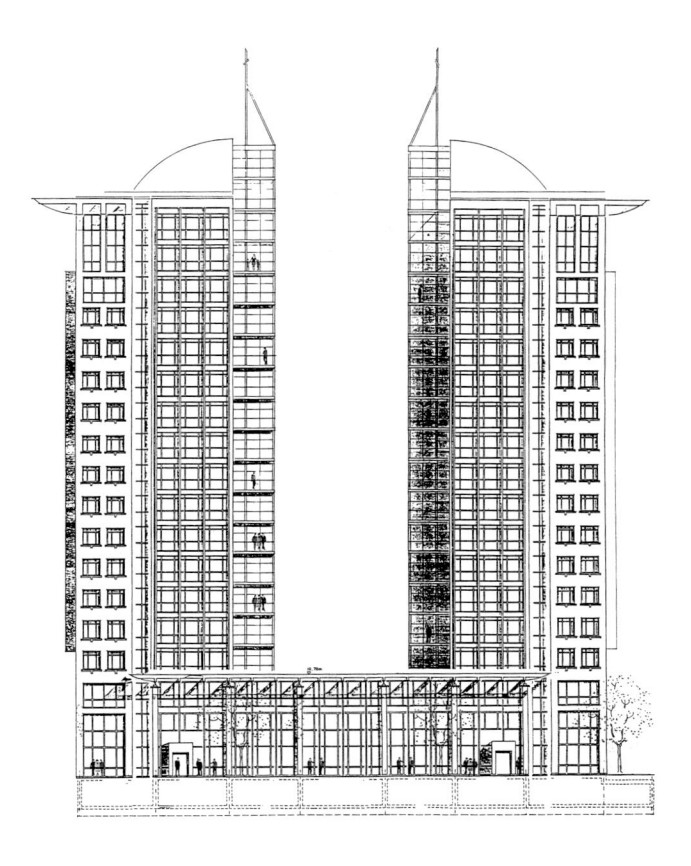

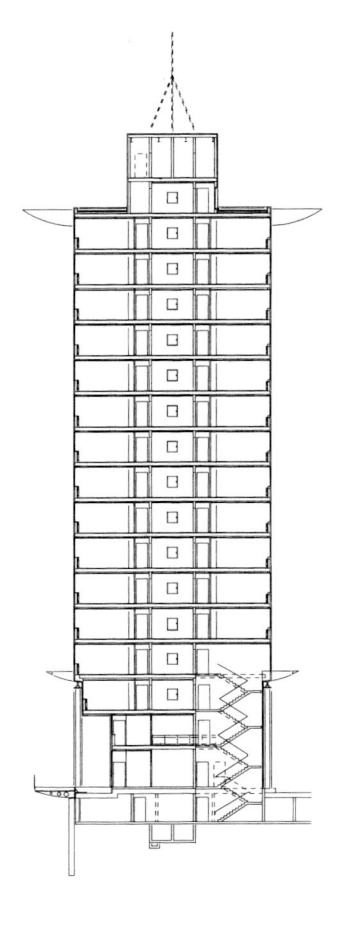

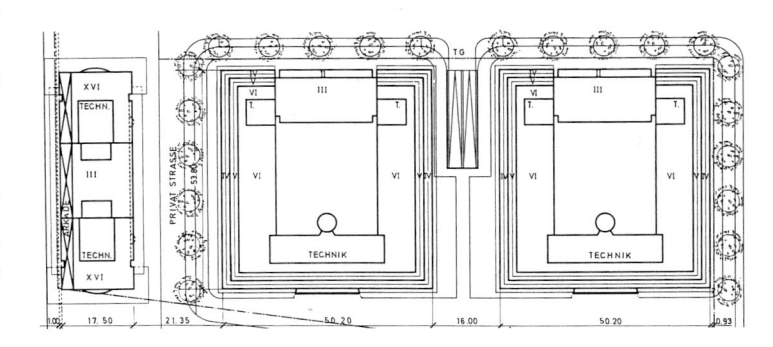

**Ansicht der Bürotürme
von der Eichenstraße von Süden**
South elevation of office towers
from Eichenstrasse

1:750

Lageplan Bürotürme und Karrees
Site plan of office towers and blocks

1:2000

Turmquerschnitt
Cross section of tower

1:750

Projektadresse:
Location:
Hoffmannstrasse/Eichenstrasse
in
12435 Berlin-Treptow

Client:
Grundstücksgesellschaft
Am Treptower Park
Berlin
a company of
Unternehmensgruppe
Roland Ernst

Project Stages:
Competition 1993
(1st prize Gerhard Spangenberg
1st purchase Kieferle & Partner)
Design development from
December 1993
Start of construction August 1994
Expected completion 1996

Building Use:
Shops
Offices

Upper Floors:
High-rise (XVIII):
Ground floor shops
1st-15th floor offices
16th and 17th floor services
2 blocks (VII):
Ground floor – 5th floor offices
6th floor services

Basement Floor (I):
Car park

Site Area:
12440 m²

Built Area:
2 blocks à 2036 m²
High-rise 735 m²

Gross Floor Area
(excluding underground
car park)
High-rise 11187 m²
2 blocks à 10477 m²

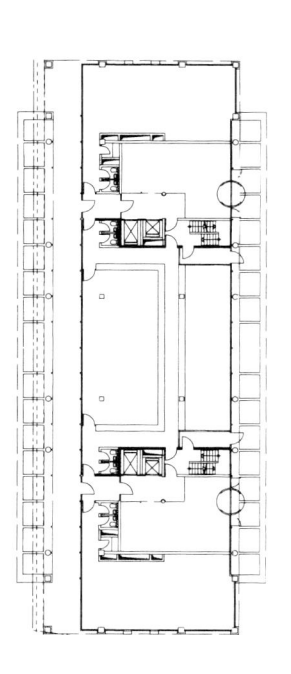

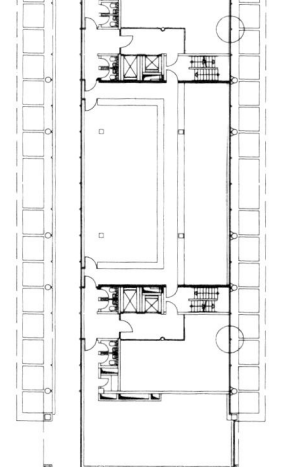

**Grundriß Erdgeschoß
Bürotürme mit Ladennutzung**
Ground floor plan
of office towers
retail

**Grundriß 1. Obergeschoß
mit Büronutzung**
1st floor plan
offices

1:750

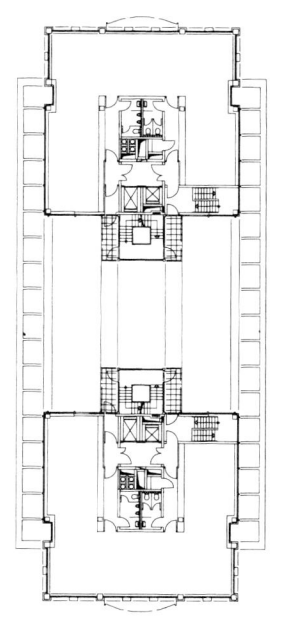

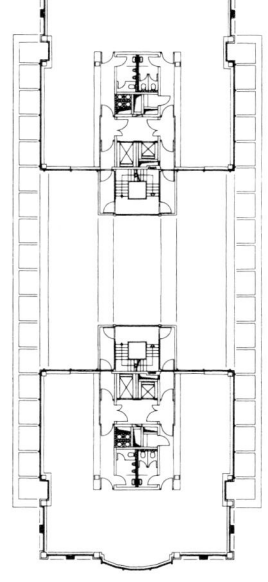

**Grundriß 3. Obergeschoß
mit Büronutzung**
3rd floor plan
offices

**Grundriß 4.-12. Obergeschoß
mit Büronutzung**
Plan of 4th to 12th floors
offices

1:750

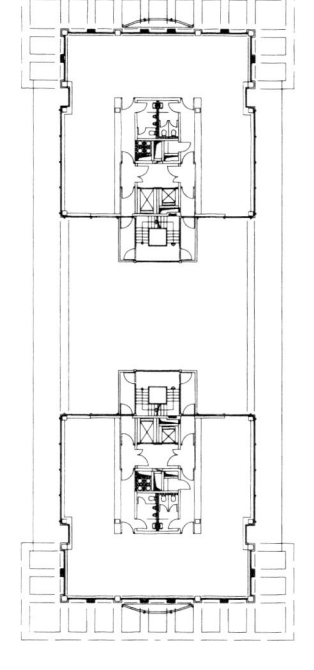

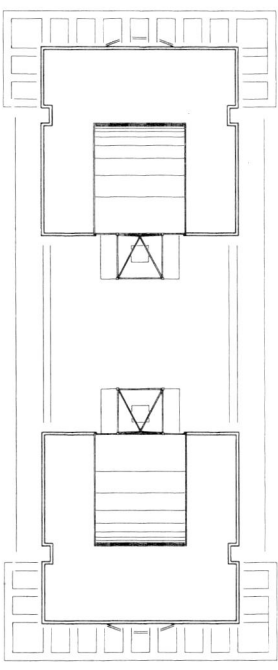

**Grundriß 14. und
15. Obergeschoß
mit Büronutzung**
Plan
of 14th and 15th floors
offices

Dachaufsicht
Top view of roof

1:750

Büro- und Dienstleistungskomplex am Treptower Park
Office and Services Complex at Treptower Park

Spreetürme und Karrees

Der Bürokomplex der Architekten Kieferle & Partner entsteht auf dem westlichen Teilgrundstück des ehemaligen DDR-Kombinats Elektro Apparate Werke (EAW). Als Teilbereich eines neuen Dienstleistungs- und Gewerbeviertels folgt das Projekt den Vorgaben des städtebaulichen Entwurfs von Gerhard Spangenberg; es umfaßt eines der vorgesehenen Turmhäuser an der Spree sowie zwei U-förmige Gebäude im Süden der Türme. In dieser Lage definiert der Bürokomplex den Übergang von der industriellen bzw. gewerblichen Nutzung im Westen der Eichenstraße zu den geplanten Wohnblöcken im östlich angrenzenden Bereich.

Die Höhenentwicklung des Projektes orientiert sich mit 18 Geschossen für die an der Spree gelegenen Turmhäuser bzw. 7 Geschossen für die U-förmigen Gebäude an der städtebaulichen Gesamtkonzeption. Durch die Verbindung der Türme mit einem 3-geschossigen Sockelbau und die abgestuften Querspangen der U-förmigen Bürogebäude entsteht eine differenzierte Ausbildung der Baukörper.

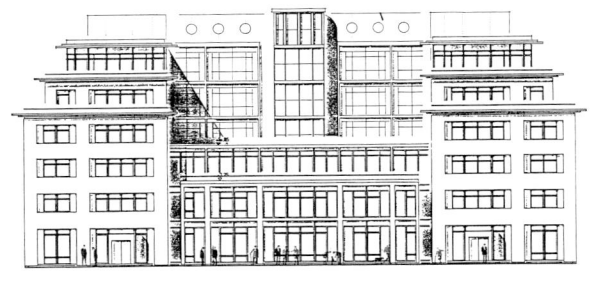

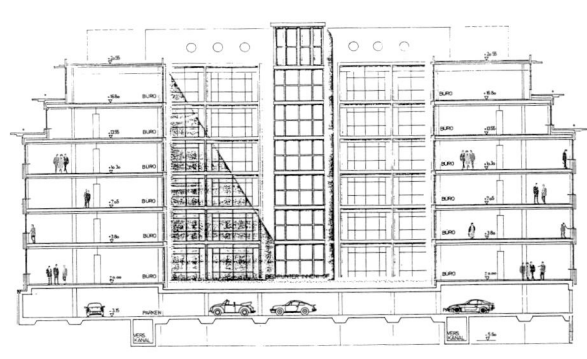

Ansicht Karree-Gebäude von der Eichenstraße von Westen
West elevation of square building from Eichenstrasse

Ansicht von Osten
East elevation

Ansicht von Süden
South elevation

1:750

Gebäudeschnitt im Bereich des begrünten Innenhofes in Nord-Südrichtung
Cross section north-south through landscaped inner courtyard area

1:750

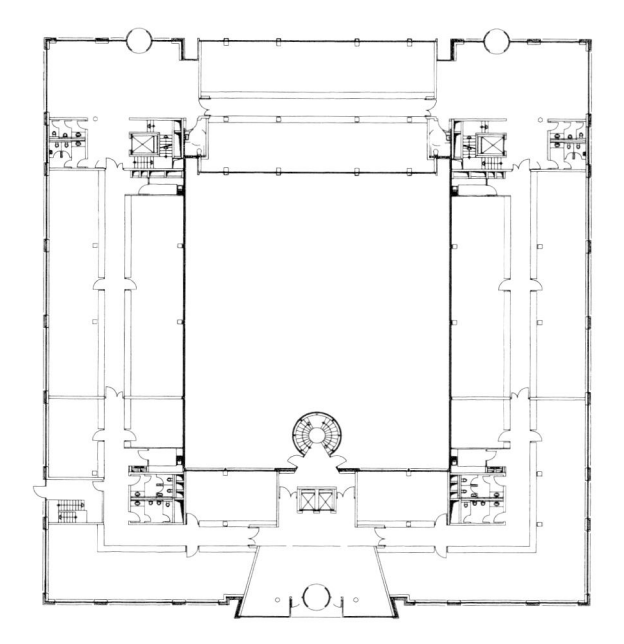

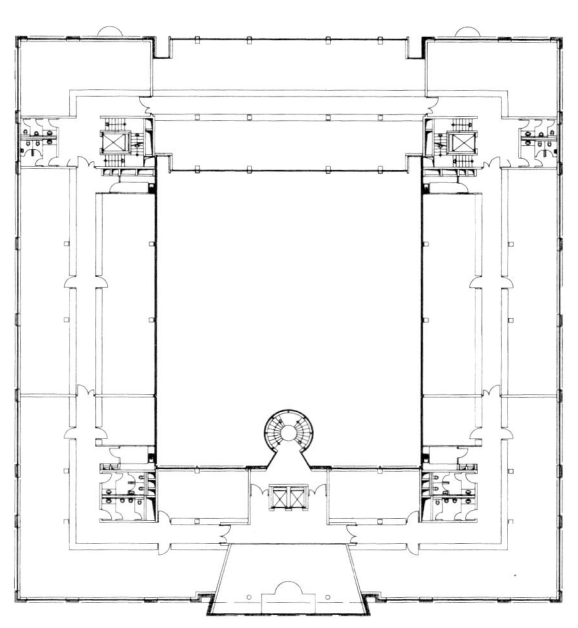

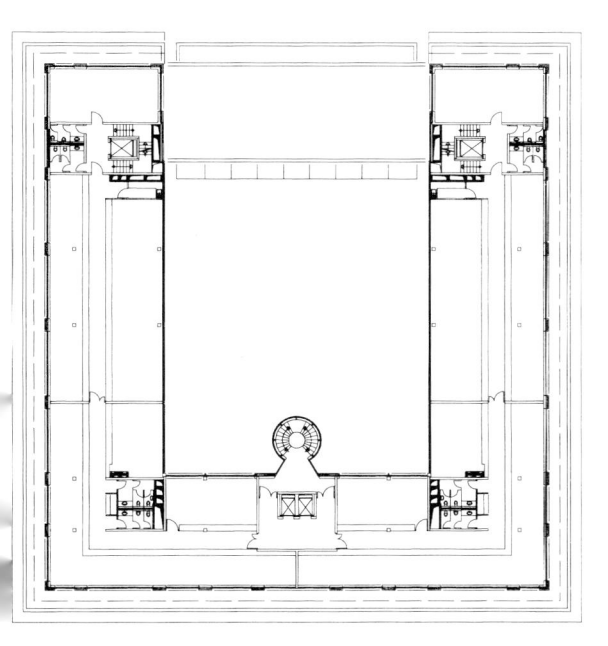

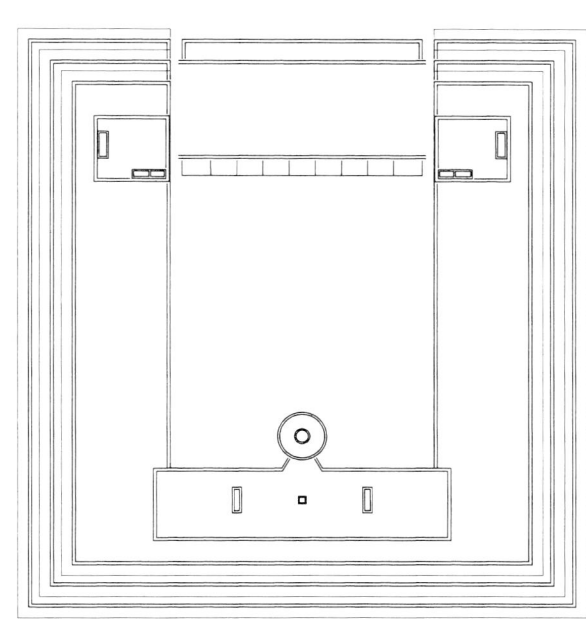

The office complex designed by Kieferle & Partner is situated on the western part of the former GDR Elektro Apparate Werke (EAW). As part of the new services and business district the project is in accordance with Gerhard Spangenberg's urban plan; it comprises one of the planned tower blocks on the Spree and two U-shaped buildings to the south of the towers. In this location the office complex defines the transition from industrial and commercial use west of Eichenstrasse to the projected residential blocks bordering on the east.

The heights of the buildings, i.e. 18 storeys for the tower blocks on the Spree and 7 storeys for the U-shaped buildings, are in line with the overall urban concept. By linking the towers with a 3-storey base structure, and by means of the cross pieces in the U-shaped buildings, the design is further refined and differentiated.

Grundriß Erdgeschoß Karree-Gebäude mit Büronutzung
Ground floor plan square building offices

Grundriß 1. Obergeschoß mit Büronutzung
1st floor plan offices

1:750

Grundriß 4. Obergeschoß mit Büronutzung
4th floor plan offices

Dachaufsicht
Top view of roof

1:750

Büro-, Hotel- und
Geschäftszentrum
Kynaststraße, Ostkreuz
Office, Hotel and
Commercial Centre
Kynaststrasse, Ostkreuz

Twin Towers

Klaus Theo Brenner
Berlin

Mitarbeit staff
Giovanna Di Loreto

Bauherr:
INCO Baupartner GmbH
Berlin

Planungstermine:
Entwurfsplanung seit 1994
Baubeginn 1997
Voraussichtlicher Bezug 1999

Nutzung:
Läden
Büros
Hotel

Geschosse (XXI):
EG + 1.OG Läden
(von der Seeseite)
2. OG Eingangsgeschoß
mit Halle und Sälen
(von der Kynaststraße)
3.-20. OG Büros und Hotel

Untergeschosse:
keine

Grundstücksgröße:
ca. 10.000 m²

Überbaute Fläche:
ca. 2.500 m²

Bruttogeschoßfläche:
ca. 37.000 m²

Das Projekt wurde auf der Grundlage des städtebaulichen Rahmenplans für das Entwicklungsgebiet Rummelsburger Bucht entwickelt. Als eines von drei Zwillingshochhäusern mit beabsichtigter Ensemblewirkung ordnet sich das Gebäude dem Bahnkörper und dem Ostkreuz zu. Das steinerne Hochhaus mit Mauerwerksfassade ist zur Bahn hin glatt und horizontal gegliedert, zur Bucht stark plastisch ausgebildet.

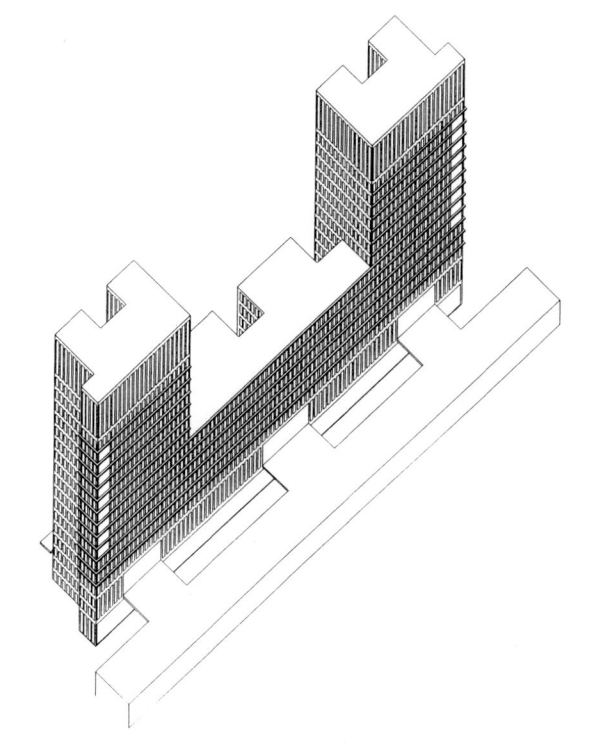

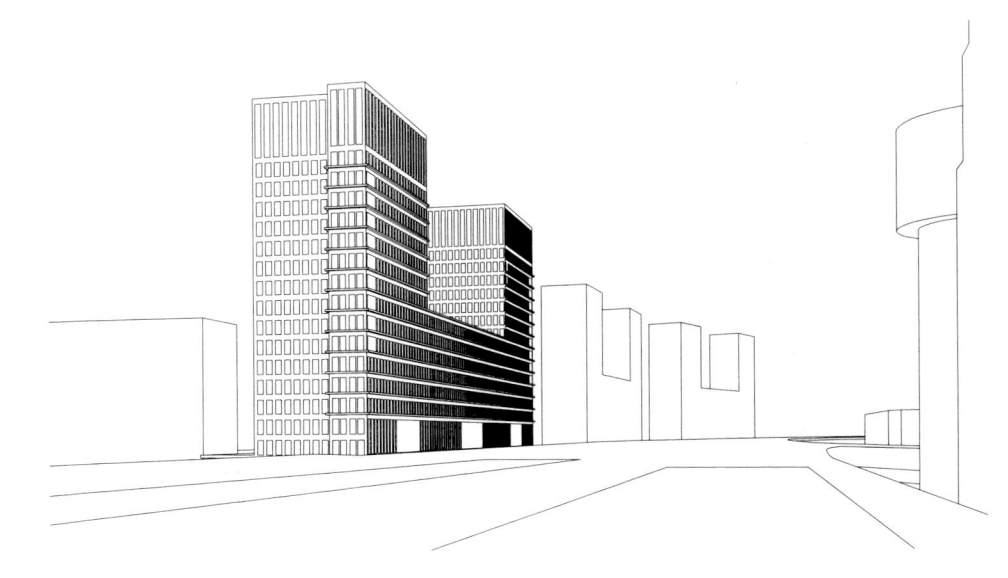

oben above
**Axonometrie
Ansicht der zur Bucht
gewandten Fassade**
Axonometric projection
of façade facing the bay

**Axonometrie
Ansicht der zum Bahnkörper
gewandten Fassade an der Kynaststraße**
Axonometric projection of Kynaststrasse façade facing the railway

**Perspektive von Südosten
Blick entlang der
Bahnpromenade**
Perspective drawing
from southeast along
Bahnpromenade

Projektadresse:
Location:
Kynaststrasse 18-25
in
10317 Berlin-Lichtenberg

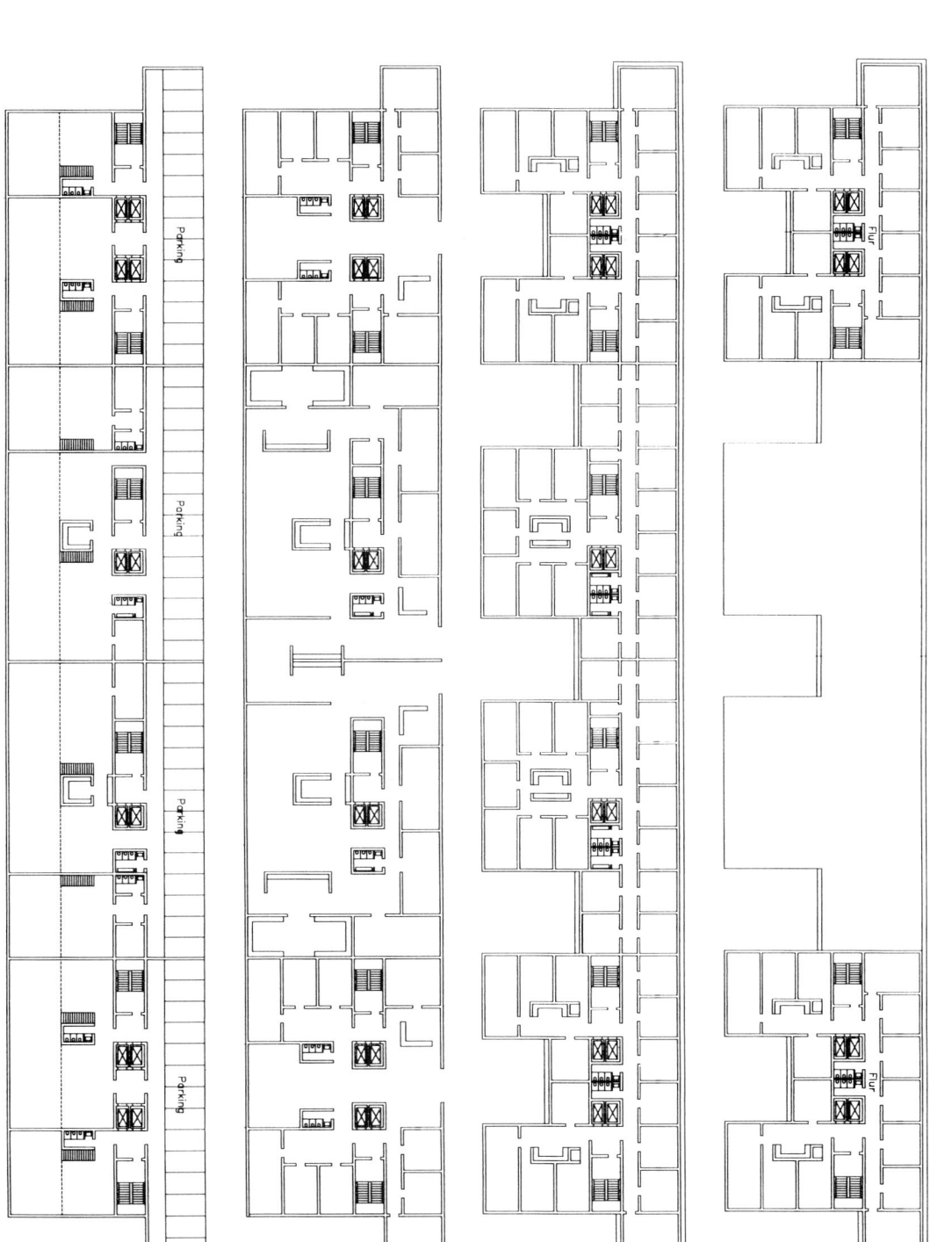

Client:
INCO Baupartner GmbH
Berlin

Project Stages:
Design development from 1994
Start of construction 1997
Expected completion 1999

Building Use:
Shops
Offices
Hotel

Upper Floors (XXI):
Ground floor – 1st floor
shops (from the lakeside)
2nd floor
entrance level with entrance
hall and functions halls (from
Kynaststrasse)
3rd-20th floor
offices and hotel

Basement Floors:
none

Site Area:
ca. 10000 m²

Built Area:
ca. 2500 m²

Gross Floor Area:
ca. 37000 m²

The project was developed in accordance with the basic urban plan for the Rummelsburger Bucht area. As one of three twin-towers designed to work as an ensemble, the building is oriented towards the railway and Ostkreuz. The stone-like high-rise with masonry façade presents a smooth, horizontally divided face towards the railway and is strongly sculptural in character on the side facing the bay.

**Grundriß Erdgeschoß
mit Ladennutzung**
Ground floor plan
retail

**Grundriß Eingangsgeschoß
Kynaststraße mit Gastronomie,
Hotelhalle**
Plan of entrance level
Kynaststrasse
restaurants, hotel lobby

1:750

**Grundriß Normalgeschoß
mit Büronutzung, Hotel**
Typical floor plan
offices, hotel

**Grundriß
11.-20. Obergeschoß
mit Büronutzung, Hotel**
Plan of 11th to 20th floors
offices, hotel

1:750

V
Potsdamer Platz: Die neue Mitte?

Potsdamer Platz mit dem Columbushaus von Erich Mendelsohn im Hintergrund, Aufnahme um 1930
Potsdamer Platz, with Erich Mendelsohn's Columbushaus in the background, photograph ca. 1930

Brüder Luckhardt und Alfons Anker, Telschowhaus, Potsdamer Straße, 1926-1928
Luckhardt Brothers and Alfons Anker, Telschowhaus, Potsdamer Strasse, 1926-1928

›Potsdamer Platz‹ bezeichnet heute ein ausgedehntes innerstädtisches Gelände, das nach Süden durch den Landwehrkanal, nach Westen durch das Kulturforum und nach Norden durch den Tiergarten begrenzt wird; wie eine städtebauliche Halbinsel schließt es nur nach Osten an den Stadtkörper der Bezirke Mitte und Kreuzberg an. Seinen Namen verdankt das Areal der an seinem nordöstlichen Rand gelegenen Brache des ehemaligen Potsdamer Platzes.

Der historische Potsdamer Platz ist Mythos und Legende zugleich. In den zwanziger und dreißiger Jahren galt er als Europas verkehrsreichster Platz und als Sinnbild modernen Großstadtlebens. Hier schienen »alle technischen Errungenschaften der Verkehrsregelung von Paris, London, New York sozusagen ausstellungsmäßig angewandt zu sein«[1]. Es gab einen aus Amerika importierten modernen Verkehrsturm, hell aufleuchtende Neonreklamen und vor allem einen ununterbrochenen und kaum zu bändigenden Fahrzeug- und Fußgängerverkehr, der auch durch Verkehrspolizisten – die »bei diesem feierlichen Akt eine Art Menuett«[2] aufführten – kaum in geordnete Bahnen zu lenken war.

Für die Architekten der Moderne war der Potsdamer Platz – wie der Alexanderplatz – einer der zentralen Orte der Auseinandersetzung mit moderner Architektur und Großstadtplanung. Hier war mit dem Columbushaus von Erich Mendelsohn 1930 eines der modernsten Bürohäuser Europas entstanden. Das Projekt von Martin Wagner mit einem mehrstöckigen Verkehrsring zur Entflechtung des Automobilverkehrs und das Hochhaus der Brüder Luckhardt in der Achse der Leipziger Straße blieben hingegen kühne Vision.

Seit dem Fall der Mauer und nach Beseitigung der Grenzanlagen, die das Gelände im Zustand einer Brache gehalten hatten, entstanden neue Projekte für den Potsdamer Platz. 1991 wurde der städtebauliche Wettbewerb durchgeführt. Preisträger waren die Münchener Architekten Hilmer & Sattler mit einem Projekt, das »nicht das weltweit verwendete Stadtmodell der Hochhausagglomeration, sondern die Vorstellung von der kompakten, räumlich komplexen europäischen Stadt«[3] vertrat. Gegen Gebäudeformen, wie sie das Europacenter verkörperte, wurde gefordert: »Städtisches Leben soll sich nicht im Inneren großstrukturierter Gebäudekomplexe, sondern auf Straßen und Plätzen entfalten«[4].

Der Entwurf zielte auf eine Neuinterpretation des Berliner Blocks, der nicht nach dem traditionellen Muster der Blockrandbebauung, sondern durch »große Häuser« von ca. 50 x 50 m Seitenlänge bebaut werden sollte. Die Traufhöhe sollte – mit Ausnahme turm-

V
Potsdamer Platz: The New Centre?

Today, the name Potsdamer Platz signifies an extensive inner-city site bordered in the south by the Landwehr canal, in the west by the Kulturforum and in the north by the Tiergarten; like an urban peninsula it links in the east to the inner-city area of Berlin Mitte and to Kreuzberg. Its name comes from the area of wasteland to the northeast which was once the original Potsdamer Platz.

The name Potsdamer Platz has historic, almost legendary significance. In the 1920s and 30s it was Europe's busiest square and the very image of modern city life. Here it seemed as if »all the technical achievements in traffic regulation in Paris, London and New York had been integrated into one perfect model.«[1] There was a modern traffic tower, bright neon advertising and above all a never-ending, almost unstoppable stream of people and traffic; traffic policemen conducted a »kind of ceremonial minuet«[2] in an attempt to direct them all into ordered channels.

For the architects of the Modern movement Potsdamer Platz, like Alexanderplatz, was a focus of the debate between Modern architecture and city planning. It was here in 1930 that one of the most modern office buildings in Europe was built - the Columbus House by Erich Mendelsohn. Other schemes were to remain simply bold visions: Martin Wagner's project for a vertically layered road system to stream the traffic, and the Luckhardt brothers' high-rise in line with Leipziger Strasse.

Since the fall of the Berlin wall and the removal of the border fortifications which turned Potsdamer Platz into an enforced wasteland, new projects have been developed for this site. In 1991 an urban planning competition was held. The prize-winners were the Munich architects Hilmer & Sattler with a project which »did not fall in line with the urban model for an agglommeration of high-rises, such as is generally found throughout the world, but sought to present a compact, spatially complex, European town model (...).«[3] In contrast to the model presented by such building forms as the Europacenter, the belief here was that »the life of a city is not played out inside large-scale building complexes, but on the streets and in the public squares.«[4]

The design aimed at a new interpretation of the »Berlin Block«, not in the traditional form of continuous block edge development, but as a succession of »large square houses« with 50 m sides. The eaves height, with the exception of the towers on Potsdamer Platz, was to be kept to 35 m, and as such was considerably higher than the traditional eaves height in Berlin.

Brüder Luckhardt, Haus Berlin am Potsdamer Platz, Entwurfsvarianten 1929-1931

Luckhardt Brothers, Haus Berlin on Potsdamer Platz, design variants 1929-1931

Martin Wagner, Übergreifender Entwurf für Leipziger und Potsdamer Platz mit angehobenem Verkehrsring, Modellfoto 1929

Martin Wagner, overall plan for Leipziger Platz and Potsdamer Platz with raised roadway, model photo 1929

artiger Akzente am Potsdamer Platz – einheitlich bei 35 m liegen und damit die traditionelle Berliner Traufhöhe deutlich überschreiten. In diesen Dimensionen schienen die Häuser geeignete städtebauliche Bausteine, um die angestrebte Vielfalt der Nutzungen als Wohn- und Geschäftshaus, Kaufhaus, Konzernzentrale, Musical-Theater, Hotel etc. architektonisch umsetzen zu können. Zwischen den Häusern angeordnete kurze und schmale Straßen sollten in großzügige städtische Räume münden: in die Neue und die Alte Potsdamer Straße, den Freiraum mit großer Wasserfläche auf dem Gelände des ehemaligen Potsdamer Bahnhofs und den Grünkeil zum Tiergarten.

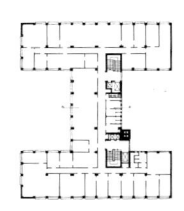

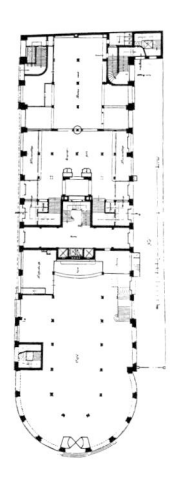

Der Entwurf von Hilmer & Sattler wurde durch Senatsbeschluß vom 10. Dezember 1991 Grundlage des Bebauungsplanverfahrens. Er wurde ergänzt und detailliert durch die Ergebnisse der Realisierungswettbewerbe, die durch drei der insgesamt vier Investoren ausgelobt und 1992 bzw. 1993 entschieden wurden. Die aus diesen Wettbewerben hervorgegangenen Preisträger waren Renzo Piano (Paris) für Daimler Benz/debis, Giorgio Grassi (Mailand) für ABB sowie Helmut Jahn (Chicago) für Sony.

Helmut Jahn bricht mit der Bebauung des dreieckigen Grundstücks am Kemperplatz die orthogonale Blockstruktur des Masterplans kaleidoskopisch auf und organisiert die Bauteile um ein ovales, mit einem Zeltdach überspanntes öffentliches »Forum«. Neben dem großen Dach des Forums werden weitere architektonische Akzente des Komplexes durch das Hochhaus am Potsdamer Platz und durch den Sony-Trakt am Kemperplatz gesetzt. Der zentrale ovale Baukörper zeichnet sich mit geschwungener Fassade zum ›Grünkeil‹ ab; diese sich zum Tiergarten weitende Grünfläche nimmt mit ihrer auf konzentrischen Ringen aufgebauten Gestaltung die Gebäudeform des Forums auf.

Giorgio Grassi und Renzo Piano hingegen führen den Bebauungsplan von Hilmer & Sattler formal und funktional konsequenter fort. Grassi entwickelt für das langgestreckte Grundstück am Ostrand des Planungsgebietes eine Addition von Baukörpern mit H-förmigem Grundriß. Er greift damit einen Gebäudetyp auf, den Bruno Paul 1929/30 bei seinem Kathreiner-Haus zur Beantwortung unterschiedlicher stadträumlicher Situationen – Randbebauung zur Potsdamer Straße und sich öffnende Hofform zum Kleistpark und den Königskolonnaden – realisiert hatte. Auch Grassi nutzt diese Gebäudetypologie, um die Baukörper über Höfe zur Köthener Straße und zum Park auf dem ehemaligen Bahnhofsgelände zu öffnen. Mit der durch zwei der drei Gebäudeflügel gebildeten Blockrandbebauung werden hingegen schmale Straßen zwischen den einzelnen Gebäuden definiert. Damit wird der von Hilmer & Sattler beabsichtigte Kontrast zwischen weiten und engen Stadträumen variiert und ausgearbeitet.

Nach Norden findet das Bebauungsband von Giorgio Grassi seinen Abschluß in einem geschwungenen Baukörper, der die Erinnerung

These dimensions seemed to represent the appropriate building unit size to give sufficient architectural scope for accommodating the variety of intended uses - apartments, offices, department stores, company headquarters, theatres, hotels etc. Short, narrow streets between the individual blocks were to lead into wider city spaces: to the Neue and the Alte Potsdamer Strasse; to the area with open water on the site of the former Potsdamer Station; and towards the green wedge leading to the Tiergarten. In a Senate decision of December 10, 1991 Hilmer & Sattler's plan was made the basis for the overall development. It was extended and refined in accordance with the results of the project competitions held by three of the four investors groups and decided in 1992 and 1993. The prize-winners from these competitions were Renzo Piano (Paris) for Daimler-Benz/debis, Giorgio Grassi (Milan) for ABB and Helmut Jahn (Chicago) for Sony.

Helmut Jahn's plan for the triangular site on Kemperplatz breaks the orthogonal block structure of the master plan into a kaleidoscope of elements arranged around an oval, public »Forum« covered by a tent-like roof. Other points of architectural focus in the complex are the high-rise on Potsdamer Platz and the Sony building on Kemperplatz. The central, oval building volume presents a curved façade to the »green wedge«; the concentric rings in the design of this area of green, extending and widening towards the Tiergarten, echo the shape of the Forum.

Giorgio Grassi's and Renzo Piano's projects, however, represent a more logical continuation of Hilmer & Sattler's plan in form and function. For the long, narrow lot on the east side of the site Grassi has developed a design consisting of an additive sequence of building volumes on an H-shaped ground plan. This building type was also used by Bruno Paul in the Kathreiner Building, 1929/30, in response to the diverse urban situations encountered at the site - block edge development towards Potsdamer Strasse and a more open courtyard formation towards Kleistpark and the Königskolonnaden. Grassi, too, uses this type to open up the building, via courtyards, towards Köthener Strasse and the park on the former station site. The block edge development formed by two of the three building wings is defined by narrow streets between the individual buildings. This achieves variation in the contrast intended by Hilmer & Sattler between wide and narrow urban spaces.

Giorgio Grassi's line of buildings is completed on the northern edge by a curved structure which is reminiscent of the legendary »Haus Vaterland«. To the south of the extended Bernburger Strasse the strip of land which was originally intended for use by the investors is now to be dedicated to school and kindergarden use. Opening onto this area in the south is a spatially and functionally related U-shaped residential block. Based on

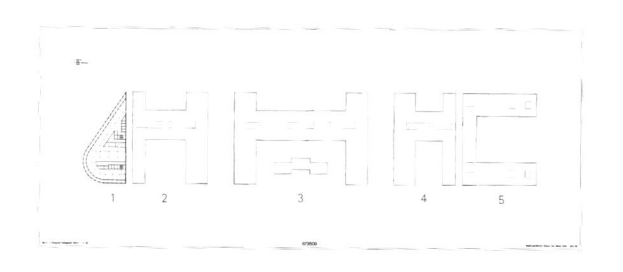

Giorgio Grassi, A+T-Komplex, Lageplan
Giorgio Grassi, A+T complex, site plan

1
Schweger & Partner
2/3
Giorgio Grassi
4
Jürgen Sawade
5
Diener & Diener

Giorgio Grassi, A+T-Komplex, Gesamt-isometrien mit Blick von Nordwesten
Giorgio Grassi, A+T complex, overall isometric projections with views from northwest

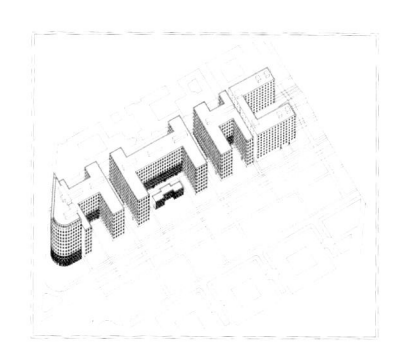

Renzo Piano, Lageplanskizze Potsdamer Platz/Leipziger Straße, Wettbewerbs-planung 1992
Renzo Piano, site plan sketch Potsdamer Platz/Leipziger Strasse, competition planning 1992

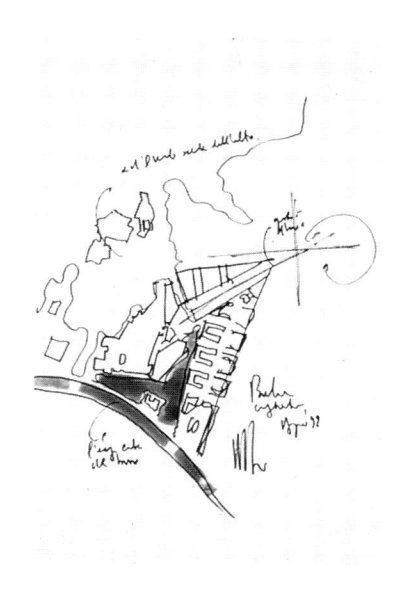

debis-Komplex, Blick auf die Hochhäuser von Hans Kollhoff und Renzo Piano an der Einmündung der Alten Potsdamer Straße in den Potsdamer Platz, Modellfoto
debis complex, view of Hans Kollhoff's and Renzo Piano's high-rises at the junction of Alte Potsdamer Strasse with Potsdamer Platz, model photo

debis-Komplex, Blick vom Landwehrkanal auf das Gebäude von Arata Isozaki und die debis-Hauptverwaltung von Renzo Piano, Modellfoto
debis complex, view from the Landwehrkanal of Arata Isozaki's buildings and Renzo Piano's debis headquarters, model photo

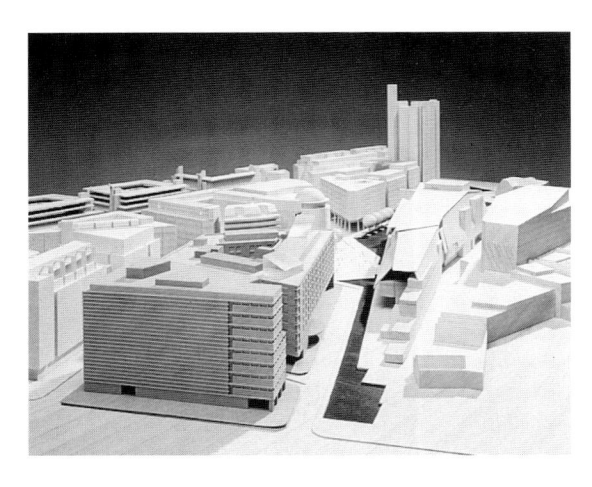

debis-Komplex, Blick in der Achse der neuen Wasserfläche an den Erweiterungsbauten der Neuen Staatsbibliothek entlang, Modellfoto
debis complex, view across new area of water by the building extensions to the new national library, model photo

an das legendäre Haus Vaterland wachhält. Südlich der verlängerten Bernburger Straße steht das bandartige Grundstück nicht mehr – wie anfangs gedacht – den Investoren zur Verfügung, da hier Schul- und Kitastandorte vorgesehen sind. Zu ihnen öffnet sich mit räumlichem und funktionalem Bezug der südliche U-förmige Wohnblock. Auf der Grundlage des Gesamtentwurfes von Giorgio Grassi erfolgte die weitere architektonische Planung der einzelnen Gebäude durch Hinzuziehen von drei weiteren Architekturbüros, die ebenfalls am Wettbewerb beteiligt waren: Schweger + Partner, Diener & Diener und Jürgen Sawade.

Auch Renzo Piano hält sich in seinem Gesamtentwurf für debis im wesentlichen an die Blockstruktur von Hilmer & Sattler, verklammert sie jedoch zum Teil durch eine zentrale, überdachte Shopping Mall. Piano findet darüber hinaus eine entscheidende Neuformulierung des westlichen Abschlusses des Quartiers zur Staatsbibliothek. Die Staatsbibliothek wird auf ihrer nach Osten gewandten Rückseite durch Neubauten ergänzt, die sich vom orthogonalen System der Blockstruktur lösen und mit dem Gebäude von Scharoun zu einer städtebaulichen Einheit verschmelzen.

Innerhalb des Quartiers definieren sie eine zentral gelegene Piazza, die den Stadtraum der Alten Potsdamer Straße auffängt. Rund um die Piazza liegen die Nutzungen, die bis in die Nachtstunden die urbane Lebendigkeit des Quartiers sichern sollen: ein Hotel mit eigenen Geschäften, Restaurants und Konferenzbereich, ein Musical-Theater, eine Spielbank und Wohnungen.

Auch in dem insgesamt 4-geschossigen unterirdischen Bauwerk des Quartiers ist der Platz ein wichtiger Knotenpunkt, da hier die zentrale Lieferzone mit Andockstellen für LKW liegt und über den angrenzenden Tiergartentunnel erschlossen wird. Ein unterirdisches Wegenetz, über das auch die gesamte Entsorgung abgewickelt wird, verbindet diesen Bereich mit den blockbezogenen Nutzungen. Die Einfahrt in den Tiergartentunnel erfolgt von der Uferstraße des Landwehrkanals; die Rampen schneiden in die Wasserfläche ein und sind so aus der Fußgängerperspektive geschickt kaschiert.

Angrenzend an die Einfahrt in den Tiergartentunnel liegt mit dem debis-Gebäude von Renzo Piano am Landkanal eines der Hochhäuser, die ihr Volumen aus der Blockstruktur heraus entwickeln und das Viertel zu den angrenzenden Stadträumen hin zeichenhaft markieren. Am Potsdamer Platz bilden die beiden Hochhäuser von Hans Kollhoff und von Renzo Piano eine Torsituation und schieben sich wie Keile in den Platz hinein. Sie flankieren die Alte Potsdamer Straße, die eine wichtige Erschließungsfunktion für das Quartier übernimmt: Als attraktive Fußgängerpromenade führt die dank ihres historischen Lindenbestandes als Naturdenkmal eingetragene Straße vom neuen unterirdischen S-, U- und Regionalbahnhof am Potsdamer Platz bis zur Piazza und wird

Giorgio Grassi's overall plan the further development of the individual buildings was carried out by three other architectural offices who had also been participants in the competition: Schweger + Partner, Diener & Diener and Jürgen Sawade.

Renzo Piano, too, generally adhered to Hilmer & Sattler's block structure in his overall design. In part, however, he fills in these blocks by creating a central, covered shopping mall. His solution for the western edge of the district towards the Staatsbibliothek (national library) represents a decisive new formulation. Behind the Staatsbibliothek, towards the east, new buildings shake free from the orthogonal block system and blend with Scharoun's building to form an urban entity.

Within the district they mark out a central piazza taking up the urban space of the Alte Potsdamer Strasse. Around the piazza are various types of building use that are intended to promote the urban vitality of the district through into the early hours of the morning: a hotel with its own shopping facilities, restaurants, a conference area, a musical theatre, a casino and apartments. The piazza is intended to »be a diverse and tension-filled focus in the whole district for the eclectic and the disciplined in architecture, for commercial and cultural functions, for water and gardens. In this way it becomes a nerve centre for city life, and a source of inspiration in the overall planning.«

Also in the 4-level subterranean part of this complex the square is a key point of intersection; here is the central delivery zone with loading bays for trucks. From here is also direct access to the nearby Tiergarten tunnel. Supplies for the buildings above enter and leave the area via a subterranean road network. The entrance to the Tiergarten tunnel is via the road along the banks of the Landwehr canal; the ramps extend into the water and are thus cleverly concealed from view to pedestrians.

Bordering on the Tiergarten tunnel entrance is the debis Building by Renzo Piano on the Landwehr canal; it is one of a number of high-rises which develop their volumes out of the block structure and demarcate the district from neighbouring areas of town. On Potsdamer Platz the two high-rises by Hans Kollhoff and Renzo Piano form a gateway situation, projecting like a wedge into the square. These towers flank the Alte Potsdamer Strasse which fulfils an important linking function for the district. This street forms an attractive pedestrian promenade and, thanks to the old lime trees lining the route, it is protected by a preservation order as a natural monument. It leads from the new Potsdamer Platz underground station, serving S-Bahn, U-Bahn and the regional network, up to the piazza, and is linked to Margarethenstrasse and the Kulturforum via the Staatsbibliothek.

An interesting aspect of the high-rises by Piano and Kollhoff is their differing use of glass and stone. Kollhoff's design foresees

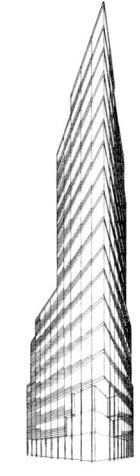

Renzo Piano, Hochhaus am Potsdamer Platz, Skizze
Renzo Piano, high-rise on Potsdamer Platz, sketch

Hans Kollhoff, Hochhaus am Potsdamer Platz
Hans Kollhoff, high-rise on Potsdamer Platz

Renzo Piano, Bürogebäude an der Piazza, Entwurfsskizze
Renzo Piano, office building on the Piazza, design sketch

Renzo Piano, Hochhaus mit debis-Hauptverwaltung, perspektivische Skizze
Renzo Piano, high-rise with debis headquarters, perspective sketch

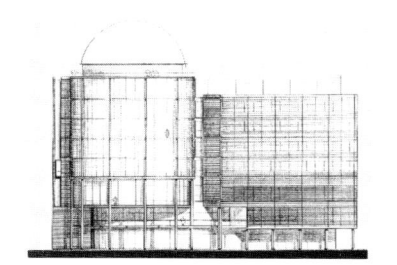

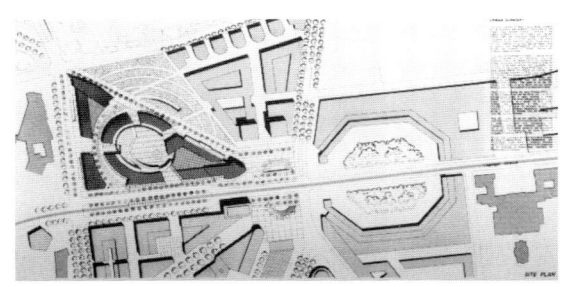

oben above
Otto Rehnig,
Esplanade,
1907-12,
historische
Aufnahme
Otto Rehnig,
Esplanade,
1907-12,
contemporary
photograph

Mitte center
Murphy/Jahn,
Sony-Gelände
Potsdamer Platz,
stadträumliches
Konzept,
Wettbewerb
1992
Murphy/Jahn,
Sony site on
Potsdamer Platz,
urban planning
concept,
competition
1992

Murphy/Jahn,
Piazza des Sony-
Gebäudes,
Innenraum-
perspektive,
Wettbewerb
1992
Murphy/Jahn,
Sony building
piazza, interior
perspective,
competition
1992

durch die Staatsbibliothek hindurch an die Margarethenstraße und das Kulturforum angebunden.

Interessant ist bei den Hochhäusern von Piano und Kollhoff auch die unterschiedliche Verwendung der Materialien Glas und Stein. Kollhoff sieht ein im Bereich der Obergeschosse mit Klinker, in der Sockelzone mit graugrünem Granit verkleidetes, steinern wirkendes Bauwerk mit Lochfassade vor, dessen Volumen sich von den 22 Geschossen des Turmes auf die Traufhöhe des Quartiers zurückstaffelt. Piano schafft am Potsdamer Platz ein transparent und leicht wirkendes Hochhaus mit doppelschaliger Vorhangfassade, das mit dem Kontrast von Glas und Ziegelpaneelen spielt. Auch bei anderen Bauten im Viertel setzt Piano Glas und Ziegel gemeinsam als Gestaltungsmittel ein: Bei seinem Bürogebäude an der Piazza kontrastiert ein gläserner Zylinder mit der benachbarten Ziegelfassade, beim debis-Gebäude am Landwehrkanal löst sich die Ziegelfassade des Blocks schrittweise nach Süden auf und geht in die Glasfassade des Hochhauses über.

Am 3.3.1993 wurde das Bebauungsplanverfahren II-B5 für den Bereich des Potsdamer und Leipziger Platzes förmlich eingeleitet. Für die architektonische Umsetzung wurden neben den bereits genannten Architekten für einzelne Bauten des debis-Komplexes auch Arata Isozaki, Richard Rogers, Rafael Moneo und Lauber & Wöhr hinzugezogen. Die geplante Geschoßfläche von rund 1,1 Mio. m² verteilt sich nach dem Bebauungsplanentwurf auf 50 % Büroflächen, 20 % Handel, 20 % Wohnen und 5-10 % Gastonomie, Kultur und Hotels. Diese urbane Nutzungsmischung benötigt zudem eine übergreifend geplante, aber im Quartier selbst untergebrachte technische und soziale Infrastruktur: eine Grundschule, 4 Kindertagesstätten und eine Energiezentrale. Darüber hinaus muß das öffentliche Verkehrsnetz deutlich ausgebaut werden, um den prognostizierten Verkehrsfluß zu bewältigen und den Individualverkehr auch in diesem Gebiet auf 20 % zu begrenzen.

Bauaufgabe und Ort dieses neuen Quartiers am Potsdamer Platz sind in Europa einzigartig. Mitten im Herzen einer europäischen Hauptstadt entsteht auf historischem Boden ein vollkommen neues Stück Innenstadt für 20.000 Beschäftigte und ein Vielfaches an täglichen Besuchern, Kunden und Geschäftspartnern. In seiner Lage zwischen City West und City Ost bildet es eine städtebauliche Klammer, die die Stadt – über den ehemaligen Grenzbereich hinweg – zu einer funktionalen und räumlichen Einheit verbindet. Dennoch entsteht mit dem Geschäftsviertel nicht die einzige neue Mitte der Stadt Berlin, sondern ein eigenständiges Hauptzentrum, das seinen Platz in der über die Jahrhunderte hinweg polyzentrisch gewachsenen Stadt behaupten muß.

1 H. Walden, »Der Potsdamer Platz«, in: »Weltbühne«, 1927, Bd. 1, S. 77.
2 ebd.
3 Hilmer & Sattler, Erläuterungen zum Wettbewerbsprojekt Potsdamer Platz.
4 ebd.

clinker brick in the upper storeys, with grey-green granite cladding on the base section; the whole effect is of a monolithic volume, with a punctuated façade stepped downwards from the 22nd storey to the general eaves height of the district. Piano's plan is for a transparent, light high-rise with double-skin curtain wall, which makes use of contrasting brick and glass panels. Piano uses this combination of glass and brick in other buildings in the district: in his office building on the piazza he contrasts a glass cylinder with the neighbouring brick façade; in the debis Building on the Landwehr canal the brick façade of the block gradually dissolves towards the south and merges with the glass façade of the high-rise.

On March 3, 1993 the development plan II-B5 was started for the area of Potsdamer Platz and Leipziger Platz. In addition to the architects already mentioned individual buildings in the debis complex are also to be built by Arata Isozaki, Richard Rogers, Rafael Moneo and Lauber & Wöhr. The proposed floor area of about 1.1 million square metres is divided in accordance with the development plan into 50 % office space, 20 % trade, 20 % residential and 5-10 % restaurants, cultural facilities and hotels. This mix of use requires an overall infrastructure plan for the district, to include an elementary school, 4 kindergardens and a central energy unit. In addition the public transport links must be considerably improved in order to be able to cope with the expected increase in traffic and to reduce to 20 % the number of private cars.

The nature and location of this new district taking shape on Potsdamer Platz are unique in Europe. In the very heart of a European capital, on historic ground, a completely new section of the inner city is being created for 20,000 workers, many more visitors, customers and business partners. Located between the City West and City East, on ground where the Berlin wall once stood, it knits the city together into one functional and spatial unit. Yet this business district does not represent the only new centre in Berlin - it is just one main, independent centre which must assert its own identity in a city which has known centuries of polycentric growth and development.

Renzo Piano, Südeinfahrt in den Tiergartentunnel, Fotosimulation
Renzo Piano, south entrance to the Tiergarten tunnel, photo montage

1   H. Walden, »Der Potsdamer Platz«, in: »Weltbühne«, 1927, vol. 1, p. 77.
2   ebd.
3   Hilmer & Sattler, Explanatory notes Potsdamer Platz competition project.
4   ibid.

Daimler-Benz
Gebäude Buildings
B1/B3/B5/B7/C1/D1/D2
Weinhaus Huth
und Gesamtkonzept
and Overall Concept

Potsdamer Platz

Renzo Piano Building Workshop
Paris, Genova
mit with
Christoph Kohlbecker
Gaggenau

Mitarbeiter Büro Piano
Staff Piano office
B. Plattner (Projektleiter project manager), S. Baggs, E. Baglietto, R. Baumgarten, G. Bianchi, P. Charles, G. Ducci, C. Hight, S. Ishida, M. Kramer, N. Mecattaf, J. Moolhuijzen, F. Pagliani, L. Penisson, E. Rossato Piano, J. Ruoff, C. Sapper, S. Schäfer, M. van der Staay, R. V. Trufelli, L. Viti

Bauherr:
debis Gesellschaft für
Potsdamer Platz Projekt und
Immobilienmanagement mbH
Berlin

Planungstermine:
Wettbewerb 1992, 1. Preis
Masterplan April 1993
Entwurfsplanung seit 1994
Baubeginn 1994
Voraussichtlicher Bezug
1997-1998

Nutzung:
debis-Verwaltung
150 Wohnungen
Büros
Läden und Gastronomie
Musicaltheater
Spielbank

Geschosse:
B1 (XVII):
EG + 1. OG Läden
2.-16. OG Büros
Weinhaus Huth (VI):
EG Läden, 1. OG Restaurant
2.-5. OG Wohnungen
B3 (VIII):
EG + 1. OG Läden
2.-7. OG Büros
B5 (X):
EG + 1. OG Läden, 2.-9.
OG Wohnungen
B7 (VIII):
EG – 2. OG Läden
3.-7. OG Büros
C 1 (debis) (XXII/VII):
EG-21. OG Büros
D1 (III): Spielbank
D2 (IV): Musicaltheater

Untergeschosse:
B1/B3/B5/B7 (IV):
1. UG Einzelhandel
2.-4. UG Tiefgarage, Technik
C1 (II):
1.+2. UG Parken, Technik

Grundstücksgröße:
67.157 m²

Überbaute Fläche:
49.600 m²

Bruttogeschoßfläche:
340.000 m²

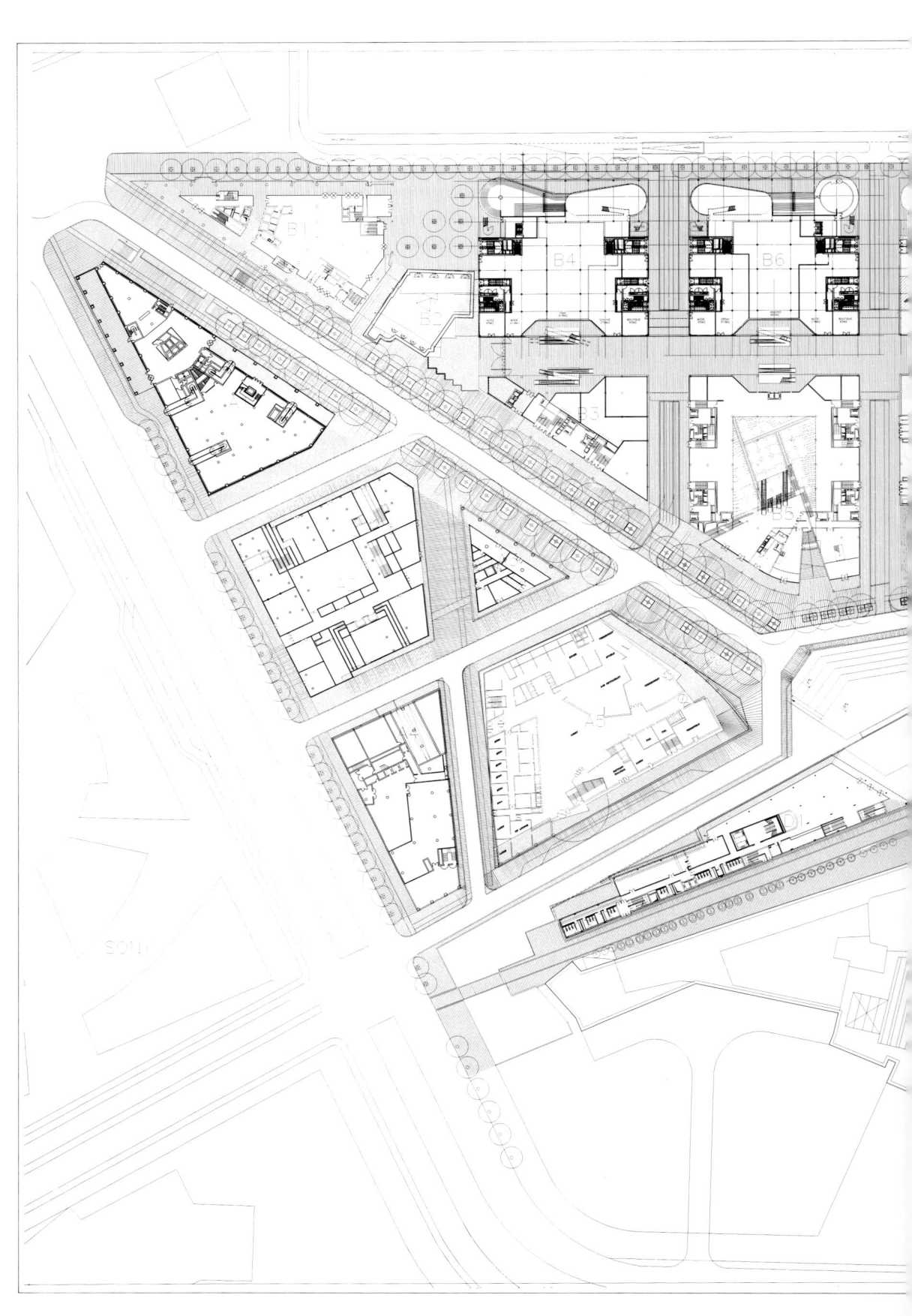

Mitarbeiter Büro Kohlbecker
Staff Kohlbecker office
H. Falk, A. Hocher, R. Jatzke,
M. Kohlbecker, M. Lindner,
N. Nocke, A. Schmid, W. Sprang

Project Projektadresse:
Location:
Potsdamer Platz
in
10785 Berlin-Tiergarten

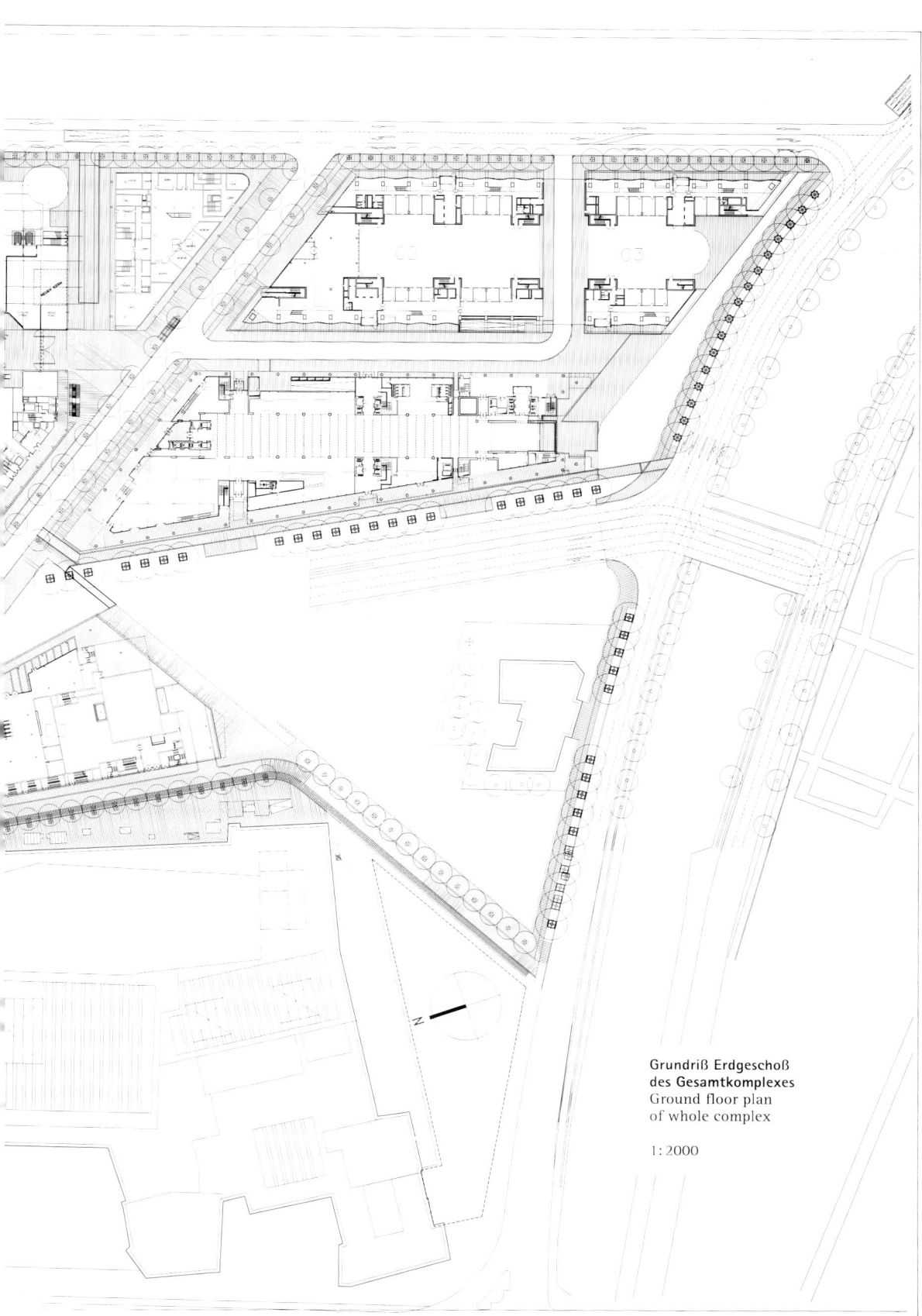

Client:
debis Gesellschaft für
Potsdamer Platz Projekt und
Immobilienmanagement mbH
Berlin

Project Stages:
Competition 1992, 1st prize
Master plan April 1993
Design development from 1994
Start of construction 1994
Expected occupation date 1997-1998

Building Use:
debis administration
150 apartments
Offices
Shops and restaurants
Musical theatre, casino

Upper Floors:
B1 (XVII):
Ground floor and 1st floor shops
2nd-16th floor offices
Weinhaus Huth (VI):
Ground floor shops
1st floor restaurant
2nd-6th floor apartments
B3 (VIII):
Ground floor and 1st floor shops
2nd-7th floor offices
B5 (X):
Ground floor and 1st floor shops
2nd-9th floor apartments
B7 (VIII):
Ground floor – 2nd floor shops
3rd-7th floor offices
C1 (debis) (XXII/VII):
Ground floor – 21st floor offices
D 1 (III): Casino
D 2 (IV): Music theatre

Basement Floors:
B1/B3/B5/B7 (IV):
1st basement retail
2nd-4th basement car park
and building services
C1 (II):
1st and 2nd basement car park,
building services

Site Area:
67157 m^2

Built Area:
49600 m^2

Gross Floor Area:
340000 m^2

Grundriß Erdgeschoß
des Gesamtkomplexes
Ground floor plan
of whole complex

1:2000

Daimler-Benz
Gebäude Buildings
B1/B3/B5/B7/C1/D1/D2
Weinhaus Huth
und Gesamtkonzept
and Overall Concept

Potsdamer Platz

Das debis-Bebauungskonzept des Büros Piano baut auf der Blockstruktur des städtebaulichen Entwurfs von Hilmer & Sattler auf. Der Potsdamer Platz erfährt eine Betonung durch Turmhäuser; ein weiteres Hochhaus steht im Bereich der Wasserbecken am Landwehrkanal. Ausstrahlend von den Hochhäusern am Potsdamer Platz wird die Blockstruktur durch eine zum Landwehrkanal führende Shopping-Mall und die als Fußgängerstraße wiederbelebte Alte Potsdamer Straße durchschnitten. Das Kulturforum erfährt hinter der Staatsbibliothek Ergänzung durch ein Musical-Theater, den Erweiterungsbau für die Staatsbibliothek und einen Ausstellungspavillon. Diese Neubauten definieren einen Stadtplatz, in den die Alte Potsdamer Straße mündet.

Um wieder urbanes Leben im Bereich des Potsdamer Platzes entstehen zu lassen, wurde eine intensive Nutzungsmischung mit Büros, Einzelhandel, Gastronomie, Hotels, Konferenzbereichen, Musical-Theater, Ausstellungspavillon und Wohnungen festgelegt.

Das Büro Piano wurde nach Vorliegen der Bebauungskonzeption u.a. mit der Planung des Sitzes der debis-Hauptverwaltung beauftragt. Dieser Baukörper kombiniert Rechteckblock und Hochhaus. Um ein lineares Atrium mit Hauptzugängen von der Eichhornstraße und von der Uferstraße des Landwehrkanals liegen im Erdgeschoß öffentlichkeitsbezogene Nutzungsbereiche wie der Mercedes-Showroom zur Eichhornstraße, die Empfangszone zum Landwehrkanal, aber auch Meetingroom, Bibliothek, Restaurant und Einzelhandel.

debis-Gebäude (C1)
Ansicht von Süden
debis Building (C1)
South elevation

debis-Gebäude
Ansicht von Norden
mit Schnitt im
Bereich des Atriums
debis Building
North elevation
with section through
atrium area

1:750

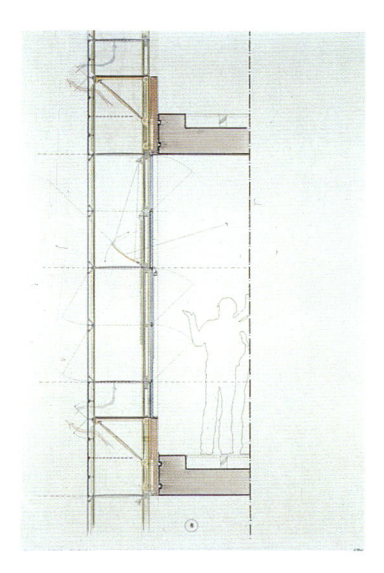

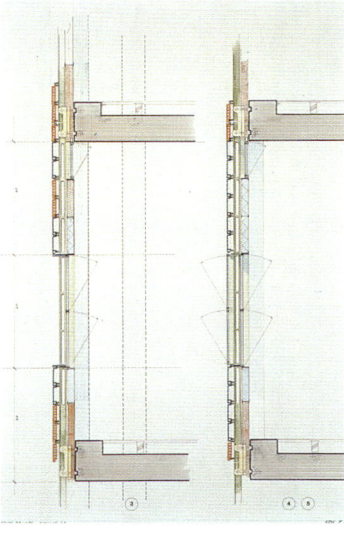

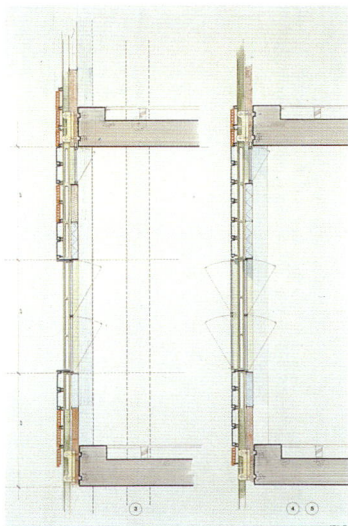

**debis-Gebäude
Südlicher Abschluß mit zweischaliger
Fassadenkonstruktion
Ausschnittsmodell**
debis Building
Southern end with double-skinned
façade
Model of detail

**debis-Gebäude
Fassadenschnitt
mit zweischaliger
Außenwandkonstruktion**
debis Building
Façade section
with double-skinned
structure of outer wall

**debis-Gebäude
Fassadenschnitt
mit Terrakottaverkleidung**
debis building
Façade section with
Terracotta cladding

The debis development concept designed by Piano continues Hilmer & Sattler's basic urban concept and block structure. The towers add emphasis to Potsdamer Platz; a further high-rise stands near the water basin at Landwehrkanal. Slicing through the block structure is a shopping mall starting at the high-rises on Potsdamer Platz and leading to the Landwehrkanal, and the Alte Potsdamer Strasse, now enlivened as a pedestrian zone. Behind the Staatsbibliothek the Kulturforum is supplemented by a music theatre, the extension to the national library and an exhibition pavilion. These new buildings mark out a town square and the end of the Alte Potsdamer Strasse.

To inject urban life again into the area around Potsdamer Platz it was decided to specify an intensive mix of uses, including offices, shops, restaurants, hotels, conference facilities, a music theatre, exhibition pavilion and apartments.

After presenting the urban concept Piano was commissioned with further projects, such as the planning of the debis headquarters. This building is a combination of a square block and a high-rise. On the ground floor various public-oriented areas are positioned around a linear atrium with main entrances from Eichhornstrasse and Uferstrasse on the Landwehrkanal; these areas include a Mercedes-Benz showroom on Eichenstrasse, a reception area on the canal side, and also meeting rooms, a library, a restaurant and shops.

**Daimler-Benz
Gebäude** Buildings
**B1/B3/B5/B7/C1/D1/D2
Weinhaus Huth
und Gesamtkonzept**
and Overall Concept

Potsdamer Platz

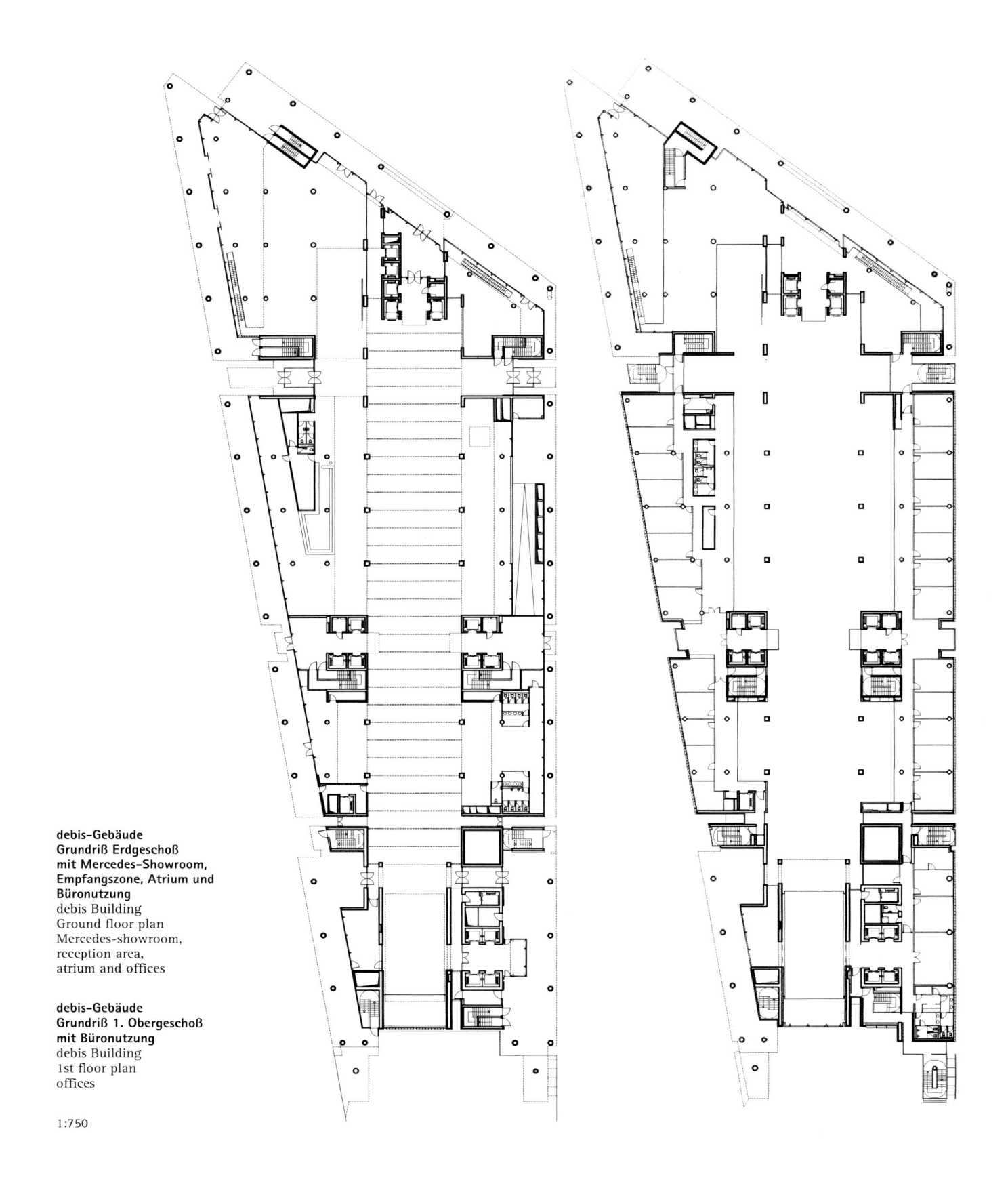

**debis-Gebäude
Grundriß Erdgeschoß
mit Mercedes-Showroom,
Empfangszone, Atrium und
Büronutzung**
debis Building
Ground floor plan
Mercedes-showroom,
reception area,
atrium and offices

**debis-Gebäude
Grundriß 1. Obergeschoß
mit Büronutzung**
debis Building
1st floor plan
offices

1:750

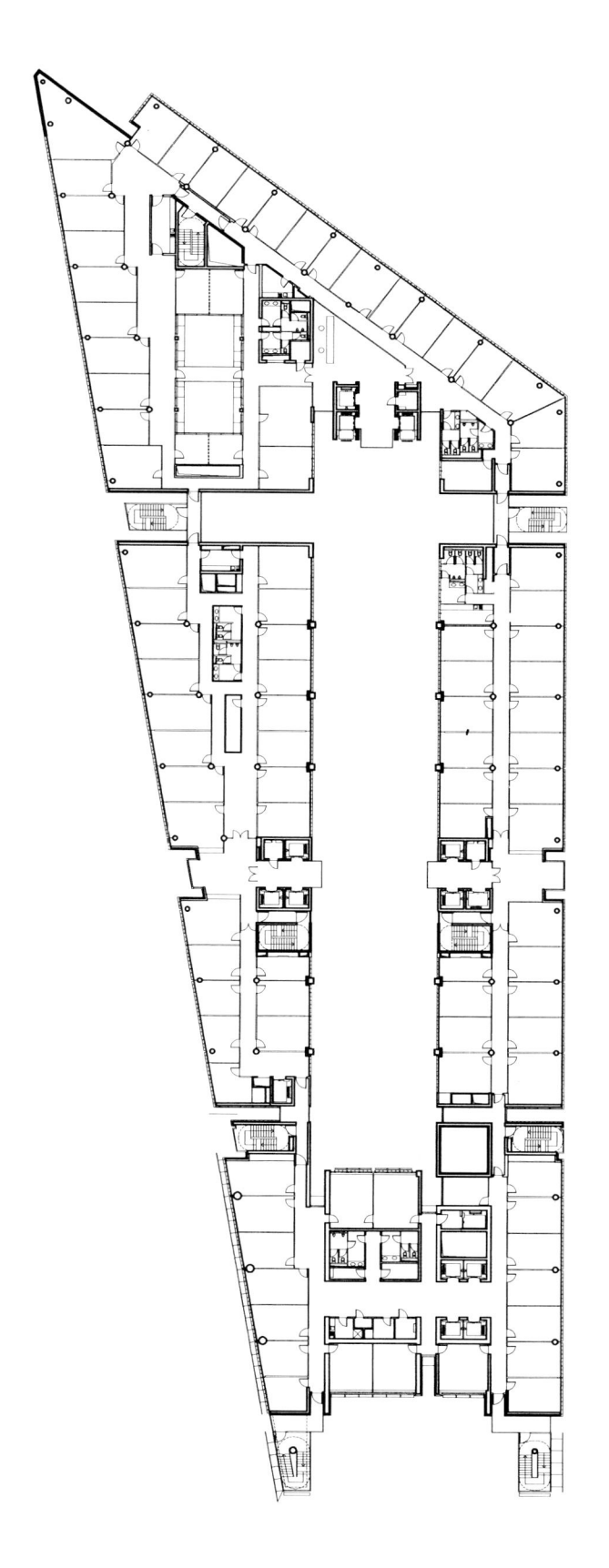

debis-Gebäude
Grundriß 5. Obergeschoß
mit Büronutzung
debis Building
5th floor plan
offices

1:750

Daimler-Benz
Gebäude Building A 1   Potsdamer Platz

Hans Kollhoff
Berlin

Mitarbeit staff
Jasper Jochimsen
(Projektleiter project manager)

Bauherr:
debis Gesellschaft für
Potsdamer Platz Projekt und
Immobilienmanagement mbH
Berlin

Planungstermine:
Städtebaulicher
Ideenwettbewerb 1991
Realisierungswettbewerb 1992,
5. Preis
Entwurfsplanung seit 1993
Baubeginn 1994
Voraussichtlicher Bezug 1997

Nutzung:
Läden mit
1.200 m²
Büros mit
28.500 m²

Geschosse (XXII):
EG Läden, Eingangshalle,
Restaurant
1.–21. OG Büros

Untergeschosse (IV):
Technik, Tiefgarage, Lager

Grundstücksgröße:
3.100 m²

Überbaute Fläche:
2.600 m²

Bruttogeschoßfläche:
ca. 31.000 m²

**Blick vom Potsdamer Platz
von Osten
Modellaufnahme**
View of Potsdamer Platz
from the east
Model photo

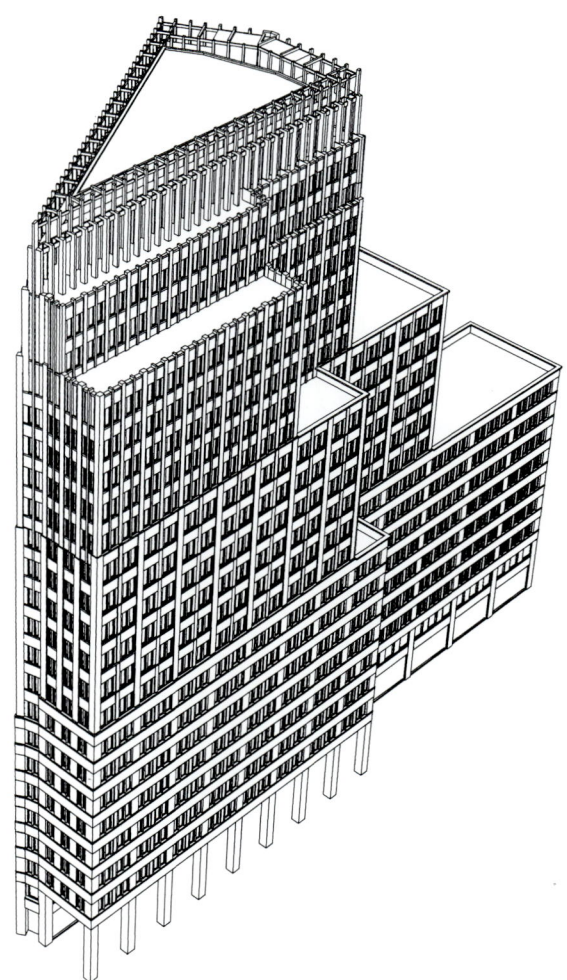

Axonometrie von Nordosten
Axonometric projection
from northeast

Projektadresse:
Location:
**Potsdamer Platz
Alte Potsdamer Strasse
Neue Potsdamer Strasse**
in
10785 Berlin-Tiergarten

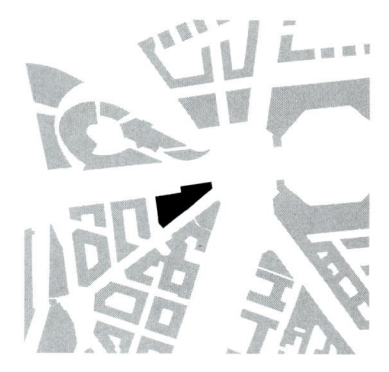

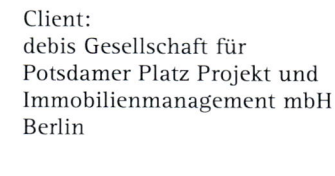

Client:
debis Gesellschaft für
Potsdamer Platz Projekt und
Immobilienmanagement mbH
Berlin

Project Stages:
Urban planning ideas competition 1991
Project competition 1992,
5th prize
Design development from 1993
Start of construction 1994
Expected completion 1997

Building Use:
Shops totalling
1200 m²
Offices totalling
28500 m²

Upper Floors (XXII):
Ground floor shops, entrance hall, restaurant
1st-21st floor offices

Basement Floors (IV):
Building services
Car park
Storage areas

Site Area:
3100 m²

Built Area:
2600 m²

Gross Floor Area:
ca. 31000 m²

**Blick von Südwesten
Modellaufnahme**
View from the southwest
Model photo

Daimler-Benz
Gebäude Building A 1   Potsdamer Platz

An der nördlichen Spitze des Daimler-Benz-Areals, in renommierter Lage am Potsdamer Platz, liegt das Bürohochhaus A1. Gemeinsam mit dem gegenüberliegenden Sony-Turm definiert es eine Torsituation zur Neuen Potsdamer Straße.

Der Baukörper des insgesamt 22-geschossigen Hochhausturmes wird abgetreppt und nimmt an seiner Westseite die Höhen der angrenzenden Bebauung auf. Zwischen den Gebäudeflügeln liegt ein 4-geschossiges Atrium.

Für die Obergeschosse ist Büronutzung mit unterteilbaren Mieteinheiten vorgesehen. Im Erdgeschoß befinden sich Einzelhandel und das traditionsreiche Café Josty in der Spitze zum Potsdamer Platz. Die doppelgeschossige Eingangshalle kann von der Alten und von der Neuen Potsdamer Straße aus betreten werden. Von hier hat man Zutritt zum Atrium, das für publikumsnahe Nutzungen oder als Schalterhalle dienen kann. Die Bürogeschosse erhalten eine eigene zentral angeordnete Etagenlobby.

Als Materialien werden für die Fassade Klinker und im Sockelbereich graugrüner Granit verwendet. Die Spitze des Turmes verjüngt sich kronenartig. Nachts soll das Bauwerk durch eine besondere Beleuchtung weitere »Inszenierung« erfahren.

Grundriß Erdgeschoß
mit Eingangshalle,
Ladennutzung und Gastronomie
Ground floor plan
with entrance hall,
retail space and restaurants

Grundriß 1. Obergeschoß
mit Büronutzung
1st floor plan
offices

Grundriß 2.-5. Obergeschoß
mit Büronutzung
Plan of 2nd to 5th floors
offices

Grundriß 6. Obergeschoß
mit Büronutzung
6th floor plan
offices

1:750

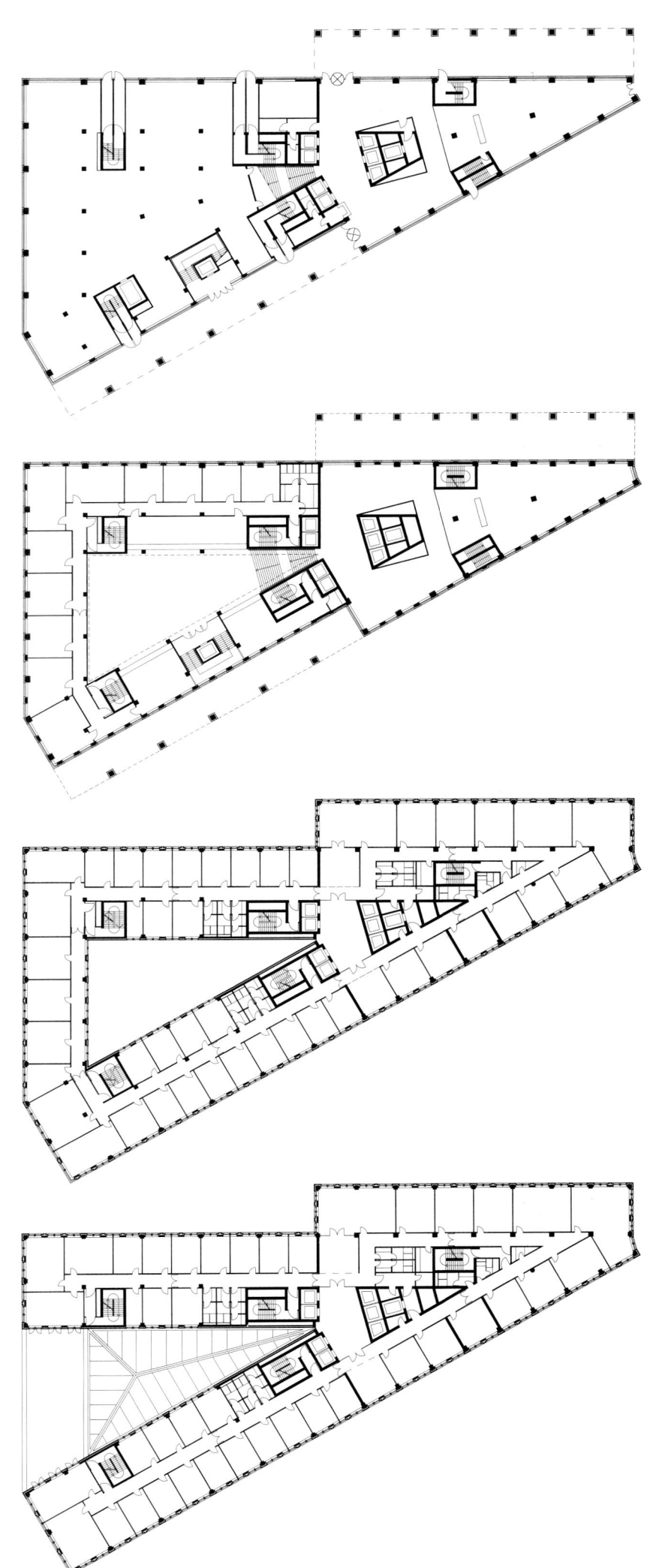

On the north side of the Daimler-Benz area, in a prominent site on Potsdamer Platz, is the office high-rise A1. Together with the Sony Tower opposite it forms a kind of gateway leading to the Neue Potsdamer Strasse.
The tower block rises in stages to a total of 22 storeys, matching on the west side the heights of neighbouring buildings. Between the wings of the buildings is a 4-storey atrium.
The upper floors are intended for use as flexible office space, divided into lettable units. At ground floor level are shops and the famous old Café Josty at the corner facing Potsdamer Platz. The double-height entrance hall can be reached from both the Alte and the Neue Potsdamer Strasse. Leading off this hall is the atrium which can be used for more public use or as a ticket hall. The office storeys have their own centrally located lobby on each floor.
Clinker bricks were used for the façades, with grey-green granite at ground floor level. The top of the tower gradually narrows to a crown. At night the building is to be illuminated for special effect.

Grundriß 7./8. Obergeschoß mit Büronutzung
7th/8th floor plan
offices

Grundriß 10./12. Obergeschoß mit Büronutzung
10th/12th floor plan
offices

Grundriß 13. Obergeschoß mit Büronutzung
13th floor plan
offices

Grundriß 20./21. Obergeschoß mit Büronutzung
20th/21st floor plan
offices

1:750

Daimler-Benz
Gebäude Buildings
B4, B6, B8

Potsdamer Platz

Richard Rogers Partnership
London

Entwurfsteam design team
Andrew Wright, Dan Macorie,
Dennis Ho, Douglas Keys, James
Leathem, Laurie Abbott, Lennart
Grut, Neil Southard, Nick Malby,
Richard Paul, Richard Rogers,
Sabine Coldrey, Wolfgang
Wagener

Bauherr:
debis Gesellschaft für
Potsdamer Platz Projekt und
Immobilienmanagement mbH
Berlin

Planungstermine:
Planungsstart 1993
Baubeginn 1996
Voraussichtlicher Bezug 1998

Nutzung:
Läden mit
17.000 m² Bruttogeschoßfläche
Büros mit
28.000 m² Bruttogeschoßfläche
Wohnungen mit
12.000 m² Bruttogeschoßfläche

Geschosse:
B4, B6 (X):
EG + 1.OG Läden
2.-9. OG Büros
B8 (X):
EG Läden
1.-9. OG Wohnungen

Untergeschosse (IV):
1. UG Einzelhandel, Technik
2.+3. UG Tiefgarage, Technik
4. UG Tiefgarage, Lager

Grundstücksgröße:
8.200 m²

Überbaute Fläche:
8.200 m²

Bruttogeschoßfläche:
57.000 m²

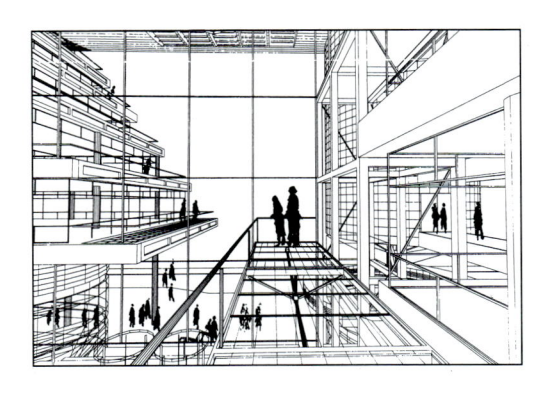

Die Blöcke B4, B6 und B8 sind konzeptionell analoge Baukörper. Nach Nordwesten grenzen sie an die zentrale Shopping Mall, nach Südosten an den neuen Park. Ihre Höfe öffnen sich zum Park; hier erhalten alle, auch die zur Mall orientierten Büros eine »erste Adresse« an der Linkstraße.
Die Eingangsebene zu den Büros liegt im 2. Obergeschoß.

Ansicht Linkstraße von Osten
Modellaufnahme (Gebäude B6)
1994
East elevation Linkstrasse
Model photo (Building B6)
1994

Blick in das Atrium
Entwurfsstudie
1993
View of atrium
Design study
1993

Blick von der Linkstraße
Entwurfsstudie
1993
View of Linkstrasse
Design study
1993

Tragwerksingenieure
Structural engineers
IBF
Dr. Falkner GmbH,
Weiske & Partner GmbH,
Ove Arup & Partner
Gebäudetechnik building services
RP+K Sozietät
Kostenplanung cost management
Davis Langdon & Everest
Förderanlagen transporting plant
Hundt & Partner

Fassaden façades
Institut für Fassadentechnik IFFT
Bauphysik statical analysis
Müller BBM, GmbH
Brandschutz fire protection
debis RISK Consult GmbH
Tageslichtanalyse
Daylighting analysis
Cambridge Architectural Research

Projektadresse:
Location:
Potsdamer Platz
in
10785 Berlin-Tiergarten

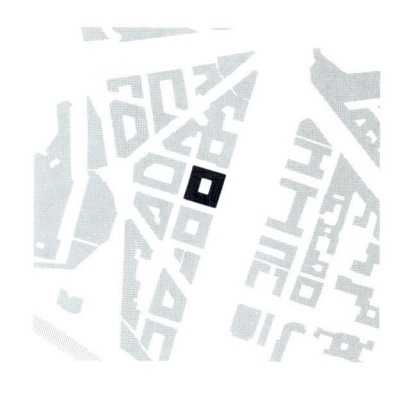

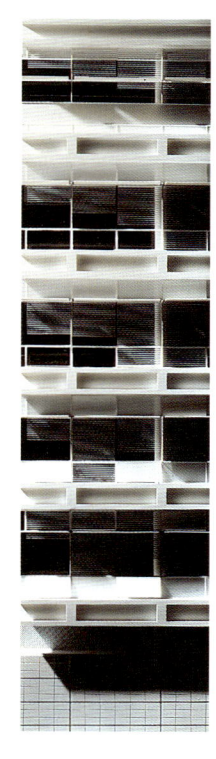

Client:
debis Gesellschaft für
Potsdamer Platz Projekt und
Immobilienmanagement mbH
Berlin

Project Stages:
Start of planning 1993
Start of construction 1996
Expected completion 1998

Building Use:
Shops totalling
17000 m²
Offices totalling
28000 m²
Apartments totalling
12000 m²
Upper Floors:
B4, B6 (X):
Ground floor and 1st floor shops
2nd-9th floors offices
B8 (X):
Ground floor, 1st-9th floors
apartments

Basement Floors (IV):
1st basement retail, services
2nd and 3rd basement car park,
services
4th basement car park,
storerooms

Site Area:
8200 m²

Built Area:
8200 m²

Gross Floor Area:
57000 m²

Blick in die Eingangshalle Gebäude B6 von Südosten Modellaufnahme
View of entrance hall (detail) Block B6 from the southeast

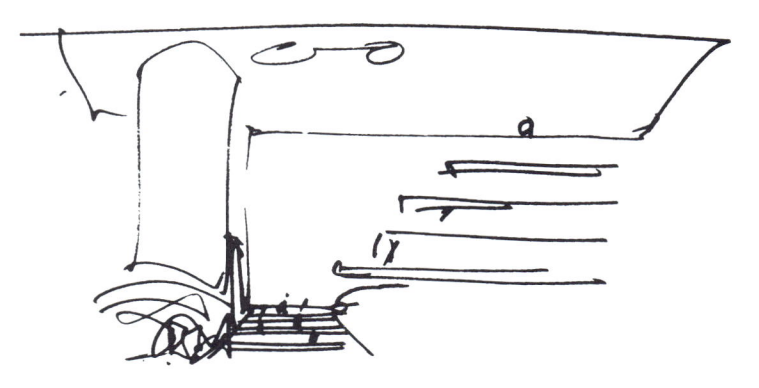

Entwurfsskizze Richard Rogers 1993
Design sketch by Richard Rogers 1993

Fassadenmodell
Façade model

Blocks B4, B6 and B8 are conceptually similar structures. To the northwest they border on the central shopping mall, to the southeast they border on the new park. Their courtyards open towards the park; here all the offices, including the ones facing the mall, have direct access to Linkstrasse.
The entrance level to the offices is on the second floor.

Daimler-Benz
Gebäude Buildings
B4, B6, B8

Potsdamer Platz

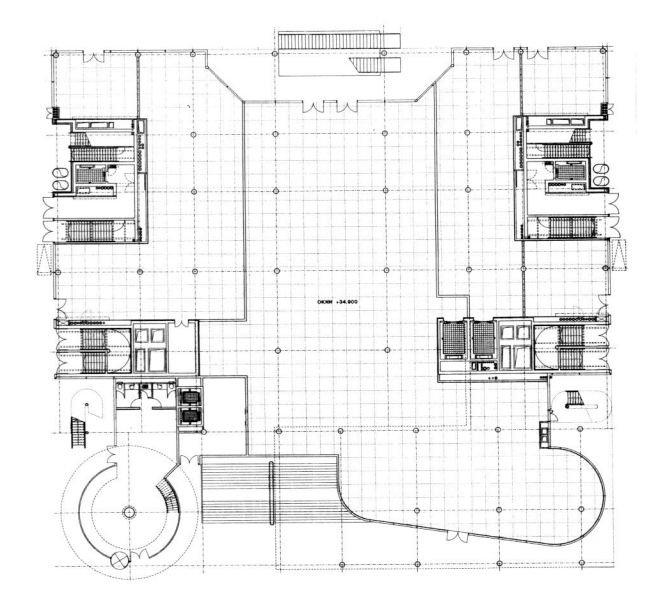

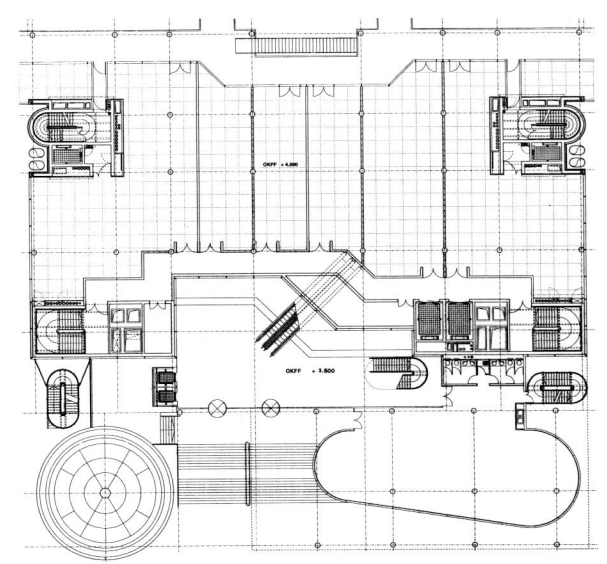

Die zu überwindende Höhendifferenz von 10 m wird durch eine Abfolge von Freitreppe, Rolltreppe und gläsernem Aufzugsturm überbrückt. Ein Atrium bildet das Entrée zu den Büros. Als Beitrag zur Verringerung des Energieverbrauchs ist es zugleich Bestandteil des umfangreichen ökologisch-energetischen Konzeptes, das entwurfsbestimmend war.
Alle drei Gebäude besitzen 7 Normal- und 2 Staffelgeschosse. Die Traufhöhe an der Linkstraße wird durch ein Vordach akzentuiert; die Blocköffnung ist (wie das Atrium) mit einer Stahlkonstruktion überspannt und wird durch einen Zylinderbau betont. Die Gebäude haben ein modulares Fassadensystem, in das je nach Nutzung und Himmelsrichtung transparente, transluzente oder opake Fassadenelemente eingesetzt sind.

Grundriß Erdgeschoß mit Eingangshalle und Ladennutzung
Ground floor plan entrance hall and retail space

1:750

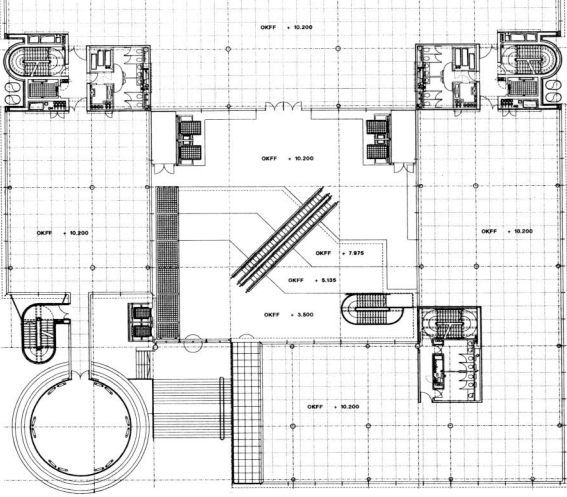

Grundriß 1. Obergeschoß mit Ladennutzung
1st floor plan offices

Grundriß 2. Obergeschoß mit Büronutzung
2nd floor plan offices

1:750

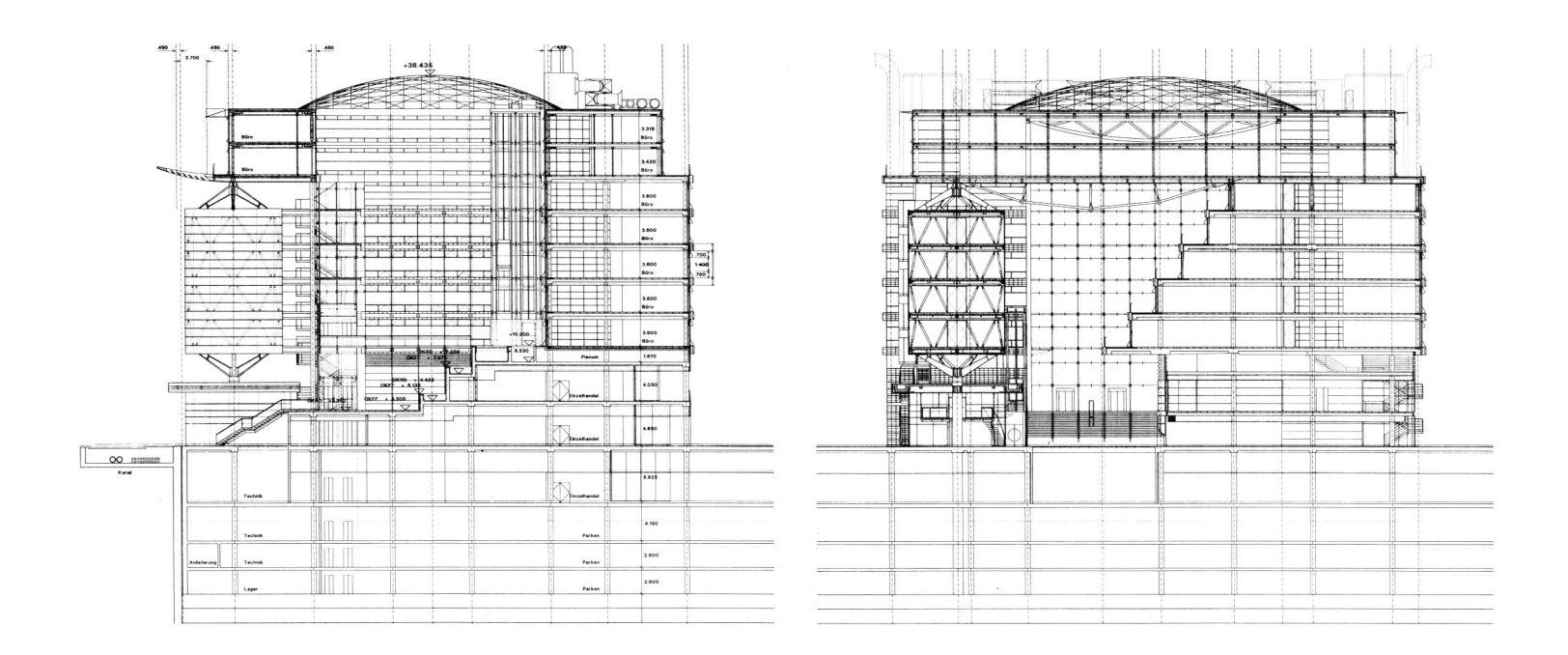

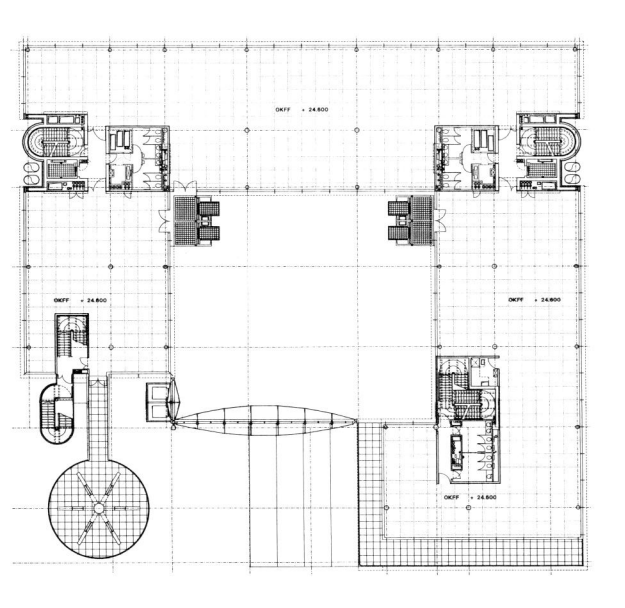

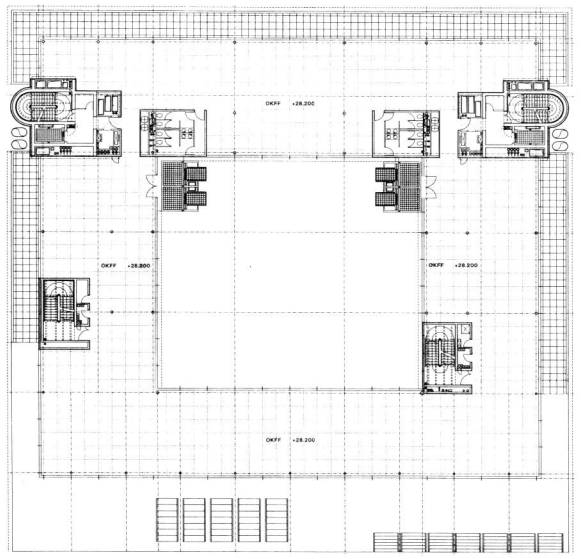

**Gebäudequerschnitt
im Bereich des Atriums
in Ost-Westrichtung**
Cross section east-west
through atrium area

**Grundriß 6. Obergeschoß
mit Büronutzung**
6th floor plan
offices

1:750

**Gebäudelängsschnitt durch
den Eingangsbereich
zum Atrium
in Nord-Südrichtung**
Longitudinal
section north-south
through atrium
entrance area

**Grundriß 8. Obergeschoß
mit Büronutzung**
7th floor plan
offices

1:750

The height difference of 10 m is overcome via flights of steps, escalators and a glass lift tower. The entrance to the offices is marked by an atrium. As a contribution to reducing the energy consumption of the building the atrium is also part of the comprehensive ecological and energy concept, which forms a decisive part of the design.

All three buildings have 7 full upper storeys and 2 further storeys stepped back from the façade plane. The eaves height on Linkstrasse is accentuated by a can-opy; the block opening (like the atrium) is spanned by a steel construction and given added emphasis by a cylindrical structure. The buildings have a modular façade system, into which are inserted, depending on use and direction, transparent, translucent or opaque façade elements.

Daimler-Benz Gebäude Buildings C2 – C3	Potsdamer Platz	Arata Isozaki & Associates Architects Tokyo mit with Steffen Lehmann & Partner Architekten Berlin	Mitarbeit staff Isozaki & Associates: Makoto Kikuchi Kenji Sato Atsushi Aiba Planungspartner Partners in planning Lehmann & Partner: Steffen Lehmann Andreas Hoffmann Mattias Barth Michelle Overly

Bauherr:
debis Gesellschaft für Potsdamer Platz Projekt und Immobilienmanagement mbH
Weinhaus Huth, Berlin

Planungstermine:
Realisierungswettbewerb 1992, 3. Preis
Entwurfsplanung seit 1993
Baubeginn 1994
Voraussichtlicher Bezug 1997

Nutzung:
Einzelhandelsfläche mit 800 m²
Büros für rund 1.200 Arbeitsplätze
Büroflächen flexibel als »Lean Office«

Geschosse (X):
EG Läden
1.-8. OG Büros, Konferenzräume
9. OG Technik

Untergeschosse (II):
1. UG Tiefgarage, Technik
2. UG Lager, Tiefgarage

Grundstücksgröße:
8.100 m²

Überbaute Fläche:
3.500 m²

Bruttogeschoßfläche:
37.000 m²

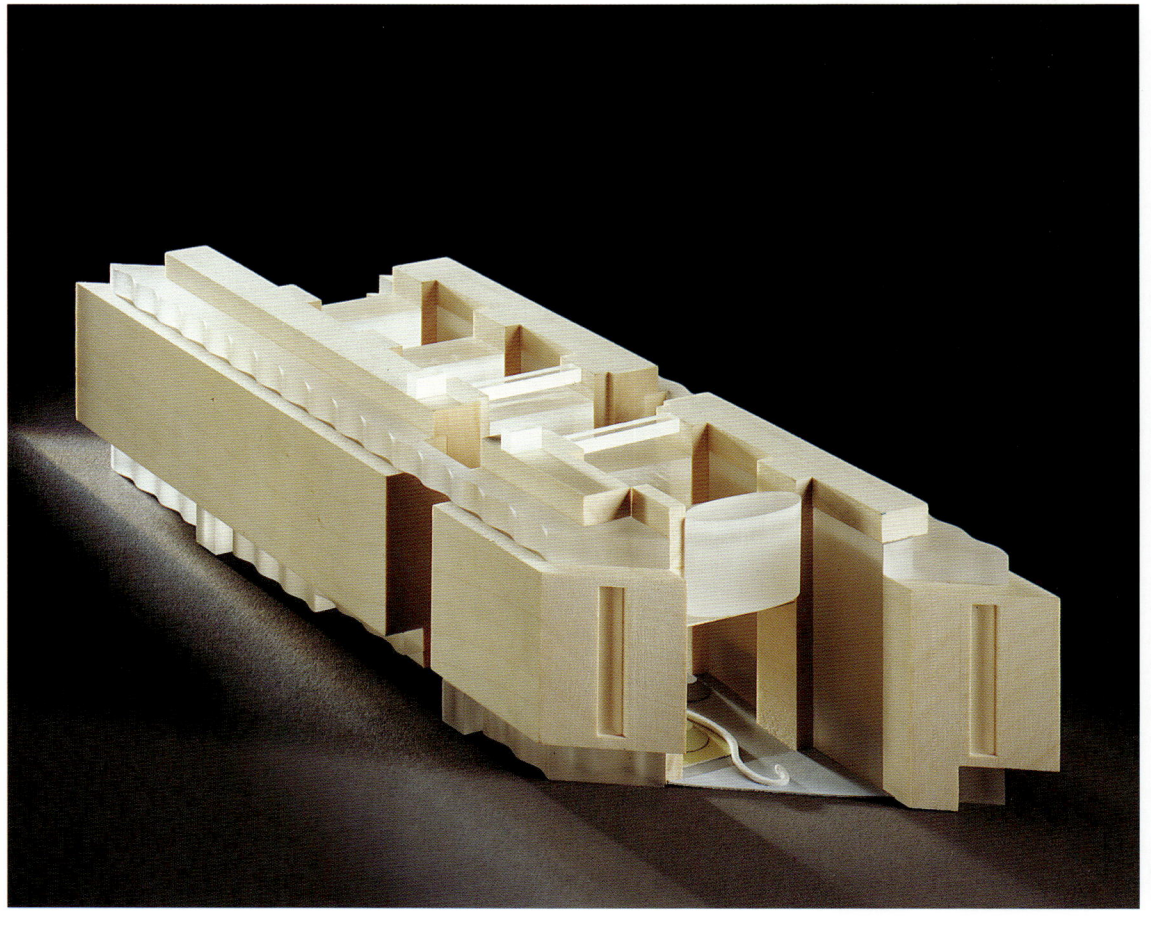

Blick von Südwesten
Modellaufnahme
Juli 1994
View from the southwest
Model photo
July 1994

Blick in den Stadtgarten von Süden
Modellaufnahme
Februar 1994
View of the Stadtgarten from the south
Model photo
February 1994

Die beiden Baukörper C2 und C3 entstehen auf einem trapezförmigen Grundstück am südlichen Ende des Daimler-Benz-Komplexes und grenzen an die Uferstraße des Landwehrkanals. Sie bestehen aus unterschiedlich langen, paarweise angeordneten Zeilen, die sich in Nord-Süd-Richtung erstrecken und die Fluchtlinie der nördlich daran anschließenden Daimler-Benz-Blöcke aufnehmen. An den schiefwinkli-

Statik statical analysis
Ove Arup GmbH, Berlin
mit with
Boll & Partner, Stuttgart
UG-Planer basement planning
Christoph Kohlbecker Architekten
Gaggenau
Fassadenplaner façade planning
JFFT, Frankfurt

Projektadresse:
Location:
Ecke Linkstrasse/
Reichpietschufer
in
10785 Berlin-Tiergarten

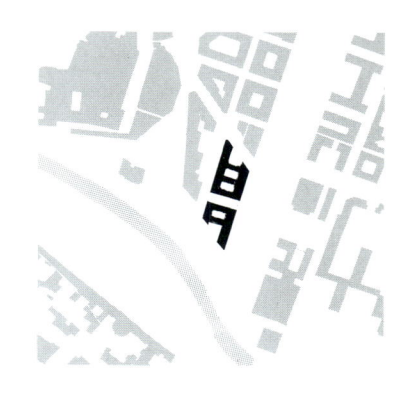

Client:
debis Gesellschaft für
Potsdamer Platz Projekt und
Immobilienmanagement mbH
Berlin
Weinhaus Huth, Berlin

Project Stages:
Competition 1992, 3rd prize
Design development from 1993
Start of construction 1994
Expected completion 1997
Building Use:
1 retail area
800 m^2
Offices for approx. 1200 staff
office space completely flexible
as a »lean office« concept

Upper Floors (X):
Ground floor shops
1st-8th floor offices, conference rooms
9th floor services

Basement Floors (II):
1st basement
car park, building services
2nd basement
storeroom, car park

Site Area:
8100 m^2

Built Area:
3500 m^2

Gross Floor Area:
37000 m^2

Blick von Süden
Modellaufnahme
März 1994
View from the south
Model photo
March 1994

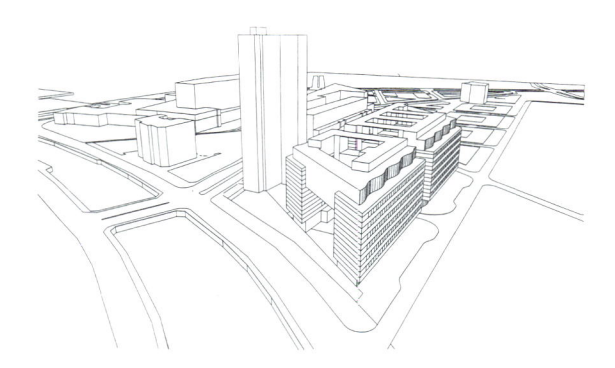

Vogelflug-Perspektive
des Komplexes am Reichpietschufer
Juli 1993
Bird's-eye view perspective of complex
on Reichpietschufer
July 1993

The site allocated for buildings C2 and C3 is trapezoid in shape, and lies at the southern end of the Daimler-Benz complex bordering on Uferstrasse by the Landwehrkanal. The two buildings consist of two rows of unequal length aligned opposite each other in a north-south direction, taking the same line as the Daimler-Benz buildings to the north. At the corners of the plot the ends of the buildings are angled.

Daimler-Benz
Gebäude Buildings Potsdamer Platz
C2 – C3

gen Grundstücksgrenzen werden die Zeilenköpfe abgeschrägt.
Zwischen den Zeilen entsteht ein öffentlich zugänglicher »Stadtgarten«, der durch die transparent gestalteten Erdgeschoßzonen hindurch von der Straße aus wahrgenommen werden kann. Über den Stadtgarten hinweg werden die Zeilen durch fünf jeweils 3-geschossige Brückenbaukörper miteinander verbunden; diese verglasten Baukörper von fast 9 m Breite sind im 5., 6. und 7. Obergeschoß zwischen die Treppenhauskerne gespannt.
Die Zeilen haben zur Straße eine durchgängige Traufhöhe von 29 m. Darüber liegen Staffelgeschosse bis zu einer Gebäudehöhe von insgesamt 37 m. Das 7. Obergeschoß und das Erdgeschoß erhalten wellenförmige Vollverglasungen, die den streng linearen Charakter der Gebäude aufbrechen sollen.

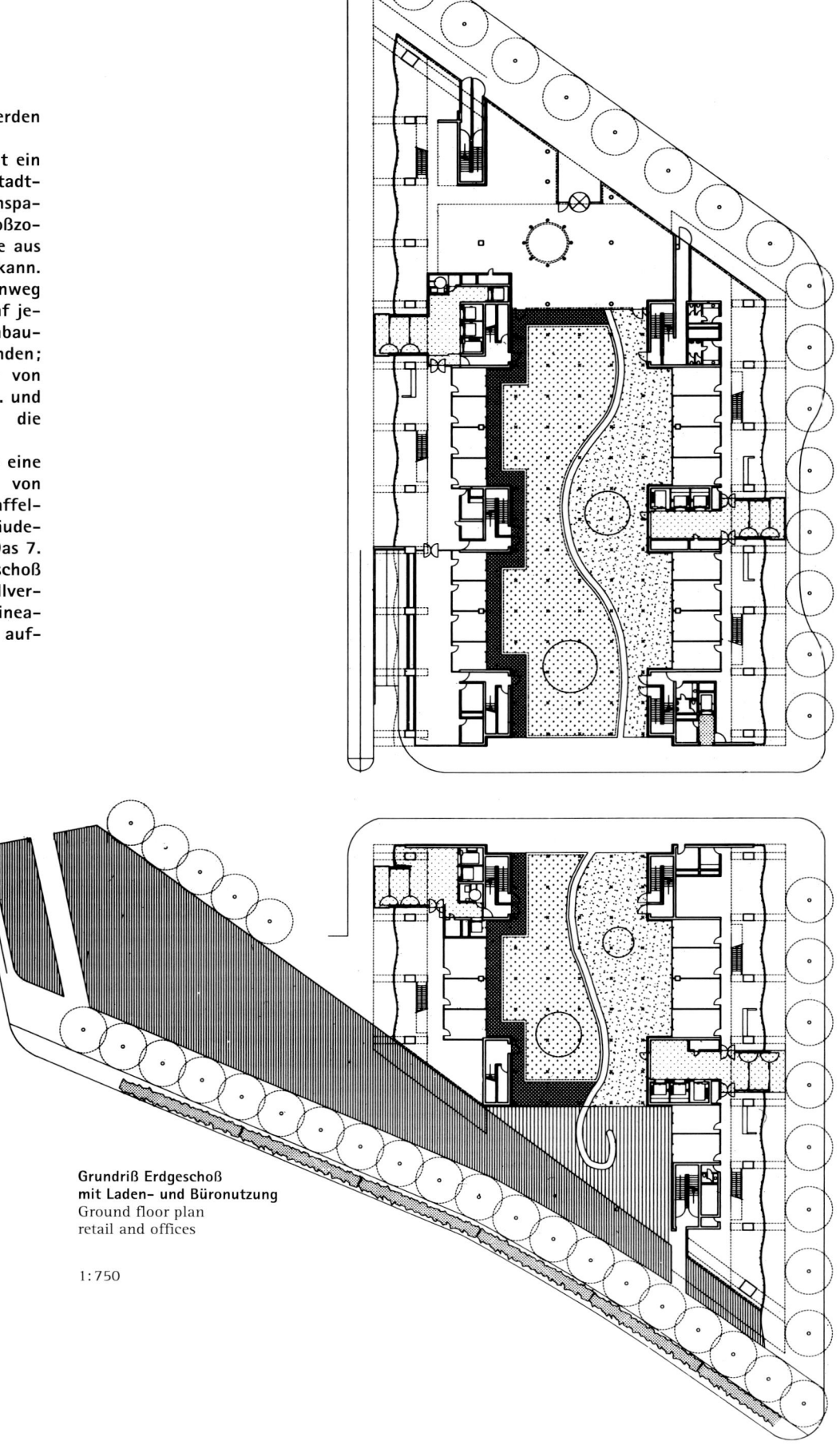

**Grundriß Erdgeschoß
mit Laden- und Büronutzung**
Ground floor plan
retail and offices

1:750

Between the rows is an »urban garden« open to the public; the transparent design of the ground floor zones reinforces the links between garden and street. Bridging this garden area are five 3-storey glazed sections, almost 9 m wide, spanning between the 5th, 6th and 7th floors at the level of the stairwells.

Towards the street the rows have a uniform eaves height of 29 m, above which the remaining upper floors are gradually stepped back from the façade plane to reach a total building height of 37 m. The 7th storey and the ground floor have undulating floor-to-ceiling glazing which is intended to break up the otherwise strictly linear character of the building.

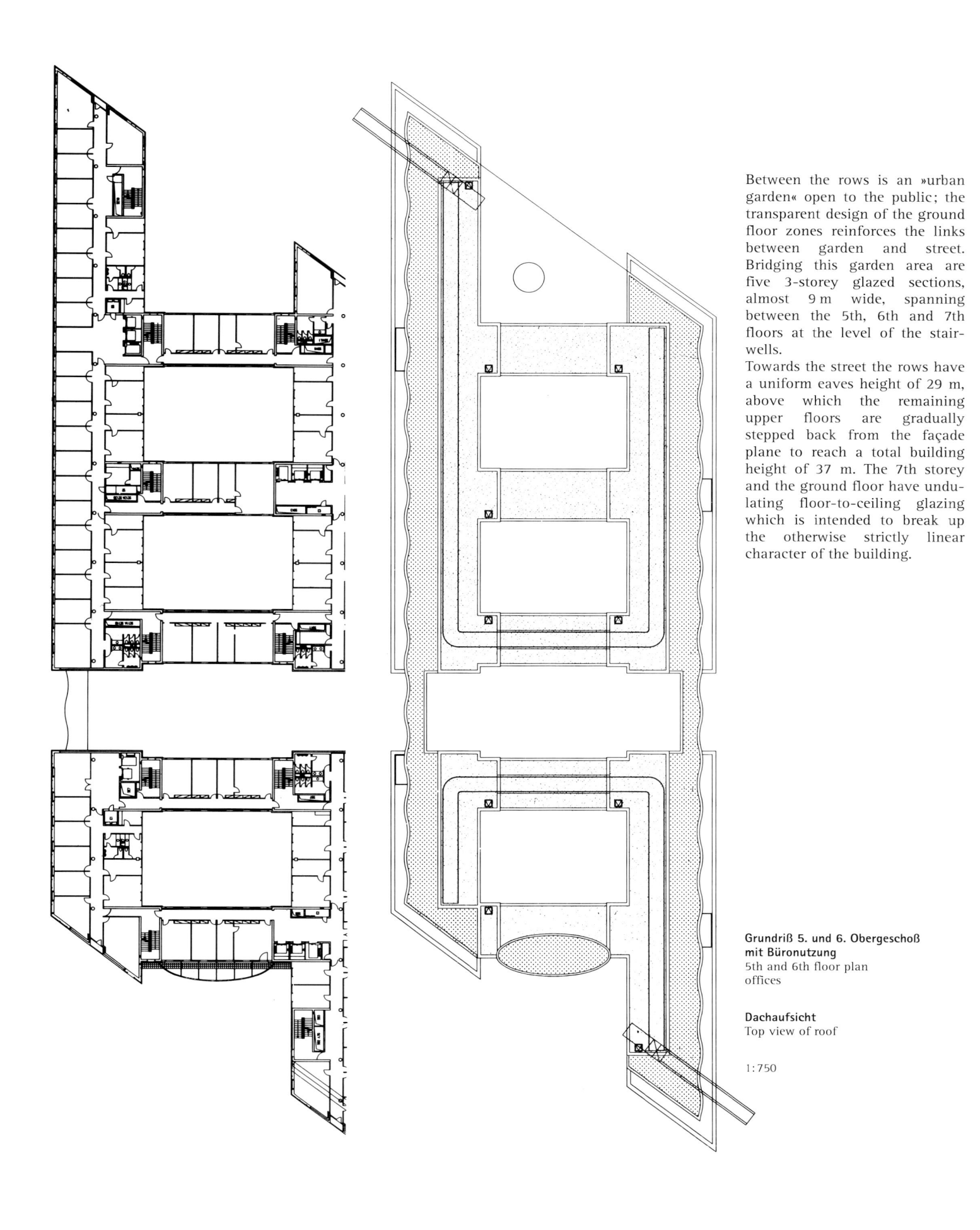

Grundriß 5. und 6. Obergeschoß mit Büronutzung
5th and 6th floor plan
offices

Dachaufsicht
Top view of roof

1:750

Daimler–Benz
Gebäude Buildings Potsdamer Platz
C2 – C3

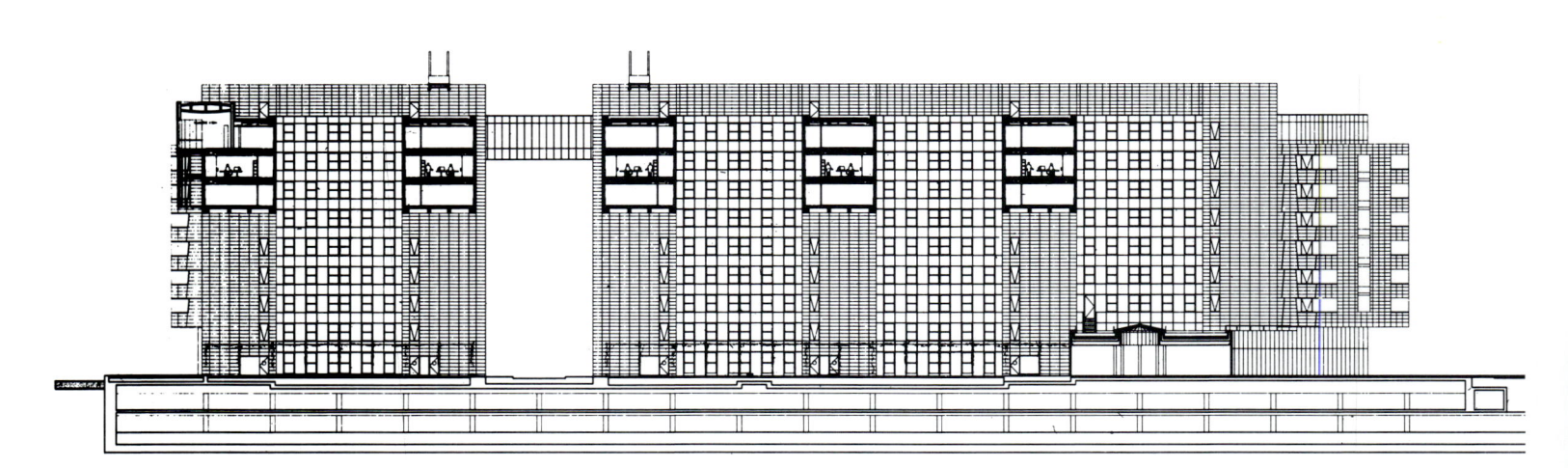

**Vorentwurfsskizze
Aquarell von Arata Isozaki**
Preliminary design sketch
Watercolour by Arata Isozaki

**Längsschnitt durch Garten, Brücken und
Läden mit Ansicht der Hoffassaden**
Longitudinal section through garden,
bridges and shops with elevation
of courtyard façades

1:750

Gebäudequerschnitt
im Bereich des Stadtgartens
Cross section
through Stadtgarten area

1:750

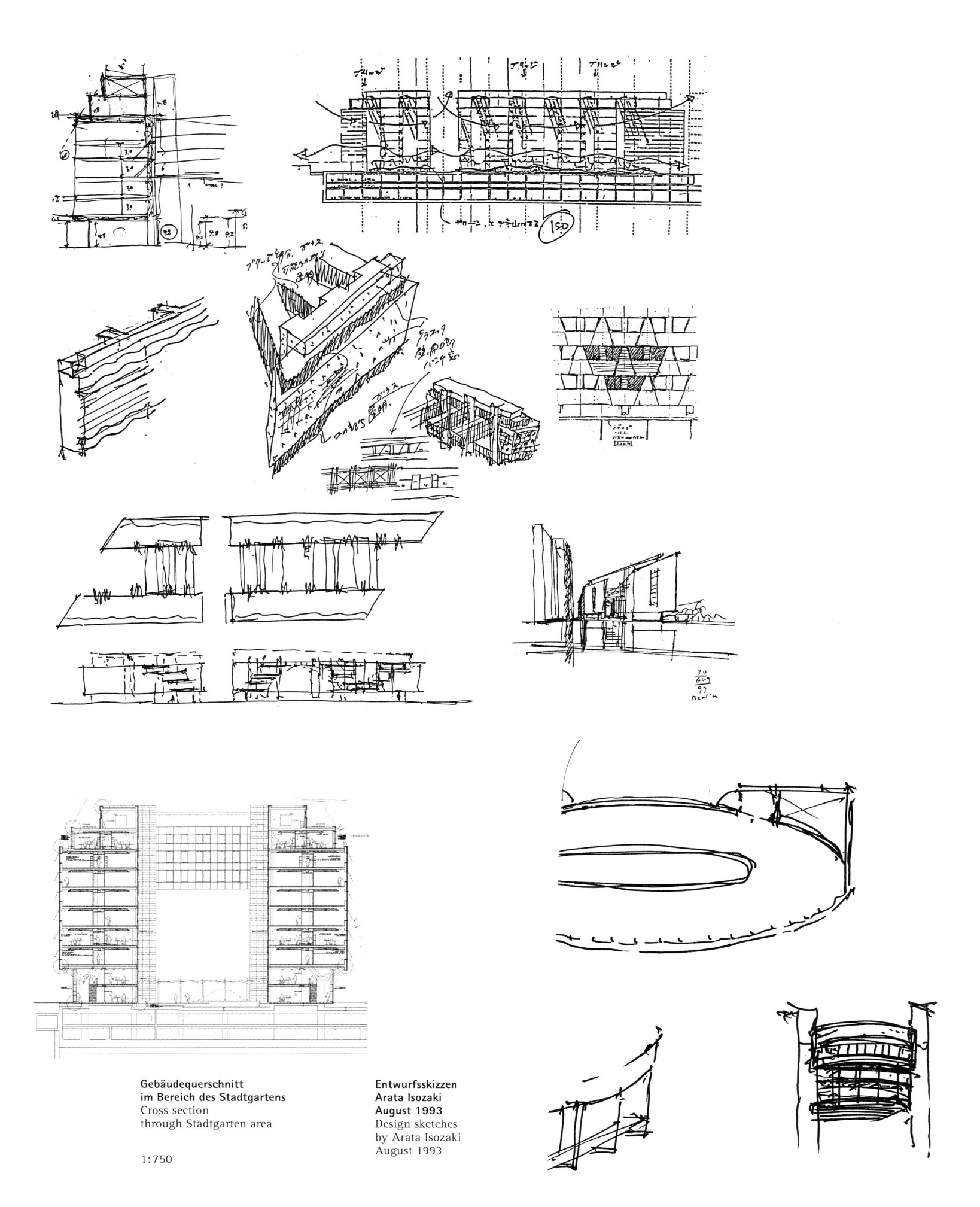

Entwurfsskizzen
Arata Isozaki
August 1993
Design sketches
by Arata Isozaki
August 1993

A+T
Gebäude Buildings 2, 3
und Gesamtkonzept
and Overall Concept

Potsdamer Platz

Giorgio Grassi
Milano

Mitarbeit staff
(**Wettbewerb** competition)
Nunzio Dego
Elena Grassi
Simona Pierini
Guido Zanella

Bauherr:
A+T
Projektentwicklungsgesellschaft
& Co. Potsdamer Platz Berlin KG
Heidelberg
eine Beteiligungsgesellschaft
von ABB und TERRENO

Planungstermine:
Wettbewerb 1993, 1. Preis
Entwurfsplanung seit 1993/94
Baubeginn 1995
Voraussichtlicher Bezug 1996/97

Nutzung:
8-10 Läden mit
ca. 100–350 m²
21-49 Büros mit
300-800 m² (unterteilbar)

Geschosse:
Gebäude 2 (VIII):
EG Läden, Gastronomie
1.-7. OG Büros
Gebäude 3 (VIII):
EG – 7. OG Büros

Untergeschosse (II):
Tiefgarage, Technik
(Planung Schweger + Partner)

Grundstücksgröße:
7.287,6 m²

Überbaute Fläche:
Gebäude 2 mit 1.772,6 m² und
Gebäude 3 mit 2.862,6 m²

Bruttogeschoßfläche:
Gebäude 2 mit 13.840,16 m² und
Gebäude 3 mit 20.587,5 m²

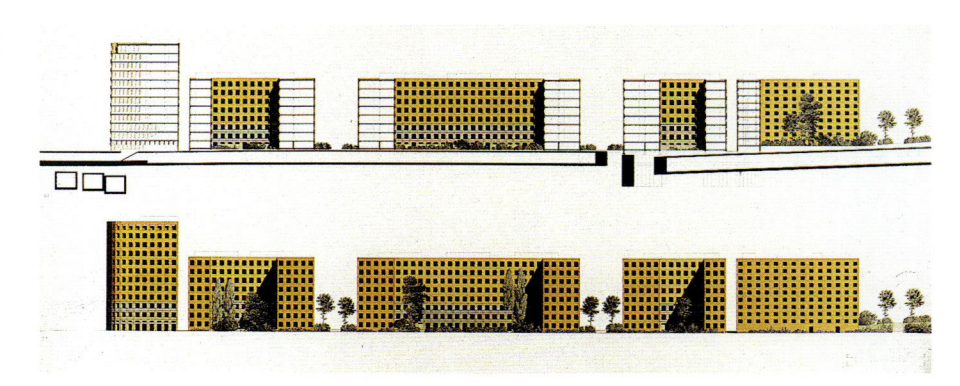

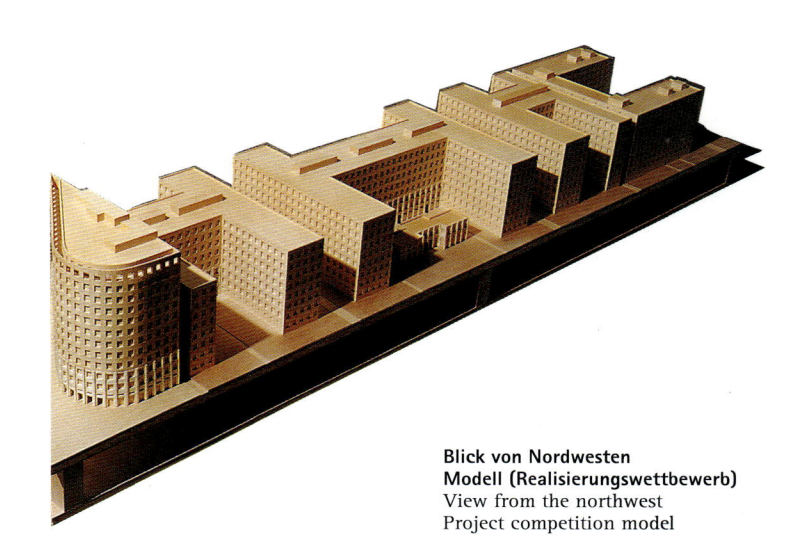

Blick von Nordwesten
Modell (Realisierungswettbewerb)
View from the northwest
Project competition model

Ansicht von der Neuen Promenade
und Längsschnitt durch
die Gesamtanlage
(Realisierungswettbewerb)
Neue Promenade elevation
and longitudinal sections
through overall complex
(project competition)

1:2000

Dachaufsicht
(Realisierungswettbewerb)
Top view of roof
(project competition)

Mitarbeit Ausführung
Staff final planning
Nunzio Dego, Elena Grassi
Mailand
Lucio Nardi
Berlin
Landschaftsarchitekt
Landscape architect
Gustav Lange
Hamburg

Projektadresse:
Location:
Stresemannstrasse/
Köthener Strasse/
Neue Promenade
in
10963 Berlin-Tiergarten

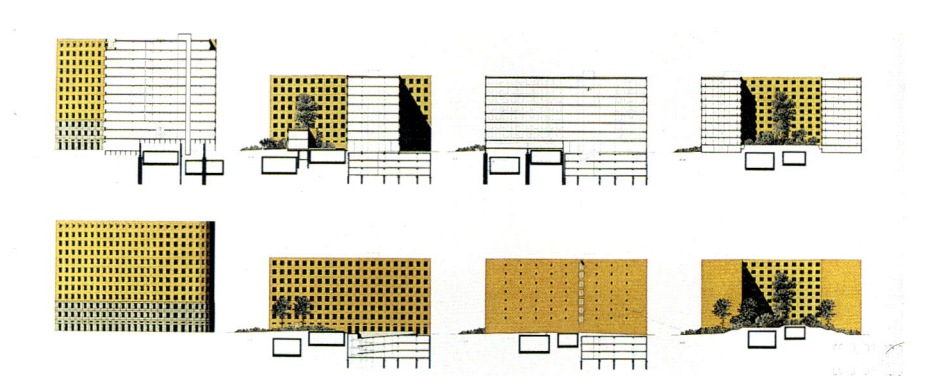

Client:
A+T
Projektentwicklungsgesellschaft
& Co. Potsdamer Platz Berlin KG
Heidelberg
a holding company of ABB and
TERRENO

Project Stages:
Competition 1993, 1st prize
Design development from
1993/94
Start of construction 1995
Expected completion 1996/97

Building Use:
8-10 shops
à ca. 100-350 m²
21-49 offices
à 300-800 m²
(divisible into smaller units)

Upper Floors:
Building 2 (VIII):
Ground floor shops, restaurants
1st-7th floor offices
Building 3 (VIII):
Ground floor – 7th floor offices

Basement Floors (II):
Car park, services
(Planning Schweger + Partner)

Site Area:
7287.6 m²

Built Area:
Building 2, 1772.6 m² and
Building 3, 2862.6 m²

Gross Floor Area:
Building 2, 13840.16 m² and
Building 3, 20587.5 m²

Ansichten und Schnitte
(Realisierungswettbewerb)
Elevations and sections
(project competition)

1:2000

Fassadenstudie
Köthener Straße und
Neue Promenade
Teilansicht und Schnitt
(Realisierungswettbewerb)
Köthener Strasse and
Neue Promenade
detail and section
(project competition)

A+T
Gebäude Buildings 2, 3 und Gesamtkonzept and Overall Concept

Potsdamer Platz

Das schmale Grundstück erstreckt sich zwischen der Köthener Straße im Osten und der von einem Stadtkanal durchzogenen neuen Grünanlage im Westen; nach Norden grenzt es an den Potsdamer Platz. Der Entwurf unterteilt das Terrain in fünf Blöcke und greift damit das Thema des ersten städtebaulichen Entwurfes von Hilmer & Sattler auf.

Am Potsdamer Platz liegt ein 12-geschossiger Kopfbau (Gebäude 1), der diese besondere städtebauliche Situation akzentuiert und den Baukörper des historischen Hauses Vaterland nachempfindet. Er erhält einen eigenen Zugang zum U-Bahnhof Potsdamer Platz. Nach Süden schließen sich zunächst drei 8-geschossige Baukörper mit H-förmigem Grundriß an, die zum Stadtraum offene Höfe bilden. Der größte der zum Kanal geöffneten Höfe nimmt den Flachbau eines Caféhauses auf. Der südliche Abschluß des Komplexes wird durch einen U-förmigen Baukörper (Gebäude 5) gebildet.

Das Nutzungskonzept sieht im Kopfgebäude am Potsdamer Platz und in den drei H-förmigen Baukörpern Büros sowie in der Erdgeschoßzone Läden vor. Der südliche, U-förmige Baukörper erfüllt mit 225 Wohnungen die Auflage eines 20prozentigen Wohnanteils des Komplexes.

Nach Vorliegen der städtebaulichen Gesamtkonzeption werden vom Büro Grassi die Gebäude 2 und 3 realisiert. Mit der Entwurfsbearbeitung der übrigen Baublöcke wurden weitere Architekturbüros beauftragt.

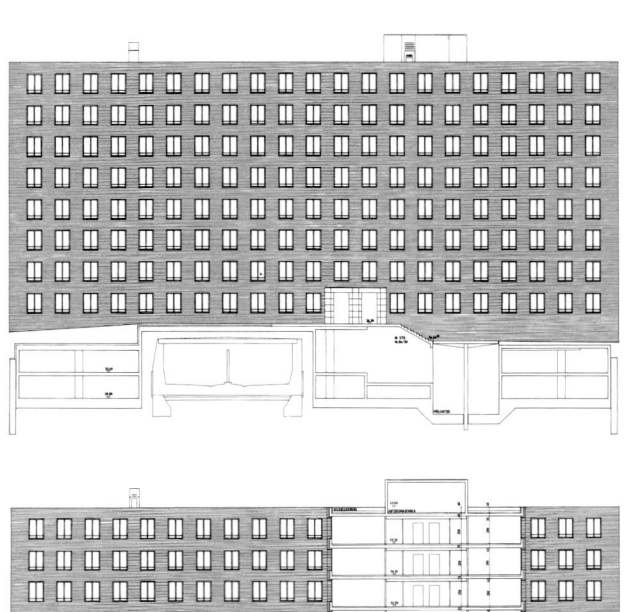

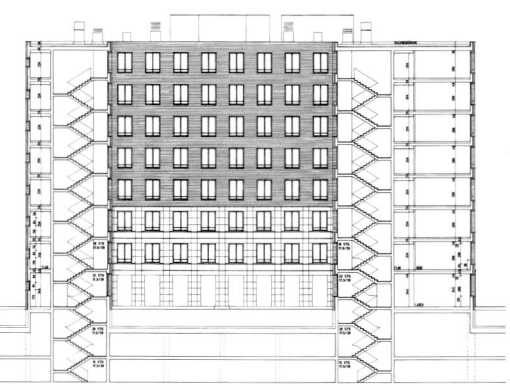

Gebäude 2
Ansicht von Süden
Building 2
South elevation

Gebäude 2
Querschnitt durch den Mittelflügel
mit Ansicht der Hoffassaden
Building 2
Cross section through the central
part with courtyard façades elevation

Gebäude 2
Ansicht Neue Promenade
von Westen
Building 2
West elevation
Neue Promenade

Gebäude 2
Gebäudeschnitt mit
Hofansicht Neue Promenade
Building 2
Section with elevation
of courtyard Neue Promenade

1:750

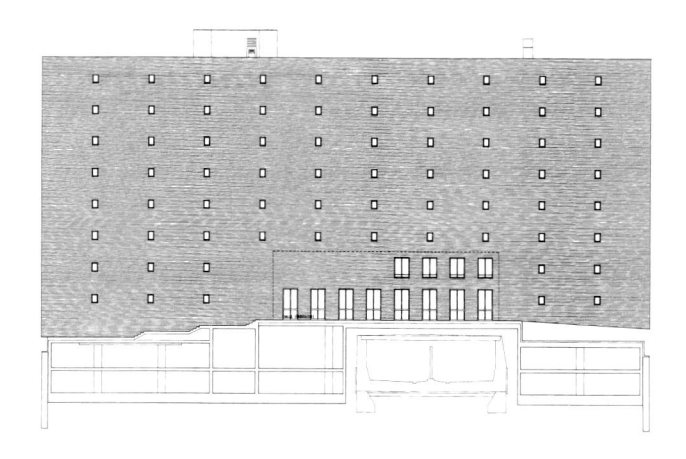

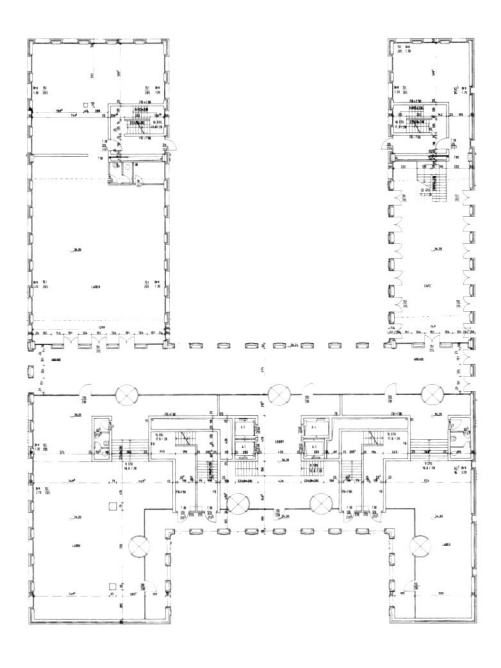

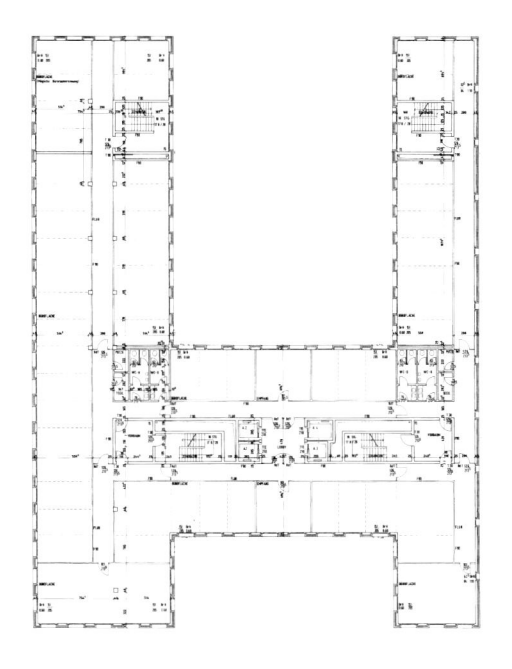

Gebäude 2
Ansicht von Norden
Building 2
North elevation

Gebäude 2
Grundriß Erdgeschoß
mit Lobby, Ladennutzung
und Café
Building 2
Ground floor plan
lobby, retail space and café

Gebäude 2
Grundriß Normalgeschoß
(4.-7. Obergeschoß)
mit Büronutzung
Building 2
Typical floor plan
(4th to 7th floors)
offices

1:750

The narrow plot stretches between Köthener Strasse in the east and a new open park area with canal on the west; to the north it borders on Potsdamer Platz. The design foresees a division of the site into five blocks and is thus a continuation of Hilmer & Sattler's theme put forward in the first urban design competition.
At the Potsdamer Platz end is a 12-storey front (building 1), which accentuates the special urban situation, echoing the form of the historic Haus Vaterland. Here the block has its own access to the U-Bahn station Potsdamer Platz. Immediately to the south of this tower are attached three 8-storey, H-shaped blocks which form open courtyards facing outwards. The largest of the courtyards facing the canal contains a low, flat building housing a café. The southern end of the complex is defined by a U-shaped building (building 5).
The plan for building use includes offices in the section facing Potsdamer Platz and in the three H-shaped blocks; at ground floor level shops are planned. The southern, U-shaped block, contains 225 apartments and thus meets the 20% residential requirements for the complex.
After presentation of the total urban concept buildings 2 and 3 are built by Grassi. Other architects have been commissioned to complete the design stages for the remaining blocks.

A+T
Gebäude Buildings **2, 3**
und **Gesamtkonzept**
and Overall Concept

Potsdamer Platz

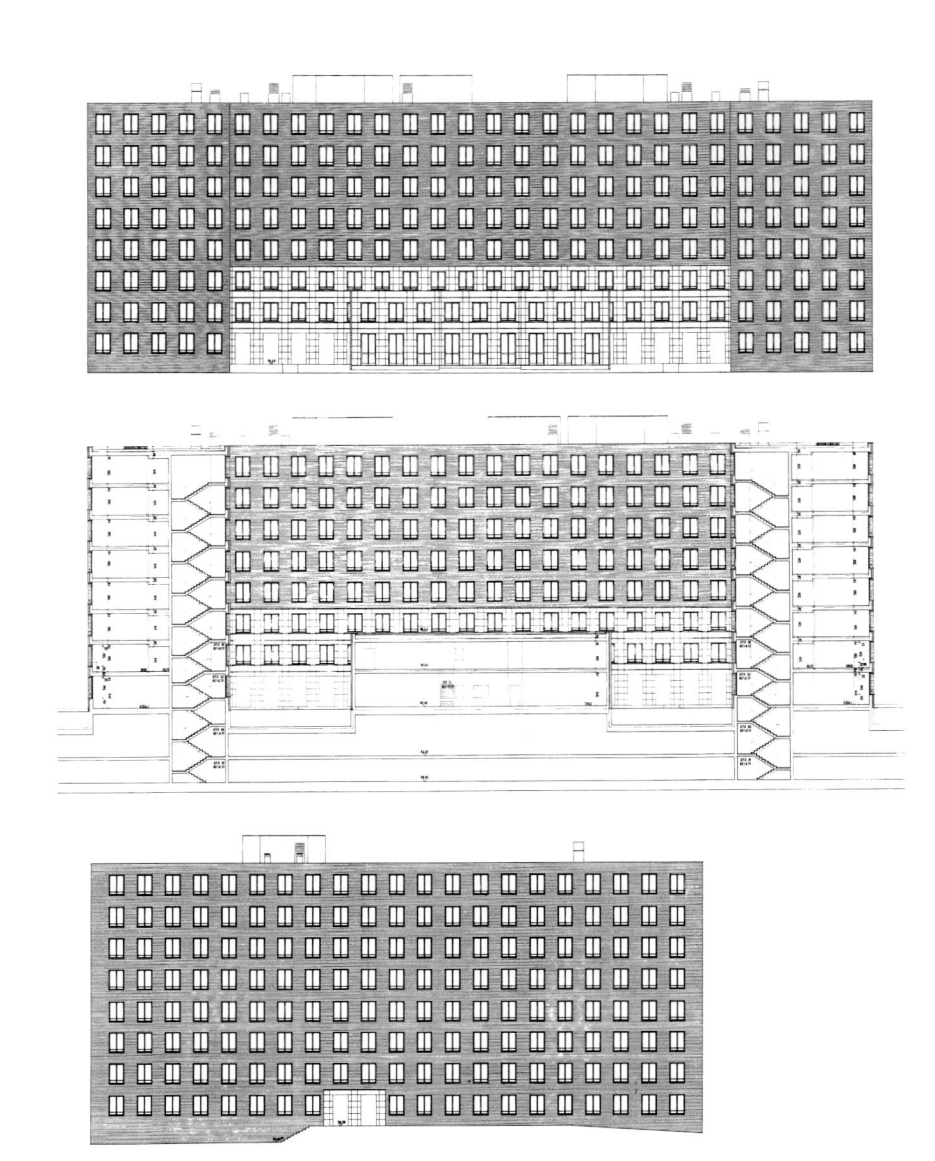

Gebäude 3
Ansicht Neue Promenade
von Westen
Building 3
West elevation
Neue Promenade

Gebäude 3
Gebäudeschnitt mit Hofansicht
Neue Promenade
Building 3
Section
with elevation
of courtyard
Neue Promenade

1:750

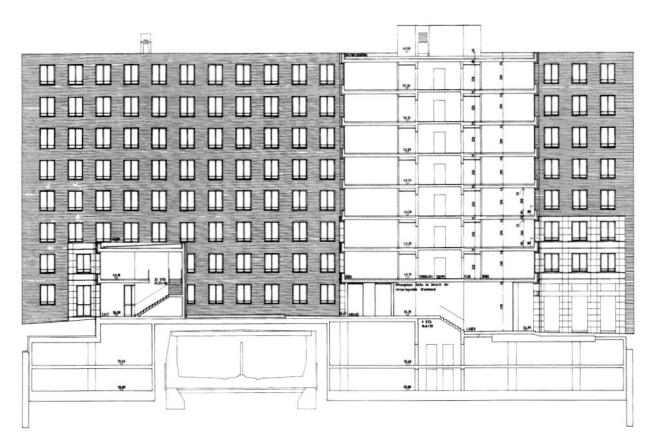

Gebäude 3
Ansicht von Norden
Building 3
North elevation

Gebäude 3
Querschnitt durch den
Mittelflügel mit Ansicht
der Hoffassaden
Building 3
Cross section through
the central part with
courtyard façades elevation

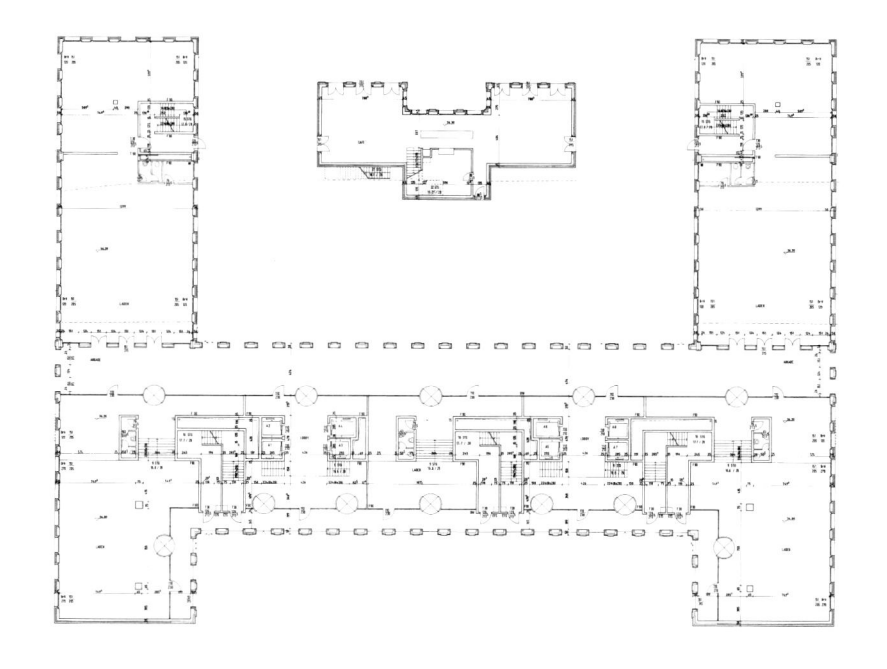

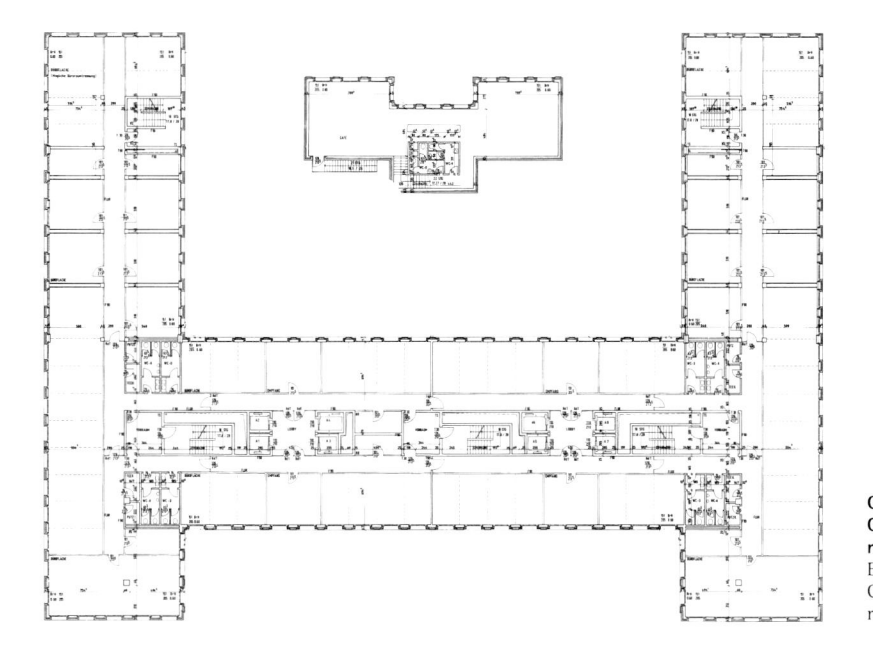

**Gebäude 3
Grundriß Erdgeschoß
mit Ladennutzung und Café**
Building 3
Ground floor plan
retail space and café

**Gebäude 3
Grundriß 1. Obergeschoß
mit Büronutzung**
Building 3
1st floor plan
offices

1:750

A+T
Gebäude Building 1
(Kopfbau End Building)

Potsdamer Platz

Architekten Schweger + Partner
Berlin
Peter P. Schweger
Franz Wöhler
Hartmut H. Reifenstein
Bernhard Kohl
Wolfgang Schneider

Mitarbeit staff
Marcus Brettel
Frank Finkenrath
Torsten Fischer
Ingrid Forza-Spiller
Stefan Grieshop
Charlotte Huhnholz
Ilona Kopp
Heino Lattemann
Annette Rakow
Claus Schenning
Uwe Thiesemann
Thomas Voigt

Bauherr:
A+T
Projektentwicklungsgesellschaft
& Co. Potsdamer Platz Berlin KG
Heidelberg
eine Beteiligungsgesellschaft
von ABB und TERRENO

Planungstermine:
Wettbewerb 1993
Entwurfsplanung seit 1994
Baubeginn 1995
Voraussichtlicher Bezug 1997

Nutzung:
Verkaufsfläche mit
insgesamt 200 m²
Büros (variable Größe) mit
5.510 m² Hauptnutzfläche

Geschosse (XII):
EG Läden
1. OG Technik
2.-11. OG Büros

Untergeschosse (II):
zweigeschossige Tiefgarage
(458 Pkw-Stellplätze), Lager,
Technikflächen

Grundstücksgröße:
1.042,52 m²

Überbaute Fläche:
1.042,52 m²

Bruttogeschoßfläche:
12.100 m²

Perspektive
Neue Promenade
von Westen
Perspective drawing
of Neue Promenade
from the west

Perspektivische
Entwurfsskizze
Blick in den »Stadtschlitz«
Perspective
design study
view of »Stadtschlitz«

Landschaftsarchitekt
Landscape architect
Gustav Lange
Hamburg

Projektadresse:
Location:
Köthener Strasse
in
10963 Berlin-Tiergarten

Client:
A+T
Projektentwicklungsgesellschaft
& Co. Potsdamer Platz Berlin KG
Heidelberg
a holding company of ABB and
TERRENO

Project Stages:
Competition 1993
Design development from 1994
Start of construction 1995
Expected completion 1997

Building Use:
Sales area totalling
200 m²
Offices (variable size) totalling
5510 m² main floor space

Upper Floors (XII):
Ground floor shops
1st floor services
2nd-11th floor offices

Basement Floors (II):
Two-level car park:
458 parking spaces; storeroom,
services areas

Site Area:
1042.52 m²

Built Area:
1042.52 m²

Gross Floor Area:
12100 m²

Perspektive
Neue Promenade
Ecke Stresemannstraße
von Norden
Perspective drawing
of the corner Stresemannstrasse
of Neue Promenade
and from the north

A+T
Gebäude Building **1**   Potsdamer Platz
(Kopfbau End Building)

Den städtebaulichen Vorgaben von Giorgio Grassi folgend, liegt Gebäude 1 als 12-geschossiger Kopfbau am Potsdamer Platz. Es ist das höchste Gebäude des A+T Komplexes und erhält, nicht zuletzt aufgrund seiner charakteristischen tropfenförmigen Rundung, eine autonome architektonische Form und Struktur. Dies gilt auch für die Fassade, die zum Potsdamer Platz ab dem 3. Vollgeschoß eine vollflächige Verglasung aufweist. In Anlehnung an die Fassadenmaterialien der anschließenden Blöcke sind der 3-geschossige Sockelbereich und die Südfassade mit hellrotem Backstein verkleidet. Eine 2-geschossige Halle und drei Brücken als Verbindung zwischen den Gebäuden 1 und 2 bestehen aus den Materialien der Ganzglasfassade.

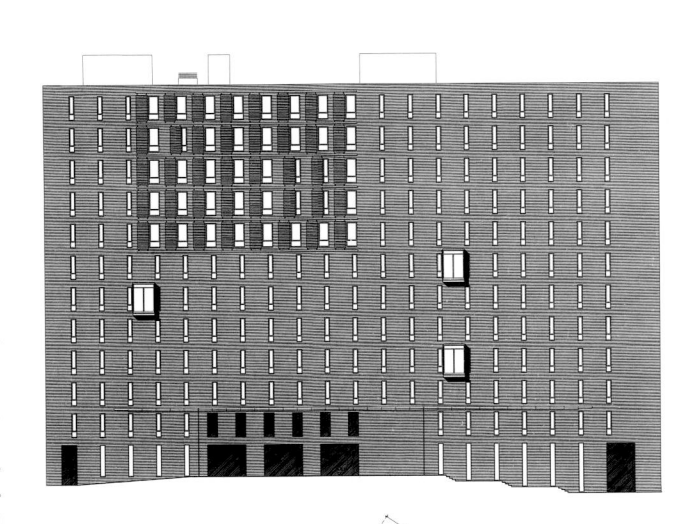

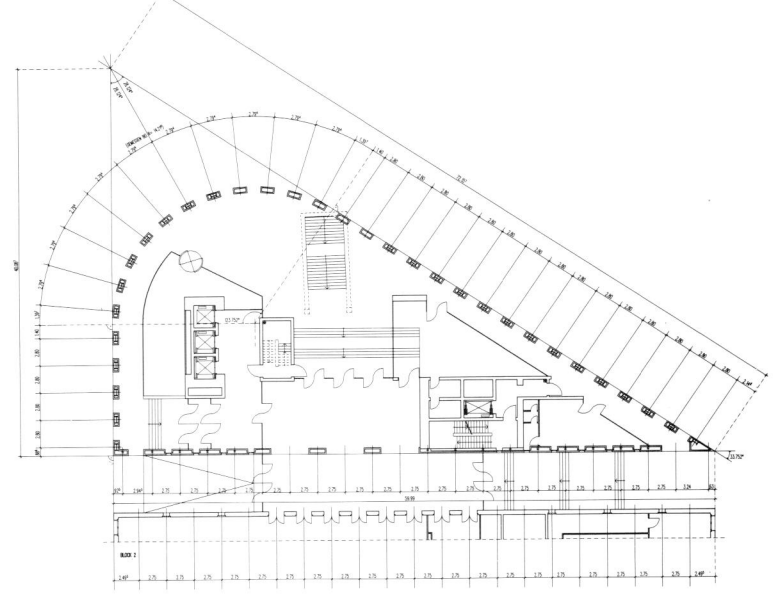

**Ansicht »Stadtschlitz«
von Süden**
South elevation
of »Stadtschlitz«

**Grundriß Erdgeschoß
mit Ladennutzung**
Ground floor plan
retail

**Grundriß 5. Obergeschoß
mit Büronutzung**
5th floor plan
offices

1:750

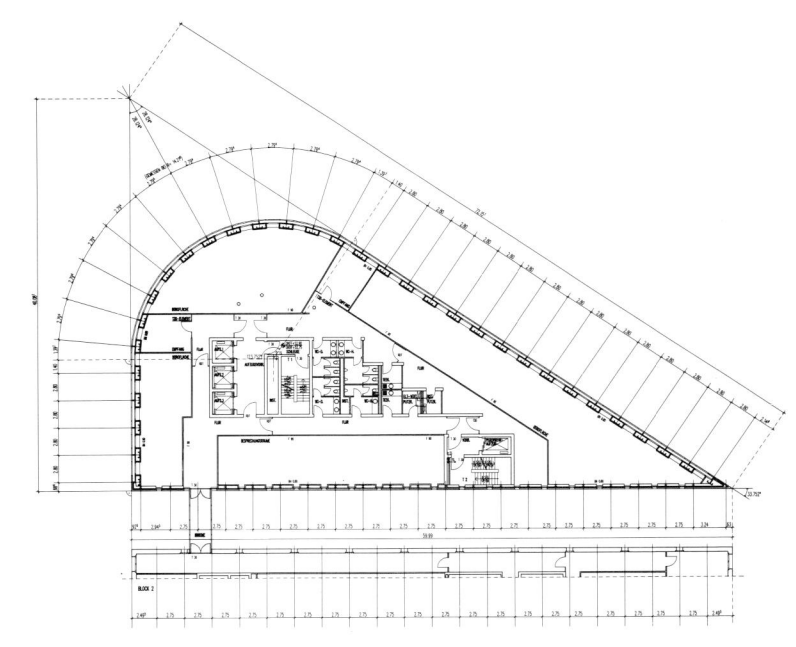

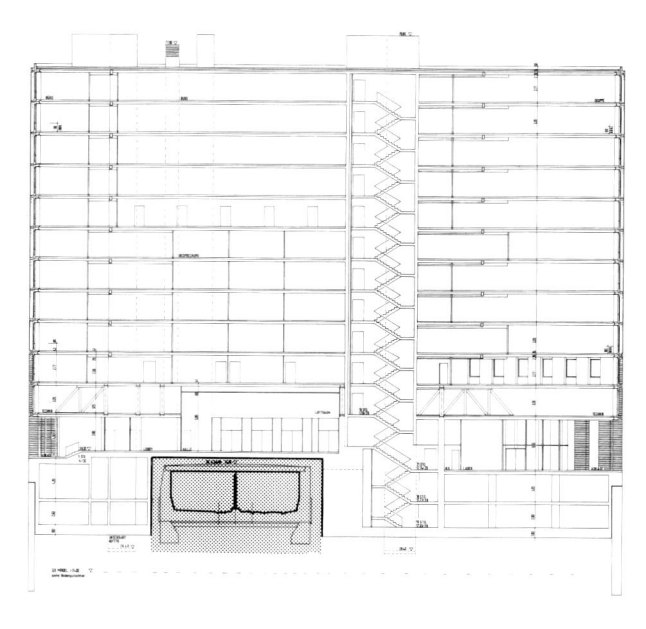

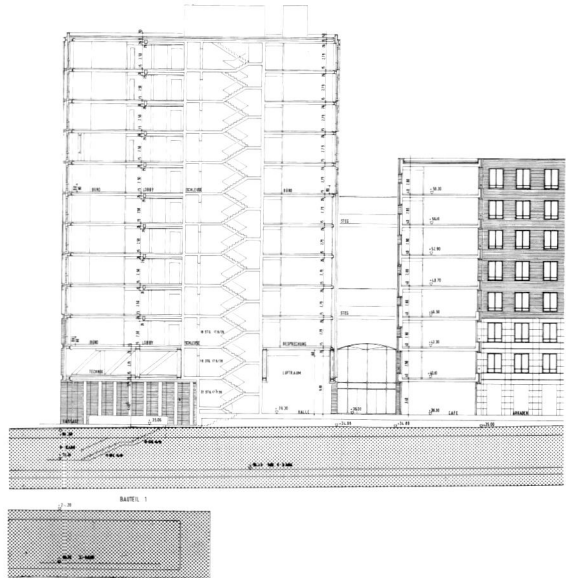

In line with Giorgio Grassi's guidelines building no. 1 facing Potsdamer Platz is a 12-storey high-rise. It is the largest building of the A+T complex and has a highly individual architectural shape and structure, two of the more distinctive features being its droplet-shaped curvature and the extensive glazing from the third floor upwards facing the square. Echoing the façades of buildings nearby, the facing material used for the 3-floor base section and for the south façade is pale red brick. The double-height hall and the three bridges linking buildings 1 and 2 are constructed in the same materials as the glazed façades.

Gebäudelängsschnitt
Longitudinal section

Gebäudequerschnitt
Cross section

A+T
Gebäude Building 4   Potsdamer Platz   Jürgen Sawade   Mitarbeit staff
                                                Berlin   Kurt Niederstatt
                                                                    (Projektleitung project manager)
                                                                    Frithjof Taras
                                                                    Joachim Kleine Allekotte
                                                                    Stephan Plog
                                                                    Boris von Glasenapp
                                                                    Landschaftsarchitekt
                                                                    Landscape architect
                                                                    Gustav Lange
                                                                    Hamburg

Bauherr:
A+T
Projektentwicklungsgesellschaft
& Co. Potsdamer Platz Berlin KG
Heidelberg
eine Beteiligungsgesellschaft
von ABB und TERRENO

Planungstermine:
Wettbewerb 1993
Entwurfsplanung seit 1994
Baubeginn 1995
Voraussichtlicher Bezug 1997

Nutzung:
4 Läden mit
160 m², 190 m², 300 m², 370 m²
176 Büros à 30 m²

Geschosse (VIII):
EG Läden
1.-7. OG Büros

Untergeschosse (II):
Zweigeschossige Tiefgarage
(Planung Schweger + Partner)

Überbaute Fläche:
1.733 m²

Bruttogeschoßfläche:
13.250 m

Unter Berücksichtigung der H-Typologie entsteht ein 8-geschossiges Gebäude mit 5-geschossigen Köpfen zur Köthener Straße. Abmessungen und Fassadengestaltung mit Ziegelmauerwerk und tiefliegenden Lochfenstern folgen den Vorgaben für den Gesamtkomplex. Die Südfassade erhält abweichend davon mauerwerksbündige Glasbausteine. Bei den Hoffassaden ist eine Kontrastierung durch hellen Naturstein mit bündig liegenden Fenstern vorgesehen.

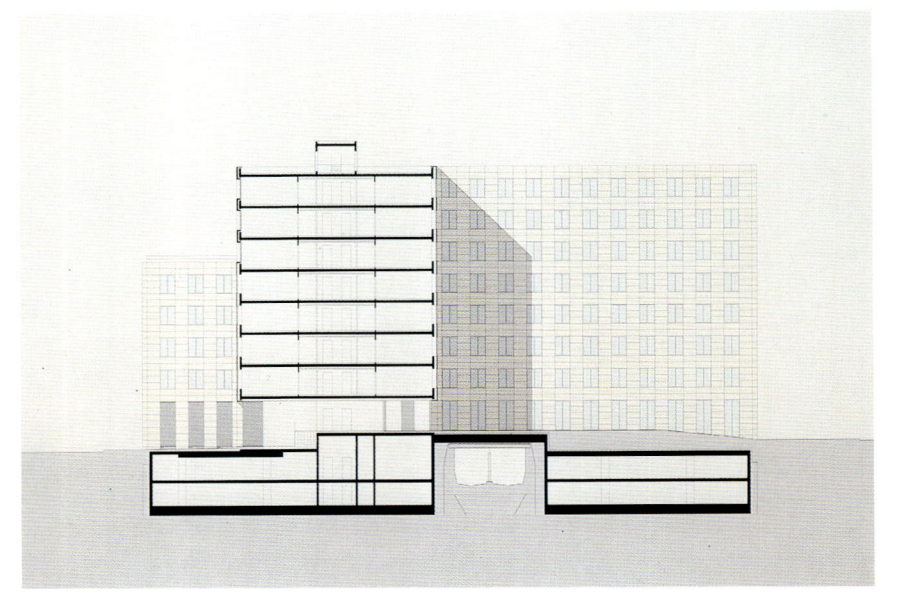

Ansicht von Norden
(links Köthener Straße
rechts Neue Promenade)
North elevation
(left Köthener Strasse
right Neue Promenade)

Gebäudeschnitt
durch den Querflügel
mit Hofansicht des Südflügels
Section
through the transverse wing
with courtyard elevation
of south wing

1:750

rechte Seite right side
Grundriß Erdgeschoß
mit Ladennutzung
Ground floor plan
retail

Grundriß 1.-4. Obergeschoß
mit Büronutzung
Plan of 1st to 4th floors
offices

Grundriß 5.-7. Obergeschoß
mit Büronutzung
Plan of 5th to 7th floors
offices

1:750

Projektadresse:
Location:
**Köthener Strasse
in
10963 Berlin-Tiergarten**

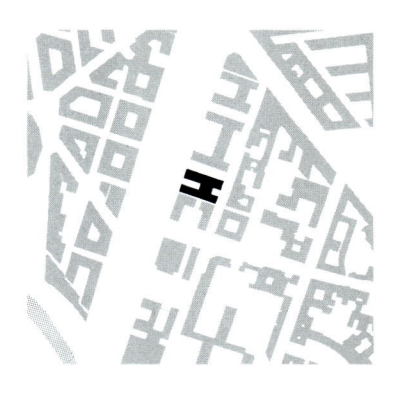

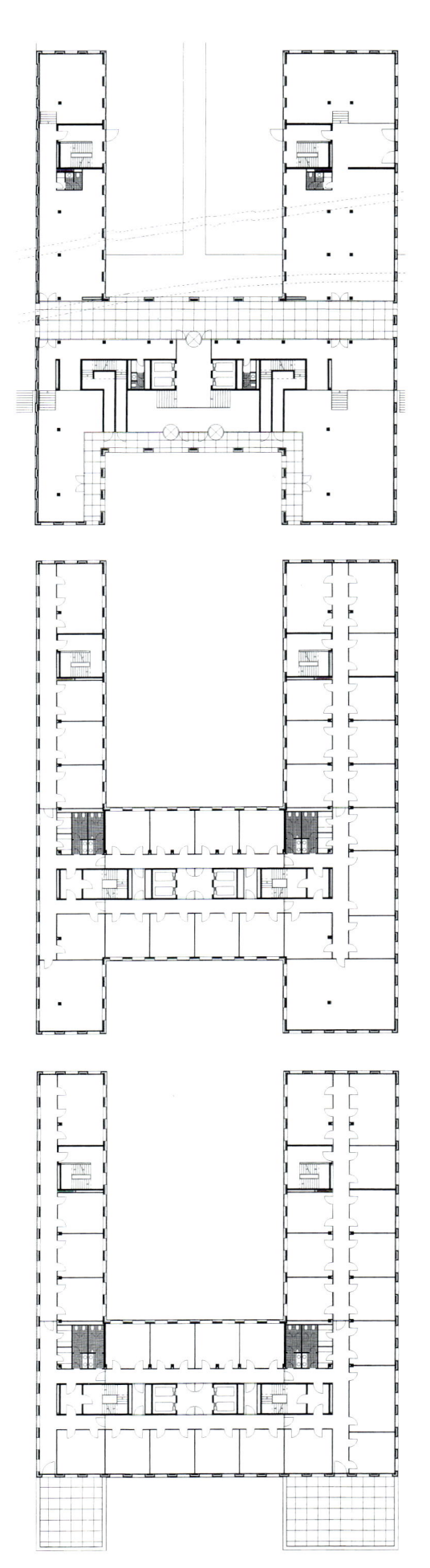

Client:
A+T
Projektentwicklungsgesellschaft
& Co. Potsdamer Platz Berlin KG
Heidelberg
a holding company of ABB and
TERRENO

Project Stages:
Competition 1993
Design development from 1994
Start of construction 1995
Expected completion 1997

Building Use:
4 shops
à 160 m², 190 m², 300 m² and 370 m²
176 offices
à 30 m²

Upper Floors (VIII):
Ground floor shops
1st-7th floor offices

Basement Floors (II):
Two-level car park
(Planning Schweger + Partner)

Built Area:
1733 m²

Gross Floor Area:
13250 m²

The 8-storey H-shaped block lowers to 5 storeys on the end sections facing Köthener Strasse. The building's dimensions and the brickwork façades with their regular pattern of deep inset windows follow the guidelines for the whole complex. The south façade, however, has glass blocks positioned flush with the brickwork. Contrast is generated on the courtyard façades through pale coloured natural stone and windows level with the façade plane.

**Ansicht Neue Promenade
von Westen**
West elevation
Neue Promenade

**Ansicht Köthener Straße
von Osten**
East elevation
Köthener Strasse

1:750

A+T
Gebäude Building 5 Potsdamer Platz

Diener & Diener Architekten
Basel
Roger Diener
Marcus Diener

Bauherr:
A+T
Projektentwicklungsgesellschaft
& Co. Potsdamer Platz Berlin KG
Heidelberg
eine Beteiligungsgesellschaft
von ABB und TERRENO

Planungstermine:
Wettbewerb 1993, 2. Preis
Entwurfsplanung seit 1993
Baubeginn 1995
Voraussichtlicher Bezug 1997

Nutzung:
2 Läden mit
insgesamt 400 m²
90 Wohnungen

Geschosse (IX):
EG Läden, Eingangshalle
1.-8. OG Wohnungen

Untergeschosse (II):
Tiefgarage, Technik
(Planung Schweger + Partner)

Grundstücksgröße:
3.070 m²

Überbaute Fläche:
2.420 m²

Bruttogeschoßfläche:
15.100 m²

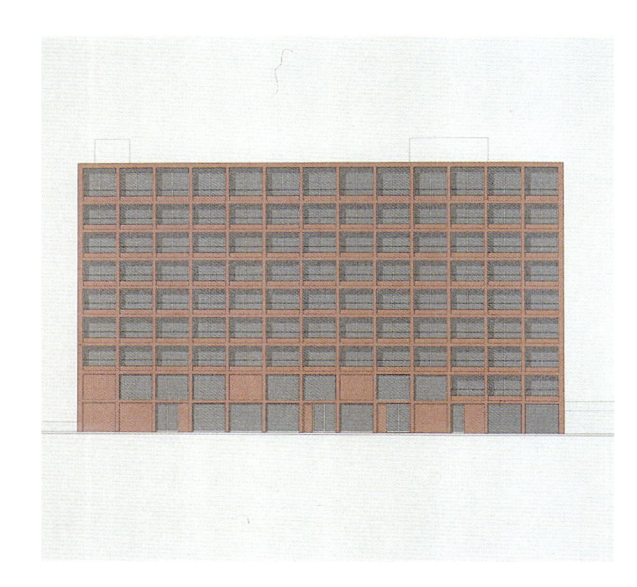

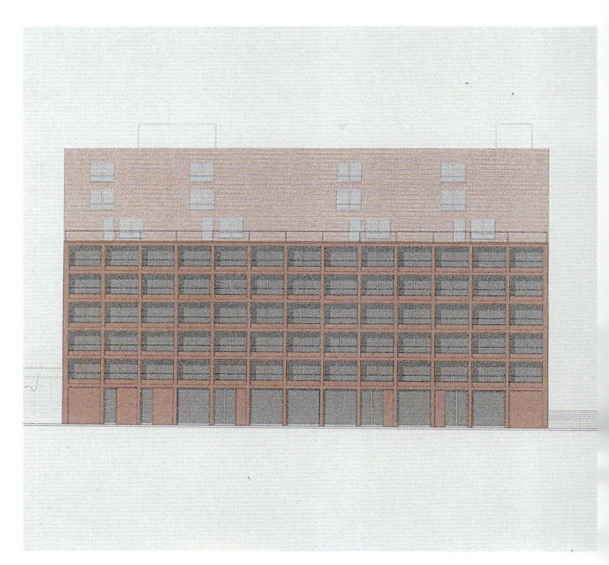

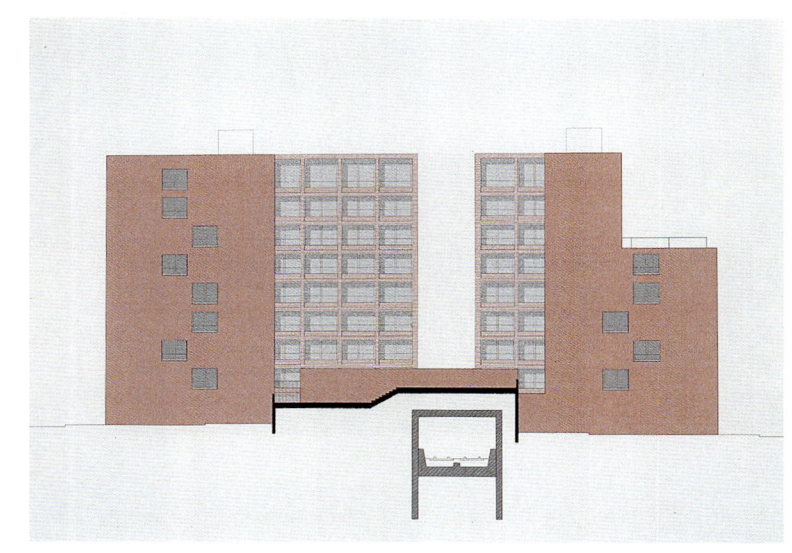

Den südlichen Abschluß bildet eine 9-geschossige, an der Köthener Straße 6-geschossige Wohnanlage. Die beiden Häuser sind der U-Form des städtebaulichen Entwurfes von Grassi einbeschrieben. Durch zwei dicht aneinandergerückte L-förmige Bauten wird der Block geöffnet und in Beziehung zum angrenzenden Schulgrundstück gesetzt. Auch im konstruktiv-architektonischen Ausdruck heben sich die Wohnhäuser von den Bürogebäuden ab.

Ansicht Neue Promenade
von Westen
West elevation
Neue Promenade

Ansicht Köthener Straße
von Osten
East elevation
Köthener Strasse

Ansicht von Süden
mit Schnitt
durch den U-Bahntunnel
South elevation
with section
through the U-Bahn tunnel

1:750

Projektadresse:
Location:
**Köthener Strasse/
Neue Promenade
in
10963 Berlin-Tiergarten**

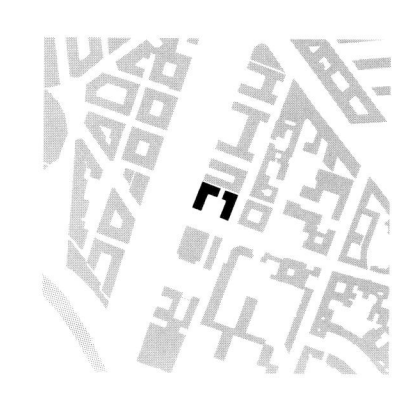

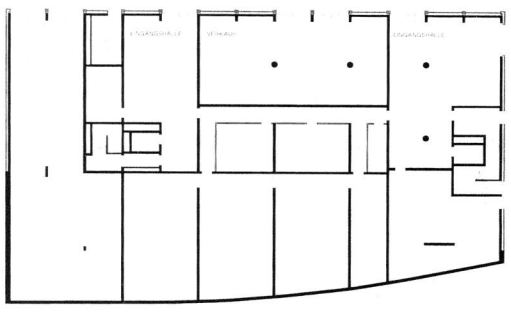

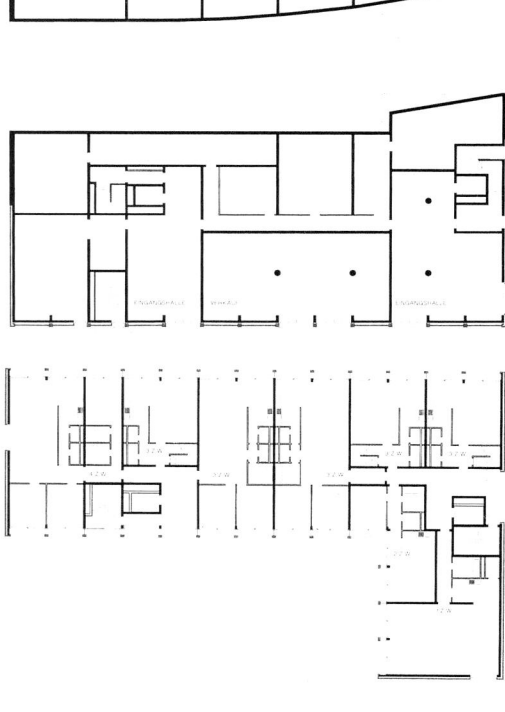

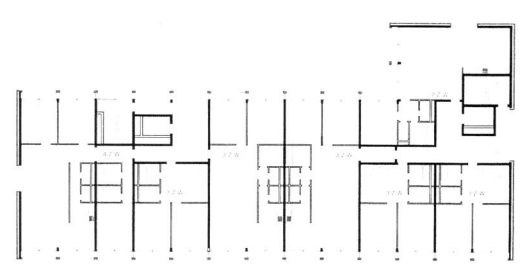

Client:
A+T
Projektentwicklungsgesellschaft
& Co. Potsdamer Platz Berlin KG
Heidelberg
a holding company of ABB and
TERRENO

Project Stages:
Competition 1993, 2nd prize
Design development from 1993
Start of construction 1995
Expected completion 1997

Building Use:
2 shops totalling
400 m²
90 apartments

Upper Floors (IX):
Ground floor shops, entrance hall
1st-8th floor apartments

Basement Floors (II):
Car park, services
(Planning Schweger + Partner)

Site Area:
3070 m²

Built Area:
2420 m²

Gross Floor Area:
15100 m²

**Grundriß Erdgeschoß
mit Eingangshalle und Ladennutzung**
Ground floor plan
entrance hall and retail space

**Grundriß Normalgeschoß
mit Wohnungen**
Typical floor plan
apartments

1:750

At the southern end is located this 9-storey (6 storeys on Köthener Strasse) residential complex. Both buildings follow the U-shaped ground plan of Grassi's urban design. The complex is to be opened up by the figure of the two closely positioned L-shaped buildings, thus creating a relation to the adjacent school site. Also in terms of architectural expression the two residential blocks differ from the office buildings.

Schluß:
Vom Bauboom zum Bautypus

Mit einem Gesamtbauvolumen, das 1994 ca. 27 Mrd. DM betrug, ist Berlin eine der größten Baustellen der Welt. Allein die zusammenhängenden innerstädtischen Brachen im Bereich zwischen Spreebogen, Landwehrkanal und den ehemaligen Ministergärten an der Leipziger Straße, die durch den Flächennutzungsplan und die Bebauungsplanentwürfe (für Regierungsnutzungen im Norden und geschäftsstädtische Kernnutzungen im Süden) festgeschrieben wurden, umfassen ein Territorium, das ein Vielfaches der Fläche der neuen Geschäftsstadt der Londoner Canary Wharf darstellt.

Angesichts des enormen Tempos, mit dem Ende des 20. Jahrhunderts architektonische und städtebauliche Planungen in Berlin umgesetzt werden, gilt es aus dem Rausch des ersten Baubooms zu erwachen und sich bewußt zu machen, welchen tiefgreifenden Wandlungsprozeß die Stadt mit der Gesamtheit dieser Realisierungen durchläuft. Jedes einzelne Gebäude, ob Büro- und Geschäftshaus, Kaufhaus, Hotel oder Wohnhaus, prägt den Maßstab und das Stadtbild, die Nutzungsstruktur und die Lebensqualität der künftigen Metropole Berlin. Daß dies im Positiven wie im Negativen gilt, zeigt das weitgefächerte Spektrum der im Anhang dieses Buches dargestellten Projekte, die – am Beispiel des Büro- und Geschäftshauses – exemplarisch das vielgestaltige Baugeschehen in der Stadt widerspiegeln.

Wegen der städtebaulichen Tragweite, die das Büro- und Geschäftshaus gerade in der Innenstadt besitzt, ist es eine auch kulturelle Verantwortung, Sorge zu tragen, daß nicht länger das schnell amortisierte Renditeobjekt im Vordergrund steht. Das Büro- und Geschäftshaus muß sich aus allzu oft vorherrschender Trivialität befreien. Es muß mehr sein als ein Vehikel flüchtig visualisierter Botschaften und surrogathafter, konsumierbarer Bilder. Es muß urbane Würde zurückgewinnen und als Großstadtarchitektur einer durchkomponierten räumlich-tektonischen Ausarbeitung folgen, sowohl in seiner inneren Gebäudestruktur als auch im Bezug der Baukörper zur Stadt. Insbesondere die Übergangsbereiche zwischen außen und innen – der Eingang, das Foyer, die Fassade – und die mit der Stadt verflochtenen baulichen Elemente – die Arkade, die Passage, der Turm, die Ecke, die Baukörpergliederung – müssen sorgfältig durchdacht und gestaltet sein. Geschieht das nicht, dann werden Gebrauchs- oder besser Verbrauchsarchitekturen das Stadtbild dominieren, die sich eher an der Schnellebigkeit oberflächlicher Visualität und an graphischen Fassadenbehandlungen orientieren als an urbaner Qualität und architektonischer Komposition.

Conclusion:
From Building Boom to Building Type

With a total building volume of approximately 27 thousand million DM in 1994 Berlin is one of the biggest building sites in the world. One inner-city area alone is many times the size of the new Canary Wharf business district in London: this is the area between the »Spreebogen« (the bend in the River Spree), the Landwehrkanal and the former ministerial gardens on Leipziger Strasse. As set out in the zoning plan and the draft development plans, the north of this area will be given over to governmental use and core business activities will be concentrated in the south.

Given the enormous speed at which architectural and urban plans are being realised in Berlin at these latter years of the 20th century, it would be appropriate to step back a little from this first wave of building enthusiasm and take a more considered look at the deep and lasting changes which are happening in the city as a result of these plans. Every individual building, whether office block, department store, hotel or apartment block, has an effect on the scale and the urban face of Berlin, they affect the structure of building use and the quality of life in this future metropolis. The fact that this can imply positive and negative aspects is shown in the wide spectrum of projects in the appendix of this book; commercial and office buildings are a good example of the many aspects of building in the city today.

The role that office and commercial buildings play in the urban character of the inner city in particular places a certain cultural responsibility on all concerned to ensure that quick-return property investments do not unduly dominate. Office and commercial buildings must free themselves from an all too frequent triviality. They must be more than just a vehicle for fleeting messages and a surrogate reflection of consumer images; they must regain their urban dignity, developing into a city architecture with carefully composed spatial and tectonic relationships, both in terms of inner structure and, on a larger scale, as building volumes in the wider urban environment. Special attention must be given to the transition areas between inside and outside – the entrance, the foyer, the façade – and to those elements in a building which interact with the town – the arcade, the covered mall, the tower, the corner and the inner structure. If these factors are overlooked, then the urban image will come to be dominated by everyday, or even run-of-the-mill consumer architecture, driven more by a need to reflect transitory visual fashions and façade treatments than a concern for a longer-lasting overall urban quality and architectural composition.

Immer wieder zu hörende Parolen wie »anything goes« oder in ihrer Anwendung auf amerikanische Städte entstandene Theorien wie »Learning from Las Vegas« sind nicht nur verfehlt, sondern fatal in einer Stadt, die so sehr der europäischen Städtebautradition verpflichtet ist und den modernen Städtebau an der Schwelle zwischen 19. und 20. Jahrhundert so entscheidend geprägt hat wie Berlin. Im Angesicht wieder aufflammender, durch die Chaosforschung aus Naturwissenschaft und Mathematik befruchteter Theorien, die das Chaos als immanenten und zu beförderden Wesenszug der Stadt darstellen, sollte es genügen, sich die fatalen Einflüsse der Chaos- und Zerstörungslehren des Futurismus auf die europäische Architektur und Stadt der Moderne vor Augen zu führen. Gerade in einer physisch so geschundenen Stadt wie Berlin muß Architektur zu Regel, Komposition und – in der Traditionslinie des einst »steinernen Berlin« – zu Körperhaftigkeit, Materialität und Tektonik zurückfinden, um ihrer Doppelrolle als Baustein der Stadt und als Lebens- und Arbeitswelt gerecht zu werden.

In die Auseinandersetzung mit der Großstadtarchitektur am Beispiel des Büro- und Geschäftshauses fließt ein breites Spektrum ineinandergreifender Themen und Strategien ein. Deren entwurfliche Beantwortung verbindet viele der im Hauptteil dieses Buches gezeigten Architekturen. Hierzu zählen:

– die Einordnung des Gebäudes in den städtebaulichen Kontext und sein Bezug auf die Charakteristika des Ortes, die städtebaulicher oder topographischer Art, aber – als genius loci – auch historisch oder kulturell überliefert sein können;
– Rationalität im Ausdruck und in der Gebäudestruktur als konsequente Ableitung vom Rhythmus der Büroraumfolgen, vom Achsraster und damit vom Typus;
– die Reduktion der Mittel und die Beständigkeit der Materialien in ihrer sowohl architektonischen als auch ökonomischen Bedeutung, verbunden mit der Möglichkeit, daß Bauwerke natürlich altern können und mit ihrer Patina an Schönheit gewinnen, statt dem Verschleiß preisgegeben zu sein;
– Materialität und Tektonik im Sinne von ›gefügter Materie‹, gleich ob aus Stein, Glas, Metall oder anderen Materialien, und damit die Abgrenzung gegen Architekturansätze ohne eigenständige analoge Stadtidee;
– die Auseinandersetzung mit der Fassade nicht nur in ihren Proportionen und ihrer Maßstäblichkeit, sondern auch in ihrer Materialbeschaffenheit und Detaillierung, ihrer konstruktiven Qualität und ihrer plastischen Ausformung, der das Spiel von Licht und Schatten zusätzlich Tiefe und Struktur, aber auch Lebendigkeit verleiht;
– die Nutzungsmischung mit Läden, Büros, Wohnungen und ggf. kulturellen Einrichtungen auch innerhalb eines Gebäudes in verti-

Catchphrases such as »anything goes« or, in the context of American cities, theories such as »Learning from Las Vegas«, are not only out of place but destructive in a city such as Berlin which is so firmly rooted in the European architectural tradition, and one which has had such a decisive influence on modern town planning at the end of the last century and beginning of this. In the face of rekindled views, promoted by current chaos theories in science and mathematics, that chaos is to be seen as not only inherent but also as a positive aspect of the urban scene, we need only to look at the catastrophic legacy of the destructivist theories of Futurism in European architecture and in the Modernist view of the city. In a city such as Berlin, with its history of psychological trauma, architecture must surely revert to norms, to composition and – in the tradition of the one-time solid, »stone« city of Berlin – to the physical, the material and the tectonic; only in this way can architecture fulfil its dual role as a factor in the urban image of the city and as a social and working environment.

A wide spectrum of interacting themes and strategies enters into the debate on city architecture, taking the example of office and commercial buildings. The design response to this links many of the architectural examples shown in the main section of this book. These themes include:

– the integration of the building into the urban context and its reference to the characteristics of its location, which can be both urban and topographical, and also – as a genius loci – historical and cultural in origin;

– a rationality of expression and building structure, deriving from the rhythm of the sequence of rooms, the axial spacing and thus the building type itself;

– the reduction of the architectural means and the longevity of the materials in both architectural as well as economic terms, linked with the possibility that buildings can age naturally, their patina adding to the overall attraction instead of merely showing signs of wear and tear;

– the material and the tectonic in the sense of »formulated material«, whether of stone, glass, metal or other materials, and as such the delimitation against architecture with no corresponding urban concept of its own;

– the concern with the façade not only in terms of its proportions and scale, but also as regards its material composition and detailing, its structural quality and its sculptural form, enlivening the façade by adding depth and relief;

– the mix of uses with shops, offices, apartments and sometimes also cultural facilities, distributed vertically inside a building, together with the aim of ensuring independent access to these different functional zones;

– the development of the office and commercial building type,

kaler Schichtung, verbunden mit dem Ziel einer gegenseitig störungsfreien Erschließung;
– die Weiterentwicklung der Gebäudetypologie des Büro- und Geschäftshauses, unter anderem mit der Aufwertung der Attikageschosse in ihrer mit dem Aufzug gewonnenen Bedeutung als moderne Beletage;
– die Nutzung der Terrassierungen und Dachflächen als Gärten und Panoramaterrassen über den Dächern der Stadt für Wohnungen, Chefetagen und Konferenzbereiche;
– die Versöhnung von Individualität des Bauwerks und Kollektivität der Stadt als Wesensmerkmale der Großstadtarchitektur und das Entfalten architektonischer Qualität innerhalb der Bindungen des Städtebaus und des Typus.

Das neue Stadtbild von Berlin wird die Vielfalt der Architektur nur allzu deutlich widerspiegeln. Diskussionen darüber, ob eine Trauflinie bei 22 m oder 30 m liegen soll, ob eine Fassade aus Glas oder aus Stein sein muß, ob ein Bauwerk ein Hochhaus sein kann oder sich in eine einheitliche Silhouette fügen muß, werden in Berlin als Grundsatzdispute geführt und mit einer Leidenschaft diskutiert wie nirgendwo anders. Dabei geht die Diskussion allerdings meist an den entscheidenden Fragen vorbei: der Frage nach einer auf den jeweiligen Ort bezogenen Auseinandersetzung, der Frage nach der Qualität der Architektur und der Frage nach der Überwindung des Exzeptionellen auf der Grundlage der Weiterentwicklung des Typus.
»Das Vorhandensein eines Typus«, schrieb Fritz Schumacher 1940 in ›Künstlerische Aufgaben der Großstadtarchitektur‹, »ist (...) der sicherste Beweis für den restlosen Ausgleich zwischen praktischen und künstlerischen Forderungen. (...) Echte Schöpferkraft wird dem Streben nach dem Typus niemals aus dem Wege gehen. Ist er noch nicht gefunden, so wird sie suchen, ihm näher zu kommen; ist er gefunden, so wird sie suchen, ihm ein edles neues Gewand zu geben. Niemals aber zeigt sich echte Schöpferkraft in dem viel verbreiteten Streben, etwas anders zu machen, bloß um es anders zu machen. Wer den Typus verschmäht, weil er glaubt, innerhalb seiner Grenzen nicht genug zur Geltung zu kommen, offenbart seinen Egoismus.«[1]
Die Ausarbeitung eines ausgereiften Typus des Büro-/Wohn- und Geschäftshauses, der auch die Forderungen nach einer Funktionsmischung innerhalb eines Gebäudes und nach einer Nutzung der Terrassierungen und Dachflächen in engem Bezug auf den Grundriß erfüllt, ist in Berlin noch nicht abgeschlossen. Mit seiner Weiterentwicklung sollte die Chance verfolgt werden, innerstädtischen Bauwerken eine zusätzliche architektonische Qualität zu verleihen.

1 Nachgedruckt in: »An dieser Hoffnung habe ich bis zuletzt festgehalten ... Fritz Schumacher über Probleme der Großstadt« (architextbook Nr. 6), Berlin 1986.

including the upgrading of the attic storeys, which since the invention of the lift have been able to establish their new significance as a modern »Bel étage«;
– the use of terracing and roof surfaces as gardens and panorama terraces above the city skyline, for apartments, management floors and conference areas;
– the reconciliation of the individuality of a building with the collectivity of the city, as a characteristic of city architecture, and the unfolding of architectural quality within these links and within the building type.

The new urban image of Berlin will reflect all too clearly the architectural variety. Questions such as whether the eaves height should be 22 metres or 30 metres, whether façades should be of glass or concrete, or whether a building can be a high-rise or fit in more with the unified silhouette, are currently being debated in Berlin with an intensity unparalleled elsewhere. Yet generally this debate is missing the key questions – ones directed towards the specifics of a particular location, or the quality of the architecture itself, or the question of overcoming the exceptional on the basis of a continued development of the building type.
In his book entitled »Künstlerische Aufgaben der Großstadtarchitektur« (Creative Tasks for City Architecture), published in 1940, the author, Fritz Schumacher wrote:
»The existence of a particular building type is (...) the surest proof for the complete balance between practical and artistic demands. (...) Real creativity will never shy away from striving for a building type. If a type does not exist it will attempt to seek it out; when one is found, it will seek to give it a new, noble face. Never does real creativity appear in the widespread striving to do something differently, simply for the sake of it. Those who reject the type because they see in it a restriction of their talents, are revealing their egoism.«[1]
The development of a mature building type combining a functional mix of offices, apartments and commercial space in one volume and utilising terracing and roof areas, all with close reference to the ground plan, is not yet completed in Berlin. Its further development should exploit this opportunity of attaining additional architectural quality in inner-city buildings.

1 Reprinted in: »An dieser Hoffnung habe ich bis zuletzt festgehalten ... Fritz Schumacher über Probleme der Großstadt« (architextbook no. 6), Berlin 1986.

**Das Business Center
Checkpoint Charlie Friedrichstrasse
Block 105**

Skidmore, Owings & Merrill; New York
mit with Pysall Stahrenberg & Partner;
Berlin

Mauerstrasse 93
10117 Berlin-Mitte

Am ehemaligen Grenzübergang Checkpoint Charlie schließt ein Komplex mit insgesamt fünf Baukörpern den historischen Stadtgrundriß: zwei Neubauten mit integriertem Altbestand entlang der Mauerstraße; ein Rundbau zur Kreuzung Friedrichstraße/Mauerstraße mit einem ihn flankierenden Kopfbau an der Mauerstraße sowie ein L-förmiger Bau entlang der Zimmerstraße. Die Anzahl der Geschosse liegt zwischen 6 und 9 OGs sowie 1 bis 3 UGs. Den Rundbau als zentrales Element des Komplexes markiert ein aus der Fassade springendes Treppenhaus. Die Gebäude enthalten Büros, Läden und Wohnungen.

A complex of five buildings completes the historical urban plan at the former border crossing point, Checkpoint Charlie. Two new buildings integrate older structures along Mauerstrasse; a round building on Friedrich-/Mauerstrasse is flanked by an end building on Mauerstrasse, and there is an L-shaped building along Zimmerstrasse. The number of storeys varies between 6 and 9 upper storeys and 1 to 3 basement levels. The round building as a central element of the complex marks out a stair tower projecting from the façade. The buildings contain offices, shops and apartments.

**Das Business Center
Checkpoint Charlie Friedrichstrasse
Block 106**

Philip Johnson Architects; New York
Philip Johnson, John Manley,
Christian Bjone, Karin Bruckner

Pysall Stahrenberg & Partner; Berlin
Joachim Grundei, Justus Pysall jr.,
Peter Ruge

Friedrichstrasse
10117 Berlin-Mitte

Der Gebäudekomplex besteht aus einer 7-geschossigen Blockrandbebauung, der eine öffentliche Grünfläche zugehört. Das Gebäude ist als Büro- und Geschäftshaus konzipiert. Einer der beiden Innenhöfe bildet den organisatorischen Mittelpunkt des Entwurfs. Die Erschließung erfolgt von der Friedrichstraße über eine Passage im EG-Geschäftsbereich. Die Fassaden werden durch vertikale und horizontale Flächen strukturiert, die mit Granit verkleidet sind. Die vertikalen Flächen wechseln mit Glas-Vorhangelementen, von denen einige schräg nach oben zurückfließen.

The complex consists of a 7-storey building which forms part of a block edge and includes a green area open to the public. The building is intended for offices and retail. One of the two inner courtyards forms the organisational centre of the design. A passage in the commercial area on the ground floor provides access from Friedrichstrasse. Vertical and horizontal areas, which are clad with granite, lend the façades structure. The vertical areas alternate with curtain walls, some of which flow diagonally upwards.

**Das Business Center
Checkpoint Charlie Friedrichstrasse
Block 200**

KSP; Berlin
Kaspar Kraemer, Rolf J. Schmiedecke,
Jürgen J. K. Engel,
Michael Zimmermann

Friedrichstrasse 47-49a
10117 Berlin-Mitte

Eine ruhige, großzügig verglaste Straßenfront umgreift den gesamten Büro- und Geschäftskomplex. An der Mittelzone der Hauptfassade sind metallische Rahmen in die mit Granit verkleidete Rasterstruktur gesetzt. An der Nordfassade laufen die Fensterbänder teilweise bündig mit der Steinfassade. Im Innern des Komplexes befinden sich die Baukörper des Atriums und der Rotunde. Neben Büros und Läden beherbergt das Gebäude eine Gedenkstätte an der Ecke Friedrich-/Zimmerstraße. Die Haupterschließung erfolgt von der Friedrichstraße über ein Foyer im EG-Ladenbereich zu einem Atrium im 1. OG.

A quiet, extensive glass street front encompasses the whole office and commercial complex. Metallic frames are inset in the granite-clad grid in the central zone of the main façade. On the north façade, window strips are placed flush, in places, with the stone façade. An atrium and a rotunda are located inside the complex. Apart from offices and shops, the building also contains a memorial on the corner of Friedrichstrasse and Zimmerstrasse. Main access is from Friedrichstrasse via a foyer, on the ground-floor shop area, leading to an atrium on the 1st floor.

**Das Business Center
Checkpoint Charlie Friedrichstrasse
Block 201 A**

Lauber + Wöhr; München
Ulrike Lauber, Wolfram Wöhr

Friedrichstrasse 50-55
10117 Berlin-Mitte

Das 8-geschossige Bürogebäude Block 201 A fügt sich städtebaulich in die Vorgaben der Friedrichstraße mit Blockrandschließung und durchgehender Traufhöhe ein. Die Fassade ist in einen 2-geschossigen Sockelbereich, eine 4-geschossige Mittelzone und einen Attikabereich mit 2 Staffelgeschossen gegliedert. Die Ecke Friedrichstraße/Krausenstraße ist geschlossen massiv, die Ecke Friedrichstraße/Schützenstraße vollständig verglast.

The 8-storey office block follows urban planning guidelines for block development along Friedrichstrasse, keeping to the overall eaves height. The façade is articulated into a 2-storey base area, a 4-storey central zone and an attic area with 2 storeys stepped back from the main façade plane. The corner of Friedrichstrasse and Krausenstrasse presents a closed, solid face, whereas the corner of Friedrichstrasse and Schützenstrasse is fully glazed.

**Das Business Center
Checkpoint Charlie Friedrichstrasse
Block 201 B**

Bender Glass; Berlin
Günther Bender, Gisela Glass

Schützenstrasse 74/
Charlottenstrasse 75/
Krausenstrasse 12
10117 Berlin-Mitte

In dem Gebäude werden strukturelle Gestaltungselemente des Quartiers wie Sockelzone, Mittelteil, Gesims und deutlich abgesetzte Dachzone aufgenommen. Allen Fassaden gemeinsam ist eine additive Staffelung in zwei Schichten: einer äußeren, der Bauflucht folgenden (Sichtmauerwerk) und einer um ca. 1,80 m zurückliegenden, die - überwiegend aus Glas - alle Geschosse durchdringt. Der jeweilige Wohnungstyp (insgesamt 200 Wohnungen) wird in der Fassadengestaltung wiedergegeben (z. B. Maisonettewohnungen mit großmaßstäblicher Fassadengliederung).

Structural design elements of the district such as a base and central zone, a cornice and a distinctly contrasting roof zone have been adopted. All façades share the same double layering: an outer skin (fair-faced masonry) following the line of development along the street and a second skin, mostly of glass, at approximately 1.80 m behind this first, and extending to all floors. The respective apartment types (a total of 200 apartments) are reflected in the design of the façade (e.g. maisonette apartments with larger-scale façade articulation).

The entire block is being built over in three stages as a closed block edge structure. Three perpendicular buildings mark out four inner courtyards. Towards Schützenstrasse the existing historical buildings (19th century) and the surviving remains of the structure built by Erich Mendelsohn (1921/22) are to be restored and integrated and reconstructed in part. Echoing the tradition of the site – the former Mosse publishing house – and its surroundings the concept provides for a media centre with offices and printing works (81 %), residential space (13.5 %), shops, surgeries and galleries.

In drei Bauabschnitten entsteht eine Überbauung des gesamten Blocks als geschlossene Randbebauung. Drei Querriegel definieren vier Höfe im Inneren. Zur Schützenstraße werden der historische Bestand (19. Jh.) und die Reste der Überbauung von Mendelsohn (1921/22) restauriert und integriert sowie in Teilen rekonstruiert. Als Nutzung ist in Anlehnung an die Geschichte des ehemaligen Mosse-Verlagshauses und seiner Umgebung eine Blockgesamtkonzeption als Medienzentrum mit Büro- und Druckereiflächen (81 %) sowie Wohngebäuden (13,5 %), ferner Läden, Praxen und Galerien vorgesehen.

Mosse-Zentrum
Mosse-Centre

Fissler Ernst Architekten; Berlin
Jürgen Fissler, Hans-Christof Ernst

Schützenstrasse 18-25/
Jerusalemer Strasse/Zimmerstrasse/
Markgrafenstrasse
10117 Berlin-Mitte

The block is to be completed in a way which integrates the old buildings and also reinstates the historical street profile of the bordering streets. Parallel to Leipziger Strasse is a 45 m long glass hall which is reached via the 2-storeys-high foyer on the Friedrichstrasse side. A tower on the corner of Friedrichstrasse and Leipziger Strasse, and the 2-storeys-high arcades in the base section are intended to revive traditional Berlin block design. The two upper floors are stepped back from the façade. The residential part of the building is a vertical section along Kronenstrasse.

Unter Einbeziehung der Altbauten wird der Block komplettiert und das historische Profil der angrenzenden Straßen wieder hergestellt. Parallel zur Leipziger Straße erstreckt sich eine 45 m lange Glashalle, die durch ein 2-geschoßhohes Foyer von der Friedrichstraße erschlossen wird. Durch einen Eckturm an der Friedrichstraße/Leipziger Straße sowie 2-geschoßhohe Arkaden im Sockelbereich wird die Wiederaufnahme der Gestaltungstradition der Berliner Blöcke beabsichtigt. Die beiden oberen Geschosse sind zurückgestaffelt. Wohnnutzung liegt in vertikaler Anordnung an der Kronenstraße.

Büro- und Geschäftshaus
Quartier 203
Office Building
Block 203

von Gerkan, Marg und Partner;
Hamburg, Aachen

Friedrichstrasse/Leipziger Strasse/
Kronenstrasse/Charlottenstrasse
10117 Berlin-Mitte

The project aims to redefine the significance of the traditional lot structure in line with historic references in Friedrichstadt. The project was developed as an overall plan and several individual concepts; it replaces lot fragmentation with a »set of blocks« principle. A glass-roofed inner courtyard constitutes the unifying element of the individually designed houses. This »winter garden« serves as a central access area. Shops and restaurants are grouped around it. The apartments are located in a separate building.

Ziel des Projekts ist es, im Rahmen der historischen Bezüge der Friedrichstadt die Bedeutung der traditionellen Parzelle neu zu definieren. In dem in einem Gesamt- und mehreren Einzelkonzepten entwickelten Projekt wird die Parzellisierung durch das Prinzip des Baukastensystems ersetzt. Ein glasüberdachter Lichthof im Innern des Komplexes bildet das Verbindungselement der individuell gestalteten Einzelhäuser. Dieser »Wintergarten« dient als zentraler Erschließungsraum. Um ihn gruppieren sich Läden und Gastronomie. Wohnungen sind in einem eigenständigen Gebäude untergebracht.

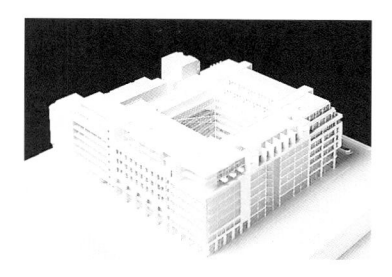

Kontorhaus Mitte

Josef Paul Kleihues (Gesamtkonzept);
Berlin
Klaus Theo Brenner; Berlin
Walther Stepp; Berlin
Vittorio Magnago Lampugnani/
Marlene Dörrie; Frankfurt a.M.

Friedrichstrasse 185-190/
Mohrenstrasse 13-16/
Kronenstrasse 60-65
10117 Berlin-Mitte

Refurbishment, upward extension and conversion of a complex built in 1905 and 1954. The existing buildings are 6 or 7 storeys high with a pitched roof and T-shaped ground plans, which link to form an overall I-shaped plan. The refurbished complex will have 7 storeys and flat roofs throughout. The cores are to be removed from the buildings, the stairs and the entire technical infrastructure are to be replaced, and ancillary buildings torn down. The façades are to be redesigned to include large shop windows on the ground floor, and the windows overlooking Taubenstrasse widened.

Das Projekt umfaßt Sanierung, Aufstockung und Umbau des Komplexes aus den Jahren 1905 bzw. 1954. Die Altbauten sind 6- bzw. 7-geschossig mit Satteldach und jeweils T-förmigem Grundriß, der einen I-förmigen Gesamtgrundriß bildet. Es entstehen durchgehend 7-geschossige Gebäude mit Flachdächern. Die Gebäude werden für den Umbau entkernt, Treppenhäuser und die gesamte technische Infrastruktur werden erneuert, Anbauten werden abgerissen. Die Fassaden werden neu gestaltet mit großzügigen Schaufenstern im EG und Verbreiterung der Fensteröffnungen zur Taubenstraße.

Büro- und Geschäftshaus
Office Building
Taubenstrasse/Mohrenstrasse

Regina Schuh; München

Taubenstrasse 20-22/
Mohrenstrasse 42-44
10117 Berlin-Mitte

The 7-storey building is vertically divided into a residential and office section to which access is gained by means of two stair-wells each with its own lift. There are shops on the ground floor. In addition there are 2 basement parking levels. The inner courtyard incorporates a playground and space for relaxing. The street fronts consist of extensive glazed surfaces contrasting with stone-clad punctuated façades. The corner is accentuated as a polygonal glass semi-cylinder.

Das 7-geschossige Gebäude ist im vertikalen Aufbau in einen Wohn- und einen Büroteil gegliedert; diese werden durch zwei Treppenhäuser mit je einem Aufzug erschlossen. Im EG befinden sich Läden. Hinzu kommen 2 Tiefgaragenebenen. Ein gestalteter Hofbereich bietet Raum für Spiel und Erholung. Die Straßenfronten bestehen aus stark verglasten Bereichen, die steinverkleideten Lochfassaden kontrastieren. Die Gebäudeecke ist als polygoner Glashalbzylinder betont.

Wohn- und Geschäftshaus
Apartment and Office Building
Alte Jakobstrasse/Seydelstrasse

Architektur + Planung; Berlin
Günter Stahn

Alte Jakobstrasse 96-99/
Seydelstrasse 18-19
10179 Berlin-Mitte

Zwei Wohn- und Geschäftshäuser
Two Apartment and Office Buildings
Michaelkirchstrasse

Kollhoff & Timmermann; Berlin
Hans Kollhoff, Helga Timmermann

Michaelkirchstrasse 22, 23
10179 Berlin-Mitte

Das Projekt liegt am Südufer der Spree an der neuen Michaelbrücke, einer Verbindungslinie zwischen City-Ost und Kreuzberg. Die Bebauung ist auf den Büroetagen zweibündig organisiert und besitzt in den beiden oberen, zurückgestaffelten Geschossen Maisonette-Wohnungen. Die Wohngeschosse werden hofseitig über einen Laubengang mit separaten Aufzugs- und Treppenanlagen erschlossen. Sie sind zur Michaelkirchstraße zu einem turmartigen Akzent hochgetreppt, mit dem das Gebäude einen Bezug zur Stadtsilhouette der City herstellt.

The site is on the south bank of the Spree at the new Michaelbrücke, a main link between City East and Kreuzberg. The offices are laid out along a spine corridor. There are maisonette apartments on the two upper stepped-back storeys. Access to the flats is from the inner courtyard via an outside corridor with a separate lift and stairs. On the Michaelkirchstrasse side, the residential floors are terraced to create a tower-like effect. Thus the building seeks to establish a relationship with the inner city skyline.

TRIAS
Büro- und Geschäftshaus
Office Building

Beringer & Wawrik; München
sowie and Zobel & Weber; München

Holzmarktstrasse 15-18
10179 Berlin-Mitte

Das Gebäude liegt nahe der Jannowitzbrücke unmittelbar hinter den hier direkt ans Spreeufer grenzenden S-Bahn-Bögen. Zur Straße schließt es als 6-geschossiger linearer Baukörper den Straßenrand. Drei V-förmige 13-geschossige Flügelbauten zur Spree hin umschließen zwei erhöht liegende Plazas, unter denen große zusammenhängende Ladenflächen liegen. Die Gebäude besitzen Vorhangfassaden mit horizontalen Fensterbändern.

The building is situated near the Jannowitzbrücke, just behind the S-Bahn tracks which run along the banks of the Spree here. Towards the street the building presents a 6-storey linear face closing the line of development along the street. Three V-shaped, 13-storey wing sections facing the Spree enclose two raised plazas under which are located large shopping areas. The buildings have curtain wall façades with horizontal bands of fenestration.

**Büro- und Geschäftshaus/
Wohngebäude**
Office Building/Apartment Building
Strasse der Pariser Kommune

Wörle und Partner; München, Berlin

Strasse der Pariser Kommune 48
10243 Berlin-Friedrichshain

Der in seiner Höhenentwicklung differenzierte Entwurf leitet sich aus den unterschiedlichen stadträumlichen Beziehungen ab. Zum Platz der Pariser Kommune bildet ein 13-geschossiges Hochhaus mit Staffelgeschoß die städtebauliche Dominante. Die im Süden anschließende Blockbebauung nimmt mit ihrer Höhenstaffelung die jeweils umgebende Bebauung auf. Die Fassade des Hochhauses besteht aus einer reinen Aluminium-Glasfassade. Die Blockbebauung erhält eine Lochfassade mit Steinverkleidung und greift damit den Charakter der Karl-Marx-Allee auf.

The differentiated height development of this design is a response to the differing urban relationships at the site. Towards the Platz der Pariser Kommune the 13-storey high-rise with stepped storey dominates the urban scene. The block adjoining to the south takes its heights from the surrounding developments. The façade of the high-rise is a pure aluminum and glass façade. The smaller block has a punctuated, stone-clad façade, in line with the character of the Karl-Marx-Allee.

Büro- und Geschäftshaus
Office Building
Stralauer Platz

Murphy/Jahn; Chicago

Stralauer Platz 35
10243 Berlin-Friedrichshain

Auf dem ehemaligen Mauergrundstück vermittelt der halboffene Entwurf zwischen Hauptbahnhof und Spreeufer. Ein 5-geschossiges und ein in Stufen 15-geschossiges Gebäude rahmen einen neu entstehenden Platz ein. Die Z-Form des Hauptgebäudes formt ostseitig einen offenen Wintergarten. Westseitig führt ein großes Tor zur »high plaza«. Zur Spreeseite entsteht auf dem terrassenförmig aufgeschütteten Flußufer eine Promenade mit Läden im EG. Das Hauptgebäude definiert den Blockrand mit einer steinverkleideten Fassade, der eine Ganzglasfassade als gleichberechtigtes Thema zur Seite gestellt wird.

On a site once divided by the Berlin Wall this semi-open design establishes a relationship between Hauptbahnhof station and the banks of the Spree. A 5-storey building and a staggered, 15-storey building frame a new square. The Z-shape of the main building forms an open winter garden on the east side. On the west a large gate leads to the »high plaza«. Towards the Spree, a promenade with ground-floor shops has been created on the terraced river embankment. The main building, with its stone-clad façade offset against an all-glass façade of equal status, defines the edge of the block.

Quasar
Büro- und Geschäftshaus
Office Building

Takamatsu + Lahyani; Kyoto, Berlin
Shin Takamatsu und Gabriel E. Lahyani

Frankfurter Allee 69/Voigtstrasse 1
10247 Berlin-Friedrichshain

Das Gebäude liegt an der großen Radialstraße auf einem Eckgrundstück. Es hat 7 Geschosse sowie ein Kellergeschoß und ein Technikgeschoß auf dem Dach. Die Fassade besitzt eine schwarze Granitverkleidung mit Edelstahlelementen. Zur Straßenecke hin sind vom 3. OG an 4 turmartige Glaskörper mit linsenförmigem Grundriß integriert. Das Tragwerk des Gebäudes ist ein Stahlbetonrahmen, bei dem das 3. OG als Kragarm für den Glas-Edelstahl-Zylinder über dem Haupteingang angebildet ist. Eine Vierendeelkonstruktion trägt die Glastürme sowie den freispannenden Eingangsbereich.

The building is situated on a corner plot on a main radial street. It has 7 storeys, a basement and a services floor on the roof. The façade is clad with black granite with stainless steel elements. Four glass tower-like structures with a lens-shaped ground plan reach up from the 3rd floor on the corner. The building has a reinforced concrete frame; the 3rd floor serves as a cantilevered support for the glass and stainless steel cylinder above the main entrance. A Vierendeel girder construction supports the glass towers and the free-spanning entrance area.

In an area otherwise dominated by slab blocks without spatial identity, this office and commercial centre is to create spatial sequences in its interaction between differently shaped open spaces and in its variety of lines of sight. At the end of Alt-Friedrichsfelde Strasse a spatially simple square seeks to counteract the dominance of the street. Apart from office space, the centre is open to many different uses: a cinema with bar, restaurants, shops and cafés. A hotel with supermarket at ground floor level and a hall on the 1st floor is reached via a bridge above the arcade at the square.

Das Büro- und Geschäftshauszentrum soll in einer Sequenz von ineinandergreifenden Längs- und Breitenplätzen sowie Sichtachsen ein Raumgefüge inmitten der Raumlosigkeit der Plattenbauten schaffen. Als städtebaulicher Abschluß der Straße Alt-Friedrichsfelde entsteht ein räumlich einfach formulierter Platz, der der Dominanz der Straße entgegenwirkt. Das Zentrum bietet neben Büroflächen eine Vielfalt von Nutzungen: Kino mit Bar, Restaurants, Läden, Cafés. Ein Hotel mit Supermarkt im EG und mit Halle im 1. OG ist über eine Brücke oberhalb der Platzpassage erreichbar.

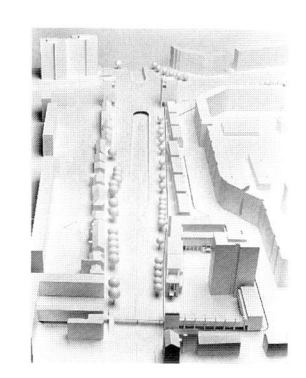

Wohngebietszentrum
Community Centre
Alt-Friedrichsfelde

K + K Architekten; Berlin
Georg Kohlmaier, Holger Kühnel

Alt-Friedrichsfelde 23, 25
10315 Berlin-Lichtenberg

The project is part of the reorganisation of the district around the S-Bahn station Ostkreuz. It is the more northerly of two office buildings which represent a further development of block architecture, taking their starting point in the listed building of Knorr-Bremse AG designed by Alfred Grenander. The building consists of a chamber-like arrangement of 8-storey slab blocks with courtyard gardens; following the S-Bahn tracks is a curved, 13-storey high-rise slab with an aluminum and glass façade. The lower slab buildings have a curtain wall façade of aluminum and brick.

Das Projekt ist Bestandteil der Neugestaltung des Quartiers am S-Bahnhof Ostkreuz. Es ist das nördliche zweier Bürogebäude, die ausgehend vom denkmalgeschützten, von Alfred Grenander erbauten Gebäude der Knorr-Bremse AG den Typus der Blockbebauung fortsetzen. Das DLZ Nord besteht aus kammartig angeordneten 8-geschossigen Riegeln mit begrünten Innenhöfen sowie einer 13-geschossigen, dem Verlauf der S-Bahn folgenden geschwungenen Hochhausscheibe. Sie hat eine Aluminium-Glas-Fassade. Die flacheren Riegelbauten haben eine vorgehängte Aluminium-Ziegelraster-Fassade.

Dienstleistungszentrum
Services Centre
Ostkreuz, DLZ Nord

J.S.K/Perkins & Will; Berlin

Schreiberhauer Strasse/
Ecke Kaskelstrasse
10317 Berlin-Lichtenberg

Trade and business premises, plus a youth club are being built in several phases. A 16-storey high-rise with two straight sides and one curved façade of ceramic and glass marks the entrance to the residential centre. Conversion work will be carried out on an existing supermarket which will be integrated into the complex. A long element with external steel frame forms the urban and functional link with a 4-storey building. An existing walkway which cuts through the lower floors forms the backbone of the whole ensemble.

In mehreren Bauteilen entstehen Handels- und Büroflächen sowie ein Jugendclub. Ein 16-geschossiges Hochhaus, das aus zwei geraden und einer gebogenen Scheibe mit Keramik- bzw. Glasfassaden besteht, bildet den Auftakt zu dem Wohngebietszentrum. Ein vorhandener Supermarkt wird umgebaut und in den Komplex integriert. Ein Bauteil mit außenliegenden Stahlfachwerkträgern bildet die städtebauliche und funktionale Verbindung mit dem 4-geschossigen Abschnitt. Eine vorhandene Fußgängerstraße, die die Basisgeschosse durchschneidet, bildet das Rückgrat des Ensembles.

Wohngebietscentrum
Community Centre
Am Tierpark, Hans-Loch-Viertel

MRL Architekten
Markovic Ronai Lütjen Voss;
Hamburg, Berlin

Am Tierpark/Otto-Schmirgal-Strasse
10319 Berlin-Lichtenberg

Characteristic features in this building type are the continuous, long street façades with continuous eaves and the »Berlin courtyard« laid out as an extended green area inside. Many openings lead from this inner courtyard area to the street and emphasise the urban balance between open, green areas and built elements. The building's depth allows flexibility in arranging the business and commercial functions contained within it. The façades are primarily of brick, alternating with ceramic strips, and iron or glass elements.

Charakteristisch für den typologischen Aufbau des Komplexes sind die zusammenhängenden langen Straßenfassaden mit durchlaufender Traufe sowie der als ausgedehnte Grünfläche angelegte »Berliner Hof« im Inneren. Zahlreiche Durchgänge öffnen den grünen Innenhof zur Straße hin und betonen ein urbanes Gleichgewicht zwischen grünem und bebautem Element. Die Nutzung des Gebäudes als Büro- und Geschäftshaus kann aufgrund der Gebäudetiefe flexibel gestaltet werden. Die Fassaden zeigen vorwiegend Ziegelstein, abwechselnd mit Keramikstreifen, sowie Elemente aus Eisen und Glas.

Büro-, Geschäfts- und
Dienstleistungszentrum
Office, Commercial and Services Centre
Landsberger Arkaden

Aldo Rossi; Milano
mit with Giovanni Da Pozzo
und and Marc Kocher
in Berlin: Götz Bellmann
und and
Walter Böhm

Landsberger Allee 106
10407 Berlin-Lichtenberg

As one possible form of Critical Reconstruction, this building creates a seemingly self-evident urban condition, one which has never existed in this form up to now. The building is designed for the requirements of its owner and main users as well as for use by additional office users and shops. The materials used for the façades follow traditional choices for commercial buildings in Berlin: along the streets the façades consist of fair-faced masonry with storey-height openings with natural wood parapets and window frames; the southeast courtyard façade is a steel and glass construction.

Als mögliche Form der Kritischen Rekonstruktion stellt der Bau einen selbstverständlich erscheinenden städtischen Zustand her, den es in dieser Form noch nicht gegeben hat. Das Gebäude wurde sowohl direkt für den Bedarf des Besitzers und Hauptnutzers als auch für zusätzliche Büronutzer und Läden konzipiert. Die Auswahl der Fassadenmaterialien knüpft an die Tradition Berliner Gewerbebauten an. Die Straßenfassaden besitzen Sichtmauerwerk mit geschoßhohen Öffnungen mit Brüstungen und Fenstern in naturbelassenem Holz, die südöstliche Hoffassade ist eine Stahl-/Glaskonstruktion.

Dienstleistungsgebäude
Services Centre
Sächsische Strasse
der of the
Berliner Landesentwicklungs-
gesellschaft mbH

Stefan Scholz in
Bangert Scholz Architekten;
Berlin

Sächsische Strasse 47
10707 Berlin-Wilmersdorf

Hauptverwaltung der Berliner Wasser-Betriebe
Head Office of the Berlin Waterworks

Boris Podrecca; Wien
mit with Gotthard Eiböck

Hohenzollerndamm 44/
Eisenzahnstrasse 36-38/
Bielefelder Strasse 13-15
10709 Berlin-Wilmersdorf

Der Entwurf komplettiert die Blockrandbebauung an der Eisenzahn- und der Bielefelder Straße. In den Innenraum der so entstehenden U-Form sind zwei Gebäudespangen eingestellt, die nach Norden durch einen Querriegel einen Abschluß finden. Der Haupteingang in der Achse des Altbaus am Hohenzollerndamm wird beibehalten. Die Fassaden der Randbebauung sind aus Stein - sowohl monolithisch wie auch als Verkleidung -, die der Bürotrakte im Hof besitzen eine Aluminium-Glas-Konstruktion; der Erschließungsquertrakt ist ganz aus Glas.

This design completes the block edge along Eisenzahnstrasse and Bielefelder Strasse. Two cross braces have been placed in the interior of the ensuing U-form. The braces end in a bar to the north. The main entrance in the axis of the existing building on Hohenzollerndamm has been retained. The façades of the block edge are made of stone - both monolithic and in the form of cladding -, those of the office blocks in the courtyard of aluminum and glass; the perpendicular circulation building is made entirely of glass.

Bürohaus am Halensee
Office Building at Halensee

Léon + Wohlhage; Berlin
Hilde Léon, Konrad Wohlhage

Halenseestrasse/Ecke Kronprinzendamm
10711 Berlin-Wilmersdorf

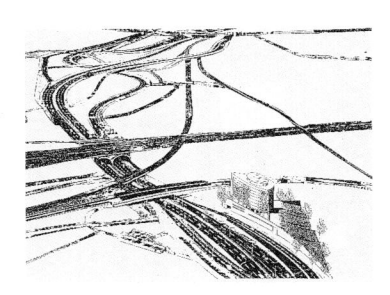

Das dreieckige Baugrundstück ist eine berlintypische, durch den Straßenbau entstandene Restfläche und ist von der angrenzenden Autobahn hochkontaminiert. Das Projekt zeigt modellhaft die Möglichkeiten eines Stadtwachtums »nach innen«. Das Gebäude konzentriert sein Volumen auf die Grundstücksspitze mit einer Auskragung von 6 m über die Autobahn. Eine Wand auf Straßenniveau mit Wasserfall schützt den Einfahrtshof vor Lärm und Abgasen. Zum Wohnviertel entsteht ein künstlich angelegter Hügelgarten. Der Hauptbaukörper hat eine gläserne doppelschalige Klimafassade.

Typical for Berlin, the triangular site is a result of urban road construction. It is highly contaminated owing to its proximity to the autobahn. This project exemplifies the possibility of »inward« urban growth. The building concentrates its volume at the corner of the site, cantilevered 6 m towards the autobahn. A wall with a waterfall at street level protects the access courtyard against noise and fumes. An artificial undulating landscaped garden marks the transition to a residential area. The main building has a ventilated double-skin glass façade.

Büro- und Geschäftshaus
Office Building
am at Emser Platz

Arno Bonanni; Berlin

Sigmaringer Strasse 18,19/
Hohenzollerndamm 187
10713 Berlin-Wilmersdorf

Der Gebäudekomplex schließt entsprechend der historischen Bebauung den Blockrand zum neugestalteten Emser Platz und betont die Ecksituation. Elemente der Umgebung wie die Lochfassade und die Traufhöhe der Nachbarbebauung werden aufgegriffen. Die in drei Zonen gegliederte Fassade besteht aus einem 2-geschossigen, mit grau-grünem Granit verkleideten Sockel, einer lichtgrau verputzten Lochfassade (2.-5. OG) sowie 2 Staffelgeschossen mit vorgehängter Aluminium-Glas-Konstruktion (6. und 7. OG.).

In line with existing development at this point, the complex closes the block edge facing the newly designed Emser Platz and provides emphasis for the corner situation. Integrated into the design are elements from the surrounding development, such as the punctuated façade and the eaves height. The façade, which is divided into three zones, consists of a 2-storey base section clad with grey-green granite, a light-grey rendered punctuated façade in the 2nd-5th storeys and two stepped-back stories with aluminum and glass curtain walls at the 6th and 7th storey levels.

Geschäfts- und Wohnhaus
Office Building
Lietzenburger/Fasanenstrasse

Moritz Müller und and Götz M. Keller; Berlin
in Zusammenarbeit mit
in cooperation with
Werner Stutz Collectif Architecture

Lietzenburger Strasse 67-71/
Fasanenstrasse 33
10719 Berlin-Wilmersdorf

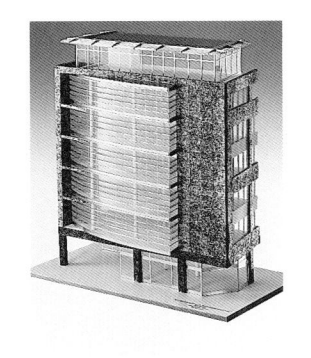

Die Bebauung des Eckgrundstücks besteht aus einem Büro- und Geschäftshaus direkt auf der Ecke und zwei Wohngebäuden mit 17 Wohnungen in der Fasanenstraße und Lietzenburger Straße. Die Fassaden gliedern sich in einen vollständig verglasten Sockelbereich, eine 5-geschossige Hauptzone mit geschwungenen, das Gebäude prägenden Fensterbändern und eine erneut vollständig verglaste Attikazone. Im Sockelbereich sind acht Läden geplant.

The development on this corner site consists of an office and commercial building situated directly on the corner and two residential blocks with 17 apartments in Fasanenstrasse and Lietzenburger Strasse. The façades are divided into a fully glazed base, a 5-storey main section with curved bands of fenestration giving a distinct character to the building, and at attic level, another glazed section. Eight shops are planned for the base section.

Büro- und Geschäftshaus
Office Building
Spichernstrasse 2

Architekten PSP
Pysall Stahrenberg & Partner; Berlin
Hans-Joachim Pysall,
Peter Stahrenberg, Joachim Grundei

Spichernstrasse 2
10777 Berlin-Wilmersdorf

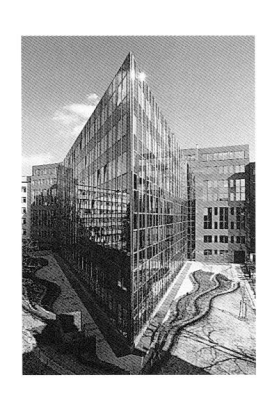

7-geschossige Randbebauung mit durchlaufenden Gesimskanten und zurückgesetztem Dachgeschoß. Ein polygonaler Einschnitt über alle Geschosse markiert straßenseitig den Eingang, von dem aus die Bebauung bogenförmig dem Straßenraum folgt. Die mit rotem Sandstein verkleidete Fassade gliedert sich klassisch in Sockel, Mittelbereich mit 2-geschossigen Fensterelementen alterniert mit Lochfenstern und ein Gesimsband mit durchlaufenden Lochfenstern. Im Blockinneren bildet ein solitärer Glaskubus einen Kontrast zur Randbebauung.

This 7-storey block edge development has a continuous cornice edge and a top storey set back from the façade plane. A polygonal break extending through all floors marks the main entrance; from this point the building curves round following the line of the street. The façade is clad in red sandstone and divided along classical lines into a base zone, a central zone with 2-storey window units alternating with pierced windows and a cornice with continuous pierced windows. On the inside of the block a solitary glass cube sets up a contrast with the block edge development.

A series of open, covered and closed spaces is created at the centre of the block, between the block edges which define the course of the street. The focal point is the Sony Forum, a multifunctional hall and a roof which is partly made of glass and partly of transparent reinforced fibreglass membrane. Highly visible city landmarks in this complex are the Potsdamer Platz high-rise, the Sony headquarters at Kemperplatz and the Forum roof. The restored beaux-arts façade of the former hotel Esplanade is integrated along Bellevuestrasse.

Zwischen der Blockrandbebauung, die den Verlauf der Straßen definiert, entsteht im Blockinneren eine Serie von offenen, bedeckten und geschlossenen Räumen. Den Mittelpunkt bildet das Sony-Forum als Multifunktionshalle mit einer teils verglasten, teils aus transparenter verstärkter Fiberglasmembran bestehenden Überdachung. Weithin sichtbare Akzente des Komplexes sind das Hochhaus Potsdamer Platz, das Sony-Hauptquartier am Kemperplatz und das Forum-Dach. An der Bellevuestraße wird die restaurierte Beaux-Arts-Fassade des ehemaligen Hotel Esplanade integriert.

Sony Zentrum Centre
Potsdamer Platz

Murphy/Jahn; New York, Chicago

Potsdamer Platz/Neue Potsdamer Straße / Kemperplatz
10785 Berlin-Tiergarten

The 7-storey building completes an existing block. It contains work areas, offices and special rooms for conferences and presentations; there is a large exhibition area off the main entrance. The inner courtyard rests on the roof (1.20 m) of the underground car park; the flat roofs are extensively planted. The stone-clad structure of the street façade has remotely adjustable inset glass louvres to provide for natural ventilation of the work areas and act as a protection against the weather and traffic noise. Adjustable louvre units afford solar shading on the courtyard side.

Das Gebäude schließt 7-geschossig die vorhandene Blockbebauung. Es enthält Arbeitsräume und Büros, Sonderräume für Tagungen und Repräsentation; über den Haupteingang wird darüber hinaus ein Ausstellungsbereich erschlossen. Durch die Garagenüberdeckung von 1,20 m entsteht ein Innenhof; zusätzlich werden die Flachdächer extensiv begrünt. In die steinverkleidete Struktur der Straßenfassade sind steuerbare Glaslamellen als Wetter- und Lärmschutzschicht und zur natürlichen Be- und Entlüftung der Arbeitsräume integriert. Hofseitig bieten bewegliche Lamellenelemente Sonnenschutz.

Verbandsgebäude der Deutschen Bauindustrie
Building of the Association of the German Construction Industry

Architekten Schweger + Partner; Hamburg
Peter P. Schweger, Franz Wöhler, Hartmut H. Reifenstein, Bernhard Kohl, Wolfgang Schneider

Kurfürstenstraße 129
10785 Berlin-Tiergarten

At the edge of the »inner-city periphery« between the Landwehr Canal and the Tiergarten district several urban connections can be distinguished: the link from City West to the new Potsdamer Platz, the end of the Landwehr Canal route from Kreuzberg and the Grosser Stern-Lützowplatz axis. The design reflects the fragmented urban surroundings: linear buildings and objects are grouped to form a square, a street and a park with the WTC, rented office space, apartments, kindergarten, restaurants, shops and a hotel. A 40 m high triangular building contains all the core functional areas of the WTC.

In der »innerstädtischen Peripherie« zwischen Landwehrkanal und Tiergartenviertel bündeln sich mehrere städtische Bezüge: Verbindung von City-West mit dem Potsdamer Platz, Ende der Landwehrkanal-Route aus Kreuzberg und Berührung der Achse Großer Stern zum Lützowplatz. Der Entwurf reagiert auf die uneindeutige städtische Umgebung: Zeilenbauten und Objekte formen einen Platz, eine Straße und einen Park, die vom WTC-Zentrum sowie durch Mietbüros, Wohnungen, Kita, Gastronomie, Läden und Hotel genutzt werden. Ein 40 m hohes dreieckiges Gebäude birgt alle Kernfunktionen des WTC.

World Trade Center Berlin

Léon + Wohlhage; Berlin
Hilde Léon, Konrad Wohlhage

Klingelhöferdreieck, Klingelhöferstrasse
10785 Berlin-Tiergarten

Planned as a response to a former bridge link at this point, the indented angle on the corner of Torfstrasse and Friedrich-Krause-Ufer is taken up as an urban situation of its own right. The building situated parallel to the S-Bahn completes the angle. A 7-storey part at right angles to the bridge route marks out a gateway situation. The design takes its reference from the existing building by Egon Eiermann, in terms of its floor heights and connection heights. There are two circulation cores with external stairwells providing for easy access to one large integrated area on each floor.

Der für die ehemals anschließende Brücke konzipierte einspringende Winkel der Torfstraße/Ecke Friedrich-Krause-Ufer wird von dem parallel zur S-Bahn liegenden Bau komplettiert. Ein 7-geschossiger Gebäudeteil orthogonal zur Brückentrasse markiert eine Torsituation. Der Entwurf setzt sich mit dem bestehenden Gebäude von Egon Eiermann auseinander und greift dessen Geschoß- und Anschlußhöhen auf. Als übersichtliche Erschließungselemente dienen zwei Gebäudekerne mit außenliegenden Treppenhäusern, die je Geschoß eine große zusammenhängende Nutzfläche fassen.

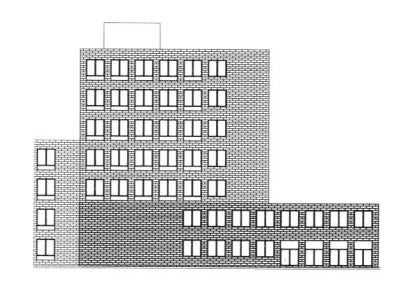

Neubau/Erweiterung Bürodienstgebäude
New Building/Extension of Administration Buildings
Landeseinwohneramt und Landesamt für Zentrale Soziale Aufgaben

Walter A. Noebel; Berlin
mit with Bettina M. Krug,
Philipp J. Bernhard

Friedrich-Krause-Ufer 23-25
13353 Berlin-Tiergarten

The 5-storey building lies in an area in which ring-roads and city-motorways cut deeply into the bordering block structure; the block edges had to give way. The building concept develops this situation. A cubic unit with clinker brick face closes - along Erfurter Strasse - the existing pattern; a long building clad with natural stone, horizontal windows and parapet panels along Wexstrasse leads to Innsbrucker Platz. By slightly setting back this new structure from the line of development, the two buildings on either side retain their original solitary character.

Das 5-geschossige Gebäude liegt in einem Bereich, in dem die Ring- und Stadtautobahn tief in die Blockstruktur einschneiden; die Blockkanten mußten weichen. Die bauliche Konzeption greift diese Situation auf. Ein kubischer Bauteil mit dunkler Klinkerverblendung schließt an der Erfurter Straße die vorhandene Bebauung, ein langgestreckter, mit Naturstein verkleideter Baukörper mit horizontalen Fenster- und Brüstungsbändern an der Wexstraße leitet zum Innsbrucker Platz über. Durch Zurücksetzen der Baufluxht behalten zwei benachbarte Gebäude ihren Charakter als Solitäre.

Büro- und Geschäftshaus
Office Building
Wexstrasse

Maedebach, Redeleit & Partner; Berlin

Wexstrasse 2/Erfurter Strasse
10825 Berlin-Schöneberg

Bürohaus
Office Building
Stresemannstrasse 111

Alsop & Störmer; Hamburg, London
William Alsop, Jan Störmer,
Holger Jaedicke, Mohamed Azhar,
Stephen Pimbley

Stresemannstrasse 111–119/
Dessauer Strasse 1–3
10963 Berlin-Kreuzberg

Der Entwurf für ein Grundstück unmittelbar gegenüber dem Martin-Gropius-Bau will vor dem historischen Bauwerk die Platzqualität innerhalb der bestehenden heterogenen Stadtstruktur verbessern. Das Gebäude folgt mit seinen 7 Geschossen den städtebaulichen Vorgaben für eine Blockrandbebauung und bleibt dennoch ein eigenständiger Baukörper. Die Annäherung der Gebäudespitze an einen angrenzenden Jugendstilbau auf 2,50 m Distanz bewirkt ein spannungsreiches räumliches Miteinander. Die Fassade erzeugt in flächiger Struktur ein Glas- und Blechfarbspiel.

The design for a site directly opposite Martin-Gropius-Bau seeks to enhance the city square atmosphere inside the existing heterogeneous urban structure vis-à-vis the historical building. With its 7 storeys the building is in line with overall guidelines for block edge development and yet still maintains a distinct identity. The 2.50 m gap between the top of the building and the neighbouring art nouveau building creates a certain spatial tension. Along the surface of the façade is an interplay of glass and coloured metal panels.

Erweiterung der GSW-Hauptverwaltung
Extension to the GSW Headquarters

Matthias Sauerbruch/Louisa Hutton;
Berlin, London

Kochstrasse 22, 23
10969 Berlin-Kreuzberg

Der Neubau erweitert ein Bürohochhaus aus den 50er Jahren für die Gemeinnützige Siedlungs- und Wohnungsbaugesellschaft. Die neue Bebauung besteht aus einem 21-geschossigen Hochhaus mit transparenten Glasfassaden, massiven Flachbauten mit Lochfassaden und Naturstein- bzw. Keramikverkleidung sowie einem Aufbau an der Markgrafenstraße, für den eine Kupferfassade vorgesehen ist. Ein markantes Gestaltungsmerkmal der Westfassade des Hochhauses ist eine Schicht von farbigen Schiebeläden aus Lochmetall unmittelbar hinter der äußeren Verglasung.

The new building forms an extension to a 1950s office high-rise used by a public housing association. The new building consists of a 21-storey high-rise with transparent glass façades, more solid low-rise structures with punctuated façades and natural stone or ceramic tile cladding as well as a structure in Markgrafenstrasse for which a copper façade is planned. A striking design feature of the west façade of the high-rise building is the layer of colourful sliding shutters made of perforated metal and located directly behind the external glazing.

Bundesdruckerei GmbH
Federal Printing Works
»Wertdruckgebäude 2«

Bayerer Hanson Heidenreich Schuster;
Berlin

Kommandantenstrasse
10969 Berlin-Kreuzberg

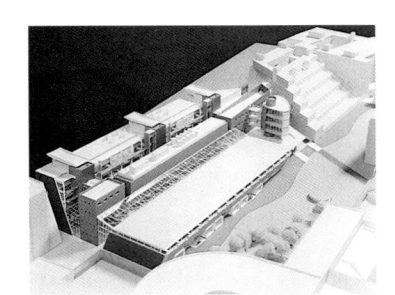

Das Projekt ist Teil einer Ergänzung des seit 1879 bestehenden Komplexes der Staatsdruckerei. Im ersten Bauabschnitt entsteht ein Druckzentrum hauptsächlich für Banknoten. Städtebauliches Ziel ist die Blockrandschließung zur Linden- und Kommmandantenstraße. Ein kleiner Platz markiert den Nordzugang zum Gelände. Obwohl es sich um einen hermetisch abgesicherten Komplex handelt, ermöglicht der Hauptbau mit seiner 78 m langen und 15 m hohen »structural-glazing«-Fassade Einblick in die Produktionsebenen. Hinter dem Industriegeschoßbau liegen ein Hochregallager und eine Produktionshalle.

The project is part of an extension to the complex of the state printing works (built in 1879). The first phase foresees a printing centre primarily for the printing of bank notes. This building will complete the block edge towards Lindenstrasse and Kommandantenstrasse. A small square marks the northern entrance to the site. Although the complex is hermetically sealed, the main building, with its 78 m long and 15 m high structural glazing façade provides a view of the production floors. Behind the slab block there is a high-stack warehouse, and a production hall.

Gewerbe Zentrum am Ullsteinhaus
Trade Centre at Ullsteinhaus

Nalbach Architekten; Berlin
Johanne und and Gernot Nalbach

Ullsteinstrasse 130
12099 Berlin-Tempelhof

Das Projekt erweitert das Produktionsgebäude von Eugen Schmohl (1924). Entgegen Schmohls ursprünglichen Erweiterungsplänen wurde als Referenz an das Baudenkmal und den angrenzenden Tempelhofer Hafen auf eine geschlossene Bauweise verzichtet. An der Ullsteinstraße führt ein 3-geschossiger Riegel den Schwung des Altbaus fort. Er trägt 3 Turmbauten mit jeweils einem Sicherheitstreppenhaus, die zum Hafen hin 3- plus 3-geschossige Hallen anbinden. Die Nutzung des Riegels sieht Büros bzw. Gewerbe vor, die Turmhäuser sind flexibel nutzbar bis zur Wohn- bzw. Hotelnutzung.

The project is an extension to the 1924 factory building by Eugen Schmohl. Contrary to Schmohl's original extension plans, it was decided not to adopt a closed mode of building in reference to the monument and the bordering Tempelhof Harbour. Along Ullsteinstrasse a 3-storey slab structure continues the curve of the existing building. It has 3 towers each with an emergency staircase which connect to 3 plus 3-storey halls facing the wharf. The slab will be used for offices and commercial purposes; the towers are more flexible, and can be used even for apartments or hotel rooms.

BEWAG-Hauptverwaltung
BEWAG Headquarters
»Am Schlesischen Busch«

Liepe und Steigelmann; Berlin
Axel Liepe, Hartmut Steigelmann

Puschkinallee 52
12435 Berlin-Treptow

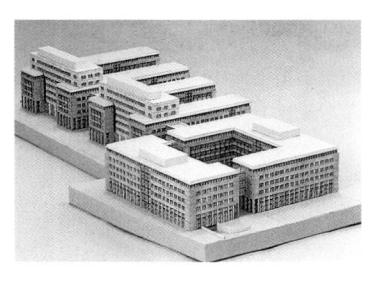

In dem traditionellen Industrie- und Gewerbegürtel entlang des Landwehrkanals und der Spree bildet das Grundstück einen Übergangsbereich zwischen offener Einzelhausbebauung im Süden und dem Park »Schlesischer Busch« im Norden. Drei klar gegliederte Einzelbaukörper sind auf mehreren Ebenen mit Brückenbauwerken verbunden. Ein vierseitig teilumschlossener Atrium-Block aus zwei Häusern bildet den Eingangshof. Zwei U-förmige Gebäude öffnen sich zum Park hin. Einheitliche Gestaltungselemente sind eine horizontale Dreigliederung sowie Ziegelverblendmauerwerk.

In the traditional industrial and trade zone along the Landwehr Canal and the Spree, the premises form a transitional link between an open, low-rise area in the south and the »Schlesischer Busch« park in the north. Three clearly articulated individual buildings are joined at several levels by bridge links. Partly enclosed on four sides, an atrium block consisting of two buildings forms the entrance courtyard. Two U-shaped buildings open towards the park. Unifying design features are a horizontal triple articulation as well as brick facing on the façades.

Situated on the former site of the Berlin wall, the building can be interpreted as both an independent entity and part of a larger group of buildings. It thus leaves open various possibilities for urban developments in the area. The height of the building is in line with the general eaves height in Berlin. The façade has stone cladding and, on the courtyard side, white ceramic stone cladding; it has a distinct base zone in a light grey colour and the window frames are clearly articulated. The inner courtyard is laid out as a garden.

Das Gebäude, auf dem ehemaligen Mauerstreifen gelegen, kann sowohl als Solitär als auch als Teil einer größeren Gebäudegruppe bestehen. Damit bleiben Möglichkeiten für unterschiedliche städtebauliche Entwicklungen in diesem Bereich offen. Die Höhe des Gebäudes entspricht der Berliner Traufhöhe. Die Fassade ist mit Stein bzw. auf der Hofseite mit weißen Keramiksteinen verkleidet; sie hat einen ausgeprägten Sockel in »lichtgebendem« Grau sowie massiv ausgebildete Fensterrahmen. Der Innenhof ist als Garten angelegt.

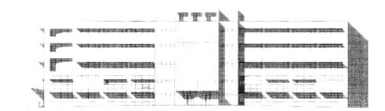

Siemens Verkehrstechnik
Siemens Traffic Technology

Douglas Clelland; London

Elsenstrasse 87–96
12435 Berlin-Treptow

The town hall site borders on two planned squares. A tower on the northwest side of the building, together with towers to be erected on the squares, marks the regional centre. The building consists of two distinct volumes linked by a large stepped glass hall. The 5-storey tower base is in line with the eaves height of the square and is fully glazed towards the Stadtplatz. The shaft of the tower above the base has a smaller ground area of 16.50 x 24 m and displays a regular punctuated façade of red clinker brick with pilaster strips on both main façades.

Das Grundstück des Rathauses grenzt an zwei vorgesehene Stadtplätze. Ein Turm an der Nordwestseite des Gebäudes markiert gemeinsam mit auf den Plätzen entstehenden Türmen das Stadtzentrum. Das Rathaus besteht aus zwei eigenständigen Baukörpern, verbunden durch eine große getreppte Glashalle. Der 5-geschossige Turmsockel nimmt die Traufhöhe der Randbebauung auf und ist zum Platz hin vollständig verglast. Der Turmschaft oberhalb des Sockels besitzt eine kleinere Grundfläche und zeigt eine regelmäßige Lochfassade aus rotem Klinker mit Lisenen an beiden Hauptfassaden.

Rathaus am Zentrum Hellersdorf
City Hall at Hellersdorf Centre

Behrendt und Stutzer; Berlin
Hartmut Behrendt, Christoph Stutzer

Spanischer Platz (vorläufiger Name aus städtebaulichem Wettbewerb)
provisional name from urban design competition)
12627 Berlin-Hellersdorf

The office and commercial complex, situated at the junction of the Marzahn, Lichtenberg and Hohenschönhausen districts, consists of 5 building sections. The main section with 22 storeys and a height of about 100 m consists of a pyramid-shaped glass structure, wedged between two high-rise slabs clad in granite. The other buildings are linked with each other and with the main building via a glazed connecting structure. These lower buildings contain offices and production areas as well as car parking spaces. A 3-storey hall forms the main entrance.

Der Büro- und Gewerbekomplex am Kreuzungspunkt der Bezirke Marzahn, Lichtenberg und Hohenschönhausen besteht aus 5 Gebäudeteilen. Der 22-geschossige Hauptteil ist ca. 100 m hoch und besteht aus einem pyramidenförmigen gläsernen Baukörper zwischen zwei mit Granit verkleideten Hochhausscheiben. Die übrigen Gebäude sind über gläserne Verbindungsbaukörper untereinander und an den Hauptbau angeschlossen. Sie nehmen Büro- und Produktionsflächen sowie PKW-Stellplätze auf. Über eine 3-geschossige Eingangshalle wird das Gebäude erschlossen.

Pyramide
Büro- und Gewerbekomplex
Office and commercial complex

Regina Schuh; München

Alte Rhinstrasse/Landsberger Allee/
Rhinstrasse 140/Strasse 13
12681 Berlin-Marzahn

Block 16 forms the southwest corner of the new »Weisse Taube« commercial district. The tower-like design of the corners with glazed façades emphasises its location. The top floor, set back a little, retreats behind the façade. The offices are arranged along central corridors; the office wings are positioned symmetrically around two square inner courtyards. The ground floor can accommodate shops or offices, as desired. The closed areas of the main façade have a pale-coloured, insulating mineral render finish; the base is clad in natural stone.

Der Block 16 bildet das südwestliche Eckgebäude des neuen Gewerbeviertels »Weiße Taube«. Seine turmartige Ausbildung der Gebäudeecken mit gläsernen Fassaden betont diese Position. Das oberste Vollgeschoß tritt dabei als Staffelgeschoß hinter die Fassade zurück. Die Büronutzung ist in zweihüftigen Flügeln untergebracht, die symmetrisch um 2 quadratische Innenhöfe angeordnet sind; im Erdgeschoß sind wahlweise Gewerbe- oder Büronutzung möglich. Die geschlossenen Hauptfassaden sind mit hellem wärmedämmendem Mineralputz versehen; der Sockel ist mit Naturstein verkleidet.

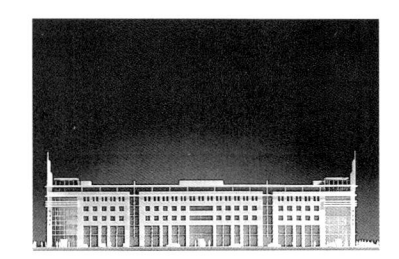

Bürogebäude Office Building
Block 16, Areal »Weiße Taube«

J.S.K./Perkins & Will; Berlin

Landsberger Allee 315–343
13055 Berlin-Hohenschönhausen

The building sets the tone for a future business district within the urban area. Deliberately »spartan« in construction, this large complex makes use of exposed concrete and industrial-standard single glazing; bare concrete staircases articulate the whole design. The building is to contain shops, offices, restaurants and sports/fitness facilities. One third of the useable area will be available for 99 apartment units. Access to the apartments and the sports facilities along the courtyard is via the inner courtyard.

Das Gebäude bildet den städtebaulichen Auftakt einer zukünftigen Gewerbezone in städtischem Gebiet. In gezielt »spartanisch« schlichter Bauweise entsteht ein Großkomplex in Sichtbetonkonstruktion mit einfacher Industrieverglasung, dessen Gliederung durch freigelegte Treppenkonstruktionen ebenfalls aus Beton erfolgt. Als Nutzung sind Läden, Büros, Gastronomie und Sport/Fitness vorgesehen; 1/3 der Nutzfläche steht für insgesamt 99 Wohnungen zur Verfügung. Vom Innenhof aus werden alle Wohnungen sowie die im Hof angeordneten Sportanlagen erschlossen.

Pankow-Center-Nord

d-company; Bern
Anatole du Fresne, Insook du Fresne,
Danny Bucco

Pasewalker Strasse 114–117
13127 Berlin-Pankow

Bürogebäude Office Building
Dovestrasse/Salzufer

Steinebach & Weber; Berlin
Karl-Heinz Steinebach, Friedrich Weber,
Brendan Mac Riabhaigh, Ingrid Pagel

Dovestrasse 2-4/Salzufer 22
10587 Berlin-Charlottenburg

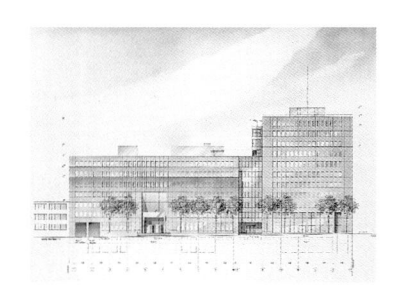

Das Grundstück liegt auf ehemaligem Industriegelände direkt an der Spree. Das Gebäude besteht aus einem Baukörper mit traditioneller Traufhöhe und darüber zurückgestaffelten Attikageschossen sowie einem 11-geschossigen Eck-Hochhaus mit zurückgesetzter Giebelformation, die an die Tradition alter Speicherhäuser erinnert. Mit dem gegenüberliegenden bestehenden Eck-hochhaus definiert es ein Tor zum Stadtteilzentrum Moabit. Die Baukörperstruktur ist klar gegliedert mit einer steinverkleideten Lochfassade.

The site is on former industrial land bordering directly on the Spree. One part of the building is of traditional eaves height, with stepped-back attic floors at a higher level; the other part is an 11-storey corner high-rise with set-back gable formation recalling the tradition of old warehouses. In conjunction with the existing corner tower block opposite it marks out a gateway situation leading to the centre of the district of Moabit. The building structure is clearly articulated, with a punctuated stone-clad façade.

Neubau Verwaltungsgebäude
New Administration Building
Landesversicherungsanstalt Berlin

Steinebach & Weber; Berlin
Karl-Heinz Steinebach, Siegfried Süssbier, Marianne Specht, Marc Stroh, Robert Goppelt, Michael Krämer

Knobelsdorffstrasse 92
14059 Berlin-Charlottenburg

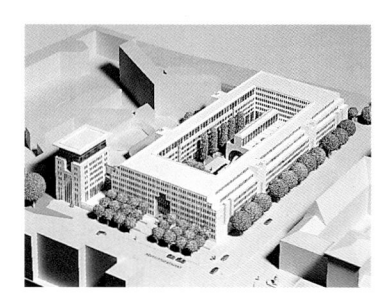

Eine »berlintypische« Blockrandbebauung mit ruhigen Konturen zu den Straßenrändern. Die Innenhofgestaltung sieht Baumalleen und Wasserflächen vor, ein Solitär nimmt ein Kasino auf. Ein freistehender 8-geschossiger »Medizinerturm« neben dem Hauptportal nimmt Bezug auf die 34 m hohen Türme der gegenüberliegenden Wohnbebauung von Salvisberg und definiert mit diesen einen neuen Stadtraum. Über verglaste Brücken ist dieser medizinische Bereich mit dem Verwaltungsgebäude verbunden. Eine Freitreppenanlage erschließt die über 6 Geschosse reichende Eingangshalle.

The building complex forms a typical »Berlin block« with quiet, unobtrusive fronts facing the streets. In the inner courtyard with tree-lined routes and ponds there is a free-standing structure containing a staff dining hall. A free-standing, 8-storey »Medics tower« next to the main gate is a response to the 34 m high towers of the Salvisberg residential development opposite; together, they define new urban relationships in the area. This medical tower is connected to the administration building by glazed bridge links. Flights of open staircases lead to the 6-storey-high entrance hall.

Wohn- und Geschäftshaus
Apartment and Office Building
Kaiserdamm 97

Jürgen Sawade; Berlin

Kaiserdamm 97/Riehlstrasse 1
14057 Berlin-Charlottenburg

Der Entwurf komplettiert den Straßenraum des Kaiserdamms und schirmt den Hofbereich und die gegenüberliegenden Altbauten zur Autobahn hin ab. Ein L-förmiger 7- bzw. 8-geschossiger Baukörper nimmt nach Süden bzw. Südosten orientierte Wohnungen sowie an der Nordwest- und Nordost-Ecke Gewerbeflächen auf. Das Gebäude erhält zum Kaiserdamm eine symmetrische Fensterband-Fassade mit Fliesenverblendung, zur Autobahn einen schallschluckenden Lochziegelsockel mit darüber liegender 8-geschossiger Industrieverglasung sowie im Hof an der Riehlstraße eine konventionelle Lochfassade.

The design completes Kaiserdamm street and offers noise-protection from the autobahn for the courtyard behind and the existing buildings opposite. An L-shaped, 7 to 8-storey block contains apartments on its south and southeast sides and commercial premises in the northwest and northeast corners. The Kaiserdamm front has a symmetrical glazing strip façade with tile facing; the autobahn façade has a sound-absorbing perforated brick base above which there is 8-storeys of industrial-standard glazing; the courtyard side on Riehlstrasse has a conventional punctuated façade.

Bildnachweis
Acknowledgements

Alle Abbildungen zu den Projekten wurden von den Architekten und Bauherren zur Verfügung gestellt.
All illustrative material for the projects was provided by the architects and clients.

30/1 Architektur im Profil, 35 Projekte für Berlin, Stuttgart, 1993, S. 49
30/2 Berlin und seine Bauten, VIII: Bauten für Handel und Gewerbe, Bd. A, hrsg. vom Architekten- und Ingenieurverein zu Berlin, Berlin, 1978, S. 175
31 ebenda, S. 176
37 BEWAG Lichtbildstelle, A 13197
44 Fotos Heinrich Helfenstein
70-71 Berlin und seine Bauten, hrsg. vom Architekten- und Ingenieurverein zu Berlin, IX: Industriebauten / Bürohäuser, Berlin, 1971, S. 130, 131; VIII: Bauten für Handel und Gewerbe, Bd. A, Berlin, 1978, S. 174
74/1 Foto Mechthild Wilhelmi
76, 84 Modellfotos Uwe Rau
100 Johann Friedrich Geist, Passagen. Ein Bautyp des 19. Jahrhunderts, München, 1978, Abb. 60, Tafel 19, Abb. 65, Tafel 25
106-109 Modellfotos und Computersimulation Gaston Bergeret, derbi, Espace & Strategie Communication (CAD)
130 Modellfoto J. Luc Signamarcheix
142/1 Ungers/Adler, 1929/1981, S.17
142/2 Lotus international, Nr. 80/1994, S. 58
143/1 Landesbildstelle Berlin, Nr. 25047
143/2 Brüder Luckhardt und Alfons Anker, hrsg. von der Akademie der Künste, Schriftenreihe Bd. 21, Berlin, 1990, S.193
144 Berlin Heute, Projekte für das neue Berlin, hrsg. von der Berlinischen Galerie, Berlin, 1991, S. 34, 66, 81
147/1 Foto Eamonn O'Mahony
147/2 Rudolf Hierl, Erwin Gutkind 1886-1968, Basel-Berlin-Boston, 1992, S. 131
153 Modellfoto Eamonn O'Mahony
156-157 Computerdarstellung Assisi, Plotterdarstellung Helfried Usner, Computergraphik
166/1 Architektur im Profil, 35 Projekte für Berlin, Stuttgart, 1993, S. 41
166/2 Brüder Luckhardt und Alfons Anker, hrsg. von der Akademie der Künste, Berlin, 1990, S. 230
167/1 P. Gössel, G. Genthäuser, Architektur des 20. Jahrhunderts, Köln, 1990
167/2 Burg, A., Crippa, M. A., Stadtbild Berlin. Identität und Wandel, Tübingen, 1991, S. 52
168 Berlin und seine Bauten, hrsg. vom Architekten- und Ingenieurverein zu Berlin, IX: Industriebauten / Bürohäuser, Berlin, 1971, S. 154; VIII: Bauten für Handel und Gewerbe, Band B, Berlin, 1980, S.67

170 Fotos Rudolf Schäfer
171/1-2 Foyer, Heft II, Berlin, 1994, S.11
172/1 Berlin und seine Bauten, VIII: Bauten für Handel und Gewerbe, Band B, hrsg. vom Architekten- und Ingenieurverein zu Berlin, Berlin, 1980, S.11
184-185 Modellfotos Eamonn O'Mahony
188 f. Modellfoto Stefan Klonk
216/2 Bauwert AG, Berlin
216/5 Jens Willebrand, Köln
217/1,3, 218/1 Hans-Joachim Wuthenow, Berlin
218/5 Ludger Grunwald, Berlin
219/3 Atelier Schneider, Berlin
219/5, 220/3, 222/2-3 Reinhard Görner, Berlin